Controlling Arms and Terror in the Asia Pacific

Controlling Arms and Terror in the Asia Pacific

After Bali and Baghdad

Edited by

Marika Vicziany

Monash University

Edward Elgar
Cheltenham, UK · Northampton, MA, USA

Published by
Edward Elgar Publishing Limited
Glensanda House
Montpellier Parade
Cheltenham
Glos GL50 1UA
UK

Edward Elgar Publishing, Inc.
William Pratt House
9 Dewey Court
Northampton
Massachusetts 01060
USA

A catalogue record for this book
is available from the British Library

Library of Congress Cataloguing in Publication Data

Controlling arms and terror in the Asia Pacific : after Bali and Baghdad /
edited by Marika Vicziany.
    p. cm.
  Includes bibliographical references and index.
    1. Terrorism–Asia. 2. Terrorism–Pacific area. 3. Arms control–Asia.
  4. Arms control–Pacific area. I. Vicziany, Marika.
    HV6433.A78C66 2007
    363.325'16095–dc22
                                              2006016209

ISBN 978 1 84542 405 3

Printed and bound in Great Britain by MPG Books Ltd, Bodmin, Cornwall

Contents

Contributors

Amitav Acharya
Professor/Deputy Director and Head of Research at the Institute of Defence and Strategic Studies, Nanyang Technological University, Singapore.

Kim C. Beazley
The former leader of the Australian Labor Party and the Opposition in the Federal Parliament in Canberra, Australia.

Farhan Bokhari
Pakistan correspondent for the *Financial Times* (London) and Honorary Research Fellow, Monash Asia Institute, Monash University, Melbourne, Australia.

Charles G.L. Donnelly
PhD candidate at the Monash Asia Institute, Monash University, Melbourne, Australia.

Asad Durrani, Lt Gen. (R)
After 34 years with the Pakistan Army, Pakistan's Ambassador to the Federal Republic of Germany (1994–97) and Saudi Arabia (2000–02).

Pervez Hoodbhoy
Professor of Nuclear and High-Energy Physics at Quaid-e-Azam University, Islamabad, Pakistan.

Carlo Kopp, PhD
Australia's best known specialist on military aviation, technology and strategic doctrine. Research Fellow at the Monash Asia Institute, Monash University, Melbourne, Australia and Lecturer, Information Technology, Monash.

Liisa Laakso
Professor of Development and International Cooperation at the Department of Social Sciences and Philosophy, University of Jyväskylä, Finland.

Oliver Mendelsohn
Former Dean of the School of Law, La Trobe University, Melbourne, Australia, and editor of *Law in Context*.

Noel M. Morada, PhD
Associate Professor and Chair, Department of Political Science, University of the Philippines Diliman, Quezon City, and Executive Director of the Institute for Strategic and Development Studies, Inc., Quezon City, the Philippines.

S.D. Muni
Former Professor of International Relations at the Jawaharlal Nehru University, New Delhi, India, and Honorary Research Fellow, Monash Asia Institute, Monash University, Melbourne, Australia.

K.S. Nathan
Senior Fellow at the Institute of Southeast Asian Studies, Singapore.

Takashi Sakamoto
Washington correspondent of *The Yomiuri Shimbun*.

Ben Sheppard
Research Associate at the King's Centre for Risk Management, King's College London, UK.

Kannan Srinivasan
Phd candidate at the Monash Asia Institute, Monash University, Melbourne, Australia.

Marika Vicziany
Professor of Asian Political Economy and Director of the Monash Asia Institute at Monash University, Melbourne, Australia.

David Wright-Neville
Associate Professor and Co-Convener of the Global Terrorism Research Unit in the School of Political and Social Inquiry at Monash University, Melbourne, Australia.

Samina Yasmeen
Associate Professor and Director of the Centre for Muslim States and Scieties at the University of Western Australia, Perth, Australia.

Abbreviations

ABM	Anti-Ballistic Missile
ABMT	Anti-Ballistic Missile Treaty
ACP	African, Caribbean and Pacific states
ADF	Australian Defence Force
AFP	Armed Forces of the Philippines
AFPSLAI	Armed Forces of the Philippines Savings and Loans Association Inc.
ALA	Asia-Latin America
AMRAAM	Advanced Medium-Range Air-to-Air Missile
APEC	Asia-Pacific Economic Cooperation
ARMM	Autonomous Region in Muslim Mindanao
ASEAN	Association of South East Asian Nations
ASEF	Asia-Europe Foundation
ASEM	Asia-Europe Meeting
ASG	Abu Sayyaf Group
ASIO	Australian Security Intelligence Organisation
ATACM	Army tactical missile systems
ATV	Advanced technology vessel
AWACS	Airborne Warning and Control System
BBC	British Broadcasting Corporation
BJP	Bharatiya Janata Party
BLT	Bodo Liberation Tigers
BMD	Ballistic missile defences
BMDO	Ballistic Missile Defence Office
BN	Barisan Nasional
BPO	Business process outsourcing
C4ISR	Command, control, communications, computing, intelligence, surveillance, and reconnaissance
CCOMPOSA	Coordinating Committee of Maoist Parties and Organisations of South Asia
CFSP	Common Foreign and Security Policy
CIA	Central Intelligence Agency
CIS	Commonwealth of Independent States
CNN	Cable News Network
CTBT	Comprehensive Test Ban Treaty

DI	Darul Islam
DRDO	Defence Research and Development Organisation
DSP	Defense Support Program
EG	Equatorial Guinea
ESDP	European Security and Defence Policy
EU	European Union
FII	Financial institutional investment
FMCT	Fissile Material Cut-off Treaty
FPDA	Five Power Defence Arrangements
FPI	Islamic Defenders Front
FY	Financial Year
GMIP	Gerakan Mujahideen Islam Pattani
GPI	Islamic Youth Movement
GPS	Global Positioning System
GSLV	Geosynchroneous Satellite Launch Vehicle
GTZ	Deutsche Gesellschaft für Technische Zusammenarbeit
HARM	High-speed anti-radiation missiles
IB	Intelligence Bureau
ICBM	Inter-Continental Ballistic Missile
ICG	International Crisis Group
ID	Identity
IGMDP	Integrated Guided Missile Development Program
IMF	International Monetary Fund
INF	Intermediate-range Nuclear Force
IPKF	Indian Peace Keeping Force
IRBM	Intermediate Range Ballistic Missiles
IRS	Internal Revenue Service
ISA	Internal Security Act
ISI	Inter-Services Intelligence
ISR	Intelligence, surveillance and reconnaissance
ISRO	Indian Space Research Organisation
IT	Information Technology
JDAM	Joint direct attack munitions
JI	Jemaah Islamiyah
JSTARS	Joint surveillance and target attack radar systems
JVP	Janatha Vimukthi Peramuna
KLO	Kamtapur Liberation Organisation
KMM	Kumpulan Mujahidin Malaysia
LOC	Line of Control
LTTE	Liberation Tigers of Tamil Eelam
MDI	Markas-ud-Dawa-wal-Irshad
MILF	Moro Islamic Liberation Front

MISA	Maintenance of Internal Security Act
MITI	Ministry of International Trade and Industries
MLSA	Mutual Logistics Support Agreement
MMA	Muttehedah Majlis-e-Amal
MNLF	Moro National Liberation Front
MRBM	Medium Range Ballistic Missile
MSRC	Malaysian Strategic and Research Centre
NASSCOM	National Association of Software and Service Companies
NATO	North Atlantic Treaty Organisation
NGO	Non government organization
NMD	National Missile Defence
NPA	New People's Army
NRI	Non-resident Indian
NWFP	North West Frontier Province
OCC	Office of the Comptroller of the Currency
ODA	Official development assistance
PAS	Parti Islam
PLO	Palestine Liberation Organization
POTA	Prevention of Terrorism Act
PPP	Pakistan People's Party
PSLV	Polar Satellite Launch Vehicle
PULO	Pattani United Liberation Organisation
PWG	People's War Group
RAAF	Royal Australian Air Force
RBI	Reserve Bank of India
RGS	Relay ground station
RMA	Revolution in Military Affairs
RNA	Royal Nepal Army
RSBS	Retirement and Separation Benefits System
SAARC	South Asian Association for Regional Co-operation
SALT	Strategic Arms Limitation Treaty
SAR	Sekolah Agama Rakyat (Malaysian Islamic Schools)
SDF	Self Defense Force (Japan)
SDI	Strategic Defence Initiative
SLBM	Submarine launched ballistic missile
SLFP	Sri Lanka Freedom Party
SLOC	Sea lanes of communication
SLV	Satellite Launch Vehicle
SNF	Short-range Nuclear Force
START	Strategic Arms Reduction Treaty
TADA	The Terrorist and Disruptive Activities (Prevention) Act 1985

TAPO	Tashkent Aircraft Production Organisation
TFDP	Task Force Detainees of the Philippines
TJ	Tehrik Jaffariya Pakistan
TMD	Theatre Missile Defences
TRACECA	Transport Corridor Europe Caucasus Asia
ULFA	United Liberation Front of Assam
UMNO	United Malays National Organisation
UNICEF	United Nations Children's Fund
UNSC	United Nations Security Council
USAID	United States Agency for International Development
VX	A nerve gas of the V series of nerve agents
WEU	Western European Union
WMD	Weapons of Mass Destruction
WTO	World Trade Organisation
ZOPFAN	Zone of Peace Freedom and Neutrality

Acknowledgments

This monograph was conceived during the Monash Asia Institute's third Asia Pacific Regional Security Dialogue, held in Beijing in March 2004 in partnership with the Institute of Asia-Pacific Studies of the Chinese Academy of Social Science. The dialogue observed Chatham House rules. Many of the key issues are discussed in the present volume, which focuses on the interplay of non-state and state actors in the region. The project was unusual in its determination to bring these two themes together and understand how these different dimensions intersect. Typically the 'Global War against Terror' is discussed separately from the general security architecture of the world, which is still determined by nation states and their defence and foreign policies. Our objective here is to assess the relative contribution that each makes to regional security. A second volume, focusing on what China's security specialists think about regional security, has also been planned.

In order to ensure good representation to many voices, the conference organizers invited participants from academic life, government and military affairs from no fewer than ten countries, all of which are important regional players. We all benefited from the exchange of views and hope that continuing discussions will contribute towards ongoing dialogue in this period of rapidly changing security scenarios. A special word of appreciation is due to our generous and enthusiastic hosts in Beijing, in particular Professor Zhang Yunling and Professor Han Feng. We also thank the Japan Foundation (Sydney and Tokyo offices) and the Ford Foundation (Beijing office) for supporting the dialogue process in a manner that enabled us to bring together a wider range of participants than before. The Monash Asia Institute provided expertise, financial and logistical support as it did for all the dialogues we have organized since India and Pakistan tested their nuclear devices in 1998. Information about these can be read on our website, www.arts.monash.edu.au/mai/ Finally, we thank Edward Caruso, Mick Kannegiesser and Emma Hegarty for their roles in editing, layout and general production management; Gary Swinton (School of Geography, Monash University) for his sketch of the Asia Pacific, and the Edward Elgar editorial team for their oversight of the publication.

Sketch: The Asia Pacific region

PART 1

Regional policies and strategies

1. What has changed, and what has not changed, since 9/9?[1]

Marika Vicziany

'9/11' has become a byword for mass casualty terrorism. But what is 9/9? As the world has come to live with terrorism, the precise sequence of terrorist acts is easily forgotten. Increasingly, images of suicide bombings and car, van or truck bombings all blend together into a confusing pastiche of violence that increasingly covers a larger and larger geographical canvas. On 9/11 it was New York, Washington and Philadelphia and since then we have had terrorist attacks in Baghdad, Bali, Jakarta, Madrid, London and Amman. In other parts of the world so far spared attacks by terrorists, there have been arrests of suspects assumed to be plotting attacks. As the definition of what constitutes terrorism or the threat of terrorism has evolved, the stereotypical profile of terrorists has shifted to uncertain territory. Today's terrorists can be 'home grown' rather than foreigners; converts rather than born into the cause that they seek to promote; female rather than male. They can be 'Western' females with blonde hair rather than matching the racial profiling that is popular in the United States;[2] they can be wives acting in concert with spouses rather than individuals bound only by ideology or anger (BBC News 2005);[3] and they can be small groups of angry people acting in concert only with themselves, rather than taking instructions from coherent, hierarchical, pan-global organizations such as Al Qaeda or Aum Shinrikyo. And their reasons for turning to violence are limitless, as the work of Khosrokhavar (2005) on Islamic suicide bombers has shown. Most important of all, as is argued in various chapters of this volume, terrorism is not a weapon used by Islamists alone – it has long been used as a tactic by various ethnic, religious and socioeconomic reform movements in the Asia Pacific.

SO WHAT WAS 9/9 AND WHY SHOULD WE TAKE SPECIAL NOTICE OF IT?

On 9 September 2004 a van drove past the Australian Embassy in Jakarta and exploded, killing three suicide bombers and 12 innocent bystanders.

Hundreds of people were injured and extensive damage to property occurred. The incident came three years after 11 September 2001, when suicide bombers flying four civilian jet aircraft killed about 3000 people when they crashed into the World Trade Center, the Pentagon and a field in Shanksville, Pennsylvania (*9/11 Commission Report* 2004, pp. 32–3).

This chapter begins by looking at the meaning of 9/9 and the new understanding of regional terrorism that has emerged as a result of an analysis of the origins and persistence of terrorism in Indonesia. Communal conflict has generated local jihads, and it is these local jihads that provide the fuel for regional and global jihads. Typically, such jihads are not new – they have a long history that goes back to the colonial era.

The next section compares this with a parallel situation in Iraq where again local situations have fuelled jihads with regional and global consequences. The chief difference in the Iraqi case is that communal conflict occurs between different sects of Islam, rather than between Christians and Muslims as in Indonesia. On the other hand, as is true of Indonesia, terrorism in Iraq has developed unpredictable characteristics very different from the monolithic image of terrorism projected by the global 'war on terror'. Despite these complexities, the 'war on terror' has emerged as the defining feature of the post-Cold War era.

The third section of this chapter examines the interplay between the war on terror and the interest of nation states in the Asia Pacific. The argument here draws on the evidence of the chapters in the present volume. The self interests of national elites emerge as primary considerations in how the global 'war on terror' has been conducted. This has meant that some nation states have sponsored terrorism while many have fought it in a half-hearted manner because other national interests are more important. The paradoxical fallout from this has been the persistent rise of China's influence in the Asia Pacific and the growing ineffectiveness of a US security strategy that relies too much on coercion and too little on persuasion.

9/9 and the 'New Terrorism'

9/9 was not significant in terms of the total casualties relative to 9/11. It did not represent a unique attack in Indonesia, for two years earlier, in 2002, a van packed with explosives detonated near two restaurants at Kuta beach in Bali, killing about 202 people. And, between the bombing in Kuta and that at the Australian Embassy in Jakarta, the Marriott Hotel in Jakarta had been attacked in August 2003. Twelve people died on that occasion. Nor was 9/9 significant as marking the end of bombings in Indonesia. Bali was again the scene of terrorism on 1 October 2005, when some 23 persons were killed and about 150 seriously injured. Compared with suicide attacks in London,

Amman and Iraq, 9/9 was also a relatively contained affair: on 7 July 2005, four British-born Muslim youths killed 52 London commuters by detonating their backpacks in the London underground and on a bus. And in Amman, Jordan, on 11 November 2005, Islamic militants carrying suicide packs attacked three hotels and succeeded in killing 52 people. In both cases, hundreds of people were injured.

So why should we pay special attention to 9/9? The answer is that the bombing of the Australian Embassy in Jakarta provides critical insights into what is happening to terrorism in the Asia Pacific region. Understanding the scenario in the Asia Pacific, in turn, might give us clues as to the changing nature of terrorism in other parts of the world. Until recently, the Asia Pacific had not been regarded as the natural home of modern terrorism; rather, this was something that was assumed to be part of the rhythm of life in the Middle East or Afghanistan or Russia. This perception is now catching up with history.

The New Terrorism

The characteristics of the Australian Embassy bombing on 9 September 2004 do not conform to what one might have expected on the basis of what happened on 9/11. First, 9/9 was organized by Jemaah Islamiyah (JI). However, the masterminds were not Indonesians but Malaysian nationals, namely Azahari Husin and Noordin Mohammed Top (ICG 2005a, pp. i–ii). Second, the suicide bombers themselves were Indonesian nationals recruited from Ring Banten, an offshoot of Darul Islam (DI),[4] a complex movement dating from the 1950s with the primary goal of establishing an Islamic state in Indonesia. Third, 9/9 involved collaboration between JI and DI in carrying out the attack; it is possible that other groups were also involved. Until 9/9 their collaboration had been limited to joint military training exercises and providing their fugitives with mutual refuge (ICG 2005a, p. 27). Fourth, despite this collaboration there was no evidence to suggest that 9/9 represented the work of a highly coordinated terrorist movement. This was not the kind of Al Qaeda-type operation that seems to have formed a core assumption behind the initial stages of the 'war on terror'. Rather it seems that there were many South-east Asian terrorist groups in a constant state of flux, factional splits and re-formations. Collaboration appears to have been intermittent and loose, and, as the long tradition of DI suggests, when people come together it is ideology and deeply personal, even family, links rather than anything else that bind them. Fifth, the analysis that has emerged from a study of 9/9 compels us to pay close attention to the deep historical roots and resentments that keep terrorism alive at the local level. These paradigms have relevance beyond Indonesia, but the Indonesian case is discussed first, followed by a short section on Iraq.

Recent analysis by the International Crisis Group (ICG) of terrorism in Indonesia takes us well beyond the initial concern for how individuals in JI and DI have been influenced by, or linked to, the mujahidin in Afghanistan (Jones 2005). There has been a new appreciation of how the traditions of militancy have been formed and passed from one generation to the next. The image of unruly hotheads rushing into action has been tempered by a better understanding of jihad as a 'holy war' accompanied by the strategy of hijrah, or flight into a safe region to avoid detection, wait patiently and rebuild one's strength for the final jihad (ICG 2005a, p. 6). This complexity is both good and bad for the objective of controlling terrorism. It is good because it opens up a longer timeframe during which the root causes of anger can be addressed, but it is also bad because the focus on the long term facilitates the inter-generational transfer of anger and militancy as a political strategy.

We also now have a better insight into why terrorism is often associated with crime, especially in the case of Islamic militancy. The concept of fa'i is one that justifies the practice of 'robbing non-Muslims in order to fund the jihad' and preparations for it (ICG 2005a, p. 5). It is also a doctrine that strengthens the resolve of the less militant but more moral members of JI and DI – these individuals may be naturally inclined to resist robbery and murder, but the objectives of establishing an Islamic order in the long run might help them to compromise on their ethical stand. Fa'i legitimizes immoral acts as part of a wider and longer struggle for an Islamic state.

The same moral order of Islam allows Muslims to protect themselves and other Muslims from attacks by non-Muslim communities. 9/9 was possible because, despite the crackdowns by army and police and the imprisonment and execution of some militant leaders, the spirit of jihad has been kept alive by domestic communal conflict in Indonesia between Christians and Muslims in Aceh, Sumatra, Kalimantan and Sulawesi. As Sidney Jones (2005) has remarked, the assassination of five people in Ceram on 16 May 2005 and the deaths of 22 on 28 May 2005 as a result of a bomb explosion in the market of Tentena did not attract international attention (presumably because no foreigners were killed), yet these conflicts have kept local jihads alive and the jihadis well practised in the art of terror. Both areas have been the focus of the revival of Christian–Muslim conflict since the late 1990s. Local jihadis have teamed up with jihadis rushing in from outside to protect Muslims against the 'enemies of Islam'. As the biography of Asep shows, these different jihadi strands have a long history of coming together, separating, reforming, and coming together again across inter-state and regional boundaries that appear to be infinitely porous (ICG 2005b, pp. 8–9). Controlling and addressing the root causes of communal strife within particular Indonesian provinces, therefore, constitutes one of the most important instruments against regional terrorism. Among the strategies suggested by ICG are reintegrating jihadis and Christian militants into the normal life of Indonesia and engaging with these veterans of violence in other ways that give them a stake in society (ICG 2005b, p. 19). Imprisonment and execution, on the other hand, strengthen the beliefs of jihadists and create a new generation of martyrs who can join a long and glorious tradition of fighters who continue to inspire further acts of extreme violence.

The interconnections between local communally based jihads, on the one hand, and jihads focused on foreigners and their indigenous collaborators in Jakarta and Bali, on the other, have been established by evidence that has survived the bombings. For example, on 9 November 2005 Azahari bin Husin was killed during a police shootout in the east Javan town of Batu. The house in which he had been hiding yielded ID cards, tapes, explosive manuals and materials, and diaries that enabled the Indonesian police to link the bombings in 2005 with the three previous attacks in 2002, 2003 and 2004 (Powell 2005a, p. 6). Azahari was one of JI's best experts on explosives and it was he who trained Heri Golun, the suicide bomber who blew up the van outside the Australian embassy (Powell 2005b). Mohammed Top escaped on this occasion, no doubt ready to regroup and identify the next target. Azahari's companion explosives specialist, Dulmatin, is still free, probably somewhere in the Philippines (Fitzpatrick 2005, p. 15). The two men arrested at the scene of the bombings are now in prison awaiting their sentence.

Whom do Azahari, Dulmatin and Top represent? There is a growing view that splits have emerged within JI because too many Muslims have been killed in the terrorist attacks. Indonesia is not like other parts of Asia: though it is not an Islamic state it is a predominantly Muslim country and home to the largest community of Muslims in the world. Muslims killing Muslims in these circumstances has made the majority of members of DI and JI intensely uncomfortable and caused them to disassociate themselves from the terrorist tactics that have become so widespread since Osama bin Laden announced his fatwa in February 1998 (Jones 2005). As the disaffection between Azahari and Top and JI grew, it is possible that these two JI leaders came to represent their own factions bound together by the history of serving as mujahidin in Afghanistan (Powell 2005b, citing Sidney Jones). In short, militant Islamists in South-east Asia are a severely constrained, unpopular minority. Yet they can inflict much harm because, even if they lacked the support of JI's high command, Azahari and Dulmatin have trained enough bomb-makers to create havoc in Indonesia and elsewhere. To contain that havoc a number of strategies have been recommended by ICG and others, in particular policies to incorporate local jihadis into the mainstream of life and, for those who refuse to be reconciled, tough anti-terror legislation and surveillance.

LOCAL AND INTERNATIONAL JIHADS IN ASIA, EUROPE AND IRAQ

The connection between local jihads and those fought at the regional and international level provides us with a framework that helps us to understand terrorist movements outside Indonesia. Yasmeen makes this connection in her study of sectarian conflict in Pakistan (see Chapter 6). Donnelly's account of terrorism in the Philippines also places great importance on localized struggles that, prior to 9/11, constituted more simple insurgencies that had few if any regional and international connections (see Chapter 13). Even the case of the London bombings of July 2005 can be placed within this paradigm, although the source of anger cannot be related to longstanding conflicts over land, privilege or religion. Instead, there is growing evidence to support the idea that in Europe the demanding standards of religious fundamentalism attract in particular young people who experience local alienation. Fundamentalism is especially appealing in European towns and cities that tolerate racism against non-white migrants and their locally born and raised children. Islam is not alone in having this appeal – in the United Kingdom, for example, Hindu fundamentalist organizations have been attracting young people to summer youth camps for quasi-military training in India. It has been shown that these fundamentalist groups have also been raising money in the United Kingdom and the United States for 'charitable' activities in India; namely, funding the fundamentalist campaigns that saw the emergence of anti-Muslim pogroms in the Gujarat in early 2002 (Vicziany 2004, pp. 109–12).

In short, the old mujahidin factor and the legacy of the war against the Soviet Union in Afghanistan is greatly muted now, compared with 9/11 and earlier terrorist attacks by Islamic militants against 'the West'. The war in Iraq is no exception. For instance, the evil of Western attacks against Muslims can be expressed most vividly in Iraq because the ongoing war is perceived to be the direct outcome of initiatives taken by the world's leading hegemon, the United States. The behaviour of the US military has fed perceptions of a religious war between Christians and Muslims – the human rights abuses in Abu Graib are only overshadowed by the alleged abuse to which the Koran itself was subjected. The disrespectful treatment of the Koran has provided a universal symbol to which many practising and non-practising Muslims can relate.[5] Iraq has, therefore, become a beacon for the mujahidin who have flooded in from Europe, Saudi Arabia, Egypt, Lebanon and Syria. The numbers may not be large, but even if they represent a minority of insurgents (perhaps no more than 15 per cent) they can inflict enormous damage, given their emotional detachment from local Iraqis.

But who are these mujahidin? According to Saudi and Israeli sources, the mujahidin attracted to the idea of fighting the United States and its allies in Iraq are all new recruits to the jihad. They are typically young men, lacking previous or existing links with Al Qaeda, and lacking any experience or knowledge of the Islamic struggles in Chechnya, Afghanistan or elsewhere. They are overwhelmingly of Arab ethnicity and responding to the war in Iraq, which has acted as a catalyst for their Islamic consciousness. In the words of Peter Bergen (quoted by Bender 2005), 'The [US] president is right that Iraq is a main front in the war on terrorism, but this is a front we created'. And this war is now the chief training ground for a new generation of militants.

Yet another characteristic distinguishes these militants from the previous generations – they are with few exceptions Sunnis challenging the new Shia-dominated government that they accuse of playing into the hands of the United States. The leadership of the Sunni insurgency appeared to have hardened with the rise of Abu Musab alk-Zarqawi (McGirk 2005, p. 25), whose appeal to terrorists was possibly greater than bin Laden's, owing to his origins as a poor boy from the Jordanian slums. The election results of December 2005 are, moreover, unlikely to resolve the risk of escalating sectarian conflict. In the current line-up the formerly privileged Sunnis have won 55 seats compared with 53 by the Kurds and 128 by the Shia parties (Chulov 2006, p. 9). The new political dominance of the Shia reflects their numerical dominance in the Iraqi population (about 65 per cent). This represents a tectonic shift in decision making inside Iraq, and the Sunni minority are predictably reluctant to give up their previous access to jobs, influence and resources. It is a shift that continues to be strongly, and violently, resisted: the lead-up to the December elections was marked by unprecedented violence. On one day alone, 14 September 2005, Shia–Sunni tit-for-tat street fights resulted in 11 bomb blasts, the death of 180 people and the wounding of another 560 (Vincent 2005). The insurgency has escalated in 2006 with the destruction on 23 February of the Golden Mosque in Samarra, one of the holiest Shia sites. Fifty Sunni mosques were destroyed in retaliation, and according to one report as many as 1300 people died in the sectarian conflicts that broke out ('1,300 dead in Iraq sectarian violence' 2006). Talk of a new 'religious war' in Iraq has now taken on a serious tone.

Rising sectarian conflict between Sunni and Shia is a feature of domestic terrorism in Pakistan too, as Yasmeen notes in this volume. However, in contrast to Iraq, the Shia in Pakistan constitute a minority of about 20 per cent or some 26 million people. The Sunni–Shia divide is a very old one but since 9/11 it has re-emerged with new importance. 9/11 was organized by Al Qaeda. The US reaction to Al Qaeda, the Taliban and other sympathizers has split the Muslim world along new lines. When the American President declared 'war on terror' his primary targets were the Sunni leaders in Al Qaeda. This has not been lost on Shia throughout the Middle East and South Asia. In Pakistan there has been a call by Shia thinkers for militant members of their communities to abandon their hatred of the United States and instead harness the US fight against Al Qaeda and the Taliban as part of Shia resistance to Sunni dominance. In the words of Zafar Hashmi, the time is now long overdue for Pakistani Shias to abandon their call 'Death to America' (Hashmi 2005).

What is most interesting about these shifting alliances built on the quicksand of sectarian conflict among Muslims is that there has not been a generalized Muslim response to the US presence in Iraq, despite growing evidence for the view that the US government has cynically manipulated information about global terror in order to justify pre-emptive military intervention in the Middle East. It has now emerged that French intelligence as early as 2001 insisted that there was no evidence to substantiate the claim that Iraq was buying raw materials for a nuclear weapons program (AFP 2005). The 9/11 Commission found no evidence of any 'collaborative operational relationship' between bin Laden and the Iraqi dictator, or of any cooperation by Iraq in attacks on the United States by Al Qaeda (*9/11 Commission Report* 2004, p. 66). The Carnegie Endowment also concluded that there 'was and is no solid evidence of a cooperative relationship between Saddam's government and Al Qaeda' (Cirincione et al. 2004, p. 48). If there were any collaboration it was between bin Laden and the Saudis in the form of financial support (*9/11 Commission Report* 2004, p. 66). The Carnegie report identified four different types of misrepresentation of evidence that, in a situation where 'intelligence assessments were unduly influenced by policy makers' (Cirincione et al. 2004, p. 50), led to unwarranted conclusions about Saddam's regime and ultimately to the US invasion. Iran had also been identified in President Bush's 'axis of evil' speech, but the 9/11 Commission 'found no evidence that Iran or Hezbollah was aware of the planning for what later became the 9/11 attack' (*9/11 Commission Report* 2004, p. 241).

STOP WORRYING AND LOVE THE BOMBINGS?

The war in Iraq is cited above, not only because it throws up questions about the connection between local sectarianism and transnational and trans-regional terror, but also because it raises fundamental questions about the extent to which terrorism rather than other factors constitutes the main threat to global security. To paraphrase the subtitle to Kubrick's film, *Dr Strangelove*, are we 'learning to stop worrying and love the bombings'? Has terrorism been serving some unpredictable yet useful purposes? Has terrorism strengthened the hand of the state? In particular, has the global 'war on terror' served the purpose of increasing US political and economic hegemony?

Acharya (Chapter 5) in this collection reflects on how a syndrome of fear has overtaken the global stage, driven largely by the most powerful nation in the world, which is also the most fearful. As Acharya notes, 'The hegemon's fears beget fear of the hegemon' and fear of the hegemon fuels further fear and hatred, in particular among Islamic militants who see this perpetual, low-intensity conflict as the path towards a pan-Islamic global state. During recent fieldwork in western China I discovered that Huntington's book, *The Clash of Civilisations*, had been translated not only into Mandarin but also into some minority languages including Uygur, the language of one of China's Muslim communities. One person who had read Huntington said that he had done so because when the inevitable war between Islam and the West broke out he wanted to know why he was fighting on the side of Islam. The fact that Huntington was an American academic seemed to be highly relevant to this person, despite my protestations about Huntington's work being both misunderstood and simultaneously a work that had occasioned great debate in 'the West'.

Since 9/11 the hegemon's fears have been sharply preoccupied with Islamic militants, with the result that Islam has virtually become synonymous with terrorism as far as the US government and media are concerned. Yet as Muni and Sakamoto remind us, in other parts of the world, terrorism is a far more complex and multi-layered phenomenon. In South Asia the word 'terrorism' has come to include a wide range of old and new militancies: peasant wars for land reform, ethnic nationalities fighting against the encroachment of numerically dominant 'foreigners', Maoists fighting kings, Buddhists fighting Hindus, and Islamic terrorists fighting for Kashmir (see Chapter 14). Sakamoto (Chapter 18), who writes on Japan's experience with terrorism, serves to remind us that the first and only organization in Asia to use 'weapons of mass destruction' was Aum Shinrikyo – a millenarian Buddhist movement bent on the universal destruction of a world order that they perceive to be evil. Despite the horrors of Aum Shinrikyo's sarin gas attack on the Tokyo subway and other criminal activity, Aum continues to exist and function in Japan today, and has even experienced some modest growth in membership. The Japanese public is 'learning to live with the threat of terrorism' without the state adopting any stringent position against it.

In contrast to the Japanese experience, the United States, western Europe and Australia have increasingly turned to draconian anti-terrorism legislation to protect the public against mass casualty violence. However, the fear of attacks by Muslim extremists has now been joined by an equally palpable fear, namely that the new acts will erode civil liberties. Mendelsohn notes that until now the new powers of the Australian state have been used with restraint, but there is no certainty that this will remain the case (see Chapter 4). In South-east Asia, anti-terrorist legislation has had a chequered history, but the erosion of civil liberties is perhaps less of an issue simply because Malaysia, Singapore and the Philippines have all been authoritarian states in the post-colonial period (see Chapters 4, 11 and 13). As Donnelly notes in the case of the Philippines, the expanded authoritarianism of the state risks further entrenchment of a privileged elite that may ultimately lack the credibility to bring the Muslim minorities of Mindanao into the mainstream.

The self-serving stance that the Asian elites have taken on the global 'war on terror' is addressed by Yasmeen in the case of Pakistan. Yet, as she notes, the precarious balancing act that leaders like General Musharraf have embarked on is fraught with danger. In order to satisfy the US demand for the apprehension of international terrorists, Musharraf has arrested dozens of suspects, but he has done so in a manner that aims to avoid alienating Islamists who remain his most powerful weapon against the secular opposition parties that contest the legitimacy of his military rule. Musharraf's half-hearted clamp-down on terrorists is not the only problem in controlling terrorism in South Asia. At a much more fundamental level, Hoodbhoy (Chapter 8) and Bokhari (Chapter 7) note that school textbooks in Pakistan and Afghanistan continue to promote jihad as one of the attributes of a good citizen. The problem of ideological indoctrination, it seems, lies not with the much maligned religious schools or *madrassahs* but rather with the government schools that use these official textbooks. The paradox does not end there either: some of these textbooks have been designed and financed with the support of Western governments and aid agencies.

The global 'war on terror' has been an incomplete and lopsided effort, despite the rhetorical flourishes about stamping out mass casualty terrorism. Tolerating government textbooks that harden children to the horrors of violent jihad is only one of the many details that has slipped through the network of surveillance. Another equally devastating form of blindness is addressed by Srinivasan (Chapter 2), that is, how the mechanisms for capital flight from poor countries to the West are the very same mechanisms that have made it possible for terrorist organizations to accumulate capital in 'safe havens' from where funds can be shifted as needed to finance transnational violence. Srinivasan argues that US legislation prevents US banks from accepting money earned from a list of 200 classes of domestic crime. But when it comes to accepting foreign deposits the same strict criteria are ignored; only 15 of these 200 classes of crimes are applied to funds generated in foreign jurisdictions. Unless 'dirty money' is defined in a consistent manner, regardless of the jurisdiction in which it is created, the United States and other Western governments that tolerate tax havens and 'private banking business' are encouraging not only the impoverishment of poor countries but also the terrorism that the global 'war on terror' is supposed to stop. These contradictory policies also feed negative perceptions of the United States and its allies by suggesting that not even the fear of terrorism is strong enough to prevent rich nations from sucking into their orbits whatever global wealth has been generated, regardless of the means by which it was created.[6] Again, the economics underpinning the war in Iraq, in particular the role of the US Defense Department in distributing jobs to contractors, reinforces these impressions.

Of course, narrow national self-interest continues to dominate not only the policies of the West but also those of the nations in the Asia Pacific. As Nathan, Muni and Wright-Neville argue in this volume, the mutual suspicion and fear that state actors in the region have of each other has made regional collaboration on controlling terror and arms exceedingly difficult. The cultural complexity of the Asian nations has also constrained the hand of government, despite the authoritarian traditions in the region. The pressures of nation building in the case of Malaysia and Indonesia, both countries with large Muslim populations, have ensured a more moderate tone in condemning Islamic extremism, much to the irritation of the United States and its allies. The difficulty of reconciling domestic political interests with US priorities is especially revealing in the case of the Philippines, one of America's most loyal allies (see Chapter 12). The outcome of these conflicting national interests is that the 'war on terror' has not replaced the more fundamental questions that remain about the future security architecture of the Asia Pacific.

Perhaps the most dramatic example of national self-interest as the driver of a new security architecture in the Asia Pacific is the creeping arms race that has emerged in the region. Even modestly ambitious nations such as Singapore and Malaysia have started to restructure their defence forces in a manner that reflects their new concerns with what is happening in their neighbourhood (see Chapter 11). In particular, they are building capacities to ensure some say in determining the way in which security of the sea lanes and the distribution of the resources of the seas will be decided. In India and China we see examples of highly ambitious procurement programs designed to increase the range and capacity of the military hardware of two emerging economic powers. Kopp's careful study of these trends also reminds us that Russia, a major supplier of military equipment to India and China, is not to be left out of any consideration of regional security in the Asia Pacific (Chapter 16). Increasing the air power of these emerging giants also propels the proliferation of missiles. Sheppard (see Chapter 15) documents the missile competition between India and Pakistan. Given the nuclear status of both countries, the growing missile capability of India and Pakistan is a serious development. China, as much as the United States, is concerned about this.

Since the Kargil 'war' between Pakistan and India in May 1999, China has become less and less supportive of Pakistan's demand that India be a party to solving the Kashmir crisis through international intervention. When the Pakistani Prime Minister, Nawaz Sharif, went to China in late June 1999 for a scheduled five-day visit, the meetings were reduced to one day, largely because China wished to signal its determination to find a peaceful solution to Kashmir (Singh and Davis 1999). Sharif had gone to Beijing to get sympathy for Pakistan's Kargil initiative as a way of pushing India into multilateral negotiations. Despite these low-level hostilities between India and Pakistan, as Durrani argues in Chapter 9, the 'composite dialogue' of 1997 survived. The bilateral agreement in 1997 was to end the Indo-Pakistani deadlock by separating the different issues that divided them. Eight separate working parties were set up with the right to begin resolving individual issues within their brief, even when other issues being addressed by other parties lagged behind. As Durrani notes, 'The very fact that the framework evolved in 1997 had survived nuclear tests, the Kargil episode, a military coup, 9/11 and the stand-off of 2002 proves that it was wisely conceived'. In April 2005 the Indian and Pakistani governments moved towards developing people-to-people links even in the case of Kashmir, with a new bus service carrying passengers between the two divided parts of Kashmir. China's position on all these developments has been to encourage rapprochement in the language of friendly reconciliation that has moved beyond China's traditional support for Pakistan in the direction of developing India as a major regional trade partner. By the end of 2005, Indo-China trade was worth about US$17 billion, making China into India's most important economic partner after the United States.

China's policies vis-à-vis South Asia stand in contrast to those of the United States, which in recent years has been giving extensive military aid to the King of Nepal in his war against Maoist insurgents, who are fighting a classical, peasant battle for land rights and recognition of the needs of the indigenous Nepalese Buddhist minorities (Vicziany 2006, pp. 387–8). There is widespread concern that US policy in the Himalayas is designed to establish a US foothold in the region. On a wider canvas, there is growing alarm about US determination to develop a national missile defence system. Beazley (Chapter 17) presents an argument against Australian support for the US missile system, in contrast to the official position that remains ambiguous. The consequences of ambiguity are serious (see below).

In another sharp contrast to US policies towards the Asia Pacific, Laakso (Chapter 3) explains why it has been easy to forget that the European Union has now become a political player in the Asian region as a result of releasing its first security policy statement in December 2003. As Laakso notes, the competing national priorities of EU members and the lack of obvious instruments for pursuing a coordinated political strategy on Asia make it easy to underrate the role that the European Union could play in the region. Despite this she argues that 'the European Union could exercise remarkable power on the ground ... and is capable of developing a soft footprint in Asia in contrast to the more strident polices of the United States'. It is the strident policies of the United States that are creating openings in the Asia Pacific for the more moderate language and strategies of the Europeans. The multi-polarity of EU approaches to security, in particular its emphasis on toning down the language of belligerence and focusing on confidence-building exercises, makes the new leaders of Asia much more comfortable and willing to negotiate their way through situations in contrast to digging in their heels in response to the often overbearing and pre-emptive military language of the United States. In the past that militarist tone was linked to the extensive on-ground presence of US troops in Asia and Europe. The new technology, however, makes it possible to achieve the same objectives with much reduced ground forces. Less is more, in this case (Noonan 2005), with the result that the withdrawal of US troops from the Asia Pacific arena is unlikely to produce a softer language.

HOW THE CHAPTERS IN THIS VOLUME ARE ORGANIZED

The chapters in this collection have been touched on in the previous sections in order to place them in a wider, global framework and show how the different issues dealt with in this volume are interrelated. However, the organization of the chapters follows a slightly different order. The remainder of Part 1 brings together four chapters that address the question of regional security in the Asia Pacific in broad policy terms. Srinivasan analyses the ineffectiveness of anti-money-laundering legislation, Laakso highlights the potential of new EU security policies, Mendelsohn looks at national differences in anti-terrorism legislation and Acharya provides a critique of the US 'war on terror'.

The second part of this volume takes the form of various country case studies beginning with four chapters about Pakistan. Research on Pakistan remains paltry, and yet Pakistan is now at the interface between the changing security scenarios in the Asia Pacific to its east and Central Asia to its west. It is for this reason that we have included four different perspectives on Pakistan. Three of the chapters focus on the domestic situation in Pakistan, and all the authors link the internal situation to wider regional concerns. The second group of chapters pertains to South-east Asia. All four deal with counter-terrorism in its many aspects. The third group of chapters deals with South Asia and shift the focus sharply to great power politics. This is hardly surprising for the following reasons: first, terrorism is a very old problem in South Asia and not especially related to 9/11 or Islamic militancy; second, the key players in South Asia, namely India and Pakistan, are both nuclear weapons states in addition to having a 50-year history of conventional confrontation; and third, both Pakistan and India have reformulated their relationships with the world's leading powers – namely the United States and China. For these reasons, South Asia not only throws the whole question of terrorism as defined since 9/11 into sharp relief but also compels us to question whether terrorism is more of a threat to regional and human security than great power rivalry. Chapter 14 explicitly links the two issues together by drawing attention to the problem of state-sponsored terrorism.

The final four chapters in this volume help to complete the analysis by returning to two fundamental questions: the role of the United States in the Asia Pacific and weapons of mass destruction. Beazley (Chapter 17) argues that building US security via National Missile Defence (NMD) undermines China's sense of security and therefore has the potential to give way to 'destabilizing strategic competition'. NMD stands in sharp contrast to EU policies of engagement. Again the words that President Bush uttered after 9/11 continue to haunt us: 'Why do they hate us?' Despite 'blowback', the by now well-documented adverse responses to US foreign and defence policies (Johnson 2002), the US administration still cannot see how it has created a domino effect. The result of US efforts to contain all military acquisitions except its own can be seen in Chapter 16, which documents the range and extent of Chinese purchases of Russian military hardware. Chinese acquisitions are increasingly matched by India, which, as Sheppard (Chapter 15) notes, is also involved in a competitive relationship with Pakistan's missile program. As one authority on the Indian nuclear program stated in 1998, India's nuclear capacity is not directed at Pakistan; rather it is China specific.[7] This is not very comforting to Pakistan, however, because the size of India's response to China greatly outweighs what India needs to contain Pakistan. This dynamic three-way relationship brings us back to the fundamental question: what is driving China's military acquisitions and productions program? The unambiguous answer is US security policies in the Asia Pacific.

Sakamoto's chapter on Aum Shinrikyo is appropriately located at the end of this collection. It serves as a timely reminder that millenarian movements of all persuasions can manifest a destructive character not unique to militant Islamists.

CONCLUSION

What is happening in the Asia Pacific and what is the connection between controlling terrorism and controlling arms? Chapter 12 provides a dramatic example of the dynamic nature of this relationship. When the Philippine government withdrew its troops from Iraq in order to rescue a Filipino worker from execution by the Iraqi terrorists who had kidnapped her, President Macapagal-Arroyo decided to woo China. This was done to bolster the Philippines' relationship with the rising superpower and also to contain US criticism of the decision to place the life of migrant Filipino workers above the interests of the US 'war on terror' in the Middle East. This double blow for the United States also signals tacit consent for the rise of China as a regional power. Had the United States been more sympathetic to the dilemmas facing the Philippine government, the Philippines would not have been propelled into the arms of China – at least not so quickly. As this case suggests, the US strategy of controlling terrorism has acted against its strategy of containing the arms race and containing the influence of China.

A more recent example can be cited to show how US impatience, coupled with high-tech military intervention, is directly undermining the credibility of the fragile regimes that the Western allies are supporting in Pakistan and Afghanistan. On 13 January 2006, in hunting for the deputy leader of Al Qaeda, US forces in Afghanistan fired into three Pakistani villages in a pre-dawn raid. It is alleged that the Pakistan government was not informed and that at least 18 Pakistani villagers died, including five children. Protest rallies followed, the largest in Karachi with some 5000 people. The most important Islamic party responded by attacking the Musharraf government for being 'American slaves' (Witte and Khan 2006). Musharraf's own Foreign Minister provided a fuller explanation of why Pakistanis were so angry: 'Such an action creates immense internal problems for us as the perception grows that the US has no respect for our sovereignty' (Kasuri, cited in Witte and Khan 2006). The infringement on Pakistani sovereignty overshadowed the news that perhaps two senior Al Qaeda commanders were also killed (Khan 2006).

Controlling arms and terror in the Asia Pacific requires less draconian legislation and less military intervention. As I have suggested in this chapter, the style of US responses to arms proliferation and transnational terror has sometimes driven allies into the arms of potential challengers to US hegemony and sometimes weakened the capacity of those allies to handle complex situations that reflect the delicate domestic political situations that have evolved in the post-colonial era. It is not surprising, therefore, that during the Beijing Security Dialogue that gave rise to the present volume, the United States was identified as the number one problem in creating a better security environment in the Asia Pacific. The same militaristic style that has prevented the United States from playing a more constructive and consensual role has embellished the international importance of Islamic militants by constructing paradigms of fear that ignore both the sectarian divisions among Muslims and the potential of other Islamic voices.

If the US strategy against regional and international terrorism in the form of the global 'war on terror' is not working, what is going to work? This is an enormously complicated subject well beyond the grasp of the current chapter. However, what we can say with some confidence is that an effective strategy for countering militancy of all kinds requires governments and armed forces to understand what has driven people to desperate measures. It should not be automatically assumed that these desperate measures are directed at the West, or even the United States in the first instance. Rather, as the argument in the first two sections of this chapter has stressed, the origins of militancy typically lie at the local level – whether we are talking about Islamic, Buddhist, Hindu or Christian militancy, or militancy arising from any number of other causes. It is the local situation that needs to be addressed for, without this, local anger and violence will continue to recruit outsiders to help in the local struggle. That recruitment process carries the dangers of overspilling into regional and even global conflict. Given the current security architecture of the Asia Pacific region, the only clear loser from such a process is the United States, and the only clear winners are the rising regional powers, in particular China and India. In the meantime, we all have to live with the fallout of the creeping arms race and the ever-present fear that arms and terror will spin out of control.

NOTES

1. I am grateful to various people who read the draft of this chapter and in particular to my colleague Dr David Wright-Neville, Co-convenor of the Global Terrorism Research Unit in the Politics Department of Monash University.
2. On 9 November 2005 a baker's assistant by the name of Muriel Degauque blew herself up together with five Iraqi policemen controlling a road north of Baghdad. She was a 38-year-old convert to Islam with a history of 'rebellious' behaviour. She had married a Moroccan fundamentalist and entered on her Iraqi mission via Syria (Browne and Watson 2005). The London bombings of July 2005 also destroyed simplistic explanations about the nature and origins of modern terrorism (O'Neill 2005, p.6).
3. Mrs Rishawi entered Amman, capital of Jordan, with her husband some four days prior to attempting to blow herself up in the Raddison Hotel during a wedding reception. Al Qaeda claimed responsibility for the suicide bombings, which involved three separate sites and killed 57 people (BBC News 2005).
4. Sidney Jones has described DI, an organization characterized by many factions and splinter groups, as an extended family that collaborates and squabbles. Indonesians speak of DI as a large house that has rooms for all.
5. There has been considerable controversy about whether and how the Koran was mishandled in Abu Graib ('Newsweek was Right' 2005). Whatever the truth of the allegations, the important fact is that they have been widely reported. Even the English language Chinese press has carried stories about these accusations ('FBI Memo: Guantanamo Guards Flushing Koran' 2005).
6. Another example of a damaging contradiction arises from the war in Iraq. About 13 000 cluster munitions were used by US and British forces in Iraq. These contained some two million 'bomblets', and during the 'decapitation campaign' to bring down Saddam Hussein some 1000 civilians were killed largely by ground launchers operating in populated areas (Human Rights Watch 2003a; 2003b, pp. 80–99). In addition to the mortality caused on impact (owing to the wide dispersion of the bomblets) their coloured canisters that look like soft drinks, toys or food packets attracts the attention of children, who have been injured by collecting these unexploded bombs. Cluster munitions have been deemed to be as destructive as land mines. Despite this, cluster bombs could be purchased at a weapons fair held in London in September 2005 (Shah 2005, p. 18). It is hard for the layperson in an Asian country to understand why the United States invaded Iraq in order

to destroy 'weapons of mass destruction' when the United States and its allies market cluster munitions.
7. Statement made at the 1st Security Dialogue organized by the Monash Asia Institute in Melbourne, August 1998. The two-day conference was held under Chatham House rules and so the identity of this speaker cannot be released.

REFERENCES

9/11 Commission Report: Final Report of the National Commission on Terrorist Attacks upon the United States (2004), Official Govt Edition, Washington: US Government Printing Office.

'1,300 dead in Iraq sectarian violence' (2006), *Guardian Unlimited*, 28 February, www.guardian.co.uk/Iraq/Story/0,,1719976,00.html, accessed February 2006.

AFP (2005), 'French told CIA nukes claim was bogus', *The Australian*, 13 December, www.theaustralian.news.com.au/common/story_page/0,5744,17545760%255 E2703,00.html, accessed December 2005.

BBC News (2005), 'Jordan Shows "Would-be Bomber"', 13 November, http://news.bbc.co.uk/2/hi/middle_east/4433712.stm, accessed November 2005

Bender, Bryan (2005), 'Study Cites Seeds of Terror in Iraq: War Radicalized Most, Probes Find', *Boston Globe*, 17 July, www.boston.com/news/world/middleeast/articles/2005/07/17/study_cites_seeds_of_terror_in_iraq?mode=PF, accessed November 2005.

Browne, Anthony and Rory Watson (2005), 'Belgian waitress turned Baghdad bomber', *The Weekend Australian,* 3–4 December, 10.

Chulov, Martin (2006), 'Shi'ites, Kurds ready to talk deals on coalition', *The Australian*, 23 January, 9.

Cirincione, Joseph, Jessica Mathews, George Perkovich and Alexis Orton (2004), *WMD in Iraq – Evidence and Implications*, Carnegie Endowment for International Peace, Washington.

'FBI Memo: Guantanamo guards flushing Koran' (2005), Chinadaily.com 26 May, www.chinadaily.com.cn/english/doc/2005-05/26/content_445909.htm, accessed January 2006.

Fitzpatrick, Stephen (2005), 'JI fights on minus bomber', *The Australian,* 11 November, 15.

Hashmi, Zafar (2005), 'The Shia Strategy in Iraq and Iran', *Shia News.com*, 22 January, www.shianews.com/hi/articles/politics/0000400.php, accessed December 2005.

Human Rights Watch (2003a), 'US: hundreds of civilian deaths in Iraq were preventable', New York, 12 December, pp. 1–3, http://hrw.org/english/docs/2003/12/12/iraq6582.htm, accessed January 2006.

Human Rights Watch (2003b), *Off Target: The Conduct of the War and Civilian Casualties in Iraq*, New York, Washington, London, Brussels, http://hrw.org/reports/2003/usa1203/, accessed January 2006.

ICG (International Crisis Group) (2005a), *Recyling Militants in Indonesia: Darul Islam and the Australian Embassy Bombings*, Asia Report No. 92, 22 February.

ICG (International Crisis Group) (2005b), *Weakening Indonesia's Mujahidin Networks – Lessons from Maluku and Poso*, Asia Report No. 103, 13 October.

Johnson, Chalmers (2002), *Blowback: The Costs and Consequences of American Empire*, London: Time Warner.

Jones, Sidney (2005), 'New developments with Jemaah Islamiyah', talk as Visiting

Fellow, Institute for Southeast Asian Studies, Singapore, and Project Director, ICG, 5 July, www.icg.org accessed October November 2005. (The speech on the ICG web site is accompanied by a powerpoint presentation.)

Khan, Ismail (2006), 'Two senior Al Qaeda men killed in Bajaur raid', *Dawn*, 19 January, www.dawn.com/2006/01/19/top4.htm, accessed January 2006.

Khosrokhavar, Farhad (2005), *Suicide Bombers: Allah's New Martyrs*, trans. by David Macey, London/Ann Arbor MI: Pluto Press.

McGirk, Tim (2005), 'The rise of an evil protégé', *Time*, 19 December, 23–5.

'Newsweek was right' (2005), *The Nation*, 18 May, www.chinadaily.com.cn/english/doc/2005-05/26/content_445909.htm, accessed January 2006.

Noonan, Michael P. (2005), 'When less is more: the transformation of American expeditionary land power in Europe', Foreign Policy Research Institute, Subscription E Note of 24 May.

O'Neill, Sean (2005), 'Blasts destroyed UK terror theories', *The Australian*, 29 December, 6.

Powell, Sian (2005a), 'Second Bali bomber slips the net', *The Weekend Australian*, 12–13 November, 6.

Powell, Sian (2005b), 'The Bali bomb maker's death will be avenged', *The Weekend Australian*, 12–13 November, 24.

Shah, Saeed (2005), 'Cluster Bombs on Offer at Arms Fair Despite Sales Ban', *The Independent,* 14 September, 18.

Singh, Ajay and Anthony Davis (1999), 'The price of conflict', *Asiaweek*, 9 July, www.asiaweek.com/asiaweek/99/0709/nat1.html, accessed December 2005.

Vicziany, Marika (2004), 'Globalisation and Hindutva: India's experience with global economic and political integration', in Gloria Davies and Chris Nyland (eds), *Globalisation in the Asian Region: Impacts and Consequences*, Cheltenham, UK and Northampton, MA, USA: Edward Elgar, pp. 92–116.

Vicziany, Marika (2006), 'Nepal: economy', in Lynn Daniel (ed.), *South Asia 2006*, London and New York: Routledge/Taylor & Francis Group, pp. 386–400.

Vincent, Michael (2005), 'Al-Qaeda Declares war on Iraqi Shia population', ABC Transcripts, 15 September, www.abc.net.au/pm/content/2005/s1461303.htm, accessed December 2005.

Witte, Griff and Kamran Khan (2006), 'Attacks strain efforts on terror', *Washington Post*, 23 January, www.washingtonpost.com/wp-dyn/content/article/2006/01/22/AR2006012200759.html, accessed January 2006.

2. Money laundering and security

Kannan Srinivasan

'Money laundering' is the term used to describe the concealment of the profits of crime, as well as of the funds needed to carry out criminal acts that, for reasons of safety, consumption or the need to use the funds, may be transferred across international borders. Today money laundering is seen as a threat to security because it has been connected with the financing of serious international crime, including the narcotics trade, and acts of terror have been organized and funded in a manner that has been entirely undetectable. As Senator Carl Levin has said:

> We live in a post-9-11 world. After the attack on America, we strengthened our anti-money laundering laws, in part, because Osama bin Laden boasted that his modern new recruits knew the 'cracks' in 'Western financial systems' like they knew the 'lines in their hands.' That chilling statement helped fuel a new effort to strengthen our defenses against terrorists, corrupt dictators, and others who would use our financial systems against us. (Levin 2004)

Another view is addressed below, namely that terrorism has been financed by a unique, ancient, Middle East-Asian financial system known as *havala*.

HAVALA, PRIVATE BANKING, CAPITAL FLIGHT AND TERROR

It is claimed that *havala* is a creation of drug lords and terrorists and exists solely to serve them. The following extract from a report in *Time* is an example of this kind of thinking:

> Welcome to the world of hawala, an international underground banking system that allows money to show up in the bank accounts or pockets of men like hijacker Mohammed Atta, without leaving any paper trail. ... 'People know that salaries cannot buy the good things,' says Ali ... 'You need a little extra.' Even at a cost of enabling crime and terrorism. (Ganguly 2001)

There is no doubt that terrorist organizations have used the *havala* network. This was documented by the 9/11 Commission Report:

> ... Al Qaeda frequently moved the money it raised by hawala, an informal and ancient trust-based system for transferring funds ... Bin Ladin relied on the established hawala networks operating in Pakistan, in Dubai, and throughout the Middle East to transfer funds efficiently. (9/11 Commission 2004, p. 188)

Yet neither money laundering nor *havala* is the creation of terrorists or drug lords. *Havala*, a system of money transfers that originated in India several centuries ago, far surpasses the international banking system in the efficiency, speed and low cost of its operations. It serves a large population, most of whom are otherwise law-abiding citizens. To attempt to stop *havala* while leaving the formal system of private banks and trusts and tax havens intact would serve no purpose other than to protect the profits of the cartel of international banks (McCulloch and Pickering 2005).

Moreover, *havala* is not the actual mechanism that ensures capital flight. Indeed, that flight has already taken place through a range of mechanisms, including the over-invoicing and under-invoicing of trade. Once the money is overseas, *havala* is only a system of providing liquidity on the back of those funds. Even without *havala*, this money would have departed, and would have been placed in investment projects or money centre banks.

Havala is not the most important way to launder money. It is true that money laundering can assist acts that are criminal in *every* jurisdiction (or country) such as drugs or terror. But there are other crimes such as tax evasion that are treated as criminal in the particular jurisdictions where they originate. It is crimes such as these, which include corruption such as kickbacks for government contracts (Srinivasan 1995) and other theft of public assets, that really drive the vast global business of laundering money.

In fact terrorists are relative newcomers who have skilfully employed widely available services. Terrorists and drug lords use *havala* but they also use the main money centre banks, trusts and tax havens – all of which are effectively unsupervised and not monitored. Yet the United States has been unwilling to entertain the prospect of any meaningful regulation for this entire world of money laundering. Given this, it is worth explaining the United States' position.

MONEY LAUNDERING AND THE UNITED STATES

The United States benefits significantly from funds laundered by companies, banks and financial institutions. Together all this laundering brings in significant capital. This, along with the investments in US instruments (such as United States Treasury securities and corporate stocks and bonds) by the Asian economies, has helped the United States to finance its current account deficit.

The U.S. net international investment position at yearend 2004 was $2,484.2 billion ... largely due to substantial net foreign purchases of U.S. Treasury securities and U.S. corporate bonds ... Foreign-owned assets in the United States ... increased ... to $12,515.0 billion with foreign direct investment in the United States valued at market value. (Bureau of Economic Analysis 2005)

There was significant flight to the dollar when the Soviet Union collapsed and was looted. Raymond Baker, an eminent scholar at the Brookings Institution and author of *Capitalism's Achilles Heel* (2005), has estimated that as much as half a trillion dollars may have left Russia in the 1990s, and a significant part of that migrated to the United States (Baker et al. 2003, p. 5; Senate Money Laundering 1999, p. 85).

The widespread capital flight to the United States has been independently documented in a study that has offered examples of how this works: Russian caviar is exported to the United States at US$3 a kilo and 5642 kg were exported in 1999, while actual market prices have ranged around US$5000. In the same year Russia imported bicycle tyres at US$364 each, when the actual market price outside Russia could not have been more than US$30 (Boyrie et al. 2004). Much the same happened when the Asian economies suffered massive capital fight in the 1990s.

Baker has shown that US multinational banks and corporations developed techniques for mis-pricing, false documentation setting up fake companies and shell banks, and developing business in tax havens and secret banking jurisdictions. They play the important role of funnelling funds to the United Kingdom or the United States. These techniques were subsequently adopted by drug cartels in the 1960s and 1970s and by other criminal syndicates during the 1980s. More recently, terrorists have adopted the same mechanisms originally developed by multinationals.

Baker points out that US law tolerates money laundering when that occurs on the basis of money 'earned' outside the United States:

Anti-money laundering legislation in the United States identifies more than 200 classes of domestic crimes, called *predicate offenses*. If a person knowingly handles the proceeds of these crimes, then a money-laundering offense has been committed. However, only 12 to 15 of these offenses are applicable if the crime is committed outside U.S. borders, and these have to do principally with drugs, crimes of violence and bank fraud. (Baker et al. 2003, p. 2; House Committee Money Laundering 2000 p. 105)

US regulations do not currently respond to these money laundering systems. Although the United States has a Foreign Corrupt Practices Act (1998) that makes it illegal for Americans to bribe foreign government officials, it is not illegal to handle or solicit funds acquired from corruption committed in any jurisdiction outside the United States (House Committee Money Laundering

2000, p. 106). US regulators have turned a blind eye to the frequent failure by US banks to file 'Suspicious Activities Reports'. In a number of transactions concerning trade deals or government contracts, no matter what the size of the deal, an unvarying percentage of the transaction has been paid out of certain bank accounts to third parties that hold another account in the same bank (ibid., p. 109). This raises suspicion that these may be kickbacks – why else would the identical percentage of the amount of the deal be paid into the account of a third party unless he were some sort of facilitator or commission agent? Such transactions should invite further attention. Indeed, banks are enjoined by regulation to investigate such transactions but they generally have chosen not to do so, because US regulators do not pursue such negligence.

The United States has enacted an Advance Pricing Agreement that makes it difficult for foreign corporations with local subsidiaries in the United States to mis-price trade in order to take tax-evading money out of the country, placing the onus for demanded clarifications squarely on the suspected evader. Yet officials turn a blind eye to mis-pricing that brings tax-evading money from other countries *into* the United States. It has never addressed money being brought into America through transfer pricing, for instance. It is entirely concerned with outflows, not inflows (House Committee Money Laundering 2000, pp. 108–9).

Karin Lissakers has discussed the lending boom to the Third World during the 1970s and 1980s, and the collusion of US bankers in siphoning funds off to the private accounts of the Third World elite. The Edge Act banks were set up in Florida for the specific purpose of laundering Latin American capital flight funds. Capital removed from many developing economies, and now deposited in money centre banks, has frequently matched or exceeded the amounts borrowed by those countries. The money centre banks, with an international presence and important wholesale business, include Citibank and JP Morgan Chase. They are involved in all the important areas of financial activity, namely corporate finance, trading, distribution and portfolio business (Lissakers 1991, p. 7). Lissakers cites a World Bank estimate that Argentina, Mexico and Venezuela, and perhaps other Latin American countries in the 1980s, had private deposits abroad that exceeded their sovereign debt. A large part of these funds were held in the United States. She points out that in 1984 US Treasury Secretary Baker had the withholding tax on non-resident owners of US securities withdrawn, in order, as Rudiger Dornbusch commented, 'for foreigners to use the US financial system as a tax haven' (ibid.).

Taxes in the United States are generally withheld at source by the Internal Revenue Service (IRS) on earnings in bank deposits and portfolio investments. But the Reagan Administration amended the law to provide a special exemption to foreign investors in US securities and bank deposits from this tax withheld at source. This exemption continues today. Such foreign investors are in fact paying no taxes anywhere; in courting them, the United States has become an important tax haven.

As the conservative American business economist Lawrence Hunter has pointed out: 'For nearly two decades, US law has encouraged foreigners to invest in US banks and debt securities by imposing no tax on interest earned on foreign deposits' (Hunter 2002). He gives instances of opportunities for such investment by foreigners

> interest on bank deposits with US banks is exempted (871(i)(2)(A)) ... Enacted in 1984, the portfolio-interest exception (section 871(h)) is perhaps the greatest single example of Congress's attempt to attract offshore investment. (ibid.)

And why has this been done? It is in the interests of the United States. To quote Hunter again:

> The rationale of the portfolio-interest exception is perhaps the purest example of enlightened self-interest and realism in attracting foreign capital. ... analysts generally believe that this provision has attracted somewhat over *$1 trillion* in foreign capital to the United States. Former senior Treasury official, Stephen J. Entin (currently President of the Institute of Research on the Economics of Taxation) estimates that private foreign investment here is $8 trillion, of which about $1 trillion is bank deposits. (ibid., emphasis added by author)

According to Hunter, since America benefits it should assist such flight capitalists in keeping their money inside the United States:

> Non-resident aliens who place deposits in US banks ... may be *escaping oppressive tax burdens*, while others may be fleeing corruption and crime. In either event, the *US economy benefits greatly from gaining access to their capital.* ... This capital stimulates economic growth and creates jobs, benefiting US workers and business owners. (ibid., emphasis added by author)

This is really a straightforward admission that the purpose of these amendments is to attract flight capital, including the money of those who do not want to pay taxes. The Reagan Administration provided anonymity to foreign owners of US bonds when it converted them to bearer bonds in 1985. Bearer bonds are debt instruments in which the investor need not be registered with any authority in the world and may remain entirely anonymous and transfer such bonds to whomever the investor pleases. They are ideal for the purpose of laundering money. Yet what has been equally important has been the willingness of US authorities to tolerate the enormous expansion of the US private banking industry. Private banking in this case does not merely refer to the general private banking sector, but rather to the highly specialized business of soliciting and managing the deposits of very wealthy overseas clients. These clients keep their wealth in a place other than their domicile because the money is often criminally or corruptly acquired, or they are avoiding taxes at home.

The private banks serve only 'high net worth' individuals – the very wealthy from all over the world – with a great deal of personal attention and a guarantee of absolute secrecy. In London, for instance, the Bank of America private bank, when I visited it in 1992, was located in the mansion that Charles I gave Nell Gwynn, but was unlisted in the London telephone directory and unknown to most officers of Bank of America London. The 'banques privées' of Switzerland became known between the two world wars as the home of flight capital from other parts of Europe. Essentially, this is the role of the international private banking business. In the United States this grew significantly on Latin American capital flight and was centred on what were called the 'Edge Act' banks, located in Florida (the Edge Act permitted exceptions to the controls on inter-state banking developed during the Depression). These banks handled suitcases of cash from Latin American flight capitalists in the 1970s; they were presumed to be simply stealing their countries' wealth but often turned out to be drug dealers as well. The US private banking business grew rapidly in the 1970s, with the great financial explosion of recycling petrodollars. Since then it has defied effective regulation: it lives on the fear that it might prompt such capital to fly out again.

A dramatic example of public knowledge about money laundering in the United States is provided by the events of the summer of 2004 when the Riggs Bank scandal broke out. The Riggs Bank had been laundering money for many years, with the compliance of officials of the Office of the Comptroller of the Currency appointed to oversee it. Moreover, for years the bank had been advertising its money laundering services on its website in the following manner:

> The Riggs Bank, N.A., of Washington D.C., offers a full range of international private banking services. Our International Service Banking office provides discreet, personalized, and specially adapted activities needed by prominent foreign customers. (Riggs 2000)

As investigations by the Senate Subcommittee on Investigations showed, Riggs was involved in systematic money laundering of the proceeds of crime. This included probably the narcotics trade by General Pinochet, as well as Omar Bongo of Equatorial Guinea, and what investigators suspected was a Saudi contribution to the 9/11 hijackers (Senate Riggs Subcommittee 2004, p. 2).

The case of Riggs was significant: it was no Panamanian hole in the wall but rather the leading Washington DC-based bank, founded in 1836. Among its customers have been 22 American presidents, including Abraham Lincoln and Dwight Eisenhower, as well as prominent personalities such as General Douglas MacArthur. Riggs financed the Mexican War and the purchase of

Alaska and Samuel Morse's invention of the telegraph. It was instrumental in the setting up of the US Federal Reserve. The head of its investment banking division was Jonathan Bush, brother of the former president and therefore uncle of the present one, and formerly head of the family investment bank, J. Bush and Co. The bank and its promoters have had enormous influence and access in the nation's capital. President Bush even stopped during his Inauguration Parade to greet chairman Albritton (Inauguration Day 2001), and the annual dinner in honour of Confederate General Robert Lee was the first public appearance by President Bush and Vice-President Cheney after the 9/11 terrorist attacks (O'Brien 2004).

Senator Carl Levin, ranking Democratic Senator on the Subcommittee on Investigations and former Chair of this committee, pointed out that, with 60 accounts and US$700 million in them, Equatorial Guinea was the bank's largest customer (Levin 2004). Levin describes how Riggs went out of its way to help the EG president set up an offshore shell corporation in the Bahamas called Otong (ibid.). An offshore shell corporation is one that is set up in jurisdictions that levy no income tax and have a minimal investigative regime. This arrangement is also used by many major corporations that are operationally based in the United States or European Union in order to avoid taxation. The headquarters in, say, New York becomes a subsidiary of a Cayman Islands corporation. Obviously, with such shell corporations in the Bahamas, Riggs knew that they were laundering the president's money. At least one of these deposits was personally brought into the Riggs Bank by the Riggs account manager who handled the EG accounts. According to Levin (2004), 'He carried the funds in a suitcase of plastic-wrapped dollar bills weighing 60 pounds or more. If that kind of cash deposit doesn't make a bank sit up and ask questions, I'm not sure anything will.'

US regulators were aware of Riggs' non-compliance with the US anti-money laundering law, but did nothing. Even the possibility that Riggs' negligence and greed may have aided the 9/11 bombers of the World Trade Center did nothing to impart a sense of urgency to federal regulation. Levin is no conspiracy theorist but a mainstream Democrat, known for working closely with Republican Senator McCain in running the powerful Armed Services Committee, as well as the Subcommittee on Investigations with Senator Coleman. As he goes on to say, 'In November 2002, media stories began alleging possible connections between certain Riggs accounts associated with Saudi Arabia and two of the 9-11 hijackers' (Levin 2004). Yet, amazingly, it still took another year for the agencies to impose a US$25 million civil fine on the bank for money laundering.

Another example of the linkages between the highly respectable Riggs Bank and international crime is given by Levin's report on how the bank assisted the Chilean dictator Pinochet, who had been accused of murder, torture, corruption, and narcotics and arms trafficking. Riggs went out of its way to solicit his business. In 1994 top Riggs officials travelled to Chile and asked Pinochet 'if he would like to open an account at the Riggs Bank here in Washington, D.C.' (Levin 2004). Unsurprisingly, 'Mr. Pinochet said yes. The bank opened an account for him personally, helped him establish two offshore shell corporations in the Bahamas … Mr. Pinochet eventually deposited between $4 and $8 million in his Riggs accounts' (ibid.).

Riggs' 'Know your Customer Profile' for Pinochet's business interests states:

> The client is a private investment company domiciled in the Bahamas used as a vehicle to manage the investment needs of a beneficial owner, now a retired professional, who achieved much success in his career and accumulated wealth during his lifetime for retirement in an orderly way. (Senate Riggs Subcommittee 2004)

The client is a company, and the term 'beneficial owner', the language of private banking, describes the real client, whose identity is kept secret in all dealings in the bank itself. So Citibank private bank, for instance, will not tell the Citibank investment bank the identity of investors, but only the names of corporations that they own.

'Success in his career' is a euphemism for a trail of murder and torture, which began with Pinochet's overthrow of a legally elected government. The profile provides the following description as the source of wealth and hence the source of funds in the account: 'High paying position in Public Sector for many years' (ibid., p. 25).

In 1998 Mr Pinochet was arrested in London on charges of crimes against humanity. A Spanish magistrate issued an order seeking to freeze his bank accounts. The order, requiring the attendance of Pinochet on trial for murder of Spanish nationals in Chile, was enforced in the United Kingdom under reciprocal arrangements. Riggs ignored the order of the court and secretly helped him move money from London to the United States. The law enforcement authorities were not alerted to these movements. In 2000, after a British newspaper alleged that Mr Pinochet had over US$1 million in accounts at Riggs Bank, Riggs altered the name on his personal account from 'Augusto Pinochet Ugarte' to 'A.P. Ugarte'. The US Office of the Comptroller of the Currency (OCC) did not even consider taking enforcement action when it was made aware of major irregularities. And the OCC examiner-in-charge of Riggs thereafter took a job with Riggs Bank (Senate Riggs Subcommittee 2004, pp. 18–37).

The Riggs Bank example has been cited here because this institution had such a prominent and respectable history. However, it is far from being a lone example of how money laundering works. Most US banks have made no effort to hide the 'special' laundering facilities that they provide. For example, a brochure for Citibank's private bank advertises the attractions of the secrecy jurisdictions of the Bahamas, the Cayman Islands, Jersey and Switzerland (Senate Money Laundering 1999, p. 7). This brochure goes on to advertise the advantages of using a PIC or private investment corporation. One advantage is: 'your ownership of the PIC need not appear in any public registry' (ibid.).

As Levin observes, given that the United States prohibits US banks from setting up 'secret' accounts that cannot be scrutinized by the authorities, the reaction of the US private banks has been to go offshore to destinations where such legal scrutiny does not apply. Being multinational banks, these US banks have no problems in servicing the needs of their clients by managing these offshore financial deposits (Senate Money Laundering 1999, p. 7). Citibank is one American bank willing to provide just this kind of service to its clients. It is the largest bank in the United States, it has one of the largest private bank operations, and it also has the most extensive global presence of all US banks. In the words of Levin, it also had 'a rogues gallery of private bank clients' (ibid.).

Given Senator Levin's expertise, it is worth recounting his list of the members of Citibank's rogues' gallery:

- Raul Salinas, brother of the former President of Mexico; now in prison in Mexico for murder and under investigation in Mexico for illicit enrichment;
- Asif Ali Zardari, husband of the former Prime Minister of Pakistan; now in prison in Pakistan for kickbacks and under indictment in Switzerland for money laundering;
- Omar Bongo, President of Gabon; subject of a French criminal investigation into bribery;
- sons of General Sani Abacha, former military leader of Nigeria, one of whom is now in prison in Nigeria on charges of murder and under investigation in Switzerland and Nigeria for money laundering;
- Jaime Lusinchi, former President of Venezuela, charged with misappropriation of government funds;
- two daughters of Radon Suharto, former President of Indonesia, who has been alleged to have looted billions of dollars from Indonesia;
- and, it appears, General Albert Stroessner, former President of Paraguay and notorious for decades for a dictatorship based on terror and profiteering (Senate Money Laundering 1999, p. 7).

And these are just the clients we know about. Other banks have similar accounts. When important international criminals have been assisted by the single most important American bank, one can see how unlikely it is that American regulators will be able to intervene selectively against certain categories of crime.

Levin also discusses Bankers Trust and how its officials feared that they would be murdered by their clients if they revealed their names to the US Government.

> The legal counsel for Bankers Trust private bank asked the Subcommittee not to make public any information about an account of a certain Latin American client because the private banker was concerned that the banker's life would be in danger if the information were revealed. (Senate Money Laundering 1999, p. 8).

Clearly the fact that its business could not be revealed even to the US Senate was an acknowledgement that the bank was participating in criminal activity. This important document gives one an idea of the extraordinary scale of the US private banking business, and how focused it is on Third World elite clients that have often made their fortunes by stealing from their countries. Robert Roach, an investigator, showed how the family of Salinas, President of Mexico, spirited its money out of the country via Citibank, to London and Zurich. The president's brother, later arrested for murder, had no legitimate business that could account for such earnings. There was no curiosity about where this money came from; instead, his banker Ms Elliott wrote to her colleagues in June 1993 that the Salinas account 'is turning into an exciting, profitable one for us all. Many thanks for making me look good'. (Roach testimony, Senate Money Laundering 1999, p. 15)

The Patriot Act and its Weaknesses

The Patriot Act, as well as other legislation, seems to make foreign criminal acts illegal in the United States. Yet, as Raymond Baker points out, the Patriot Act's definition of 'specified unlawful activity' provides the loophole needed for money laundering operations. He argues that,

> for crimes committed in the U.S., the definition is very extensive. For crimes committed outside the U.S., it's very restricted, essentially to drug trafficking, terrorism, corruption, bank fraud and some treaty violations. ... foreign tax evasion and handling the proceeds of foreign tax evasion is not a specified unlawful activity under U.S. law. (email by Baker to author, 28 April 2005)

Anti-money-laundering legislation in the United States identifies 'predicate offences' where a person knowingly handles the proceeds of any of 200 classes of crime if committed domestically. Yet the proceeds of all but 15 such crimes are exempt by US law, including the Patriot Act 2001, if the crimes are committed overseas. These include such acts as racketeering, securities fraud, credit fraud, forgery, embezzlement of private funds, burglary, trafficking in counterfeit and contraband goods, slave trading and prostitution. So it is perfectly legal for an American private banker to knowingly solicit the deposit of a South Asian trafficker in women or in illegal immigrants. This amounts to an invitation to those who profit by such crimes to bring their money to the United States.

The definition of what constitutes the 'proceeds of a foreign crime' is given in Section 320 of the Patriot Act (2001), which states that:

f) There is extraterritorial jurisdiction over the conduct prohibited by this section if –
(1) the conduct is by a United States citizen or, in the case of a non-United States citizen, the conduct occurs in part in the United States; and
(2) the transaction or series of related transactions involves funds or monetary instruments of a value exceeding $10,000.

Note that, should the crime be entirely committed outside the US continent, the proceeds of the crime may presumably be safely banked in America. Foreign governments headed by corrupt politicians will not file suit in the United States to test these laws and to curb their own corruption. And the US government does not of its own accord examine whether the proceeds of corruption transit through or are deposited in US banks. The same businesses of private banking, tax havens and other financial services that have sucked in money from around the world to the United States have also enabled such attacks on it that Raymond Baker calls money laundering 'capitalism's Achilles heel'.

UK TAX HAVENS

London is an important financial centre and an important recipient of laundered funds; a significant part of these come from the world's tax havens, led by the Crown Colonies, the offshore possessions of the Queen of Great Britain and Ireland. These are nominally independent, having delegated powers such as the conduct of diplomatic relations to the UK government. In reality, this is a legal fiction as the Channel Islands function as an extension of London and permit the United Kingdom to facilitate money laundering without accepting responsibility for it. The motive of the UK government is identical to that of the United States, namely attracting foreign capital to the national economy.

The Edwards Report has played an important role in exposing the scale of money laundering in the Channel Islands. The Report points out the illusory nature of many of the directorships of the companies listed in the Channel Islands:

11.2.2 Although formally Directors, some of these 'nominee' Directors are Directors of so many companies that they could not credibly discharge the proper duties of a Director with respect to all of them, especially in cases where they have no professional or technical support. (Edwards 1998)

Virtually the entire local population seems to be company directors. It is difficult to believe the scale of these money-laundering facilities, so again I quote from the Edwards Report. Para 11.2.3 describes the population of Sark, the capital, and the distribution of the directorships of these companies:

In Sark itself, where the total population is 575, information fairly readily publicly available in the autumn of last year indicated that:
• total Directorships held by Sark residents may have been around 15000 or more;
• 3 residents appeared to hold between 1600 and 3000 Directorships each;
• a further 16 residents appeared each to hold more than 135 Directorships each; and a further 30 residents appeared each to hold between 15 and 100 Directorships. (ibid.)

The Edwards Report concluded that the residents of Sark, the smallest of the four Channel Islands located some 80 miles south of the English coast, were hardly entrepreneurs who were driving global industries. Sark is best known as a tourist destination renowned for its fishing, lovely walks and gardens. Given this, Sark's residents were most probably front men who were acting on behalf of the real clients located in some other country. Para 11.2.5 of the Edwards Report notes that:

Whatever the precise figures may be, the perception has arisen that many of the Directors on Sark are Directors in name only, not in substance, and the real Directors – or owners of the accounts – are other people altogether. (ibid.)

INDIA AND MONEY LAUNDERING

The United States and the United Kingdom account for the bulk of the world's money-laundering capital movements, but this has depended critically on money-laundering operations in other parts of the world; in particular, India has always been an important conduit for capital flight as discussed below.

One study estimates that several billions of dollars are laundered annually through Indian trade. The authors developed a global price matrix and analysed every single India–United States import and export transaction for the years 1993, 1994 and 1995, to identify where abnormal pricing occurred and the magnitude of consequent capital flight (Zdanowicz et al. 1996). In the most recent year studied, 1995, capital flight from India to the United States effected through the mis-pricing of trade between the two countries is estimated as being up to US$5.58 billion. Were this maximum figure in the range to hold true for other countries with which India trades today, Indian money laundering through trade would exceed US$50 billion annually, although I do not have any estimate for money laundering and capital flight, either in India or globally. After careful analysis Zdanowicz et al. give examples of the scale of such 'abnormal pricing' (see Table 2.1).

Zdanowicz et al. are internationally accepted as the authorities on the mis-pricing of trade, and the consequent capital flight and revenue loss, having completed authoritative studies on Russia and the United States. Their work is now funded by grants from the US Senate.

What has been the official response to this serious study? No specific data have been disputed in the last nine years, in any published paper. But according to Reddy, now Governor of the Reserve Bank of India (RBI), the variation of prices is caused not by money laundering but the inability of Indians to bargain on the global stage:

> Schneider argues that a more probable interpretation of the results for India based on abnormal pricing model can be that the deviation in unit prices of Indian imports and exports with that of average US/World prices reflects India's *poor bargaining position* [sic] in international markets along with other rigidities. (Reddy 1997, p. 5)

Reddy quotes a study by someone called 'Bhatnagar' (no other identification is provided), commissioned by the Planning Commission, which he insists confirms the validity of an equally vague person simply called 'Schneider' (again no other identification is provided). This official publication of the Reserve Bank offers no clue as to the identity of either Schneider or Bhatnagar, despite their importance to Reddy's claims. According to this study, claims Reddy, the reasons exports fared poorly abroad were the 'lack of overseas presence, packing handicaps [sic], lack of price intelligence, poor image of Indian products, incomplete product range, production process not being modern' (ibid.).

The lack of Indian competitiveness may make sense in the case of some Indian exports, but does it make any sense when we analyse the price paid for imports of foreign goods into India? Is it true that Indian firms are buying Beechcraft and Grumman Gulfstream corporate jets at appreciably more than the list price because they cannot bargain? Even in the matter of Indian exports, it is doubtful that all cases of low prices are due to poor bargaining. For example, are Indian firms selling tea at lower prices than Kenya because of their ignorance of true prices or poor bargaining power?

Table 2.1 False pricing in Indo-US trade ($US)

US data item	Value of capital flight by	
	over-invoicing US–India *imports*	under-invoicing India–US *exports*
New aircraft, passenger transports, non-military, of an unladen weight exceeding 15 000 kg (1994)	$58 379 906	
Used or rebuilt military aircraft, of an unladen weight exceeding 15 000 kg (1994)	$21 088 351	
Spark–ignition reciprocating or rotary internal combustion piston engines for civil aircraft used or rebuilt (1994)	$4 435 698	
New multiple-engine airplanes, non-military, of an unladen weight exceeding 2000 kg but not exceeding 4536 kg (1994)	$3 700 715	
Used or rebuilt aircraft, non-military, of an unladen weight exceeding 2000 kg but not exceeding 15,000 kg (1994)	$3 643 918	
Precious and semi-precious stones (except diamonds), unworked (1994)	$3 536 512	
Turbojet aircraft turbines (engines) for use in civil aircraft, of a thrust exceeding 25 kn (1994)	$3 307 794	
Processing unit, which may contain in same housing 1 or 2 of the following units: storage, input or output, with colour cathode ray tube (CRT) (1994)	$3 283 336	
AC generators (alternators) exceeding 40 000 kva (1994)	$2 796 971	
Digital ADP Mach containing in same housing at least a CPU and an input–output unit whether or not combined without CRT (1994)	$2 599 389	
Radio transceivers, Nesoi, for frequencies exceeding 400 mhz (1995)	$12 100 808	
Insulated coaxial cable and coaxial electrical conductors (1995)	$10 860 447	
Turbojet aircraft turbines (engines) for use in civil aircraft, of a thrust exceeding 25 kn (1995)	$8 447 717	
Precious and semi-precious stones (except diamonds) unworked (1995)	$6 636 407	
Unmounted chips, dice and wafers, for digital monolithic integrated circuits of silicon (1995)	$6 165 775	

Table 2.1 Continued

US data item	Value of capital flight by	
	over-invoicing US–India *imports*	under-invoicing India–US *exports*
Digital processing unit which may contain in same housing 1 or 4 of the following units: storage, input or output, with colour cathode ray tubes (1995)	$5 975 521	
Internal combustion engine generators, Nesoi (1995)	$2 818 182	
AC generators (alternators) exceeding 10 000 kva but not exceeding 40 000 kva (1995)	$2 633 722	
New multiple engine airplanes, non-military, of an unladen weight exceeding 2000 kg but not exceeding 4536 kg (1995)	$2 590 995	
Machines for production and assembly of diodes, transistors and similar semiconductor devices and electronic integrated circuits (1995)		$480 352 554
Emeralds cut but not set for jewellery (1995)		$47 558 898
Diamonds except industrial, unworked or simply sawn, cleaved or brutd (1995)		$25 478 963
Rubies, sapphires, emeralds and rock crystals unworked or simply sawn or roughly shaped, not strung, mounted or set (1995)		$18 896 984
Exercise cycles (1995)		$9 226 814
Disc harrows (1995)		$80 757 317
Furnaces and ovens for diffusion, oxidation, or annealing of semi-conductor wafers (1995)		$24 785 810
Rubies cut but not set for jewellery (1995)		$12 755 724

Source: Data extracted from Zdanowicz et al. (1996).

Indian Weaponry Imports and Money Laundering

There is some evidence of inflated prices in Indian defence deals. This suggests kickbacks and money laundering. I have drawn upon submissions by Rear Admiral Suhas Purohit, former Deputy Chief of Naval Logistics, to explain this procedure. He investigated such over-invoicing and money laundering in Indian naval purchases over a period in the 1990s. Russia and the former Commonwealth of Independent States (CIS) are an important source of Indian

Table 2.2 Samples of Indian naval equipment procurement 1993–98 (Rs)

Item description	Official delegation price	Intermediary or agent price
D (408) B crystal	35	17 805 (500 times) (machinery sales corporation)
Relay PEC-9	95	11 192 (118 times) (HC supplies)
Lower cover 383-1-38	1 475	38 725 (26 times) (machinery sales corporation)
Contact 8BC-553-005	145	7 755 (53 times) (HC supplies)
LO pressure cut out (M) CT 1.5A	608	27 876 (46 times) (Makalu)
SN-23 pump (complete)	62 569	2 082 556 (13 times) (HC supplies)

Source: Purohit (2004).

defence procurement, replacing India's defence imports from the Soviet Union. A firm called Makalu, controlled by a former Indian Naval Chief of Staff, exploited this market in the CIS states for procuring equipment spares of Soviet-Russian origin. The very same equipment was significantly cheaper when purchased by Indian logistics delegations visiting Russia or the Ukraine, as Table 2.2 shows.

Deals have generally been conducted through intermediaries in London or New York, even though there is no requirement for this, since the goods supplied would come from Russia and the CIS states. However, London plays a role in these procurements because it is an important private banking centre, and important arms dealers are located in London for this reason. Purohit showed that even when suppliers were important Russian equipment manufacturers such as the Baltic Shipyard, the invoices were still routed through firms such as M/S GS Rughani in London.

The United States may also have become important for the same reasons, since it is a major global player in the arms business, as also in non-resident Indian (NRI) finance. A deal from Kiev for the Kamov-28 helicopter was a tripartite one that included the happily named Banking Investment Saving Insurance Corporation, registered in the United States. This third party turned out to be superfluous and only a conduit for kickbacks (Purohit 2004). Purohit made these investigations officially while Deputy Head of Naval Logistics with the rank of Rear Admiral, and it was the fact of his questioning the nature of official procurement that led to his victimization. Procurement that he organized while in office was significantly less expensive. The government has been unable to reply to his documentation of corrupt deals and has therefore only prevented the petition (filed seven years ago) from coming up for hearing by seeking repeated adjournments. When the nature of Purohit's investigations came to light, he was himself investigated for corruption and his promotion to Chief of Naval Logistics stopped. The investigations revealed no malpractice on Purohit's part and he was cleared of all charges.

Money In, Money Out

The economic rationale of international trade suggests that, when the value of a country's domestic currency falls, its exports become cheaper on the global markets and so more competitive. But Indian trade seems to go against this trend. There are several instances of India's exports growing despite the value of the rupee appreciating. One explanation could be that exporters bring back money parked abroad when the rupee is appreciating. When there was a real appreciation in the exchange rate, earnings from exports continued to grow in those very years when they should have declined as exports became uncompetitive. For example, exports rose by 20.3 per cent in 1993–94, even though the rupee appreciated that year. In the 1993–94 period, foreign investment in the stock market boomed, and the 'other capital' account showed a US$2.15 billion inflow. More recently, too, when the rupee has appreciated in real terms, India's exports have boomed.

So we should consider whether sums of hot money have flowed into India by the over-invoicing of exports and in the name of NRI remittances. It should also be asked whether there is any connection with the appreciation and depreciation of the Indian rupee; and whether trade, including the export and import of invisibles, including services and software, performs the important function of moving funds in and out of India for the purpose of speculation. Zdanowicz and others argue that there is significant capital flight. However, they do not examine whether the flow of trade in goods and services significantly serves the purposes of laundering money or speculating on the value of the currency. Also, they have not examined the connection with the depreciation of the currency.

In keeping with such systematic over-invoicing and under-invoicing, very large sums of money have entered India unlinked to any specific transactions. This reverse capital flight is welcomed by the authorities, since it is believed to be the benign obverse of money going out. At first these were treated as capital flows for the purpose of balance of payments accounting. Since they could not be linked to any particular investors, the RBI placed them in the statistical overflow category called 'other' in the capital account. Soon 'other capital' flows became the single largest item in the external capital account of the Government of India according to official statistics. 'Other capital' grew rapidly till 1995. Then, just as inexplicably, this category declined from 1996 in official records – but 'private transfers' correspondingly grew.

Why this change? The decision to term these unexplained flows 'other' capital flows was arbitrary – if they were returning capital flows, they would go into the capital account but needed to be accurately described. Equally arbitrarily, a former high official in the Ministry of Finance told me, the RBI relocated some of the suspicious 'other capital' to the heading 'private transfers', which comes under the current account. This eliminated inconvenient discussion about the 'other flows' and improved the current account. As we shall see, my analysis, made originally at a time when such flows were significant even in a period of the depreciating rupee, has become even more relevant when the rupee has appreciated over the last three years and unexplained flows have become a torrent (Srinivasan 1995).

Perhaps as a result of shifts in the labelling of suspicious flows, the figures in the RBI annual reports between 1995 and 1998 have been repeatedly revised. For instance, for FY 1997 (in India this is the year 1997–98) 'other capital' flows were originally shown as being +US\$0.83 billion in the 1998 Annual Report (Reserve Bank of India Annual Report 30 June 1998, Appendix VI, 1, p. 184). This fell to –US\$714 million in the 2001 Annual Report (Reserve Bank of India Annual Report, 28 August 2001, India's Overall Balance of Payments, Appendix VI.1).

Even in the Annual Report for 1998 the figures for as far back as 1994 were marked 'preliminary' (Reserve Bank of India Annual Report, 30 June 1998, p. 184), indicating that they may continue to be changed even though there is no technical reason for such persistent and unpredictable revisions. Data are directly collected from reporting bank branches by the RBI – they do not report to their own head offices. The RBI in turn refuses to answer questions on the nature of these inflows. Now it could be argued thus: to some extent exports might fall immediately after devaluation if many export contracts were fixed in rupee terms earlier (since the contract will now be worth less in dollar terms; indeed, even contracts fixed in dollar terms might be renegotiated by foreign buyers when they learn of the devaluation) and if the nature of demand for other Indian exports is inelastic in relation to price. The 'benefit' of devaluation, in terms of higher exports, would be garnered with a lag (the 'J curve', because it goes down before going up).

But suspicious inflows are now a flood. The category of current account 'miscellaneous' inflows, which rose from a few million dollars in the 1980s[1] to about US\$4 billion in the early 1990s, has risen to US\$39.83 billion in 2004–05 (Reserve Bank of India 2005b, Table 43 PP S618-9). At the same time, 'miscellaneous' outflows (other than business process outsourcing (BPO) and software) have grown from US\$6.10 billion in 2001–02, the first year of liberalization, to US$24.97 billion last year (ibid.). What is this money moving in and out of the country? The RBI provides no explanation. The reporting system of these flows through the banks was one of the first casualties of India's economic liberalization of the 1990s, in which financial liberalization preceded everything else. Also, it was presumed that the fewer questions asked the better concerning foreigners or non-residents sending money into India (Reserve Bank of India 2005a, India's Invisibles, pp. 195–204).

Both Inward and Outward Capital Flows?

It is important to examine whether there are continuous flows of capital flight and reverse capital flight; whether money is taken out of the country for safekeeping, and the assets therefore protected from Indian inflation and income tax, and then re-circulated into India as a foreign inflow of financial institutional investment (FII) or software export earnings or other invisibles or trade remittances. Given that the Indian markets are narrow and shallow and insider trading is effectively unregulated, important investors have earned returns of 50 to 100 per cent in recent years. FIIs are now allowed to invest in real estate by proxy by trading in real estate firms; in the last six months, Bombay real estate shares have risen by 100 per cent. One Calcutta brokerage house offers an illegal debt instrument to FIIs with an assured annual return of 25 per cent. This is well above those in developed markets, providing great opportunities for arbitrage. The 2005 market boom, entirely driven by FIIs, has seen a dramatic rise in the index. Concern has been expressed even in official circles that the Indian markets have been the focus of money laundering.

It should be determined whether this chain is broken (that is, becomes a one-way flow) only when there is some crisis, such as the one of 1991. In that situation, Indian capital/money leaves the country through the *havala* system, but it does not return. Or at least there is no return flow until the domestic economy has resettled and again provides lucrative opportunities for 'foreign investment'. But, as Karin Lissakers (1991, p. 159) has pointed out in the case of Latin America, such 'swallow money' is 'repatriated flight capital invested in very liquid instruments and ready to fly out at the slightest provocation'. It cannot easily be deployed in the long-term development of the Indian economy. Now there is some question as to whether the extraordinary growth of Indian software export earnings also really reflects returning capital flight.

Since the mid 1990s foreign exchange earnings of the Indian software industry have grown at breakneck speed. While there is no doubt that the Indian IT sector has had genuine success, there are indications that software export earnings have been used as a channel for laundering money. The absence of physical exports makes it particularly difficult to differentiate genuine exports from money laundering. At any rate, there is virtually no attempt at official monitoring, exemplified by the fact that a private-sector body, NASSCOM (the National Association of Software and Service Companies), is the source of all the data on the sector. The government has no independent mechanism for gathering data, including export earnings. Indeed, there are important problems in reconciling data from different sources. The US Department of Commerce figure for India's software exports to the United States in 2002–03 was US$1.6 billion, whereas the Indian data put it at US$6.3 billion (Ravindran 2005). Much of this discrepancy may be explained by the differing definitions of software exports used by US and Indian agencies, whereby services delivered by Indian firms on site in the United States are counted as exports by the latter but not by the former (Reserve Bank of India 2005c). Nevertheless, questions remain and further investigation is certainly warranted. For example, during this very period, 2002–03, NASSCOM figures claimed that software exports from India to all destinations were of the order of US$9.5 billion, whereas the top 20 Indian companies accounted for only US$4.5 billion of this. One respected observer of the sector argues that this is unbelievable:

> What it means is simply this, that the top 20 Indian software companies exported less than half of what the industry as a whole exported. I find this strange because I can't think of any other industry where the top 20 contribute so little. Is the structure of our industry an aberration? (Assisi quoted in Ravindran 2005)

The existence of a large number of unheard-of software exporters raises the possibility that many companies claiming to export software may be doing nothing of the sort; rather they are only recycling money. The top Indian IT companies, such as Wipro and Infosys, are well respected, with transparent accounts. It is market knowledge that many smaller IT companies are not.

THE DAMAGE DONE BY CAPITAL FLIGHT AND MONEY LAUNDERING

It is widely accepted that criminal money laundering involved in narcotics and terror promotes great instability and is an important basis for cooperation between states. But as far as capital flight is concerned, much discussion has been conducted on how tax evasion is as fundamental a right as free speech, and how capital flight should act as a corrective to bad economic management. It has been inadequately understood how capital flight, which we argue uses the same methods as money laundering, has impoverished so much of the Third World. Raymond Baker and Jennifer Nordin (2005) point out that the outflow of 'dirty money' from poor countries far surpasses the inflow of aid:

Even if foreign aid doubles, as the United Nations and Blair's commission recommend, the outflow of dirty money is still vastly larger. Annual foreign aid totals $50 billion or so, while dirty money is upwards of $1 trillion per year, half of which passes from developing and transitional economies to the West.

Baker provides a graphic instance of the implications of this: 'For every $1 the West distributes in assistance across the top of the table, we take back some $10 in illegal proceeds under the table' (ibid.). In fact the impoverishment of many states through such crime contributes to the discontent that contributes to terrorism.

CONCLUSION

The United States and the United Kingdom define money laundering to include funds employed in terrorism and narcotics, but exclude funds involved in tax evasion, capital flight, mis-pricing and transfer pricing in trade, or kickbacks – in order to protect capital inflows to them. As a result, all the international agencies follow suit. The net outcome of such self-serving legislation and 'control' has been that intervention is both selective and useless, since the drug deals, the arms deals and the funds to terrorists cannot be separated from all the other unregulated flow of capital traffic.

In their funding structures and transfer mechanisms, these 'criminal' funds are indistinguishable from so-called 'legitimate' capital flight and money-laundering transactions. Moreover, it is often the same private banks, the same tax havens and the same loopholes which enable the efficient transfer of both 'legal' and 'illegal' funds out of Third World countries. It is easy enough for a private banker to claim: 'I am not laundering money for drugs, just arms deals, or tax evasion money, or corruption.' All this is treated as acceptable. India, for instance, undertakes no surveillance of external money laundering at all, leaving it to the markets to do their work. This is in tune with the global trend – there is no regulation of the private banks, the tax havens, the trusts, or law firms and accountants who serve them.

It is impossible to act against the concealment of wealth which is criminal in *all* jurisdictions unless states are prepared to act against concealment that is criminal in *any* jurisdiction. It is impossible to segregate the range of illegal acts that, when presented as financial transactions, appear identical. The effort to permit one sort of crime while cracking down on another has doomed the entire effort to control crime. If one wants to act against one, one must act against all.

A monitoring of international export and import prices on the lines of the studies we have cited would indicate over-invoicing and under-invoicing and could go a long way towards restricting such capital flight. Customs and income-tax scrutiny and regulation of trade could significantly limit the scope of such concealed flows, as is evident in the success the United States had in its intensive regulation of foreign multinationals, especially Japanese, engaged in transfer pricing to avoid US taxation in the 1980s and 1990s. Global capacity can be built to regulate corruption and money laundering. Anti-money-laundering initiatives are possible. These should include regulation for the legal profession, accountants, the tax havens and the private banks. None of this can be accomplished, however, without substantial international cooperation and the exchange of information on funds that flee any jurisdiction to be concealed elsewhere in some 'safe' haven. This kind of cooperation is being urged in the 'war on terror', but this war has had a limited and misplaced focus – there should be a war on money laundering, capital flight and illegal ways of generating funds. Until this is addressed, money laundering for the specific use of terrorism cannot be controlled or stamped out.

The difficulty in implementing the strategy described above is that those who facilitate money laundering and capital flight services, and employ such funds, constitute a significant lobby, and it may be difficult to win support for a policy of intervention. Opposition to such intervention would include many important multinationals, especially the oil companies that have got used to doing a certain sort of business; large contracting and engineering firms; and many of the world's largest banks (especially those in private banking focused on what they call high net worth individuals across borders) and legal and accounting firms. This is a pretty formidable constituency. Under these circumstances, it may not be possible to act against money laundering and capital flight or against the other criminal activity they facilitate, which includes the trade in narcotics and the financing of terror.

NOTE

1. In older annual reports that I have seen, but the official website has no report predating 1998.

REFERENCES

9/11 Commission (2004), 'The National Commission on Terrorist Attacks upon the United States', chaired by Thomas Kean, www.9-11commission.gov/report/911Report.pdf, accessed 16 July 2005.
Baker, Raymond (2005), *Capitalism's Achilles Heel: Dirty Money and How to Renew*

the Free-Market System, New Jersey: John Wiley & Sons.

Baker, Raymond, Brionne Dawson, Ilya Shulman and Clint Brewer (2003), 'Dirty money and its global effects', Center for International Policy, International Policy Report, January, http://ciponline.org/financialflows/dirtymoney.pdf, accessed 1 November 2005.

Baker, Raymond and Jennifer Nordin (2005), 'While dirty money flows, the poor stay poor', *International Herald Tribune Wednesday,* 13 April, http://ciponline. org/financialflows/poorstaypoor.htm, accessed 1 November 2005.

Boyrie, Maria, Simon J. Pak and John S. Zdanowicz (2004), 'Estimating the magnitude of capital flight due to abnormal pricing in international trade: the Russia–USA case', Ciber Working Paper, Centre for International Education and Business Research, Florida, International University, US, July, www.personal.psu.edu/faculty/s/j/sjp14/, accessed 1 November 2005.

Bureau of Economic Analysis (2005), 'United States Department of Commerce, International Economic Accounts', www.bea.gov/bea/di1.htm, accessed 15 August 2005.

Day, Kathleen (2001), 'Allbritton resigns as Riggs CEO: son to take charge of famed bank', *Washington Post,* 15 February, http://pqasb.pqarchiver.com/washingtonpost/68611517.html, accessed 1 November 2005,

Edwards, Andrew (1998), 'Review of financial regulation in the Crown Dependencies, 1998', London: Her Majesty's Stationery Office, www.archive.official-documents. co.uk/document/cm41/4109/4109-i.htm, accessed 20 September 2005.

Ganguly, Meenakshi (2001), 'A banking system built for terrorism', *Time,* 5 October, www.time.com, accessed 1 November 2005.

House Committee Money Laundering (2000), *Combating Money Laundering Worldwide,* House of Representatives, Committee on Government Reform, Subcommittee on Criminal Justice, Drug Policy and Human Resources, www. gpo.gov/congress/house; www.house.gov/reform; www.gpo.gov/congress/house; www.house.gov/reform, accessed 15 August 2005.

Hunter, Lawrence A. (2002), *Guidance on Reporting of Deposit Interest Paid to Non-resident Aliens: Testimony before the Internal Revenue Service Proposed Rule Making: REG-133254-02 and REG-126100-00,* US Congress, 5 December 2002, www.freedomworks.org/informed/issues_template.php?issue_id=1935&isitsearc h=1&search1=LAWRENCE, accessed 21 July 2005.

Levin, Carl (2004), 'Money laundering and foreign corruption: the Patriot Act U.S. Senate Permanent Subcommittee on Investigations', 15 July, http://levin.senate. gov/newsroom/release.cfm?id=223965, accessed 22 July 2005.

Lissakers, Karin (1991), *Banks, Borrowers and the Establishment: a Revisionist Account of the International Debt Crisis,* New York: Basic Books.

McCulloch, Jude and S. Pickering (2005), 'Suppressing the financing of terrorism: proliferating state crime, eroding censure and extending neo-colonialism', *British Journal of Criminology,* 45, 470–86.

O'Brien, Timothy (2004), 'A Washington bank, a global mess', *New York Times,* 11 April 2004, www.nytimes.com/2004/04/11/business/yourmoney/11riggs.html, accessed 22 July 2005.

Patriot Act (2001), http://thomas.loc.gov/cgi-bin/bdquery/z?d107:H.R.3162, accessed 1 November 2005.

Purohit (2004), filed as a Writ Petition before Delhi High Court, 1998.

Ravindran, Pratap (2005), 'Budget on the soft trial', *Hindu Businessline,* 8 March, www. thehindubusinessline.com/2005/03/08/stories/2005030800180800.htm,accessed 1 November 2005.

Reddy, Y.V. (1997), *Capital Flight: Myths and Realities*, 21 June, www.rbi.org.in/ scripts/BS_SpeechesView.aspx?Id=27, accessed 1 November 2005.

Reserve Bank of India, various Annual Reports, www.rbi.org.in/scripts/Annual ReportPublications.aspx, accessed 1 November 2005.

Reserve Bank of India (2005a), *India's Invisibles*, Bulletin, March, 195–204, www.rbi. org.in/scripts/BS_ViewBulletin.aspx?Id=5978, accessed 1 November 2005.

Reserve Bank of India (2005b), *India's Overall Balance of Payments in Dollars*, Bulletin, July 2005, Table 43, www.rbi.org.in/scripts/BS_ViewBulletin.aspx, accessed 1 November 2005.

Reserve Bank of India (2005c), *Computer Service Exports from India: 2002–03*, Reserve Bank of India Bulletin, September, www.rbi.org.in/scripts/BS_ViewBulletin. aspx?Id=6911, accessed 15 August 2005.

Riggs (2000), www.riggsbank.com

Senate Money Laundering (1999), *Private Banking and Money Laundering: a Case Study of Opportunities and Vulnerabilities*, Hearings before the Permanent Subcommittee on Investigations of the Committee on Governmental Affairs of the United States Senate One Hundred Sixth Congress, First Session, 9 and 10 November, http://frwebgate.access.gpo.gov/cgi-bin/getdoc.cgi?dbname=106_ senate_hearings&docid=f:61699.wais, accessed 1 November 2005.

Senate Riggs Subcommittee (2004), *Money Laundering and Foreign Corruption: Enforcement and Effectiveness of the Patriot Act: a Case Study Involving Riggs Bank*, United States Senate Permanent Subcommittee Investigations, Chair Norm Coleman, Riggs Bank Minority Staff Report, 15 July, http://frwebgate.access.gpo. gov/cgiin/getdoc.cgi?dbname=106_senate_hearings&docid=f:61699.wais, accessed 1 November 2005.

Srinivasan, Kannan (1995), '"Private banking" and depreciation of the rupee', *Economic & Political Weekly*, XXX(45), 2849–50.

Zdanowicz, John S. et al. (1996) 'Capital flight from India to the United States through abnormal pricing in international trade', *Finance India*, December, X(4), 881–904.

3. The role of the European Union in Asian security

Liisa Laakso

The European Union (EU)[1] is not a very visible security actor in Asia and is mainly regarded as an economic partner. As the biggest trading block in the world, it is, for instance, India's largest source of foreign direct investment and accounts for more than a quarter of India's exports and imports (EU 2002b, p. 13). Since the mid 1990s, however, the EU has increasingly emphasized the political dimension of its relations with Asia (Wiessala 2002).

In 1996 a new forum, the Asia–Europe Meeting (ASEM), was established. Already two years earlier the European Commission had issued a document, *Towards a New Asia Strategy*, where the aim of supporting peace and security was mentioned. The strategy paper was updated in 2001 with *Europe and Asia: A Strategic Framework for Enhanced Partnerships*, paying attention to the deepening integration within the EU (Demiri 2003). The strategy notes that the EU should play a proactive role in regional cooperation in Asia; support conflict prevention efforts; and strengthen cooperation in immigration and in the fight against transnational crime, drugs, trafficking in human beings, trafficking in arms, money laundering, and the exploitation of migrants and corruption (EU 2001a, p. 17). The general aim was to reinforce the EU's presence in Asia by contributing 'to peace and security in the region and globally, through a broadening of [the EU's] engagement with the region' (EU 2001a, p. 3). The Commission's subsequent *Strategy Paper and Indicative Programme for Multi-country Programmes in Asia for 2005–2006* covers trade, investment, higher education, the environment, support to the Association of South-East Asian Nations (ASEAN) and support to the South Asian Association for Regional Co-operation (SAARC) (EU 2004a).

The European Parliament has emphasized the EU's role in Asian security in the areas of conflict prevention, peacekeeping and even peacemaking. In its report on the Commission's strategy paper the European Parliament urged the Commission to start a dialogue within ASEM on security matters. It recommended that a comprehensive approach to conflict prevention and peacekeeping be included in the ASEM process by supporting political dialogue between North and South Korea, as well as between the People's Republic of

China and Taiwan. The report also called for a withdrawal of all missiles and the gradual disarmament of the coast across the Taiwan Straits (EU 2002a).

In December 2003 the EU adopted its first ever security strategy, *A Secure Europe in a Better World* (EU 2003). It advocated a wide concept of security covering such global challenges as poverty, disease, criminality, competition over natural resources, and conflict broadly defined. As key security threats it listed terrorism, proliferation of weapons of mass destruction (WMD), regional conflict, state failure and organized crime. All of these are treated as global phenomena and the examples given refer to areas outside Europe, not least to Asia. Nuclear activities in North Korea, nuclear risks in South Asia and the activities of terrorists and criminals in Central and South-east Asia are said to threaten European countries and their citizens. The document mentions the Aum Shinrikyo terrorist sect's use of sarin gas in Tokyo in 1995 as 'the last example of the use of the WMD' (EU 2003 p. 3). Kashmir and the Korean Peninsula are given as examples of regional conflicts, and Afghanistan under the Taliban as an example of state failure. Describing the threat of organized crime, the strategy notes that 90 per cent of the heroin in Europe comes 'from poppies grown in Afghanistan – where the drugs trade pays for private armies' (EU 2003 p. 5). The southern Caucasus has particular importance as it 'will in due course also be a neighbouring region' (EU 2003 p. 8) of the EU. Japan, China and India are mentioned as countries with which the EU should develop 'strategic partnerships' (EU 2003 p. 14), and ASEAN is referred to as one of the regional organizations that can make an important contribution to 'a more orderly world' (EU 2003 p. 14). Finally, the strategy document notes that European forces have been deployed to places as distant as Afghanistan and East Timor (EU 2003 p. 1).

Given this broad 'strategy' the policies that the EU can formulate and implement will necessarily vary, with regard both to decision-making arrangements within the EU and to the instruments at its disposal. The EU has the choice to proceed on the basis of inter- governmental arrangements, which means that the powers are vested in the governments of the member states, or through autonomous action and preparatory work at the level of EU institutions, most notably the Commission. The instruments are also highly varied and could, in turn, be civilian (covering economic, cultural and knowledge-based cooperation) or involve military and police work where the EU has developed common capabilities since 1999.

Establishing coherence between different instruments and different levels of decision making is a demanding goal. Different policy areas cut across not only diverging national interests but also the interests of sub-national and supra-national groups, including industry, labour movements and NGOs. The latter are not active solely at the national level but interact with the EU-level authorities as well. Despite this one has to note that, were these various actors and interest groups to be coordinated, the European Union could exercise remarkable power on the ground. With increasing engagement, such a multilevel actor is capable of developing a soft footprint in Asia in contrast to the more strident polices of the United States.

Given these complexities, where and how might the EU contribute to Asian security? In the following discussion this issue is considered under various headings: development cooperation, promotion of regional integration (including Asian involvement in ASEM), and a more palpable security partnership with Asia.

SECURITY THROUGH DEVELOPMENT COOPERATION

The EU is an important player in international development cooperation. It provides about half of all official development assistance (ODA). The EU member states constitute the largest collective number of votes in the World Bank, the IMF and the WTO. Like many other donors, the EU regards eradicating poverty as the main objective of its development policy. This objective also relates to security. According to 'The European Community's Development Policy', 'poverty, and the exclusion which it creates, are the root causes of conflict and are endangering the stability and security of too many countries and regions' (EU 2005a, p. 1). Better security is thus seen as an important motivation for poverty eradication. Development cooperation can also address more specified tasks and programs in the fields of conflict prevention, peace-building activities and security sector reform. Security sector reform, in particular, is an emerging area of cooperation for the EU. The reform process can be supported with civilian capabilities, but it can also involve assistance to military or military-related activities, which so far have been excluded from the OECD criteria for ODA (see International Alert and Saferworld 2004, p. 20).

For all these reasons, development cooperation is particularly sensitive to the EU foreign and security policy goals. The goals might be similar or complementary, but they can also differ. The EU's resources for development cooperation amount to €7 billion a year, whereas its resources for the Common Foreign and Security Policy of the EU (CFSP) are only about €60 million (EU 2005b). With the growing importance of the EU's CFSP, there is a possibility that the security of the EU and its member states will be financed by funds reserved for the development of other regions. Various NGOs have been concerned about this possibility (see Bond 2004).[2]

So far the main emphasis of the EU's development cooperation has been in the former colonies of the European states. This has largely been arranged under the Cotonou Agreement between the EU and African, Caribbean and

Pacific states (ACP). For the Pacific Islands region the EU has indeed been an important development partner. For most of Asia, however, development cooperation falls under the much smaller Asia–Latin America (ALA) program. In aggregate, EU development cooperation in Asia is still marginal, receiving only about 19 per cent of total EU aid. This is surprisingly little, given that the majority of the world's poor live in Asia (Montes and Migliorisi 2004, p. 16).

Nor can the objective of poverty alleviation explain how the EU distributes its development assistance inside Asia. For example, in 2005 the EU planned a four-fold increase in its development aid to Pakistan, which was already getting more aid relatively speaking than Bangladesh, where poverty is more widespread (*Deutsche Welle* 2005; Bond 2002). Besides, the EU has criticized human rights abuses and the lack of democracy in Pakistan. These are not mentioned in its development cooperation agreement with Pakistan, although the Treaty of the European Community specifies 'the general objective of developing and consolidating democracy', 'the rule of law' and 'respecting human rights and fundamental freedoms' as objectives that the Community should take into account in all its policies affecting developing countries (EU 2002c, Article 177). It is evident that Pakistan is currently being rewarded for its war against terrorism and supported because of the regional role it is playing, especially with regard to Afghanistan. Also, commercial links are being emphasised. As John Quigley (2004, p. 13) notes, 'the suppression of human rights concerns to trade principles represents a worrying trend for Europe's common foreign policy'. In Bangladesh, by contrast, the EU is mainly focused on funding social sector initiatives in the area of health and education. However, it would like to become more engaged with issues about governance and the institutional reforms that are needed for democratization, including the reform of the police.

Thanks to its regional importance, India is another strategic partner of the EU. Here too the EU's relations with India have developed beyond trade and economic cooperation to the field of security and defence policy. The Commission's Communication on *An EU–India Strategic Partnership* (EU 2004b) emphasizes cooperation in conflict prevention, the fight against terrorism, and non-proliferation of WMD. Concrete initiatives include plans to train the civilian experts of peacekeeping missions, activities designed to facilitate conflict prevention or post-conflict management, joint support of UN conflict prevention and peace-building efforts, and greater cooperation between EU and India in UN peacekeeping missions. To achieve such cooperation, consultation will need to take place before major UN debates on peacekeeping and conflict management. In the fight against terrorism and organized crime, the aim is to deepen cooperation through the exchange of information and expertise, and to conduct a dialogue on preventive policy against illegal immigration, smuggling of migrants and trafficking in human beings. On the question of Kashmir, the EU is promising to 'offer its own unique experience as an example of building peace and forging partnerships' (EU 2004b, Annex p. 15).

The main constraint on EU development cooperation is the coordination of EU strategies so that policies are not weakened by contradictions. For example, in its general development policy the EU emphasizes employment creation as a means to eradicate poverty, but in its trade policy it often prevents Asian industrial products from entering its markets by anti-dumping policies (Bond 2002, p. 15). Agricultural subsidies are the biggest barrier preventing Asia's developing countries from becoming integrated into the world economy on an equal footing with the EU. In the words of Terence O'Brien (2004, p. 113) 'the EU bears a lion's share of the responsibility for the lack of progress on export subsidy discipline'. Although the WTO General Council agreement in July 2004 has been praised as a breakthrough on agricultural subsidies between the industrialized countries and developing countries, much is still to be done before the trade relations between the EU and Asia can become fair.

SUPPORT FOR REGIONAL SECURITY

The EU has been eager to promote its own model of regional integration elsewhere in the world. As was noted above, regional conflicts are mentioned in the EU security strategy as being among the key security threats. Security, stability and human rights are commonly mentioned in agreements between the EU and other regional groupings. Furthermore, the cooperation is not limited to the level of government but also includes cooperation with the organs of civil society; in particular, universities and NGOs. Also, the term 'region' is not an unambiguous one for the EU but has different meanings, evident for instance in the term 'sub-region', which cannot even be translated into all official languages of the EU.

Although security is a new theme in the EU's dealings with extra-European regional organizations and states, it has always been an important motivation for integration within Europe. According to Jean Monnet, one of the architects of European integration, cooperation in such vital areas such as coal and steel production (that is, the establishment of the European Coal and Steel Community, from where the European integration process began) made peace into a priority for the whole of Europe. Integration was based on common markets and economic benefits, and the instruments utilized were purely civilian and limited to trade relations and cross-border investments. In developing such intergovernmental cooperation the very foundations of regional security were created in Europe. Karl Deutsch (1957) grasped this by formulating his concept of the 'security community'. By this he meant the creation of a group of states where war had become inconceivable because all the members of the group agreed that force no longer needed to be used to resolve disputes among themselves.

And indeed regional integration with intensive economic cooperation seems to correlate with peaceful relations also in Asia. Although there are political problems between the member states of ASEAN, there has been no war between them since the organization was established in 1967. The link between economic cooperation, common interests and peace has been constantly emphasized (Acharya 2001; Kivimäki 2001). It is no wonder that the EU has been eager to develop inter-regional relations with ASEAN.

The EU and ASEAN are, however, very different regional organizations and thus their dialogue has not always been an easy one. While the EU is developing towards strengthening supra-national authorities and puts emphasis on normative issues like human rights and governance as membership criteria, ASEAN is a less legalistic and essentially an inter-governmental organization that approaches security 'the Asian way' through the principle of non-interference (Kim 2000; Hernandez 2000, p. 121). Instead of a binding treaty, ASEAN was established by the 1967 Bangkok Declaration on voluntary cooperation. Human rights concerns played no role in ASEAN's establishment and initiatives such as the ASEAN Programme on the Rights of Children and the ASEAN Human Rights Commission are still weakly institutionalized (Wiessala 2004, p. 6).

The EU–ASEAN Co-operation Agreement of 1980 ignored human rights completely. Dialogue mechanisms became significant only after 1995, when the Council of the EU called for the inclusion of a human rights clause in all trade and cooperation agreements between the EU and a third country (EU 2001b). However, human rights have been a difficult topic to discuss within the framework of EU–ASEAN cooperation, especially as far as individual member states of ASEAN are concerned. Burma, which became a member of ASEAN in 1997, is the most outstanding example of this problem (Wiessala 2004, p. 5). The inaction of ASEAN states on Burma, and also on the subject of human rights violations in Cambodia and Indonesia, is very different from the EU approach towards human rights violations, for instance, in Turkey, which is a candidate for becoming a member state of the EU. ASEAN, however, might be changing in this regard. As a sign of the new thinking and new opportunities for a partnership between the EU and ASEAN, Acharya (2004, p. 101) notes that Indonesia has now called for the non-recognition of unconstitutional dismissals of governments while simultaneously calling for the establishment of democracy as the normative goal for ASEAN.

Despite the differences on human rights, there are several areas of co-operation that the EU could pursue with its regional counterparts. These include trans-boundary problems, such as trade, environment and migration flows. Also, SAARC, with which EU relations are at an early stage of development, is important. The EC's *Strategy Paper and Indicative Programme for Multi-country Programmes in Asia for 2005–2006* identifies closer economic integration between SAARC members, cooperation on trade, investment and monetary, as well as environmental, issues as measures that can be supported (EU 2004a). Primarily, the EU's SAARC program provides finance for technical assistance, training, studies and the exchange of information in these areas. For the nascent integration process within SAARC, the support given by the EU might be pivotal since it can, as an external and 'resource-rich' actor, counter-balance the dominance of the regional hegemonic power, India (Acharya 2004, p. 101). The EU is also supporting the preparation for a Pacific Free Trade Area. This involves providing assistance to the Pacific Forum Island Countries to analyse, define and negotiate a Free Trade Agreement. It has even been suggested that the EU 'as the model of interstate integration and sovereignty-dilution', could play a role as a facilitator in guiding China and Taiwan towards a union (van Kemenade 2004, p. 12).

Another important region in Asia for the EU's security policy is Central Asia, which is coming closer to the EU as the EU expands its membership eastwards. The EU and member states have been involved in the region through the EU's support for the Transport Corridor Europe Caucasus Asia (TRACECA). France, for example, has participated in a group mediating between Azerbaijan and Armenia, and Germany and the United Kingdom have been involved in searching for a resolution of the Abkhaz conflict. Since 1991 the EU has provided assistance to the region through the Tacis Programme, which covers 12 countries of Eastern Europe and Central Asia (Armenia, Azerbaijan, Belarus, Georgia, Kazakhstan, Kyrgyzstan, Moldova, Russia, Tajikistan, Turkmenistan, Ukraine and Uzbekistan). The main aim of this program has been to facilitate the transition from socialist to liberal market-oriented systems in these countries. This includes support to address the social consequences of transition. A regional and cross-border strategy has been utilized to create links between neighbouring countries in the fields of environmental reform, nuclear safety, trade and transport, immigration and the fight against criminality (EU 2005c). Among other things the EU has attempted to create a 'filter system' against the drug trade from Afghanistan along the Silk Route. The first filter is in Central Asia, the second in the Caucasian countries and the third in the newly independent states of Ukraine, Moldova and Belarus (Coppieters 2003, p. 166).

In 2003 the EU Council appointed a Special Representative to the South Caucasus with the task of enhancing conflict resolution in the region and assisting in political and economic reforms (Coppieters 2003, p. 163). What is perhaps self-evident but still noteworthy with regard to the EU's policies in Central Asia is that, unlike the process of integration within the EU itself, there are no membership criteria for states wishing to belong to the EU neighbourhood. The only constraint is geographical proximity to the EU's boundaries. As Bruno Coppieters notes, the EU can well be creating a hegemonic asymmetric relationship through its cooperation with the states in this region. This is a distinct possibility if the EU's support becomes essential for security and development on the EU's periphery (Coppieters 2003, p. 171). In 2005 the EU's financial and other assistance is still below that of the United States. Despite this 'the EU can add value to the stabilization of South Caucasus by adopting a low-profile and low-expectation but long-term political approach' which, according to Dov Lynch (2003, p. 191), amounts to an 'indirect strategy' towards enhancing regional peace.

Acharya (2004, p. 95) notes that the 'experience of Europe and Asia building regional institutions, despite being marked by differences, shows common barriers to building multipolarity through regional institutions'. Such multipolarity does not require a uniform and single model of integration, but it can stem from mutual acceptance of differences and variations (ibid., p. 102). And, indeed, the EU's approach involves elements of this kind of normative approach at least as far as its commitment to inter-regional cooperation is concerned. Typically, it has responded to the lack of expected results, namely deepening integration within its regional counterparts, which has been quite usual, by intensifying its cooperation instead of diminishing it (see Coppieters 2003, p. 159).

The Asia–Europe Meeting

ASEM is a major forum set up in 1996 to formalize the EU's interest in cooperating with Asia (see Dent 2001). The idea originated in the Commission's 1994 strategy paper. Singapore played an important role in brokering the establishment of ASEM. The influence of the European Parliament and non-governmental agencies, such as the Asia–Europe Foundation (ASEF), was also important. Today ASEM brings together the EU member states, ASEAN members and China, Japan and South Korea, with the main objective being better regional security (Hwee 2000; Forster 1999).

ASEM provides a forum for informal inter-regional dialogue to enhance cooperation in political, economic, social and cultural fields. All the objectives of the EU's Asia strategy are incorporated in the ASEM forum's brief (Reiterer 2001). However, as is often the case with high-level diplomatic summits, it is not always easy to conduct constructive political dialogue on the most difficult issues. Instead, day-to-day political phenomena have dominated the discussions. Thus the Asian financial crisis was the major issue for ASEM II (1998), the war against the Taliban for ASEM III (2000) and the 9/11 terrorist attacks for ASEM IV (2002) (Wiessala 2004, p. 5).

However, the new global security issues that have emerged since 9/11 have pushed ASEM into deepened political dialogue. ASEM IV adopted the *Copenhagen Cooperation Programme on Fighting International Terrorism* and endorsed the initiative to hold an anti-terrorism symposium. It adopted the *Copenhagen Political Declaration for Peace on the Korean Peninsula*, aimed at inter-Korean reconciliation. It also held a session under the heading 'Dialogue on Cultures and Civilizations', emphasizing the importance of respect for the equal dignity of all civilizations. Despite this, Burma has officially remained outside the ASEM framework since 2003. The EU has imposed economic sanctions and has suspended development cooperation with the Burmese government. Burma's participation in ASEM, along with such ASEAN members as Cambodia and Laos, has raised discussion but with little results as far as changes inside these countries are concerned.

Violation of human rights in China is a further source of tension between the EU and the countries of Asia. However, the opinions within the EU on China seem to diverge. In its 2002 Report on *A Strategic Framework for Enhanced Partnerships*, the European Parliament urged the Council and the Commission to find ways to involve Taiwan in ASEM in order to foster democracy in the region and contribute to a dialogue between China and Taiwan. By 2005 EU–China relations seemed to be taking a turn for the better with the EU's plan to lift the arms embargo on China, which was imposed after the Tiananmen Square massacre in 1989. Lifting the embargo has become a symbol of the EU's determination to deepen its relationship with China as a strategic partner. It is likely that European economic objectives were a more important consideration than any gains the EU could get from selling arms to China. In the words of President Jacques Chirac of France, 'Europe intends to remove the last obstacles to its relations with this important country'.[3] However, owing to strong opposition from the United States, moving closer to China has not been easy for the EU (Landler 2005). Furthermore, the European Parliament has opposed the lifting of the embargo and has repeatedly echoed concerns about China's threatening stance towards Taiwan.

THE EU AS A SECURITY PARTNER

The EU has the potential to act as a moderating force in Asia. For example, the EU mission to Pyongyang, led by Swedish Prime Minister Göran Persson in 2001, was widely seen as an attempt to calm the atmosphere in the aftermath of President George Bush's criticism of North Korea. Europeans can also play a role in conflict mediation. In 2005 the former Finnish President Martti Ahtisaari, through his Crisis Management Centre, mediated talks between the Indonesian government and the representatives of the Free Aceh Movement to end the Aceh conflict. This mediation received financial support from the EU, and it seemed to be a natural partner to send monitors to the region in case the parties were able to negotiate a treaty (Merikallio 2005).

Beyond this, it is often claimed that the EU needs the United States as the 'security provider' in Asia. The EU is not an emerging superpower; rather it is a complex security actor, owing to its multilevel character with all the different agencies that formulate, decide and implement its policies. One also needs to remember that each of the member states in the EU has its own security policy and that in aggregate these policies diverge. The EU includes two nuclear weapons states (France and the United Kingdom), NATO members, states that are not NATO members but have a security agreement with it, and states that do not have a security agreement with NATO (Malta and Cyprus). Not surprisingly, there are different ideas about the role of the EU in Asia and in world politics in general, starting from the old French 'Gaullist' vision of European independence vis- vis the United States where a strategic Sino–EU partnership could be especially significant (van Kemenade 2004, p. 6).

Throughout the Cold War the United States and NATO dominated the security policy of Western Europe. But in the early 1990s there was a need to design a new defence architecture. NATO did not wither away, and indeed the Central and Eastern European states wanted to join up. These new conditions made it important for the EU to develop complementary instruments rather than mere proposals about a new kind of military alliance to replace NATO. As a result, since 1999 the EU has developed common civilian and military crisis management capabilities, and these could be deployed also in Asia.

The development of the EU rapid reaction forces has received a lot of attention. Despite this – and the EU's call for a 'strategic culture that fosters early, rapid and when necessary, robust intervention' (EU 2003, p. 11) – there are no explicit declarations in the security strategy or elsewhere about when the member states could or would use military force to defend themselves or their interests (Bono 2004, pp. 450–53). The EU's rapid reaction forces are part of the strategy of fulfilling the so-called 'Petersberg tasks'.[4] These include humanitarian as well as peacekeeping and peacemaking tasks incorporated into the Amsterdam Treaty of the EU in 1997 on the initiative of two non-NATO new member states, Sweden and Finland. The normative content of the 'Petersberg tasks' was important for Germany as well, as its defence forces have been regulated since the end of World War II to ensure that they have no capacity to engage in combat (Laakso 2005).

These developments in the EU have resonated with developments in another 'civilian power' of the post-World War II order – Japan. Again, Japan's post-World War II security policy was restricted to self-defence by its constitution, imposed by the victors. Despite this, Japan has deployed its troops to support UN peacekeeping operations and is actively developing its capacities further in that direction. Given this, and the substantial experience of EU states in peacekeeping, it is likely that the EU will be an important partner for Japan in this field in the future (Hoshino 2004, pp. 90, 91).

While it is possible and perhaps even likely that the EU will launch military operations in Asia in the coming decades, these will be based on a multiplicity of considerations reflecting the inter-governmentalism that prevails in the EU. For the EU, the use of armed force is typically an 'either–or' issue that requires clear legal authority. It is not something that could be operationalized within the context of the EU's multi-tiered structure. Multiple actors operating at multiple levels cannot easily share accountability related to decisions of this kind. However, in the case of failing states, or states that are threatened by failure, it is pertinent to speak of an overall reform of the EU's security approach. Military means have been used to strengthen both the armed forces and the police, even though the latter in the European setting is conventionally regarded as civilian.

So far the only EU mission in Asia has been civilian in nature: the EU Rule of Law Mission to Georgia (EUJUST THEMIS) launched in the context of the European Security and Defence Policy (ESDP) in July 2004. It has been regarded as a significant step forward in the development of the civilian strand of ESDP. EUJUST THEMIS involves civilian experts who will advise ministers and senior officials at the level of the central government. The purpose is to support the Georgian authorities to address problems in their justice system and to enhance the reform of the system (EU 2004c).

CONCLUSION

Given the changed global and regional security environments, the EU has increasingly emphasized the political dimensions of its relations with Asia. On the one hand, the EU's attempts to conduct political dialogue on human rights, in particular, has not been very successful. Yet there are several fields where the EU is proceeding with its Asian partners. A particularly important area of cooperation takes place between the EU and Asian regional arrangements. This cooperation is not contradictory to multilateralism and the role of the UN, for instance, but can be seen as a contribution to multipolarity in world politics.

In many respects the EU needs Asia to give substance to its CFSP, which involves a very wide concept of security. However, the activities within such a security policy are not necessarily high profile by nature. Indeed, for the EU the most suitable approach to security in Asia seems to be a low-profile but long-term indirect strategy to affect the conditions of peace. With such an approach the EU is not likely to become a visible actor in Asia, even though it explicitly aims to build awareness of the EU in the Asian region.

Also, the EU is not an emerging superpower. Rather it is a complex security actor with a multi-layered character. There are many differences between the EU member states, which means that they are by no means willing to lose all their separate bilateral Asian policies in exchange for an integrated EU policy. Nevertheless, even as a multi-levelled actor the EU can be flexible and open to new approaches in a way that government actors can seldom be. It can build its strategy on various levels, with member states and NGOs. By the same token, it has multiple capabilities at its disposal, giving it a wide range of instruments for engaging with Asia. What is pivotal to the power of the EU is internal coherence. The search for coherence compels the EU to look at the local consequences of its trade policy in Asia. It also has to adjust its agricultural subsidies to a level that enables the Asian producers to utilize their relative advantage and bring their products to the European market.

Within the EU, building up a more active Asia policy and global policy, more generally, underscores the urgency of better coordination between different policy sectors. This, however, should not mean watering down the meaning of these policies. Development cooperation, in particular, should be strengthened as part of the CFSP with its own objectives and modus operandi. The EU has a lot of potential to increase its development cooperation programs for poverty reduction and thereby also enhance Asian security. This broadly based approach is likely to be more productive of good results than a more narrowly defined security policy focused on the needs of Europeans – the latter would risk the use of development aid to reward governments fighting terrorism without addressing the underlying issues that determine human security in Asia.

NOTES

1. The EU is used here to cover most notably the Council of the European Union (representing the governments of the 25 member states), the European Commission (executive body) and the European Parliament (elected by the member states' citizens). The European Community, also an often-used term, refers to activities where the member states have delegated powers to the Commission.
2. Bond is a British network of aid agencies that represents some 300 organizations engaged in advocacy work and publishing on poverty and development.
3. He said this in Brussels on 22 February 2004, after President Bush had expressed 'deep concern' about the issue when attending the NATO Summit and EU Heads of Government Meeting.
4. The Western European Union (WEU), a security policy body within the European communities before the treaty of the European Union, agreed in 1992 in a meeting in Petersberg, Germany, to widen the tasks for which the military units of the WEU member states may be employed.

REFERENCES

Acharya, Amitav (2001), *Constructing a Security Community in Southeast Asia*, London and New York: Routledge.

Acharya, Amitav (2004), 'An Asian perspective, regional security arrangements in a multipolar world: the EU's contribution', *Chaillot Paper*, 72 (November), pp. 93–102.

Bond (2002), *Tackling Poverty in Asia*, www.bond.org.uk/pubs/eu/tackling-asia.pdf, accessed 21 June 2005.

Bond (2004), 'Civil society statement on the OECD Development Assistance Committee senior level meeting, December 8–9, 2004', www.bond.org.uk/advocacy/gsd/daction1204.htm, accessed 21 June 2005.

Bono, Giovanna (2004) 'The EU's military doctrine: an assessment', *International Peacekeeping*, 11 (3), 439–56.

Coppieters, Bruno (2003), 'An EU Special representative to a new periphery', *Chaillot Paper*, 65 (December), pp. 160–70.

Demiri, Eleni P. (2003), 'Reorientation of EU relations with Asia', University of Kent, www.eliamep.gr/_admin/upload_publication/342_1en_occ.PDF, accessed 21 June 2005.

Dent, Christopher (2001), 'ASEM and the "Cinderella complex" of EU–East Asia economic relations', *Pacific Affairs*, 74 (1), 25–52.

Deutsch, Karl (1957), *Political Community and the North Atlantic Area*, Princeton, NJ: Princeton University Press.

Deutsche Welle (2005), 'EU plans four-fold raise in aid to Pakistan', 27 April, www2.dw-world.de/southasia/pressreview/1.135312.1.html, accessed 21 June 2005.

EU (2001a), *Europe and Asia: A Strategic Framework for Enhanced Partnerships*, Communication from the Commission, 4 September, http://europa.eu.int/comm/external_relations/asia/doc/com01_469_en.pdf, accessed 21 June 2005.

EU (2001b), 'The EU's human rights & democratisation policy', http://europa.eu.int/comm/external_relations/human_rights/intro/index.htm, accessed 21 June 2005.

EU (2002a), *Report of the European Parliament on the Commission Communication on Europe and Asia: A Strategic Framework for Enhanced Partnerships*, 1999–2204 Session, 16 July.

EU (2002b), *EC Country Strategy Paper: India*, 10 September, http://europa.eu.int/comm/external_relations/india/csp/02_06en.pdf, accessed 21 June 2005.

EU (2002c), *Treaty Establishing the European Community*, Official Journal of the European Communities, C 325 of 24 December.

EU (2003), *A Secure Europe in a Better World: European Security Strategy*, http://ue.eu.int/uedocs/cmsUpload/78367.pdf, accessed 21 June 2005.

EU (2004a), *Policy, Planning and Coordination Strategy Paper and Indicative Programme for Multi-country Programmes in Asia 2005–2006*, http://europa.eu.int/comm/external_relations/asia/rsp/rsp_asia.pdf, accessed 21 June 2005.

EU (2004b), *An EU–India Strategic Partnership*, Communication from the Commission to the Council, the European Parliament and the European Economic and Social Committee, with Annex (Commission staff working document), 16 June, COM(2004) 430 final.

EU (2004c), 'Facts on EUJUST THEMIS European Union Rule of Law Mission to Georgia', 26 October, http://ue.eu.int/uedocs/cmsUpload/Factsheet%20THEMIS%20041026.pdf, accessed 21 June 2005.

EU (2005a), 'The European Community's development policy', statement by the Council and the Commission, http://europa.eu.int/comm/development/body/ legislation/docs/council_statement.pdf#zoom=100, accessed 21 June 2005.

EU (2005b), 'General budget', http://europa.eu.int/eur-lex/budget/www/index-en.htm, accessed 21 June 2005.

EU (2005c), 'The EU's relations with Eastern Europe & Central Asia', http://europa. eu.int/comm/external_relations/ceeca/tacis/, accessed 21 June 2005.

Forster, Anthony (1999), 'The European Union in South-east Asia: continuity and change in turbulent times', *International Affairs*, 75 (4), 743–58.

Hernandez, Carolina G. (2000), 'Regional cooperation in the Asia Pacific: political and security dimensions', in M. Jerneck and U. Niemann (eds), *Asia and Europe: Regional Co-operation in a Globalising World*, lectures from the Third ASEF Summer School, www.asef.org/downloads/3rdASEFSS.pdf, pp. 117–25, accessed 21 June 2005.

Hoshino, Toshuya (2004), 'Japan: a Japanese view on the global role of the European Union', Chaillot Paper, 72 (November), pp. 83–92.

Hwee, Yeo Lay (2000), 'ASEM: looking back, looking forward', *Contemporary Southeast Asia*, 22 (1), 113–31.

International Alert and Saferworld (2004), *Strengthening Global Security through Addressing the Root Causes of Conflict: Priorities for the Irish and Dutch Presidencies in 2004*, London, www.international-alert.org/index.php?page=home accessed 21 June 2005.

Kim, Jong Wang (2000), 'Democracy and Asian Values', in M. Jerneck and U. Niemann (eds), *Asia and Europe: Regional Co-operation in a Globalising World*, Lectures from the Third ASEF Summer School, www.asef.org/downloads/3rdASEFSS.pdf, pp. 141–9, accessed 21 June 2005.

Kivimäki, Timo (2001), 'The long peace of ASEAN', *Journal of Peace Research*, 38 (1), 5–26.

Laakso, Liisa (2005), 'A capability-implementation gap in the making: multi-level governance and the emerging European crisis management policy', in G. Walzenbach (ed.), *Alternatives to European Governance?*, Aldershot: Ashgate, pp. 190–221.

Landler, Mark (2005), 'Europeans see pluses in ending China ban', *The New York Times*, 24 February, cited in Forum Europe NDA, www.newdefenceagenda.org/ index.html?http://www.newdefenceagenda.org/news_detail.asp?ID=351&frame= yes~main accessed 21 June 2005.

Lynch, Dov (2003), 'The EU towards a strategy', in D. Lynch (ed.), *The South Caucasus: a Challenge for the EU*, Chaillot Paper, 65 (December), Institute for Strategic Studies, Paris, pp. 171–91.

Merikallio, Katri (2005), 'The Aceh peace talks', *Suomen Kuvalehti*, Finland, 15 May, www.suomenkuvalehti.fi/?id=5616, accessed 21 June 2005.

Montes, Carlos and Stefano Migliorisi (2004), *EU Donor Atlas Mapping Official Development Assistance*, Development Strategies with IDC, Europa – Europe Aid Cooperation Office.

O'Brien, Terence (2004), 'New Zealand: does distance lend enchantment?', Chaillot Paper, 72 (November), Institute for Strategic Studies, Paris, pp. 103–13.

Quigley, John (2004), 'EU commends Pakistan's democratic progress', *EurAsia Bulletin*, 8 (1/2), European Institute for Asian Studies, www.eias.org/publications/ bulletin/2004/janfeb04/ebjanfeb04.pdf, accessed 21 June 2005.

Reiterer, Michael (2001), 'ASEM – the Third Summit in Seoul 2000: a roadmap to consolidate the partnership between Asia and Europe', *European Foreign Affairs Review*, 6 (1), 1–30.

van Kemenade, Willem (2004), 'EU's commitment to the "one-China policy": trade and security trade-offs?', European Alliance for Asian Studies Conference, *Taiwan–China Cross Straits Relations – Outlook for Regional Security in East Asia*, Paris, 23 November, www.eias.org/conferences/chinatwstraits251104/kemenadeparis. pdf, accessed 21 June 2005.

Wiessala, Georg (2002), *The European Union and Asian Countries*, London: Sheffield Academic Press.

Wiessala, Georg (2004), 'Promoting human rights in EU–Asia relations: Burma, China and Indonesia', *The EurAsia Bulletin*, 8 (1/2), 3–6.

4. The legal response of India, Malaysia, Singapore and Australia to 9/11

Oliver Mendelsohn

The US, and then later the wider, 'war on terror' was born out of the awful symbolism and sheer destructiveness of the attacks on the World Trade Center and the Pentagon on 11 September 2001. One of the central aspects of this 'war' has been a change in legal regimes around the world. By far the greatest change has been to the legal regime of the United States itself, and this is best symbolized by the prison established for 'enemy non-combatants' (sometimes also called 'illegal' non-combatants) in Guantanamo Bay, Cuba. In the months after 9/11 some 680 of these people were collected from Afghanistan and a range of other locations and dumped in an offshore prison built on a piece of land controlled by the United States in Cuba. The offshore location of the prison was crucial to the Bush administration's effort to deny these prisoners the rights that people within the territory of the United States would normally be entitled to under either civil or military law. For many critics both within and outside the United States, Guantanamo Bay has come to represent the most toxic abuse of US constitutionalism since the incarceration of Japanese-Americans during World War II.

There is no analogue to Guantanamo Bay to be found outside the United States. By this I mean that no other country has been induced by the 'war on terror' to make such significant departures from its own constitutional traditions as has the United States. This is the major underlying proposition of this chapter, though space precludes consideration of a sufficient number of individual cases to argue the proposition comprehensively. The more precise focus of the chapter is the post-9/11 legal action of India, with comparative reference to Malaysia, Singapore and Australia. India and, in a considerably more muted way, Malaysia and Singapore are seen to have opportunistically taken advantage of the US war on terror for political objectives at least partly different from those of the United States. The US war on terror suited the regimes in power in India, Malaysia and Singapore, by legitimating longstanding authoritarianism in the treatment of political opposition that is dubiously 'terrorist' in nature. Australia is something of a different case, and is included here as counterpoint and because it has received little international attention. This nation is seen to be struggling to retain the full breadth of its liberal democratic principles in the face of mounting demands for a stronger security apparatus to combat terrorism. It seems to be government itself, including the security establishment, rather than public opinion that is driving the demands.

THE INDIAN LEGAL ORDER AND TERRORISM

The Indian Experience of Terrorism

For some three years after the events of 9/11 the principal military pre-occupation of the Indian state was with the 'militants' or 'terrorists' operating primarily in and from Indian Kashmir. The Kashmir issue, of course, is not new. It has carried on from the time of the partition of the subcontinent in 1947, and has been the direct issue of two of the three official wars fought between India and Pakistan since partition. The most recent major crisis was a mobilization of some million troops (roughly 700 000 of them Indian) in the middle months of 2002. India had justified the mobilization as a direct response to the penetration by five terrorists into the Indian Parliament compound in December 2001 – three months after 9/11. Thirteen people died in a gunfight, including the terrorists, but no Member of Parliament was injured. The government of India was quick to name the organizations responsible for the action as the terrorist groups Lashkar-e-Toiba and Jaish Mohammad, both of them based in Pakistan and committed to the cause of 'liberating' Indian Kashmir. In short, India blamed Pakistan for the attack. A number of people were convicted of offences in connection with the action, and one was hanged under the (now repealed) *Prevention of Terrorism Act* 2002.

India has had a long acquaintance with armed insurrection and with 'terror' or violence as a political tool. For example, immediately after Indian Independence there was a strong insurrectionary communist movement in the Telengana region of southern India, and this was only suppressed with considerable force (Sundarayya 1979). In the Himalayan region of Nagaland, tribal people have conducted an insurrectionary and separatist movement from virtually the time of Indian Independence up to the present. One of the most persistent armed movements dates back to the late 1960s, when a band of revolutionary Marxists organized some violent action in the Naxalbari region of rural West Bengal. The Naxalites, as they came to be called, saw their activities as the beginning of a revolution across India (Banerjee 1980). This movement was eventually put down, but a decade or so later it was reborn in a number of districts of the neighbouring and extremely poor state of Bihar and later still in parts of central India and the southern state of Andhra. The movement has persisted for some 30 years now (Mendelsohn and Vicziany 1998, pp. 44–76). Although there has been considerable exemplary violence on the part of the Naxalites that could reasonably be called 'terrorist', it is easy to sympathize with the movement's goals of land reform, social respect and abatement of sexual violence in some of India's most unequal and poorest regions.

In the 1980s the most serious challenge to the Indian state was from Sikhs who wanted to establish a separate state to be called 'Khalistan' or the 'land of the pure'. The storming of the Golden Temple of Amritsar by the Indian army in 'Operation Bluestar' caused the death of some 1000 Sikh 'militants' (the term generally used at the time). This event cost Prime Minister Indira Gandhi her own life, when one of her Sikh bodyguards murdered her in retribution. The bloody attack on militant Sikhs resonates strongly two decades after the event and has some parallels with militant Hindu treatment of Muslims at Ayodhya in 1992 (the Babri Masjid affair) and in Gujarat in 2002, and more generally for the last 15 years or so. The parallel is a core of sectarianism within the majority Hindu population. But highly militant and obscurantist representatives of the Hindu majority practising violence in defence of 'mother Hinduism' are seldom labelled 'extremists' or even 'militants' and certainly not 'terrorists'.

By and large, and with the major exception of the militant Sikh challenge in the 1980s, the Indian state has learnt to live with chronic political violence on the part of organized minorities. Why, then, was Kashmiri 'terrorism' (a reasonable enough term for some of the Kashmiri militants' activities) taken so seriously in the period from early 2002 to mid 2004? The answer to this question may have something to do with an upsurge in the activities of the Kashmiri activists themselves, but it also has a lot to do with Indian relations with Pakistan and with relations between the Hindu majority and the large Muslim minority within India itself. The two fresh factors affecting these issues over the last several years have been the advent of 9/11 with all its political and military fallout; and the rise to power of the BJP, a party that unashamedly champions the cause of militant Hinduism. For the BJP the US-led 'war on terror' was a godsend, since it facilitated the repackaging of India as a prime victim of Islamic terrorism with Pakistani roots. It has not been difficult to mount an argument that there are close links between the terrorists of 9/11 and the people who have been conducting terrorist activities in and around Indian Kashmir.

It is true that all the major parties in India have maintained an uncompromising stand on Kashmir, and none of them has been in general conciliatory towards Pakistan. In this sense India as a whole has seen great diplomatic advantage post-9/11 in trying to shift an international perception that India is as much to blame as Pakistan for the two nations' chronic enmity. But the

BJP is in a special position on the issue of Pakistan by virtue of its lack of sympathy with Muslims within India. The BJP has differed from Congress and the left-of-centre parties in its rejection of the idea of 'secularism' as an appropriate guide to government in India and in its rationale as a party of the Hindu majority. The BJP rose to power as the voice of 'Hindutva', an emotive idea of India as an essentially Hindu nation. Inevitably, this conception of India has been seen by the more than 130 million Indian Muslims as antagonistic to them. It is fair to say that since the advent to power of the BJP, Indian Muslims are under more suspicion than ever before that they constitute a fifth column for Pakistan. So when bombs go off in Mumbai, as they did again on 25 August 2003, killing some 50 people, the forces of Hindutva (including the militant Shiv Sena) are quick to attribute them to 'Muslims', regardless of whether they are Indians, Kashmiri separatists or Pakistanis. The object of the exercise is to assert a seamless identity between the enemy nation of Pakistan and Indian Muslims, who are 'really' Pakistanis in Indian clothing.

The period of BJP-led government in New Delhi (including a full term from 1999 to 2004) has seen perhaps the worst violence between Hindus and Muslims since partition in 1947. Some 2000 Muslims were killed in Gujarat State in February 2002.[1] This was superficially a spontaneous popular riot but the more considered view is that it was orchestrated, certainly exploited, by elements within the BJP government of Gujarat following the death in a train fire of 59 Hindu activists (Concerned Citizens' Tribunal 2002). The death of these Hindus was claimed to have been deliberately brought about by Muslim zealots, and the official explanation of the ensuing riots was that they were a spontaneous response to the cruel train murders (themselves reminiscent of appalling incidents on trains during partition).[2]

It can be said then that the US-led campaign against terror suited the BJP-led government of India, since it made their own preoccupations more respectable. Indeed, US approval may even have emboldened elements within the ruling party – the BJP is by no means a single monolith – in their descent into opportunistic political violence within India.

The Tension between Liberty and Authoritarianism in Independent India

In order to understand the roots of India's legal engagement with 'terror', it is necessary to provide some historical background to more recent legislation and enforcement. Some of the less agreeable aspects of this engagement derive from a tension at the very heart of the Constitution of India. On the one hand the Constitution of 1950 represents a mature statement of some of the finest constitutional norms.[3] Thus it contains a bill of judicially enforceable Fundamental Rights guaranteeing the classic civil and political liberties. Of greater novelty, the Constitution of 1950 goes on to enunciate certain 'Directive Principles of State Policy', not judicially enforceable but designed to guide the government in developing a society fit for the newly independent nation. For example:

> The State shall, within the limits of economic capacity and development, make effective provision for securing the right to work, to education and to public assistance in cases of unemployment, old age, sickness and disablement, and in other cases of undeserved want. (Article 41)

The Constitution also lays down the basis of a democratic order, marrying the principles of Westminster-style responsible government and US-derived federalism. In addition to specifying the powers and procedures of parliament and of the (essentially powerless) president, the Constitution establishes a strong Supreme Court. This Constitutional basis has enabled the Court to become clearly the most distinguished court in Asia. These are some of the 'progressive' elements of the Indian Constitution.

But there is also another tradition of government reflected in and perpetuated by the Constitution. This tradition can be called 'colonial authoritarianism' and is best exemplified by the capacity of the president (directed by the prime minister of the day) to establish a 'state of emergency' throughout the country. Article 352 authorizes the president, if satisfied that the security of India is threatened 'by war or external aggression or internal disturbance', to proclaim an emergency. During its continuation the government can suspend the Fundamental Rights (including freedom of speech and association, and protection against arbitrary arrest) (Article 357). No elections need be held during the emergency (Article 83(2)). Even without a national emergency being declared, the central or Union Government can set aside the democratically constituted government of any state (Article 356). During the period of 'president's rule' the federal principle is suspended and all functions of government are directed by the centre through whichever channels it chooses to use. Clearly then, in the basic design of the Constitution there is sufficient suspicion of the democratic principle to allow for its suspension in difficult times.

This suspicion that democracy may not always be maintainable is rooted in the colonial experience of government and is not limited to providing for the total suspension of democratic principles at particular times. One of the routine devices of British rule was preventive detention, anathema to any modern order that embodies a conception of 'due process'. Preventive detention is embraced in Independent India at least as enthusiastically as it was by the colonial state. It is only the identity of the enemies of the state that has changed.

A 'state of emergency', the centrepiece of constitutional authoritarianism, was invoked for the first time by Prime Minister Nehru during the war with

China in 1962. Despite the brevity of this war, the emergency was not lifted until six years later. Its continuation had proved advantageous to the Congress government, particularly through the access it afforded to powers of detention under the Defence of India rules. Prime Minister Indira Gandhi again used the device of proclaiming an emergency in 1971 during the war with Pakistan, and once more the emergency persisted long after the war was over.

The 1975–77 Emergency (the only state of emergency to remain in popular memory) was the first to be justified by 'internal disturbance' and it had far more drastic consequences than the two earlier emergency periods. It led to systematic censorship of the press, widespread imprisonment of political opponents, suppression of organized opposition, and the implementation of authoritarian programs such as compulsory vasectomies and brutal slum clearances (Tarlo 2003). The government had justified its declaration of a state of emergency by the strength of extra-parliamentary opposition to the regime. Whatever the truth as to the 'indiscipline' of Indian political opposition – a favourite refrain of Mrs Gandhi – her proclamation of a constitutional emergency was clearly a desperate response by a prime minister who had become embattled on many political fronts.

During the Emergency the parliament passed the 42nd amendment to the Constitution, which stripped the Supreme Court of much of the power it had either been given by the Constitution or won for itself in battles during the first quarter-century following Independence (Dhavan 1978). Above all, the 42nd amendment purported to prohibit the Court from deliberating on the validity of amendments to the Constitution made by Parliament. Here was a classic contest of executive and judiciary, in the context of a regime busy remaking itself in the image of left-wing authoritarianism (Austin 2000, pp. 370–88).

When Indira Gandhi lifted the state of emergency in 1977 and held an election she was swept from power. The new Janata government swiftly moved to repeal the 42nd amendment and generally to restore democratic norms. Although the Janata government soon fell apart and Indira Gandhi returned to power in the election of 1980, her Emergency has remained an object of oppositional inspiration among the political and civil elites. In the years following the Emergency a great raft of organizations – the women's movement is just one example – sprang up to expose and challenge arbitrary power in India. The great arena for this activity has been the courts rather than Parliament, above all the Supreme Court of India. 'Public interest' or 'social action' litigation was for the first time positively welcomed by the Court in the years following the Emergency, and this has become one of the distinctive features of Indian democracy (Baxi 1988, pp. 387–415). But parallel with these positive developments in civil society and the highest judicial institution, India continues to be disfigured by chronic police brutality, imprisonment without justification and the gross enrichment of officials (including judicial officials) at the expense of the poor. India is increasingly marked by institutional decay and unlawful behaviour on the part of officials. This is the contradictory backdrop to India's confrontation of 'terror'. The great danger is that some of the anti-terrorist measures will feed the authoritarian stream in Indian governance without necessarily being effective in the fight against terrorism itself.

The Indian Laws against Subversion and Terrorism

Post-Independence India was quick to enact the *Preventive Detention Act* of 1950. This Act remained in force until 1970, when it was allowed to lapse, but for a number of years it overlapped the Defence of India rules made under the 1962 Act of the same name. The Act and rules were the legislative response to war breaking out with China, and the rules enabled preventive detention of anyone who had acted or was likely to act in a manner detrimental to public order and national security. The rules were revived in 1971, during the war with Pakistan and its aftermath, and were maintained long enough for the imprisonment of striking rail workers in 1974 (Sherlock 2001). With an eye more firmly focused on internal disturbances not directly linked to war, the *Maintenance of Internal Security Act* (MISA) was passed in 1971. This was the principal instrument used for widespread detention of political opponents during Indira Gandhi's Emergency of 1975–77.

After the Emergency the Janata government pushed through an amendment to the Constitution that substituted 'armed rebellion' for 'internal disturbance' as a basis for declaring an emergency under Article 352 (but this was later reversed under the Congress Party in 1988). The Janata government also repealed MISA as well as the Defence of India rules. But, when Indira Gandhi returned to power in 1980, the *National Security Act* 1980 again allowed preventive detention of anyone suspected of subverting national security, public order or essential economic services.[4] Other decidedly illiberal legislation was passed at this time, including the *Essential Services Maintenance Act* 1981, providing for the suppression of strikes and lockouts in key economic sectors.

It was the Sikh situation in the mid 1980s that focused specific attention on what were now called 'terrorists'. *The Terrorist and Disruptive Activities (Prevention) Act* 1985 (TADA) provided a legislative basis for a range of counter-terrorism surveillance measures (wiretaps and so on). It provided for the death penalty in trials that could also be held in camera. On important matters, the burden of proof was reversed. There were 'Review Committees' established under the legislation which, it has to be said, did discharge a large number of detainees, as did the Supreme Court upon individual application. Overall, tens of thousands of prisoners are said to have been detained under TADA, though verification of such numbers has always been difficult.[5] There has been no definitive study of the identity of these people, but it appears that many of them, probably most, could not by any stretch of the imagination be called 'terrorists'. As is the nature of authoritarian instruments, they come to be used against a far wider sector of the population than was their justification for enactment. TADA allowed detention of anyone who committed or even facilitated the commission of 'disruptive activity', a term only vaguely defined. The Act was finally allowed to lapse by the Congress government in 1995, a rare instance when Congress has been responsible for removing legal instruments that run counter to due process jurisprudence.

With the rise to power of the BJP, the most actively divisive government since Independence, there was a renewed commitment to the approach best represented by MISA and TADA. The BJP proposed a new Prevention of Terrorism Act in 2000, but after sustained opposition by various political parties and the human rights movement the bill did not proceed. Following the World Trade Center attack, a Prevention of Terrorism Ordinance was rushed through on 24 October, and this was transformed into the *Prevention of Terrorism Act* 2002 (POTA). When the spokesman for the US State Department, Richard Boucher, was asked to comment on the Ordinance (later Act) in March 2002, he said:

> We do think it is important for governments to take steps against terrorism, to do it in a constitutional way ... We do believe that that can be done consistent with democratic principles. We have done that. The Europeans have done that. And India seems to have done that as well. (*The Hindu*, 29 March 2002)

The new Act had many features in common with TADA, though in one major respect the later Act was preferable. The vague and obnoxious phrase 'disruptive activity' was not part of the later Act, which was limited to terrorist acts (including belonging to a terrorist organization). The punishment for such activities, if they brought about death, was sentence of death or life imprisonment. The Act expanded the range of investigations possible under the ordinary law; for example, there was virtually no limit on what property could be seized (section 7). Special courts could be established to handle offences under the Act, and the trials could be held in camera. Confessions extracted outside the ordinary rules of evidence under the *Indian Evidence Act* 1872 were deemed admissible (section 32). And, importantly, the burden of proof was in effect reversed if fingerprints or the possession of arms pointed to the involvement of the accused (section 53).

Given the route along which India has passed for 30 years or more, it would not be possible to erect a case on the basis of POTA that India had entered into a new and more draconian phase of legislation justified by the hunt for terrorists. The case against this legislation, as with TADA and MISA before it, was that the most radical aspects were probably not necessary. It is not clear, for example, why proceedings should have been in camera or why there should have been open slather on confessions. The latter is a positive invitation to tyrannical police officers. There were particular concerns about providing a secret regime of trial, conviction and sentence of death. Reversal of onus of proof and other relaxation of the evidentiary burden will almost certainly lead on occasion to wrongful conviction. And surely it is not desirable that special courts be established, albeit that the judicial officers in these courts are sufficiently qualified. It is true that the Indian court system is inefficient and plagued by delay, and it is therefore possible to sympathize with a government that wishes to bypass these problems in its fight against terrorism. But there are also ways of expediting justice within the regular criminal justice administration without going down the path of a separate apparatus for those accused of terrorism.

There was, then, a strong argument that POTA was too authoritarian an instrument, even conceding the legitimacy of the concern to combat terrorism more effectively in what is undoubtedly a dangerous political and security environment for India, as well as for many other countries. It was all but inevitable, based on past experience, that if POTA had been rigorously enforced it would quite often have been directed against people who could not by any reasonable definition be thought to be 'terrorists'. In this sense the law was an unwelcome legislative reincarnation of Indian authoritarianism that had been progressively beaten down following Indira Gandhi's Emergency.

The Return of Congress and the Repeal of POTA

To almost universal surprise, Congress won more seats than the BJP in the election of 2004 and was able to form a government.[6] During the campaign, Congress had promised to repeal POTA if it won the election, a libertarianism newly discovered by a party that had instituted almost all the anti-democratic emergencies – above all Indira Gandhi's Emergency of 1975–77 – since Independence almost 60 years earlier. This stance enabled Congress to portray the BJP and its affiliates as dedicated to both sectarianism and authoritarianism. Some four months after its electoral victory, the Congress-led government repealed POTA and introduced substitute legislation.[7]

Certain key aspects of the *Unlawful Activities (Prevention) Act* 1967 (as amended in 2004) are demonstrable improvements over POTA. For example, POTA (section 32(1)) set aside the hitherto ruling provision of the *Indian Evidence Act* 1872, whereby confessions to police officers were inadmissible as evidence in court. The new Act restores the bar of admissibility of confessions to police, thereby making torture less rewarding a behaviour of gaolers and police. Under POTA a suspect could be held for up to 180 days without charge (section 49 (2)(b)), whereas now suspects must be produced before the court within 24 hours as prescribed by the ordinary criminal law. Bail could effectively be denied a suspect under POTA for a year without consideration of the court (section 49(6) and (7)), but now the ordinary provisions of the criminal law have been restored in this matter. POTA had authorized the court to draw 'adverse inference' from certain matters (including the finding of fingerprints at the site of an offence: section 53(1)(b)), thereby transferring the burden of proof from prosecution to defence. This too has been removed. And importantly, whereas it was enough for POTA that a person 'belongs or professes to belong to a terrorist organisation' (section 20(1)), under the new Act the accused is guilty of an offence only if he [sic] associates himself with the organization 'with intention to further its activities' (section 38(1)).

On the other hand, the open-ended definition of terrorist acts persists from TADA, through POTA, into the new Act (Human Rights Features, 2004). The definition is bound to sweep up many oppositional activities that are either dubiously or not at all terrorist in nature. And there remains no specified procedure for the listing of an organization as 'involved in terrorism' (section 35(1)(d)) and therefore to be included in the Schedule of the Act. Moreover, proceedings may still be held in camera 'if the court so desires' (section 44(1)).

Overall, however, replacement of POTA with the new Act is a considerable step in the right direction. The new Congress-led government has translated its recently found rhetoric of civil liberties into some valuable reform of legal instruments. No doubt this process of reform was aided by the reduced intensity of political pressure from the United States, which is now embroiled in a war in Iraq widely seen to have little to do with its 'war on terror'. The United States too continues to be roundly condemned internationally and at home for its treatment of prisoners in Guantanamo Bay and torture and mistreatment of prisoners in Iraq. The time is therefore ripe for the new government to show a more civil libertarian face. Whether or not this results in more orderly and careful administration of the criminal law in relation to political opposition remains to be seen.

The Indian Legal Order, Authoritarianism and Terror

The stance of the United States following the terrorist attacks of 9/11 can be seen to have been both influential and unhelpful to the development of India as a nation. This did not come about by virtue of a unique change of direction in the Indian polity, but rather by the ruling party's seizing of the American agenda in a way that worked to legitimate the chauvinist and authoritarian tendencies within both the party and the Indian government more generally.

An authoritarian approach to the quelling of political opposition was now reaffirmed by a ruling party that could plausibly portray itself as defender of the nation under attack from Islamic terrorism originating in Pakistan and supported by Muslim elements within India. It is only the loss of power by the BJP in an election that had little or nothing to do with this issue that has at least for the moment strengthened the anti-authoritarianism movement within India.

In India, as in other democratic nations including the United States, Britain and Australia, strong laws against terrorism have a symbolic as well as a practical effect. They symbolize the commitment of the nation to confront and defeat terrorism, irrespective of whether the laws embody procedures that will effectively deal with terrorists. To enact tough laws against terrorists is to be seen to be doing something about the practical menace of terrorism. But given the nature of Indian society – including its huge population, heterogeneity, poverty, rising expectations and colonial history – authoritarian legal instruments have inevitably been used more often than in some of the Western democracies. In other words, the authoritarianism of the Indian state has been routine and not merely symbolic and exemplary. Whether or not this has been effective in combating 'terrorism' is an issue that has scarcely been touched on in this chapter. There are really several questions here. First, there is the question of whether the special laws that deny terrorism suspects the ordinary protections of the criminal law have been more effective in bringing terrorists to justice and thus stamping out terrorism itself than the regular criminal law would have been. Second, there is the question of 'collateral damage': just how many non-terrorists have been swept into gaol or killed under the various anti-terrorism laws of the last 30 years or so? If, as seems to be the case, there are many thousands of such people, a third question is whether the tough laws are justifiable even if they are somewhat more effective than the ordinary criminal law.

Without trying to answer the above questions definitively, the main argument developed here is that great social and national detriments have flowed from the authoritarianism of the Indian state. Large numbers of real people get hurt when there are tougher laws against 'terrorism' than the ordinary criminal law would allow. In the eye of the present observer, the threat posed by the new terrorists may not be commensurate with the harm done in the name of fighting them. This is not to counsel inaction on the part of the Indian or any other state: it is the undoubted duty of the state to seek to protect its citizens from genuine terrorism. But equally, the nation is ultimately the loser if political forces divert the fight against terrorism to their own sectarian ends that have nothing to do with this fight. There is ample if not complete evidence over long periods of time that this has occurred at both national and state levels in India.

ANTI-TERRORISM LAWS IN MALAYSIA AND SINGAPORE

Malaysia and Singapore share a considerable part of their constitutional tradition with India. Like India, Malaysia and Singapore were ruled by Britain and through that connection encountered the ideas of Anglo-American constitutionalism. The concepts of the rule of law, the presumption of innocence, the separation of powers and an independent judiciary were as much a part of the constitutional tradition of Malaya and Singapore by the time of their Independence in 1957 as they had been for India ten years earlier. (In 1963 Singapore merged into the Federation of Malaya but in 1965 the island state was pushed out of what was then renamed Malaysia.) Equally, Malaya and Singapore had experienced the firm hand of colonial authoritarianism. This reached its height at the end of the colonial period during the confrontation with communist insurgents, the 'emergency', that lasted from 1948 until several years after the gaining of Independence in 1960. The parallel constitutionalism of Malaysia and Singapore (built on the rock of the Malayan Constitution of 1957) has grown out of the somewhat knotty entwining of these libertarian and authoritarian tendencies, refined over time by changing perceptions of race relations and broader social tendencies. The result has been a greater valorization of soft authoritarianism in the name of communal harmony and right-thinking values than has developed in India. This is the context into which the post-9/11 syndrome has slotted.

In the case of Singapore, a key provision of its Constitution is Article 14, which enunciates freedom of speech, assembly and association. After a standard recitation of these freedoms, the Article authorizes Parliament to make 'such restrictions as it considers necessary or expedient in the interest of the security of Singapore or any part thereof, friendly relations with other countries, public order or morality'. There is a comparable clause (Article 10(2)) in the Malaysian Constitution, also deriving from the original Constitution of Malaya 1957. Although this formulation allows for great curtailment of the civil liberties enunciated in the same Article, it is not the language itself that has brought about such curtailment. Indeed, the words qualifying the freedoms are drawn from the Constitution of India (Article 19(2)). Rather than the constitutional words themselves, it is the enactment of other laws and above all the interpretation of the courts that have allowed Malaysia and Singapore to develop their practical limitation of rights to a point where they scarcely meet the standards usually applied to liberal democracies.

Malaysia has attempted under a succession of Malay prime ministers to strike a balance between the practice of structural favouritism to Malays and the concession of sufficient opportunity to satisfy the economically more successful Chinese. This balancing act has been carefully managed, particularly since the race riots of 1969, through a coercive suppression of dissent. So the most benign explanation of the authoritarian style of Malaysian government is that it was needed to ensure that racial competition was not transformed into active disharmony. But clearly, the Malaysian government has found its arsenal of authoritarian instruments (particularly preventive detention) immensely useful in confronting opposition that is not by any reasonable conception dangerous but merely inconvenient. So it is political opportunism rather than deep social danger that has sustained the authoritarianism of the Malaysian government from before the World Trade Center attack.

Singapore, under Lee Kuan Yew and his like-minded successors, has not needed to perform the same ethnic balancing act as has Malaysia: 75 per cent of its population is ethnically Chinese and this community dominates both the economic and the political landscape of the city state. But Lee Kuan Yew had a distinctive vision of the kind of disciplined economy and overall society that he wanted for Singapore, and realization of this vision has also demanded an energetic curtailment of individual choice.

From the mid-1990s both Lee Kuan Yew and Mahathir bin Mohammed, the then prime minister of Malaysia, met the persistent international criticism of their regimes with a positive rather than defensive rationale. The code name for this rationale was 'Asian values' or sometimes, in Lee's formulation, 'Confucian' or 'Eastern' values. The argument was that some of the nations of 'the East' had developed a more disciplined approach to governance than the West had. In a long interview with Fareed Zakaria (1994, p. 110), Lee Kuan Yew characterized the United States in particular as suffering

> the breakdown of civil society. The expansion of the right of the individual to behave or misbehave as he pleases has come at the expense of an orderly society. In the East the main object is to have a well-ordered society so that everybody can have maximum enjoyment of his freedoms. This freedom can only exist in an ordered state and not in a natural state of contention and anarchy.

In expounding the values of 'the East', Lee made clear that he was talking about Korea, Japan, China and Vietnam, rather than India or 'South-east Asia' (in which he must have included the Muslim nations of Indonesia and Malaysia). In these nations a special kind of family-centric model of society and governance could be counted on to deliver rapid economic progress while maintaining social order. Nor was it a case of trading freedom for social stability and rapid economic growth – Lee seemed to be advancing a different conception of 'freedom' altogether.[8]

Lee Kuan Yew's analysis of both West and East may have been highly contested but it did seem to flow from a genuine perception of social disintegration in the West and from a particular reading of how economic development was proceeding in the East Asian world. Mahathir's political purpose in promoting 'Asian values' was considerably more instrumental.[9]

His adoption of the language of 'Asian values' was part of a larger attack on a perceived racism and continued neo-colonialism of ethnic Europeans and of the Western powers. On the other hand, Mahathir moved somewhat uneasily between his Asian and Muslim identities. He seemed to be speaking the language of Lee Kuan Yew, but we have seen that Lee's Asia was the culturally Chinese, Korean and Japanese parts of that broad region, not the Muslim parts. Moreover, Mahathir was essentially a modernizer rather than an Islamist at home and to a considerable extent his critique of the West (and of Israel and the Jews) was calculated to appeal to groups within Malaysia who favoured a more rigorously Islamic society. But he also saw himself as the most prominent politician of South-east Asia, leading the rise of this region. These tensions meant that Mahathir was more strident but ultimately less plausible than Lee as an advocate of a distinctively 'Asian' approach to governance and economic development.

The Asian financial collapse of 1997 spelled the end of Lee Kuan Yew's promotion of Asian or Confucian values. Lee was forced to concede that family-based patrimonialism had been part of the cause of the failure of the banking system and that what was needed was old-fashioned Western-style regulation of the financial sector. Whatever the merit of Confucian values in governing society in general, they had been shown to be clearly deficient in running the economy. Over the following several years there were also incipient signs of a relaxation of the tight social controls that had been valorized in the Asian values thesis. In Malaysia, however, Mahathir continued to promote what became an increasingly splenetic version of the Asian values thesis.

This is the backdrop to the post-9/11 legal scene in Malaysia and Singapore. With that attack suddenly the two South-east Asian nations morphed into mainstream collaborators in the 'war on terror'. Gone and seemingly forgotten are the days when a US Vice-President, Al Gore, could travel to Malaysia and call for '*reformasi*', the catch-cry of a Muslim opposition party protesting at the dubious trial and imprisonment of former Deputy Prime Minister Anwar Ibrahim. At that time the Democrat administration in the United States shared the liberal disquiet throughout the West at the oppressive behaviour of Mahathir. After 9/11, on the other hand, the United States showered praise on Malaysia as a soul mate in the war against terror. Mahathir was reborn as a 'moderate Muslim' leader and even welcomed to the White House in May 2002.

The legal centrepiece of coercive rule in Malaysia and Singapore is the *Internal Security Act* (ISA), which had its origins in the British colonial government's *Emergency Regulations Ordinance* 1948 enacted early in the fight against the communist uprising (Lee 2002, pp. 56–72). The most potent weapon under the ISA is the capacity of the Minister to order the preventive detention for successive periods of up to two years of anyone 'acting in any manner prejudicial to the security ... or to the maintenance of public order or essential services' of Malaysia or Singapore (section 8(1)). This provision has been much used throughout the post-colonial history of both nations, and clearly on many occasions the objective has been to suppress inconvenient dissent rather than genuine threats to the security and order of the nation. The provision continues to be the major weapon against terrorism post-9/11, but now the international community is silent on any oppressive tendencies of such action.

Legislative change in Singapore and Malaysia following 9/11 has been a matter of detail rather than of great substance. Thus Singapore enacted the *United Nations (Anti-Terrorism Measures) Regulations 2001* and the *Terrorism (Suppression of Financing) Act* 2002. These measures were largely directed against activities in relation to terrorism outside Singapore that were not adequately covered by the ISA. But when it came to taking action against members of the terrorist organization Jemaah Islamiyah (JI) some three months after 9/11, it was the tried-and-true preventive detention under the ISA that was employed. Michael Hor (2002, p. 30) notes that the United States through Defense Secretary Donald Rumsfeld sent a congratulatory message to Singapore on the action. Similarly, Malaysia used the ISA to detain a large number of alleged terrorists with ties to the Kumpulan Mujahadin Malaysia (KMM) and JI groups (Lee 2002, p. 61). The approval of the United States for these actions is of a piece with the praise of India by the State Department's Richard Boucher following enactment of new Indian anti-terrorism legislation in 2002 (see above).

Therese Lee argued in 2002 that

> Human rights in Malaysia are now newly endangered by an international community and a Malaysian public that is more willing to prioritize national security interests over individual liberties. The terrorist attacks on the United States quelled the growing momentum for a review of the ISA, and thus the ISA's potential for oppression looms in some ways larger than before. (Lee 2002, p. 63)

Lee is clearly right in the view that 9/11 has completely removed the decades-long international pressure for reform of the Malaysian (and Singapore) governments' abuse of preventive detention. On the other hand, Hor's discussion of the treatment of the JI detainees in Singapore suggests that there may sometimes be substantial ground for the regime's concern to avoid criminal trial of terrorism suspects. Hor (2002, pp. 48–50) argues that the Singapore government may have been understandably wary of turning the JI detainees into martyrs in the eyes of the Malay minority. The Singapore authorities may have been particularly concerned not to give JI a platform to stir up religious feeling and therefore social discontent. Given the success of Singapore in managing race relations – considerably greater success than that of Malaysia – Hor's discussion should warn us not to be prematurely comprehensive in our rejection of all measures that do not conform to the highest standards of due process. Aside from the question of how to promote racial harmony in multiracial societies, there remains the question of whether the ordinary standards of due process are simply too burdensome in the fight against terrorism enacted by Muslim extremists of the Al Qaeda or allied kind. A brief consideration of the Australian situation will sharpen this question.

THE CASE OF AUSTRALIA

The example of Australia neatly sums up many of the dilemmas in the contemporary fight against terrorism. Australia is a liberal democracy that has not so far been the object of a successful terrorist attack carried out on its own soil by extremists of Muslim origins. The closest Australia has come to such an event was the firebombing of night-clubs in Bali, about a year after 9/11, in which some 88 Australians and many other Westerners as well as Balinese were killed. But Australia, like much of the world, has been greatly unsettled by the several terrorist events since 9/11. Australia responded to these events by enacting new procedures for interrogating and detaining persons suspected of planning or actually carrying out terrorist acts. Prior to this legislation Australia did not have any laws specifically directed at terrorism, though it had a highly developed web of security organizations. This is not the place for an exhaustive analysis of the new laws, but a short discussion will show both the dangers to liberty and the difficulty of making judgements as to the appropriateness of the changes.

The most controversial of the legislative changes of 2002–03 were new powers to question suspects for up to 24 hours over a 28-day period – this was later increased to 48 hours if interpreters were present – and also to detain suspects without seeking to question them. By piling warrant upon warrant (only obtainable from a sitting judge), suspects can be questioned or detained for up 168 hours (*ASIO Act* 1979, sections 34D and 34F). No charges have to be laid against persons being interrogated or detained, nor do they need to be suspected of breaking the law. They need simply to be of interest to the authorities. Such persons have no right of access to lawyers or anyone else during their period of questioning or detention. The legislation received bipartisan support in Parliament, after a number of amendments moved by both major parties, but they continued to be controversial among legal and other civil libertarian groups.

There is no doubt that these changes to Australian law represent a considerable derogation from the liberty principles that prevail in the criminal justice system of Australia. The then Director-General of the Australian

Security Intelligence Organisation (ASIO) provided a spirited defence of the provisions during the mandatory review of the legislation undertaken by the Joint Parliamentary Committee on Security in May 2005 (Parliament of Australia 2005, pp. 3–4). Dennis Richardson noted that the new questioning provisions had been invoked eight times in the year and a half they had been in place, while the detention provisions had not been used at all. For Richardson, the measures represented a reasonable balance in the struggle against terrorism. He pointed out that France, to which the terrorism suspect Willie Brigitte had been deported from Australia, was able to detain persons for up to three years while charges were being prepared for trial. Brigitte himself remains in this legal limbo two years after his deportation. Richardson further noted the dependence of liberal democracies such as Australia on less hedged-about regimes in Asia. Thus in a public address in March 2005 the Director-General asked rhetorically whether the interests of the struggle against terrorism would have been better served if Hambali, the Jamaa Islamia's head of operations, had been taken into custody in Australia rather than Thailand. 'An interesting question', he observed. He concluded the address by stating, 'Too often, the starting point of some analysts and commentators is a hair shirt, which would have us believe that if only we could be perfect, so would everyone else. If only it were that simple' (Richardson, 2005).

   This meditation on the validity of variably coercive approaches to the struggle against terrorism can be viewed alongside Hor's nomination of the possible motives of the Singapore government for using the ISA powers against the Jemaah Islamiyah operatives captured in Singapore. We can readily agree that it would be wrong to assume bad faith in the relevant regimes simply because they are employing mechanisms proscribed by the ordinary criminal law. Moreover, merely because they may sometimes have acted in bad faith does not mean that they have always done so. The Australian official Richardson wants to tell us that criminal law embodying the highest standards of due process is a positive hindrance to effective confrontation of contemporary terrorism. He claims that in Australia, less than 10 per cent of those who have 'a substantive involvement' with al Qaeda, Jemaah Islamiyah and other like-minded groups 'will ever face a court of law' (Richardson 2005). The evidence will simply be insufficient to convict them of any offence. The same is true for other countries, he suggests. In these circumstances, Richardson argues that we must move beyond some of the protections of the criminal law in order to extract intelligence from suspects. Provided we retain some important provisions of due process – including the involvement of judicial officials and periodic review by Parliament – Australia will not descend into tyranny.

   Given the climate of fear that has so affected a nation like Australia since 9/11, the position represented by the Director-General of ASIO has so far won the day decisively. The Labor opposition has consistently supported the tougher new procedures for treating persons suspected of involvement with terrorism, and dissent has mainly been limited to lawyer and professional civil liberties organizations. That dissent has largely taken the form of in-principle opposition to any measure that fails to observe the full procedural guarantees of the criminal law. There has been little analysis that attempts to disprove empirically the views of the government or officials like the Director-General of ASIO. Indeed, such an exercise would be extremely difficult. How does one assess the proposition that ascertaining involvement in terrorism and the collection of intelligence will be significantly furthered by the provision of extended periods of interrogation? Instead of seeking to answer this question, the focus of lawyer-related dissent has been on the damage done to the rule of law by allowing police and security officials to lock someone away and interrogate them in secrecy for relatively long periods.

By way of a postscript, in 2005 Australia radically tightened anti-terrorism laws by enacting the *Anti-Terrorism Act (No. 2)* and providing for companion legislation by the states. The intervening event that led to this move was the London transport bombings of 7 July 2005. Perhaps, like 9/11, it was the powerful symbolism of the London attacks – bombs in the underground and a bus – and the connection that many Australians feel with London that aroused government and now also public concern so strongly. The Commonwealth gained the backing of the states – many of the criminal and police powers are in the hands of the states – and proceeded to legislate for radically stiffer investigative and detention powers to be given to the security and police apparatus. For example, the legislation allows the Australian Federal Police to apply to a court for a 'control order' lasting up to 12 months (Schedule 4). This is similar in form to an apprehended violence order, now a staple of the regular criminal law, but it allows for stricter conditions on tracking movements, travel and association. With the legislative cooperation of the states, there is a new, longer and preventive detention regime – up to 14 days, along UK lines – designed to stop further attacks in a terrorist situation and to prevent the destruction of evidence (Schedule 4, section 105). There are new 'stop, question and search' powers for the police (Schedule 5) and steps are being taken towards more rigorous security at transport hubs and other places of gathering (Prime Minister's Press Release 2005). In his September statement the prime minister also foreshadowed legislation of a new criminal offence of leaving baggage unattended at airports (ibid.). In the event, no doubt wisely, this novel and probably unenforceable measure was not included in the subsequent Act. Finally, the new Act redefined the longstanding offence of sedition in an effort to apply it more easily to persons advocating violent change (Schedule 7). This provoked the greatest concern among the many critics of the legislation.

This is not the place to analyse the recent legislation in any depth. But it can be said in summary that the new laws provide security, and particularly police, officials with very broad new powers of investigation, interrogation and detention of persons suspected of terrorist offences. Passage of the legislation immediately preceded the arrest of 17 Muslims in Sydney and Melbourne, and their being charged with a number of terrorism offences, including membership of a terrorist organization and (in the case of the Sydney detainees) with planning a terrorist attack. There appears to be considerable fear among Australia's 300 000 Muslims that the new legal and administrative measures will target them disproportionately. Clearly, a far larger number of Australians will find themselves inspected, questioned and even detained by the authorities. The potential exists for police and security officials to become considerably more oppressive under the cloak of their new powers. In the name of fighting terrorism, Australia now faces perhaps the greatest threat to the rule of law that it has experienced in the post-World War II period. At the same time, as ever, the dialectic between collective security and liberty is far from politically neutral – there is great political advantage to be had by the governing party, which is seen to be an effective guardian of the nation. In this pursuit of advantage can lie the seed of tyranny. While Australia takes its liberal democratic principles seriously, there is now active cause for concern that some of the best aspects of this society are in danger of being closed down.

CONCLUSION

This chapter has examined the impact of counter-terrorism measures on liberty in India with comparative reference to Singapore, Malaysia and Australia. In the case of India, the argument has been that the ruling BJP-led government used the drift of world affairs following 9/11 to its own advantage. The American agenda has been seen here to have strengthened the coercive, as opposed to the libertarian, stream within Indian governance, without necessarily contributing greatly to India's performance in the actual 'war on terror'. For the time being, the electoral defeat of the BJP has disrupted this drift but there remains cause for continuing concern about both liberty in general and the rights of Indian Muslims in particular.

The American-led movement against terrorism has also worked in favour of the ruling regimes in Singapore and Malaysia, since it has tended to legitimate their much criticized coercive approach to political dissent. Such legitimization will tend to retard the emergence of less authoritarian approaches to governance. But the impact of 9/11 on Malaysia and Singapore has been far less than on India, since it has confirmed the political approach of these regimes rather than let loose a more radical variant.

The final example is the more ambiguous case of Australia. Here the legal and political changes following 9/11 have again been far less than in India, and any political advantage to the party in government has accrued less blatantly than in any of the other three cases. But in Australia too the situation is viewed as something other than a simple and clearly beneficial strengthening of institutions to fight the 'war on terror' more effectively. The costs to liberty of the new police and security measures are beginning to mount to a worrying degree. Indeed, during the period of revision of this chapter for publication the Australian Parliament threw over its earlier reluctance to depart in any wholesale way from its longstanding liberty principles that had survived even the Cold War. By the end of 2005 it appeared that Australia could be categorized alongside the United States as having abandoned a significant part of its constitutional traditions in its own war against terrorism.

In her Cairo speech of 20 June 2005, US Secretary of State Condoleezza Rice said

> for 60 years, my country, the United States, pursued stability at the expense of democracy in this region here in the Middle East – and we achieved neither. Now, we are taking a different course. We are supporting the democratic aspirations of all people. (Rice 2005)

These remarks were made primarily to provide a rationale for the somewhat mysterious objectives of the war in Iraq but they have been rightly seen as potentially useful rhetoric towards the construction of a more democratic world that respects human liberty to a greater extent than it has previously. But what has been developed in this chapter is a story that seems to run counter to the very values that Secretary Rice is now promoting on behalf of the government of the United States. If it is now single-mindedly pursuing the strengthening of democracy around the world, then how can we explain its endorsement of Asian coercion? The answer, of course, is that this coercive style is praised because it is now seen to be directed against 'terror'. Unfortunately, the contradiction between a drive for world democracy and a no-holds-barred war against terror is deep and substantial. Without falling into the trap of cynicism, it is difficult to predict that the winner will be democracy and freedom.

NOTES

1. This is the figure that is regularly cited, though there are often doubts cast on its accuracy. For a broad collection of material and sources on the Gujarat riots, see the website of Online Volunteers, www.onlinevolunteers.org/gujarat/reports/index.htm

2. The BJP Chief Minister of Gujarat, Narendra Modi, jumped to the conclusion (still unverified) that the victims of the train fire in Godhra had been murdered by Muslims. His explanation, almost justification, of the ensuing riots throughout Gujarat was to point to Newton's third law: 'every action has an equal and opposite reaction' (*The Times of India*, 2 March 2002).
3. For an accessible account of the making of the Indian Constitution see Austin (1966). The most authoritative commentary on Indian constitutional law is Seervai (1991).
4. There are a number of web sites of activist or revolutionary organizations that provide quite useful material on these matters (see, for an example of the former, Amnesty International 2003).
5. In 1997, two years after the repeal of TADA, Amnesty International's annual report on India cited a government source to the effect that in March more than 42 000 people were still detained under the Act pending trial. This number had apparently declined by December 1997 to 2000, following a Supreme Court directive ordering the release on bail of various categories of detainee (see Amnesty International 1997).
6. Two early academic considerations of the 2004 election are Zoya Hassan (2004) and Gareth Price (2004).
7. POTA was repealed by the *Prevention of Terrorism Act (POTA) Repeal Ordinance* 2004 (promulgated on 21 September). On the same day the *Unlawful Activities (Prevention) Amendment Ordinance* 2004 was promulgated, amending the *Unlawful Activities (Prevention) Act* 1967. These ordinances were converted to Acts of Parliament on 9 December 2004.
8. To some extent Lee Kuan Yew was developing a version of what Isaiah Berlin called the 'positive' conception of liberty, associated with a range of thinkers opposed to European liberalism. See Berlin (1969).
9. Among the many considerations of the Asian values conception, see Goodman and Segal (eds) (1999), particularly Anthony Milner. On the relationship between the United States and Malaysia, see Camroux and Okfen (2004).

REFERENCES

Amnesty International (1997), *Report: India*, www.amnesty.org/ailib/aireport/ar97/ASA20.htm, accessed 13 February 2005.

Amnesty International (2003), <http://library.amnesty.it/isdocs//aidoceverything.nsf/IndexIASA200222000, accessed 13 February 2005.

Austin, Granville (1966), *The Indian Constitution: Cornerstone of a Nation*, Oxford: Clarendon Press.

Austin, Granville (2000), *Working a Democratic Constitution – The Indian Experience*, New Delhi: Oxford University Press.

Banerjee, S. (1980), *In the Wake of Naxalbari: a History of the Naxalite Movement in India*, Calcutta: Subarnekha.

Baxi, Upendra (1988), 'Taking suffering seriously: social action litigation in the Supreme Court of India', in U. Baxi (ed.), *Law and Poverty – Critical Essay*, Bombay: Tripathi, pp. 387–415.

Berlin, Isaiah (1969), 'Two concepts of liberty', reprinted in Isaiah Berlin, *Four Essays on Liberty*, London: Oxford University Press.

Camroux, David and Nuria Okfen (2004), 'Introduction: 9/11 and US–Asian relations: towards a "new world order"?', *The Pacific Review*, 17(2), 163–77, www.ceri-sciencespo.com/cherlist/camroux/pacificreview, accessed February 2005.

Concerned Citizens Tribunal (2002), *Gujarat 2002: Crime Against Humanity*, 2 vols, Mumbai: Citizens for Justice and Peace.

Dhavan, Rajeev (1978), *The Amendment: Conspiracy or Revolution?*, Allahabad: Wheeler.

Goodman, David and Gerald Segal (eds) (1999), *Towards Recovery in Pacific Asia, New York:* Routledge, http://www.anu.edu.au/asianstudies/values.html, accessed January 2006.

Hassan, Zoya (2004), 'Indian election 2004: a setback for the BJP's exclusivist agenda', www.ceri-sciences-po.org/archive/sept04/artzh.pdf, accessed 15 February 2004.

The Hindu, 29 March 2002.

Hor, Michael (2002), 'Terrorism and the criminal law: Singapore's solution', *Singapore Journal of Legal Studies*, July, 30–55.

Lee, Therese (2002), 'Malaysia and the Internal Security Act: the insecurity of human rights after September 11', *Singapore Journal of Legal Studies*, July, 56–72.

Mendelsohn, Oliver and Marika Vicziany (1998), *The Untouchables – Subordination, Poverty and the State in Modern India*, Cambridge: Cambridge University Press.

Milner Anthony (1999), 'What's happened to Asian values?' in David Goodman and Gerald Segal (eds), *Towards Recovery in Pacific Asia, New York:* Routledge, www. anu.edu.au/asianstudies/values.html, accessed January 2006.

Online Volunteers, www.onlinevolunteers.org/gujarat/reports/index.htm, accessed February 2005.

Parliament of Australia (2005), Official Committee Hansard: Joint Committee on ASIO, ASIS and DSD, May 19, www.aph.gov.au/hansard, accessed January 2006.

Price, Gareth (2004), 'How the 2004 Lok Sabha Election was Lost', Royal Institute of International Affairs, Chatham House, July, www.ceri-sciences-po.org/archive/ sept04/artzh.pdf, accessed 15 February 2004.

Prime Minister's Press Release on Counter-Terrorism Laws (2005), 8 September, Canberra, www.pm.gov.au/news/media_releases/media_Release1551.html, accessed February 2005.

Rice, Condoleezza (2005), 'Speech to the American University, Cairo', 20 June, www. state.gov/secretary/rm/2005/48328.htm, accessed October 2005.

Richardson, Dennis (2005), 'Address to Law Asia Conference', 23 March, www.asio. gov.au/Media/Contents/lawasia_conference.htm, accessed October 2005.

Seervai, H.M. (1991), *Constitutional Law of India*, 2 vols, Bombay: Tripathi.

Sherlock, Stephen (2001), *The Indian Railways Strike of 1974: a Study of Power and Organised Labour*, New Delhi: Rupa.

Sundarayya, P. (1979), 'Telengana', in A.R. Desai (ed.), *Peasant Struggles in India*, Bombay: Oxford University Press, pp. 532–6.

Tarlo, Emma (2003), *Unsettling Memories: Narratives of the Emergency in Delhi*, Berkeley: University of California Press.

The Times of India, 2 March 2002.

Zakaria, Fareed (1994), 'Culture is Destiny: A Conversation with Lee Kuan Yew', *Foreign Affairs*, 73 (2), 109–27.

Legislation
Australia
Anti-Terrorism Act (No. 2) 2005
Australian Security Intelligence Organisation (ASIO) Act 1979.

India
Essential Services Maintenance Act 1981
Indian Evidence Act 1872

Maintenance of Internal Security Act 1971 (MISA)
Preventive Detention Act of 1950
Prevention of Terrorism Act 2002 (POTA)
Prevention of Terrorism Act (POTA) Repeal Ordinance 2004
Terrorist and Disruptive Activities (Prevention) Act 1985 (TADA)
Unlawful Activities (Prevention) Act 1967
Unlawful Activities (Prevention) Amendment Ordinance 2004

Malaysia
Internal Security Act 1960

Singapore
Internal Security Act 1960
Terrorism (Suppression of Financing) Act 2002
United Nations (Anti-Terrorism Measures) Regulations 2001

5. Deadly discourse: reflections on terrorism and security in an age of fear[1]

Amitav Acharya

> We fear flying, we fear travelling, we fear certain countries, we fear certain religions, we fear certain people, we fear the shoes they wear, we fear cargo ships, imported goods, letters and parcels – in fact we fear everything around us ... we are going to feel this fear and the consequences for a very long time. (Mahathir 2003)

Following the 11 September 2001 attack on the United States, terrorism has been routinely described by US security officials as 'the greatest threat to peace in our time' (*Defense News* 2004). This common refrain of America's terror warriors finds plenty of followers in the community of terrorism experts and policymakers in other parts of the world, including the Asia-Pacific region. Its roots lie in the international politics of an era that may best be described as an 'age of fear' and the 'totalizing' tendency evident in most representations of terrorism one finds today. This chapter reflects on these issues as one approach to assessing the impact of 9/11, the Bali bombings and the war in Iraq on our lives.

THE AGE OF FEAR

After the 9/11 attacks we live in a world where power is no longer an adequate guarantee against fear. In fact, power begets fear. The more powerful a nation is, the more fearful it becomes. The United States is the most powerful nation on earth. But 9/11 has also made it the most fearful nation. This apparently contradictory combination, awesome power and unprecedented fear, is profoundly reshaping international security order.

The post-9/11 era is defined by three principal kinds of fear. The first kind is the most obvious and powerful type we live with today: the fear of the postmodern terrorist. Terrorism of course has a long history, but its nature, sources and implications are changing. One of the more succinct descriptions of the new and 'postmodern' terrorism came from Singapore Minister for Trade and Industry, George Yeo (2001):

> The new terrorism is of a different genre. Like in a civil war, the threat is harder to pinpoint because it is within. Families may be split with the 'good' and the 'bad' mixed together. It is globalised by the same technologies which created the global economy. It does not consist of guerrillas sheltering in the countryside making occasional incursions into the cities, but operates and draws strengths in multi-ethnic and multi-religious urban environments. It makes use of air travel and the internet. It uses similar encryption algorithms to hide its internal communications. Worst of all, its members are prepared to die for their cause.

Every time a new terrorist act takes place, our conception of what terrorism is and how it threatens us changes. September 11 was a turning point in the sense that planes were used as missiles in suicide missions. The targets were the very symbols of US military and economic supremacy. The Bali bombings turned our attention to 'soft' targets, Western tourists. The Mombasa incident, when terrorists fired missiles at an Israeli airliner, narrowly missing it, highlighted the same soft targets. Terrorism targets the hegemon and its allies. It also targets states that are not allies of the hegemon and its allies but are destinations for its citizens and tourists.

Adding considerably to the fear of postmodern terror is the fear of WMD, as articulated in Bush's axis of evil formulation. The terrorist can kill not in merely hundreds, but in thousands and millions. Many analysts today believe that it is only a matter of time before a chemical or biological attack is carried out against the United States, possibly within it, or even that a crude nuclear device is used for this purpose.

The hegemon's fears beget fear of the hegemon. This kind of fear has turned our earlier hopes for peace and freedom upside down. When the Cold War ended, realist scholars of international relations predicted greater chaos and instability. Europe was supposed to be going 'back to the future', while the Third World faced a 'coming anarchy'. Today, much of Europe remains wedded, however precariously, to a Kantian peace, while what much of the world fears is not an unknown anarchy but a known hegemony.

Hence, US hegemony – including its unrivalled hard power and the Bush administration's exercise of it, the doctrine of pre-emption, the neo-con ideology and its disregard for multilateralism – defines the second kind of fear that marks our age. The first of these elements was brought home by the swift and decisive nature of the US military victory over the Taliban. It took the United States barely a month to decimate its much-vaunted adversary. Many experts had thought that the US counter-strike in Afghanistan would be a prolonged, difficult and ultimately unwinnable campaign. How could the United States win a war in which the target was so elusive and unidentifiable?

Did not Afghanistan have a history of humiliating foreign invaders? But then there had never been another power like the United States in the history of warfare. Afghanistan offered a resounding demonstration of the 'new American way of war'. This is warfare centred on weapons with capabilities to achieve extremely long ranges, to reach targets with unparalleled precision, and to capitalize on gigabytes of positioning information gathered on the ground, in the air and from space. In this war, airpower, backed by target-spotting Special Forces, surveillance aircraft and imaging satellites with electronic systems and sensors able to peer through darkness and clouds, plays a decisive role.

This new American way of war is also thoroughly 'smart'. In the 1991 Gulf War only 10 per cent of the bombs were precision-guided, meaning they could sense and hit targets from a laser beam or pick up signals from a Global Positioning System (GPS) satellite. In the Afghan War, 90 per cent of the bombs were thus capable. The main precision-guided weapon in the Gulf War was a cruise missile costing US$1 million apiece. In Afghanistan, the main weapon of the air war was a kit, called the Joint Direct Attack Munition, which could make dumb bombs smart by attaching a GPS and tail fins to guide a bomb 9.9 miles from the aircraft to the target. It was cheap too, only costing about US$18 000 per bomb.

The war in Iraq was even more technologically impressive. This is the war in which so-called information warfare came of age. The heroes of this war were command, control, communications, computing, intelligence, surveillance and reconnaissance (C4ISR) technology, space surveillance satellites, airborne joint surveillance and target attack radar systems (JSTARS) and unmanned aerial vehicles (UAVs). The technology allowed coalition forces to deliver an integrated, real-time, optical, infra-red and radar picture on static ground objects and enemy vehicular and troop movement. It magnified the lethality of precision attack systems such as cruise missiles, army tactical missile systems (ATACMs), joint direct attack munitions (JDAMs) and high-speed anti-radiation missiles (HARMs). The 'shock and awe' campaign enabled the America-led coalition to achieve victory at a cost of just over 100 casualties, in half the time of the first Gulf War and with a third of the troops (Betz 2003).

Aside from its military might, the fear of America owes much to its diplomatic tack. Now that the unipolar 'moment' has turned out to be a fully-blown unipolar 'era', the issue of peace and freedom is closely bound up with that of US strategic primacy. And the US way of managing international order under the Bush administration has fed into the new global fear politics.

Dashing initial hopes and calls for a renewed commitment to multilateral-ism, George W. Bush did not replicate the 'New World Order' approach that his father had employed against Saddam Hussein in 1990. Instead of collective security, the United States invoked the right of national self-defence under the

UN charter to bypass direct Security Council authorization for the conduct of the military campaign. Learning from Kosovo, where alliance warfare had proven cumbersome, the United States also shunned NATO's direct involvement, although NATO had invoked its collective defence provision for the first time in history in support of the United States. While the international community was generally supportive of the US position, each of America's key regional allies have demanded and secured something in return for their backing. China and Russia were quick to press for a US understanding that domestic insurgencies should be viewed as a terrorist, rather than a human rights, issue. India secured US backing for its own war against terrorism involving Pakistani-supported Kashmir militants.

Another related factor behind the fear of the hegemon is the ideology of the Bush administration. This was aptly summed up by William Kristol, editor of Washington DC-based political magazine, *The Weekly Standard*: 'We're going to get criticized for being an imperial power anyway, so you might as well make sure that the good guys win' (Polman 2003). Originally, in the view of the socialists and liberals who opposed the Vietnam War, the neo-cons are a bunch of disillusioned patriots who parted company with the traditional conservatives who argued for an isolationist posture for America. The neo-cons advocate a more activist and interventionist foreign policy. Aside from Kristol, this group includes key administration officials such as Deputy Secretary of Defense Paul Wolfowitz and Lewis Libby, National Security Adviser to Vice-President Dick Cheney. Aided by flagship publications such as *The Weekly Standard* and *Commentary* and backed by *The Wall Street Journal, National Review* and others, the neo-cons are defined by several core attributes. Briefly put, they want empire, dismiss international law and institutions ('America is so strong, it can safely ignore other nations'), show little regard for constitutional freedoms, endorse more Israeli settlements on the West Bank and favour containment of China.

A third type of fear unleashed by 9/11 is fear of the state. This kind of fear comes from the responses of governments, led by none other than George W. Bush's and John Ashcroft's America itself, to the terrorist attacks on the World Trade Center and the Pentagon. What George Bush describes as a battle between fear and freedom can be seen in the perverse context of fearful democracies retreating from the very freedoms they seek to defend against the terrorists. In the United States as elsewhere, freedom from fear reinforces the fear of freedoms.

After 9/11 fewer people talk about the 'end of the nation state'. Instead, we hear a lot more about control over borders, control of financial flows and forced fingerprinting at airport immigration. We hear and talk about security doctrines that promise all-encompassing surveillance of all aspects of our lives. Responses to 9/11 have led to the retreat of democracy and human rights both in the East and the West.

Francis Fukuyama's 'end of history' thesis argued that the end of the Cold War had resulted in the 'final' victory for liberal democracy and free markets, with no further contestations over ideas about, and approaches to, world order (Fukuyama 1992). The Fukuyama thesis strengthened the proponents of the Kantian 'democratic peace' thesis, asserting that a world of liberal democracies would enjoy greater peace and pre-empt the clash of civilizations. This debate has been overtaken by 9/11. Fukuyama has been challenged by the emergence of a new paradigm of global fear politics in which states are reasserting themselves over societal forces and liberal democracy is in some retreat. The new fear of terrorism goes hand in hand with a renewed fear of the state.

After 9/11 fear of the state and aversion to democratic politics have both been given a new lease of life. This renewed fear of the state is brought to the surface by a report of the US Justice Department's inspector general, who serves as an internal watchdog (Fine 2003). The report reviews the handling of 762 illegal immigrants who were jailed in the immediate aftermath of the 9/11 attacks on the World Trade Center and the Pentagon, as part of a general sweep of potential suspects who might carry out another attack. (None were charged as terrorists and most have been deported.) The report found that many of the people had no connection to terrorism. They were held for long periods without being told of the charges against them and were subjected to 'unduly harsh' conditions of confinement (Hudson 2003). The report found 'significant problems' in their treatment, including continuous lock-up, being moved around in handcuffs and leg irons, and having their cell lights kept on day and night. 'While our review recognized the enormous challenges and difficult circumstances confronting the department in responding to the terrorist attacks, we found significant problems in the way the detainees were handled' (Fine 2003, p. 195). Commenting on the report, American Civil Liberties Union (ACLU) Executive Director Anthony Romero said, 'This Justice Department report will corroborate much of what we've been saying for 18 months ... The war on terrorism quickly turned into a war on immigrants' (Arena and Frieden 2003).

Writing in *The Economist* on 30 October 2003, Harold Hongju Koh, Clinton's Assistant Secretary of State for Human Rights, argued:

> Around the globe, America's human rights policy has visibly softened, subsumed under the all-encompassing banner of the 'war against terrorism'. And at home, the Patriot Act, military commissions, Guantanamo and the indefinite detention of US citizens have placed the United States in the odd position of condoning deep intrusions by law, even while creating zones and persons outside the law. (Hongju Koh 2003)

He cites a number of actions such as the creation of a 'total information awareness' program under which the government may gather information about citizens and access records – telephone, financial, educational and medical – without showing evidence of any involvement in terrorist activity. Hongju Koh believes that these setbacks are temporary, but one cannot be so sure. The fact is that measures undertaken by governments to strengthen security against terrorism can end up making states and their peoples even more insecure, whether deliberately or not.

The Age of Fear presents all of us with unpleasant choices. Addressing one type of fear solely on its own terms can aggravate the other types. For example, US leadership is needed in combating the fear of the terrorist, but the price may be an increased fear of the hegemon. To overcome the fear of the terrorist, you need homeland security, but it creates another kind of fear: fear of the surveillance state.

TOTALIZING TERROR

The discourse on terrorism and its sources has become increasingly homogenized and totalized. This totalized representation holds Islamic radicalism as the main cause of global terror and Al Qaeda, a global shadowy network, as its main agent. This view dismisses, or even mocks, poverty, the Palestinian question and other issues as causes of terror. It seldom acknowledges local roots and agents of terror, or the link between local grievances and the upsurge of terrorism. Instead, it puts the Al Qaeda network and radical Islamic ideology at the centre of the threat.

The totalizing discourse on terror also blurs the distinction between terrorism drawing upon religious fundamentalism and other forms of political violence, such as those linked to ethnic rivalry and demands for self-determination (as in Tibet and Palestine). Even in terrorist acts that are based on religious ideology, it fails to distinguish acts of revenge arising from humiliation and alienation (as in the case of the Palestinian suicide bombers in Gaza) from terrorist acts fuelled by ideological aspirations for an Islamic superstate (as espoused by the Jemaah Islamiyah or JI network). We are told that these are all somehow linked, because of the global reach of Al Qaeda.

The totalizing discourse on terror has its basis in the forces of globalization. Terrorist groups may have local roots, but their effectiveness is largely due to their opportunity to network and draw support from counterparts in other parts of the world.

Consider the Aum Shinrikyo group in Japan, whose leader, Shoko Asahara, was given the death sentence in late February 2004 for his role in the Tokyo subway gas attacks in the 1990s. Although Aum Shinrikyo's target was the Tokyo subway, it is hardly a 'Japanese' group. Its members included many Russians. It tested its weapons on a farm in Western Australia. It maintained contacts with groups in the United States to learn about making chemical weapons. It had an office in the United States. The Maoists in Nepal have similar offices in the United States and Europe, attesting to its transnational links.

But the totalizing discourse of terrorism is driven more by the politics of representation than of reality. It is a way for states and intellectual elites to collectively frame and 'securitize' (meaning: articulate as a powerful threat to national security) widely disparate causes into a single policy project, which makes the resulting sense of the terrorist threat easier to sell to the public.

Yet the price of this securitization is a distortion of our understanding about what causes terrorism and this blinds us to the responses needed. Consider the search for terror's 'root causes', the latter being a phrase that has become one of the most meaningless clichés in contemporary debates. Different leaders and experts debate whether poverty, the Palestinian issue, alienation, or lack of political space is the root cause or radical Islamic ideology. In the end, however, the explanation of what causes terrorism loses sight of the fact that it is heavily context dependent, and that there may not be a single overarching force that encourages terrorism in different parts of the world.

Hence, in some cases poverty is clearly not the cause. For example, the JI members held in detention in Singapore since December 2001 were neither poor nor illiterate. The Aum Shinrikyo members in Japan were like 'ordinary Japanese', well-educated men from a middle-class background. Yet poverty matters. The Naxalite terrorism in India feeds on poverty; one of their areas of operation is Orissa, one of India's poorest states.

Similarly, while lack of political space may not be a root cause of terrorism in Japan, it is certainly so in Egypt and much of the Middle East, as the Bush administration itself acknowledges. It is also a root cause of Maoist terror in Nepal and in Burma (the Rohingyas). Radical Islamic ideology, partly disseminating from Saudi-funded religious and educational institutions, may be a factor behind terrorist violence in some areas in South-east Asia, but it certainly is not in Sri Lanka and Nepal.

The most severe forms of terrorism, such as suicide terrorism, were invented not by Islamic groups but by the Hindu Liberation Tigers of Tamil Eelam (hereafter LTTE). Despite their long history of terrorism in Kashmir and India, Islamic terrorists in South Asia have been relatively restrained and have not resorted to suicide bombings.

The personal messianic charisma of the leader is a key factor behind terrorism sponsored by the LTTE, Aum Shinrikyo and Al Qaeda. But more mundane leaders who exploit the material grievances of their communities have led many other terrorist campaigns, such as those in Nepal and Orissa.

The search for root causes will not lead to meaningful conclusions without acknowledging these variations. The totalizing discourse on terrorism distorts not only our understanding of the causes of terror but also our responses to it. It leads to a single strategic approach, focusing on intelligence-sharing, training and other centralized strategies. The capacities of these to respond in a relevant manner are, however, seriously constrained by the diversity of causes, sequences and motives for 'terrorism'.

Globalization and advances in communication technologies give terrorist groups an opportunity to network with other groups and draw sustenance and support. But to acknowledge this is not to accept that these networks are the single most important threat or that they have a global impact. To centralize our understanding of terrorism in this way would mean neglecting other threats and security concerns, both global and local, which are more serious and urgent.

The totalizing tendency is evident in the Bush administration's view not just of the scale and intensity of (as a global threat and the most serious threat) the terrorist threat, but also of the kind of responses needed to combat this menace. (Hence Bush's famous words: 'either you are with us or you are with the terrorists' (Bush 2001).) Yet this sort of rhetoric, when put into action, not only damages US relations with countries otherwise friendly to its interests but also risks producing unintended consequences. It harks back to the Cold War, when the United States tended to view all regional security problems from the single prism of superpower rivalry and the evil empire of the Soviet Union. One consequence, as we well know now, was the Taliban.

Just as terrorism is presented as a single overarching global threat, the 'war on terror' is conceptualized and waged as a single world-wide campaign. Yet some elements of what is presented as the 'war on terror' are believable, while others are questionable. For example, many people in Asia and elsewhere supported the US war to oust the Taliban. But many of the same people refused to support the US attack on Iraq because they found its justification spurious, even though the Bush Administration presented both these actions as being part of the 'war on terror'. What seemed genuine and urgent in the case of the Taliban seemed self-serving and arrogant in the case of Iraq.

Dissenting from the 'war on terror' is not to dismiss terrorism as a highly dangerous threat to our security and wellbeing. Rather, dissent has arisen because there are genuine concerns about our understanding of terrorism's causes and the responses to it. Rejecting the 'war on terror' is to reject a tendency to conflate all sorts of challenges under a single overarching framework and to encourage a search for alternative understandings of terrorism and responses to it.

TERRORISM IN SOUTH-EAST ASIA: GLOBAL OR LOCAL?

One approach in moving beyond totalizing discourses would be to look critically at the debate over the global and local elements of terrorism in South-east Asia. Since 9/11 transnational terrorism has come to dominate the security perceptions and agendas of South-east Asian governments. South-east Asia has been termed by some analysts as the 'second front' in the global war on terror. This view rests on the belief that, with its defeat in Afghanistan, Al Qaeda elements have shifted their attention to South-east Asia. South-east Asians who trained in Afghanistan have returned home where they could respond to the Al Qaeda leadership's periodic call for terrorist strikes (both low- and high-impact), especially against entertainment spots frequented by Western tourists. In this view, South-east Asia offers an attractive home to international terrorism, thanks to a combination of factors: multiethnic societies; weak and corrupt regimes with a tenuous hold over peripheral areas; ongoing separatist insurgencies that lend themselves to exploitation by foreign elements; governments in general weakened by the financial crisis; and newly created democratic space in some of its larger polities, such as Indonesia and the Philippines, which have found it difficult to mobilize public support for security regulations to ensure preventive suppression of terrorist elements.

The discovery of a terrorist plot aimed at Singapore was revealed in December 2001. The plot specifically targeted US military installations and the personnel stationed there, thereby underscoring the intra-regional dimension of the challenge. The suspected perpetrators of the planned attacks are believed to be members of the organization Jemaah Islamiyah, whose objectives include the creation of a pan-South-east Asian Islamic state comprising the Muslim-majority areas of southern Philippines, Indonesia, Malaysia, Singapore and southern Thailand. The combination of the pan-regional blueprint, the trans-regional training and the support network of its adherents has contributed to the perception that JI represents an even larger threat to South-east Asian security by transcending local or national grievances and fault-lines.

Is South-east Asia really the second front for global terrorism? Or is terrorism locally produced, reflecting conflicts and injustices which would exist even without external aid? Some scholars, such as Rohan Gunaratna, see South-east Asian terrorism as being intimately linked to the global transnational network Al Qaeda, which orchestrates, however loosely, the training, financing and even operational leadership of local incidents such as the attack in Bali. Terrorists are like sharks, looking for fresh opportunities to exploit. Thus, when the Taliban was driven out of Afghanistan and Middle Eastern governments tightened their control, terrorists found South-east Asia, with its relatively open societies, corrupt regimes, and multiethnic settings, a convenient destination to move into (Gunaratna 2002).

A second school of thought, led by scholars like Farish Noor of Malaysia, rejects this view as being unduly alarmist and being based on a superficial understanding of the sources of conflict and violence in the region. It argues that terrorism is based essentially on local causes, such as poverty, maldistribution of wealth and lack of democracy (Noor 2002).

In reality, both views are right and both are wrong. When we look at the Bali bombings of 12 October 2002, clear evidence has emerged that the perpetrators received aid and advice from Al Qaeda. But most forms of terrorism in South-east Asia are local. Without local grievances and the weaknesses of local institutions, terrorism will not thrive. Moreover, the motivations behind terrorism can vary, from country to country, or region to region within the same country.

A report published in December 2002 by the Brussels-based International Crisis Group offers an interesting window on the varied and changing motivations of terrorist groups within Indonesia itself. The report notes that the conflicts in Maluku and Poso were an integral component of JI's recruitment and development of combat and military skills. But these two Indonesian foci were seen as attractive targets for the JI's recruitment drive because they were already sites of communal conflict predating the 9/11 attacks. In such recruitment centres, videos about the massacres in other Indonesian hotspots were often used (International Crisis Group 2002). What this signifies is that it was not an imported Al Qaeda ideology but essentially local grievances and conflicts that contributed to terrorist incidents here.

There are important variations in the nature and objectives of terrorist groups in South-east Asia. First, there are those seeking to punish rival ethnic groups in a situation of ethnic hatred and conflict, as is the case with some anti-Christian radical groups in Indonesia. The second is a more common type – it comprises those seeking independence or autonomy from post-colonial nation states. These are classical separatist movements that are now branded as terrorist by governments and analysts partly with a view to delegitimizing them. These movements feed off a hatred for those ruling regimes that are dominated by a rival ethnic group, which is perceived to be persecuting the minority group. Examples of this type include the MILF and the Abu Sayyaf in the Southern Philippines. Finally, some terrorist groups are seeking to establish a pan-Islamic state. They are motivated by religious fervour, as well as a dislike of the existing regimes, especially their pro-Western orientation. The best example of this is the JI group.

Terrorism in South-east Asia is thus neither exclusively global nor exclusively local. It is both. It breeds from local causes, but draws sustenance from the outside. Issues like the Palestine question and resentment against the global dominance of the United States give legitimacy to terrorist causes. Although many terrorist groups have religious roots, their motivations are highly political, the chief aim being to seize power in their respective states or in the region. It is important to recognize the diverse factors that motivate terrorist groups, the local roots of terrorist organizations, and the political nature of their cause, rather than present them as being driven by a single overarching global network with regional franchises. The age of fear builds from such totalizing representations. Deconstructing this representation will be essential to international order in the post-9/11 era.

NOTE

1. This chapter is based on my book: *The Age of Fear: Power Versus Principle in the War on Terror*, Singapore: Marshall Cavendish Academic; New Delhi: Rupa and Co., 2004.

REFERENCES

Arena, Kellie and Frieden, Terry (2003), 'US report critical of 9/11 detainee treatment', *CNN.com*, 3 June, http://edition.cnn.com/2003/LAW/06/02/detainees/, accessed 1 February 2006.

Betz, David (2003), 'Winning the war mirage: how the coalition did it', *IDSS Commentaries*, Singapore, Nanyang Technological University, www.ntu.edu.sg/idss/publications/commenatries2003.html, 23 May, accessed 1 February 2006.

Bush, George (2001), *Address to a Joint Session of Congress and the American People*, The White House, 20 September, www.whitehouse.gov/news/releases/2001/09/print/20010920-8.html, accessed 1 February 2006.

Defense News (2004), Special Asia Pacific Security Conference Executive News Summary, Defense News Media Group, Vancouver, United States, www.defensenews.com/promos/conferences/apsec0204/2665600.html, 22–23 February, accessed 1 February 2006.

Fine, Glenn (2003), *The September 11 Detainees: a Review of Aliens Held on Immigration Charges in Connection with the Investigation of the September 11 Attacks*, US Department of Justice, 29 April, full report, www.usdoj.gov/oig/special/0306/full.pdf, accessed 1 February 2006.

Fukuyama, Francis (1992), *The End of History and the Last Man*, London: Penguin Books.

Gunaratna, Rohan (2002), 'Gravity of terrorism shifting to region', *The Straits Times*, 15 October, http://global.factiva.com, accessed 1 February 2006.

Hongju Koh, Harold (2003), 'Rights to remember', *The Economist*, 30 October, www.economist.com/opinion/displayStory.cfm?story_id=2173160, accessed 1 February 2006.

Hudson, Audrey (2003), 'Handling of alien detainees criticized', *Washington Times*, 3 June, www.washingtontimes.com/national/20030603-122053-2320r.htm, accessed 1 February 2006.

International Crisis Group (2002), *Indonesia Backgrounder: How the Jemaah Islamiyah Terrorist Group Operates*, Asia Report No. 43, Jakarta, www.crisisgroup.org/library/documents/report_archive/A400845_11122002.pdf, accessed 1

February 2006.

Mahathir, Mohamad (2003), 'State of world not reassuring', speech at the 11th Annual Meeting of the Asia Pacific Parliamentary Forum, Kuala Lumpur, *The Straits Times* (Singapore), 14 January.

Noor, Farish A. (2002), 'Demonisation of innocent Islamic groups', *The Straits Times*, 30 October, www.global.factiva.com, accessed 1 February 2006.

Polman, Dick (2003), 'Neoconservatives push for a new world order', *Mercury News*, 4 May, www.informationclearinghouse.info/article3224.htm, accessed 1 February 2003.

Yeo, George (2001), speech prepared for the SIBOS 2001 Conference, Ministry of Trade and Industry, Singapore, 15 October, www.stars.nhb.gov.sg/public/index. html, accessed 1 February 2006.

PART 2

Case studies on security issues in the Asia Pacific

6. Islamic militancy and Pakistan: domestic and global implications

Samina Yasmeen

Pakistan's participation in the war on terrorism since 9/11 has secured it the status of the major non-NATO ally of the United States. This shift away from being identified as a pariah state has been paralleled by concerns regarding Islamic militancy emanating from Pakistan. The concerns regarding the linkages between militants in Pakistan and those operating at a global level have been heightened after the London bombings of 7 July 2005. While the Pakistan government has initiated a series of steps to control militants, these concerns persist. Views are expressed about the role played by religious schools (madrassahs) in promoting militancy at the global level. In this context, the links between Pakistani diaspora and militant outfits in Pakistan are attracting increasing attention. These views raise a number of questions. To what extent can the 'madrassah factor' explain the presence of militant ideas in Pakistan? How does militancy manifest itself in Pakistan? Can the phenomenon be controlled? If not, which factors limit the ability of the government to turn its anti-militancy initiatives into real success?

This chapter attempts to answer these questions by focusing on the causes of Islamic militancy, their manifestations, and factors on the ground that limit the effectiveness of governmental efforts. It argues that a combination of state weakness and hierarchical societal structures have created conditions in which Pakistani governments have either promoted or sustained Islamic militant groups. The end result is the emergence of two strands of Islamic militancy: one directed at alternative Islamic views within the country and the other following a regional/international agenda. The chapter argues that countering this trend requires more than merely focusing attention on religious schools. Attention needs to shift to the linkages between population growth, poverty and the quality of education provided within a hierarchical society. But the attempts to counter militancy also depend upon a shift in the regional environment that provides the needed ammunition for militants to promote their message.

STATE WEAKNESS AND HIERARCHICAL STRUCTURES: EXPLAINING MILITANCY

The phenomenon of militancy in Pakistan cannot be understood without reference to the idea of a weak state. The weakness of a state is neither purely political nor purely economic in nature. It refers to the absence of mutually agreed principles that govern the lives of citizens. It also extends to the failure to establish some basic understanding among the citizens on the identity of the state and its relationship with the external environment. Equally importantly, the notion of a weak state also encapsulates the failure to develop structures and dynamics that regulate the lives of its citizens. The *administration* of the state, under these circumstances, remains less than organized and enables often multiple centres of power to advance mutually competing agendas of domestic and foreign policy. It also creates the conditions where those at the helm of power find it necessary to seek allies in both the domestic and the international arena. This search is guided by their need to remain in power and protect their interests vis-à-vis those with a different agenda.

Since gaining its independence in August 1947, Pakistan has suffered from this weakness. Not only have its citizens differed on the identity of a state created in the name of Islam, but they have also failed to develop a mutually agreed understanding on the political structures (Haqqani 2004–05, pp. 86–7). This is not to deny that in 1973 Pakistanis agreed upon a constitution, but the weakness of the state has created a condition where the state apparatus has found it expedient to amend the constitution if and when needed. Significantly, the failure of a real understanding on principles guiding the state and society has kept the door open to periodic interventions by the military in Pakistan's politics. These interventions create the space in which the military engages in constitutional doctoring with the stated purpose of making the country/state strong. By the time military rule gives way to democratic elections, the nature of the political system has altered to the extent that politicians need to devise new strategies for operating in the system. Consequently, the state remains essentially weak without a solid political structure.

State weakness has coexisted with a hierarchical system in the country where the state, despite all its internal divisions, is separate from the wider society. The pronouncements and actions taken by the government often have little or no relevance to developments at the grass root level. This detachment is linked to the political culture of a society where power is held to be absolute (Aziz 2001, pp. 67–175; K Ahmed 2001, pp. 260–71). Those in a position of power are not made accountable for the manner in which they use (or abuse) their power. They are not expected to really share power either. But the political culture does provide for the decision-makers or centres of power to coopt members from the wider society as functionaries who promote the agenda of those in power. This creates mutually beneficial relationships between those in power and the coopted members: the latter support and advance the policies of the former with the aim of securing benefits for themselves.

Together, state weakness and the hierarchical nature of the state versus the society have created conditions where every political change opens up the possibilities and the need for the state to coopt new partners from the society. It also creates space in which those in power look for external patrons who can support the state both domestically and internationally. But the weakness of the state also creates conditions where multiple agendas and policy options are pursued simultaneously (Malik 2005, pp. 130–61). The pronouncements and actions of those at the top not only do not necessarily reflect the views of ordinary citizens, but they may also be different from the actions supported by others within the government structures.

EMERGENCE OF ISLAMIC MILITANCY

Pakistan's alliance relationships with the United States and China demonstrate how a weak state seeks external support to bolster itself. The process of Islamization pursued by General Zia-ul-Haq after the military coup of July 1977 is an example of how the state coopted allies from within the country to legitimize its rule. It is this need for legitimacy that provided the setting in which Islamic militancy emerged in Pakistan during the 1980s and 1990s.

Having removed Zulfiqar Ali Bhutto from power, General Zia needed to appeal to a drastically different view of Pakistan's identity. In an attempt to coopt orthodox Islamic groups in Pakistan, particularly Jamaat-e-Islami led by Maulana Mawdudi, General Zia shifted the focus away from Pakistan as a state for Muslims to Pakistan as an Islamic state. Given that Sunnis constituted nearly 80 per cent of the Muslim population in Pakistan, the military regime supported and sponsored the Hanafi school of thought in the country. Such a preference was bound to antagonize the Shi'ite population in Pakistan. But the situation was made more complicated by the state's cooption of Sunni elements at the grass root level to counter opposition to the military regime. Developments in Jhang are a case in point. In this area, the peasants were mostly Sunnis but the landlords belonged to the Shi'ite branch of Islam. Since these landlords opposed military rule, the Shi'ites responded by establishing Tehrik Jaffariya Pakistan (TJ), which promoted their understanding of Islam. Soon the differences escalated to such a level that sectarianism emerged as an issue in the area (Jalalzai 2005, p. 79). This also attracted external actors, Saudi Arabia and Iran, who sided with groups favouring orthodox Sunni and Shi'ite ideas respectively. The result was the extension of sectarianism to the rest of the country. Before the decade came to an end, Sunnis were calling Shi'ites non-believers (*kafirs*). The two sides were also using weapons to extend the conflict beyond theological debates. Killings of prominent members on either side became a common phenomenon. Soon, mosques patronized by either sect also became targets of attacks from the opposite side. According to one report, 703 people were killed and 2612 injured in 1268 sectarian incidents from 1987 to 2000 (Jalalzai 2005, p. 68).

But domestic factors are not the sole explanation for the rise in Islamic militancy. Regional developments following the Soviet invasion of Afghanistan, and the need for the weak Zia regime to secure patronage from external actors, also provided the context in which Islamic extremism flourished in Pakistan. Interested in bolstering his own position and receiving economic and military assistance, General Zia established a close alliance with the United States in the 1980s. As the frontline state, Pakistan provided its territory for training of mujahidin who could infiltrate into Afghanistan with the ultimate objective of rolling back the Soviets. Religious schools, madrassahs, occupied a special place in this strategy. While traditionally the madaris had provided basic religious teaching to their students, the requirements of jihad in Afghanistan added another element to their curriculum. A series of madaris, mostly connected to the orthodox Deobandi school, were selected where Islamic teachings on jihad were imparted to the students with the ultimate objective of sending them to Afghanistan.

The cooption of religious schools for strategic purposes had domestic repercussions: governmental patronage contributed to an increase in enrolments in these schools. The number of religious teachers graduating from these schools also proliferated. During a period of five years (1981–85), for instance, on average 853 Deobandi candidates appeared annually for examinations called Shahadat al-alamiyyah. This was in marked contrast to the average of 279 candidates appearing for the same qualifications during the 1960–80 period (Malik 1996, p. 227). Their induction into the wider society added a new dimension to the Zia regime's policy of Islamization: the language of orthodox Islam and the emphasis on jihad began to occupy a greater space in the society than had been the case previously.

Together these trends provided the context in which the democratically elected governments operated in Pakistan after General Zia's death in August 1988. The constitutional amendments introduced by the military regime had limited the powers of the elected prime minister in favour of the president. Meanwhile, the military retained the power to conduct Pakistan's foreign policy from behind the scenes. Elected representatives of the state were therefore weaker than envisioned by the 1973 constitution. Operating on the cultural norms of treating power as an end in itself, both Benazir Bhutto and Nawaz Sharif focused on retaining power rather than addressing the issues created by 11 years of military rule. This necessitated their tacit acceptance of the independent roles played by different institutions within the government. Intelligence agencies, including both the Inter-Services Intelligence (ISI) and Intelligence Bureau (IB), were allowed to pursue their independent agendas. The military also continued to operate as a separate and often dominant centre of power.

The weakness of the state contributed to the rise of Islamic militancy on two fronts: domestic and regional/international. Domestically, sectarian differences persisted. The geographical region in which Shi'ites and Sunnis viewed and portrayed each other as *kafirs* (non-believers) extended beyond the province of Punjab to include other provinces. Combined with the proliferation of small weapons in Pakistan ('Statement by Ambassador Masood Khalid' 2003), the tensions created a situation where both sides freely targeted professionals and theologians from the opposing sect. At the regional level, the idea of jihad persisted even after the Soviet withdrawal from Afghanistan following the Geneva Accord (1988). The Soviet withdrawal was interpreted by sections in the military and the ISI as validating the effectiveness of jihad. Drawing upon the veterans of the Afghan war, these sections embarked upon initiating jihad in the Indian part of Kashmir. Militant groups were established who drew upon tacit, or even open, support from sections of the government.

A veteran of the Afghan jihad, Hafiz Saeed Mohammad, formally launched Lashkar-e-Toiba (Army of the Pure) on 22 February 1990 (Yasmeen 2005, pp. 49–51). With Markaz-ud-Dawa-wal-Irshad (MDI) as its parent organization, the Lashkar established a significant presence in Pakistan. Its headquarters was in Muridke, a town near Lahore, from which administrative, educational, propaganda and jihadi activities were coordinated. In addition to providing social welfare services, it included an academy called Al-Mahdal-Aala-ud-Dawa-tul-Islamia, where religious training was given to both boys and girls (Musa 2001, pp. 59–62). The Lashkar also extended its operations across the four provinces of Pakistan and Azad Kashmir (the Pakistani part of Kashmir). Until 2001, it was reportedly operating 1150 offices at the provincial, district and *tehsil* levels (Raana 2002, p. 237). It was operating military training camps in Pakistan and in Azad Kashmir. By 1995 the Lashkar had also established a sister organization in the Indian part of Kashmir (M. Ahmed 2001). The Lashkar drew support from a number of sources: while the exact membership is difficult to assess, available information suggests that within Pakistan it managed to establish a strong presence in southern Punjab, northern Sindh and parts of Baluchistan. It also drew support from Kashmiris, Afghans and foreign Muslims who were willing to participate in the jihad in Kashmir. According to the available information, the group was allowed and encouraged by successive leaders in the ISI to raise funds from private sources during the 1990s. It did so by placing donation boxes in main shopping areas and mosques (personal observations since 2001). During the months of Ramadan and Hajj, its members also secured donations of animal hides, which were used to raise more funds. These activities were criticized by the Indian government that accused the Pakistan government of supporting insurgents. But, interested in retaining support of the military, successive Pakistani regimes denied the allegations. They also turned a blind eye to the presence of groups like Lashkar-e-Toiba.

The end of the democratic era did not herald an end to the policy of using jihad as a tool of foreign policy. On the contrary, the creation of another militant organization, Jaish Mohammad, during the early years of President Musharraf's government indicates that the state's weakness continued to have an impact on Pakistan's support for militancy (Yasmeen 2005, pp. 50–51). Maulana Masood Azhar established Jaish Mohammad in January 2000 after his release from an Indian prison following the hijacking of an Indian Airline aircraft. The group drew support from former members of a number of militant organizations operating with the tacit approval of the Pakistan government, including the Harkatul Mujahedeen, Harkatul Jihad-ul-Islamic and Harkatul Ansar. Masood Azhar was also linked to Osama bin Laden since their participation in the Afghan jihad. Jaish Mohammad established a strong presence in Karachi (Sindh), Multan and Bahawalpur (Punjab), Waziristan, Malakand, Kohat, Bannu and Dera Ismail Khan in the North West Frontier Province (NWFP) and Panjgor in Baluchistan (Raana 2002, pp. 153–4). It regularly issued a magazine titled *Jaish Mohammad*, which detailed the activities and 'victories' of the group in the Indian part of Kashmir.

MILITANCY IN PAKISTAN: AFTER 9/11

The terrorist attacks on the United States in September 2001 forced Islamabad to reassess its policy options. Its participation in the US-led 'war on terror' coincided with President Musharraf's emphasis on 'Enlightened Moderation' on the domestic front. As the outline of this two-pronged approach emerged in the wake of the US invasion of Afghanistan, the attacks on the Indian Parliament on 13 December 2001 revived the accusation of Pakistan's complicity in promoting militancy in the Indian part of Kashmir. New Delhi's use of the language of counter-terrorism, combined with its decision to mobilize troops on the international border with Pakistan, caused the Bush administration to put pressure on Islamabad to cease supporting militants. President Musharraf responded to the pressure by banning a number of militant groups, including Lashkar-e-Toiba and Jaish Mohammad on 12 January 2002 (*Dawn* 2002).

Despite the government's declared commitment to countering Islamic extremism, however, militant groups have not ceased to exist in Pakistan. The sectarian conflicts have persisted with varying degrees of intensity since 2002.

According to one report, in 2004 alone, 19 incidents of sectarian violence had resulted in 187 deaths and 619 casualties (Jalalzai 2005, pp. 65–8). Northern areas have been particularly affected by this domestic variant of Islamic militancy. Historically, these areas had been occupied by a predominantly Shi'ite (Ismaili) population. During the Afghan war, the Zia regime facilitated migration of Sunnis into the northern areas, thus altering the population mix. The ensuing tensions, which mirrored sectarian differences in the rest of the country, have resulted in frequent clashes between the two sects. Since early 2004, prominent Shi'ite leaders have been killed in the northern areas owing to a controversy surrounding the introduction of school curricula with a pro-Sunni bias. Baluchistan, especially Quetta, has also experienced sectarian violence during this time despite its long history of peaceful coexistence between the two sects (Khan 2004, pp. 142–4).

Militant outfits engaged in the 'freedom struggle' in the Indian part of Kashmir have not disappeared either ('Unfulfilled promises: Pakistan's failure to tackle extremism' 2004). Despite the fact that the government has banned these groups, they continue to operate in the country. Lashkar-e-Toiba has operated as Jamaat-ud-Dawa since the group was banned in January 2002. Its main publication outlet has continued to publish books and journals reflecting its commitment to jihad in Kashmir. The group also retained its visible presence in major cities until very recently: its supporters, or those coaxed into doing so, publicly displayed donation collection boxes in elite shopping centres of major cities. In Islamabad, it maintained an office off a main street facing Holiday Inn. Similarly, other militant outfits reincarnated themselves into new identities. In some cases these new identities were merely a change of name, whereas in others they referred to a splinter group created from the parent organization. Some sections of Jaish Mohammad, for instance, created Khuddam-e-Islam (Servants of Islam) under Abdul Jabbar's leadership after being expelled by the party's leader, Maulana Masood Azhar (Rana 2005).

These two manifestations of Islamic militancy have not operated in isolation from each other. In fact, those engaged in sectarian violence have often established connections with militant organizations with a regional and international agenda. The trend had been established in the 1990s when the Taliban regime reportedly allowed members of Sunni sectarian groups like Lashkar-e-Jhangvi and Sipah Sahabah to receive training in Afghanistan. In the new millennium, despite the bans imposed by the Pakistan government, these linkages have persisted. A former supreme commander of Jaish Mohammad, for instance, actively engaged in sectarian killings and was in the process of reorganizing Lashkar-e-Jhangvi when the Anti-Terrorist Force arrested him in May 2005 (Rana 2005).

These groups have also established international connections. These connections can be categorized as those focusing on the 'freedom struggle in

Kashmir' and those promoting the idea of pan-Islamism. Groups operating against the 'Indian occupation of Kashmir' had sought help from Pakistanis and Kashmiris residing in Britain even before 9/11. These links have not been severed despite the change in Islamabad's policy on Kashmir. Lashkar-e-Toiba, for instance, reportedly raised $280 000 in Britain during the years after 9/11 (John 2005, p. 9). The links based on notions of Pan-Islamism have not subsided either. On the contrary, the US reprisal attacks on Afghanistan and the invasion of Iraq have reinforced this dimension of militancy. Islamic groups within Pakistan which focus on the perceived dangers posed by a Jewish–Christian conspiracy against Muslims have skilfully employed these international developments to their benefit. As Al Qaeda has moved into Pakistan with its members being offered sanctuaries in major cities, including Rawalpindi, these groups have developed a language of global jihad for Muslims. The degree to which they use this language and the identification of appropriate 'targets' varies among the groups. But the mere emphasis on jihad has turned them into 'icons of Islamic identity'. This, in turn, has created the space in groups with similar ideals to cooperate across national boundaries. Hizb-ut-Tehrir (HuT), for instance, has focused on the idea of an Islamic Caliphate. It had been banned in Pakistan but it retained an office in London, which provided the link between disaffected young British Muslims and the ideology being promoted by the Pakistan chapter of HuT (M.A. 2005). The London bombings of 7 July 2005 are an indication of the effects of these emerging global networks of terrorism in which Pakistani militant groups continue to play a role, despite being banned by the government. But these links are not restricted to Europe: they extend to the United States and Australia as well.

CONTROLLING MILITANCY: THE CHALLENGE

The question arises as to how the spread of militancy in Pakistan and its international connections can be controlled.

Since the terrorist attacks in London, which highlighted the links between the Muslim diaspora in Britain and Muslims in Pakistan, President Musharraf's regime has focused attention on madrassahs. It has demanded that all religious schools be registered by the end of December 2005 and that international students enrolled in these be sent back home. The assumption is that madrassahs have been the main source of Islamic militancy. The role played by some of these institutions during and after the Afghan jihad corroborates these assumptions. The situation is made more complicated by the fact that, despite Islamabad's efforts in 2002 to 'streamline' madrassah education, not all the institutions have been registered with the government. The five Wafaq-ul-Madaris (networks of religious schools) responsible for providing religious education in Pakistan have registered only 2157 of the total 9212 madrassahs affiliated with them. A number of seminaries also exist outside the wafaq system (A.S. Khan 2005). This contributes to a lack of consensus on the exact number of students enrolled in seminaries across the country: while some argue that the enrolments in these institutions have not increased markedly, others claim a steady increase in the numbers of students and the related danger of extremism in Pakistan (Mir 2005).

However, a sustained focus on madrassahs ignores the realities on the ground. While the role played by religious schools in promoting militancy cannot be discounted, not all seminaries promote militant ideas (Khawaja 2005). More importantly, these schools are not the only participants in the phenomenon of militancy. The problem is deeper: it is linked to the quality of education being provided to a number of students in a hierarchical society.

With an estimated population of more than 145 million in 2002, Pakistan is the seventh most populous country in the world (United Nations Population Fund). Of these, 96 per cent are Muslims, with the 80 per cent majority belonging to the Sunni sect. Significantly, 43 per cent of the total population are below 15 years of age. The extreme income inequalities are paralleled by an increase in the level of poverty in Pakistan. According to the available data, the incidence of poverty increased from 22–26 per cent in Fiscal Year 1991 to 32–35 per cent in Fiscal Year 1999. The Pakistan government claims that the level of poverty has declined with improved economic conditions in the post-9/11 era. But this does not alter the fact that, with increasing inflation, a large section of the population live in less than satisfactory conditions. On the other hand, a small minority have access to a large proportion of the resources. Together, these factors impact on the quality of education accessed by different sections of Pakistani society.

Historically, Pakistani schools were broadly categorized in terms of the medium of instruction used by them. Students educated in the English medium were considered superior to those enrolled in schools using Urdu. This was linked to the fact that the moneyed class would generally send their children to the former category of schools, which were privately run. The less fortunate usually opted for sending their children to schools using Urdu as the medium of instruction and run by the Pakistani government. Some of them sent their children to madrassahs but their total number was smaller than the private and governmental schools. The class-determined choice of schools also had implications for jobs secured by graduates from these categories of schools. The graduates from private, English-medium schools often secured better jobs, including induction into the Civil Service of Pakistan. In time, these students formed the elite in the country. Those educated in the Urdu language, mostly through government schools, had no choice but to find second-tier jobs. The process perpetuated the hierarchical nature of Pakistani society and caused dissatisfaction among the less fortunate. Frequently, the poorest attended madrassahs.

The situation has changed in today's Pakistan. The categories of educational institutions have expanded to include private schools that provide education in English or Urdu, government schools, Pakistani campuses established by international educational institutions, and madrassahs. The quality of education provided by private English-medium schools is often very good but comes at a high price. In some cases, for instance, a person may be paying more than Rs 6000 per child to send them to a school that provides good education and prepares them to take A and O level exams conducted by Cambridge University. This enables the children to receive tertiary education in internationally recognized institutions in the United States, Canada, Britain, Australia and other developed countries. Next to this most privileged group are the graduates from private schools who enrol in the offshore campuses established in Pakistan by international educational institutions. These too are English-medium schools. In marked contrast, the standard of education provided for students in government schools or private schools with the Urdu medium of instruction is less than satisfactory. Not only do these schools lack basic facilities, but the staff also lack the necessary training to communicate knowledge effectively to their students. Consequently, students from these schools remain ignorant and ill-educated, despite being categorized as literate by the government. Lastly, madrassahs provide the category of educational institutions available to the poor in the country. Having benefited from the patronage of the Zia regime, the number of madrassahs has proliferated in Pakistan. They provide not only religious education but also food and shelter for their students, thus emerging as a favourite option for those families in greatest need but with ambitions for their children.

These different categories of educational service providers contribute to developing different levels of critical thinking, initiative and satisfaction with the existing political and economic situation in Pakistan. They also create different employment opportunities for the graduates, as already noted. The resulting disillusionment turns the less fortunate category into easy targets for ideas that question the system on religious grounds. They find solace in the endeavour to establish an Islamic system in Pakistan, and engage in activities that, in their view, will secure them rewards in the life after death. To put it differently, the variation in educational opportunities, combined with the prevalent poverty and lack of economic development, creates a situation that can easily be exploited by those intent on spreading the message of Islamic militancy. This is not to suggest that only the poor engage in the phenomenon; the fact remains that a large majority of the recruits come from a lower economic background and provide the foot-soldiers for militant organizations in today's Pakistan. Given that not all of these recruits are trained in madrassahs the process of controlling militancy in Pakistan is more difficult than the government currently realizes.

The weakness of the state also limits Islamabad's ability to control militancy. Following the pattern set by previous military regimes, President Musharraf has engaged in designing and implementing constitutional changes in Pakistan. A new political structure seems to be emerging: Musharraf introduced a system of local councils so that power could be devolved to the district level; elections to these bodies is on a non-party basis; a referendum has validated Musharraf's position as the President; and the 2002 elections saw the emergence of new political forces (for example, in the North West Frontier Provinces). Despite these changes, behind the facade of a civilian government the military retains political control. But, at the same time, the need for legitimation has caused the military to form alliances with the sections of society that serve its purpose. As part of this strategy, the Musharraf regime has both engaged with and distanced itself from Islamist elements in the country at different times. Prior to the 2002 elections, for instance, engagement took the shape of equating the qualifications of students from madrassahs with graduation from mainstream educational institutions. Following the bombings in London, the process has been reversed, with stringent equivalence standards being applied for graduates from madrassahs. These shifts, necessitated by political expediency, have strengthened the position of Islamic groups in Pakistan and weakened the credibility of government. While the decisions of 2002 enabled the Islamist Muttehedah Majlis-e-Amal (MMA) to emerge victorious in the NWFP and Baluchistan, the more recent restrictions enable these groups to use the language of defiance and the relevance of Islam as the guiding principle for their policies. Angered by the rigging of elections to local bodies in August 2005, for instance, the MMA has adopted a hostile stand vis-à-vis the Musharraf regime. It has disputed the stringent requirements of registration being imposed on madrassahs, and its continued emphasis on Pakistan's Islamic identity ensures that the space which Islamic militancy and sectarianism can occupy in Pakistan will remain.

The regional and international environment has also rendered the challenge of controlling militancy difficult. US reprisal attacks on Afghanistan created a sense of unease among those who supported the Taliban. But the carpet bombings of a neighbouring Muslim state during Ramadan were not viewed favourably by more moderate elements in the country either. This dissatisfaction with US policies has been heightened since the US invasion of Iraq in March 2003. Militant groups have responded by refining their reading of the regional environment to include the notion of 'Saddam Hussein's innocence'. They have also reportedly encouraged Pakistanis to participate in the jihad in Iraq. Hafiz Saeed, for instance, told his followers in a private meeting held in 2004 that 'Islam is in grave danger, and the mujahidin are fighting to keep its glory. They are fighting the forces of evil in Iraq in extremely difficult circumstances. We should send mujahidin from Pakistan to help them' (Swami and Shehzad 2004). Such reactions indicate that the US presence in Iraq will continue to provide a fertile ground for jihadi language among sections of Pakistani society. The military and any other successive regimes, therefore, will continue to face the challenge of curbing Islamic militancy and sectarianism.

REFERENCES

Ahmed, Khaled (2001), *Pakistan: Behind the Ideological Mask – Facts About Great Men We Don't Want to Know*, Lahore: Vanguard.

Ahmed, Manzoor (2001), 'Mujahedeen-e-Lashkar-e-Toiba: mah au saal key aaenay mein' [Mujahedeen of Lashkar-e-Toiba: through months and years], *Mujalla-tud-Dawa*, Lahore, 12 (1), 59–62.

Aziz, K.K. (2001), *Pakistan's Political Culture: Essays in Historical and Social Origins*, Lahore: Vanguard.

Dawn (2002), Lahore, 13 January.

Haqqani, Husain (2004–05), 'The Role of Islam in Pakistan's Future', *The Washington Quarterly*, 28 (1), 85–96.

Jalalzai, Musa Khan (2005), *Dying to Kill Us: Suicide Bombers, Terrorism and Violence in Pakistan*, Lahore: Al-Abbas International.

Khan, Abdul Sattar (2005), 'Many madrassas exist outside wafaq network', *The Post*, 28 August, A-1, A-6.

Khan, Tahir Mohammad (2004), *Islami Riasat-Tasawwar aur Haqaiq [Islamic State: Ideals and Realities]*, Lahore: Fiction House.

Khawaja, Inam (2005), 'Terrorism and the Madaris', *The Nation*, 29 August, 6.

M.A. (2005), 'Mission Suicide', *Newsline*, August, 24.

Malik, Iftikhar H. (2005), *Jihad, Hindutva and the Taliban*, Oxford: Oxford University Press.

Malik, Jamal (1996), *Colonialization of Islam: Dissolution of Traditional Institutions in Pakistan*, Lahore: Vanguard Books.

Mir, Amir (2005), 'Test of Will', *Newsline*, August, 42–5.

Musa, Abu (2001), 'Al-Mahdal-Aala-ud-Dawa-tal-Islamia: ta'arif, sargarmian, nizam-e-ta'lim au tarbiyat' [Al-Mahdal-Aala-ud-Dawa-tal-Islamia: introduction, educational and training programs], *Mujalla-tud-Dawa*, Lahore, January, 12.

Raana, Mohammad Aamir (2002), *Jihad-e-Kashmir Au Afghanistan [Jihad in Kashmir and Afghanistan]*, Lahore: Mashal.

Rana, Amir (2005), 'Ex-Jaish chief arrested for attacks on Christians', *Daily Times* (Lahore), 18 May.

'Statement by Ambassador Masood Khalid' (2003), Biennial Meeting of States to Consider the Implementation of the Program of Action on Small Arms and Light Weapons, New York, 7–11 July, Pakistan Permanent Mission to the United Nations.

Swami, Praveen and Mohammad Shehzad (2004), 'Lashkar raising Islamist brigades for Iraq', *The Hindu*, 13 June, www.thehindu.com/2004/06/13/01hdline.htm, accessed August 2005.

'Unfulfilled promises: Pakistan's failure to tackle extremism' (2004), International Crisis Group Report, 16 January, www.crisisgroup.org/home/index.cfm?id=2472&l=1, accessed 10 January 2006.

United Nations Population Fund, www.unfpa.org/profile/pakistan.cfm, accessed 18 January 2004.

Wilson, John (2005), 'Lashkar-e-Toiba: new threats posed by an old organization', *Terrorism Monitor*, III (4), 24 February, http://jamestown.org/terrorism/news/article.php?articleid=2369321, Washington: Jamestown, accessed August 2005.

Yasmeen, Samina (2005), 'Islamic groups and Pakistan's foreign policy: Lashkar-e-Toiba and Jaish Muhammad', in Shahram Akbarzadeh and Samina Yasmeen (eds), *Islam and the West: Reflections from Australia*, Sydney: University of New South Wales Press, pp. 45–62.

7. Musharraf and controlling terrorism

Farhan Bokhari

The most supreme 'jihad' [holy war] is offering one's life for sacrifice – the reward for which is eternal life for a martyr. (*Mutala-e-Pakistan*, 2005,[1] p. 15)

Such words have been typically heard across Pakistan from firebrand Islamic scholars who often urge their followers to take the course of jihad (holy war) as the assured route to heaven. But, surprisingly, these particular words are to be found in a school textbook. In the three years since the New York terrorist attacks prompted General Pervez Musharraf, Pakistan's military ruler, to join the US-led 'war on terror', there have been many drivers of militancy, including school textbooks that highlight the virtues of jihad. These values remain central to daily life in Pakistan. At the same time, the main challenge for the pro-US General is to demonstrate his success in cleansing Pakistani society of its legacy of militancy – this remains the source of continuing concerns among Western diplomats.

Mutala-e-Pakistan is used for teaching grade 10 students in state-owned schools across the Punjab province, which is home to more than 60 per cent of Pakistan's population of 150 million. Critics often single out the education system in such schools, as opposed to the numerically fewer private schools for the elite, as one of the possible drivers fuelling militant trends in the south Asian country. Such criticism is an example of a fundamental challenge facing Pakistan under the rule of General Musharraf. While Pakistan remains a frontline state in the war on terror, a country closely backed by the Bush administration, fresh questions over its internal situation have come to the surface following the suicide attacks in London in July 2005.

Pakistan quickly became the focus of attention following those attacks amid suggestions that one or two of the four main suspects in the first attack on 7 July visited Pakistan a year earlier and may have visited an Islamic 'madrassah' or school. Three of those suspects were of Pakistani origin – another reason for concerns over Pakistan's connection to militant activities worldwide. After initial investigations, both Pakistani and British officials emphasized that, while the suspects were of Pakistani origin, there was no evidence to suggest that their ties to their country of origin directly aided their actions in Britain.

The central question, however, for the future of Pakistan's efforts to clamp down on militancy remains the extent to which General Musharraf can succeed in rooting out terrorism from his country, beyond the actions he has taken so far. Those actions principally focus on ordering Pakistani troops to launch a vigorous campaign against militants believed to belong to Al Qaeda and Afghanistan's former Taliban regime, who took refuge in the mountainous terrain of Pakistan's tribal areas along the Afghan border after the US-backed invasion of Afghanistan following the New York terrorist attacks. In the three years since 9/11, Pakistan has successfully caught and handed over to the United States up to 700 militants, including some notable figures in Al Qaeda's hierarchy, such as Khalid Shaikh Mohammad, the group's head of operations, in 2003, and more recently, Abu Faraj Farj Al Liby, Al Qaeda's third-highest ranking leader after Osama bin Laden and Ayman Al Zawahiry (Reuters 2005a).[2]

Despite such high-profile arrests prompting widespread belief that other key Al Qaeda leaders are in hiding in Pakistan, General Musharraf is not convinced that either Osama bin Laden, leader of Al Qaeda, or Ayman Al Zawahiri, Al Qaeda's deputy leader, is hiding in Pakistan. Furthermore, he insists that Al Qaeda as an organization now lacks the vertical and horizontal integration that would be necessary for it to survive as an effective militant organization in the long run:

> My personal view is they lack the horizontal and vertical cohesion that is so essential in the homogeneity of an organisation. This is because of the successes that we have had here in Pakistan and also in Afghanistan because of which they have ceased to exist as a homogenous body. My personal judgment is that we have broken their back. (Johnson and Bokhari 2005)

After the London bombings, General Musahrraf has missed no opportunity to renew his pledge of combating militancy. In a major policy speech on the day of the second London attacks, General Musharraf urged Pakistanis to discard groups of Islamists that he said were having a regressive effect on Pakistan: 'Today, we face a battle between two distinct sets of ideas. One supports taking us towards the "Taliban" type of Islam, towards an era of darkness ... The other is about progressive values and taking us forward as a country' (Musharraf 2005a). The General used the occasion to announce yet another deadline for pushing forward a long overdue registration of Islamic 'madrassah' schools that essentially requires them to register with the government by the end of 2005.

Other measures announced at the same time, aimed against Islamic groups, included orders that have been announced before in the past three years, such as a ban on any political and religious group already banned from reappearing under another name. Furthermore, any publication dedicated to provoking violence in the name of Islam was served notice of unspecified but tough action. However, no such action has been taken against publications such as the above-noted textbook, and it is unlikely in the near future. This is not a textbook for the madrassah; it is a textbook used in government schools in the Punjab. Additionally, prayer leaders who through their sermons urged their followers to commit violence were served notice that they could be prosecuted.

In another important policy speech, on 14 August 2005, the General called upon Pakistanis, just four days before countrywide elections for municipal representatives, to reject hard-line Islamists. 'The hurdles to our progress are extremism and narrow-mindedness', said the General in the eastern city of Lahore. He said that those responsible for creating obstacles to progress had tried to impose their thoughts on others, but they had forgotten the 'original emphasis of Islam ... We cannot allow these elements to stop Pakistan's progress' (Reuters 2005b).

In a related development, General Musharraf's federal government challenged in Pakistan's supreme court the 'Hasba bill' passed by the North West Frontier Province (NWFP) provincial legislature with a view to introducing a system of preventing vice and promoting virtue as practised under the Taliban regime in Afghanistan. The supreme court turned down the 'Hasba bill' in a major step that potentially blocks other similar moves by Islamist groups.

THE MILITARY'S LEGACY

Notwithstanding General Musharraf's claims, the Pakistani military has had a long history of supporting Islamic groups dedicated to jihad and militancy. The relationship took root in the years following the 1979 invasion of Afghanistan by troops from the former Soviet Union. Within weeks of that invasion, the United States, then under the administration of President Jimmy Carter, began negotiations with the regime of General Mohammad Zia ul Haq, the military dictator who seized power in 1977.

During the decade from 1979 to 1989 – the year when Soviet troops finally withdrew from Afghanistan – the United States principally relied on Pakistan as a conduit for the supply of arms. That ten-year period saw the Afghan resistance being organized by Pakistani and US intelligence officials under the banner of jihad. This was done mainly to give a common platform to otherwise ethnically diverse groups.

In spite of the Soviet withdrawal from Afghanistan in 1989, many militant groups which were armed and motivated for a holy cause continued to exist under different titles. The Pakistani military oversaw the arming and training of such groups as successive regimes in the country gave them the encouragement to use a similar jihad concept for supporting Muslim insurgents in Indian-administered Kashmir. That policy was built around a relationship of animosity between India and Pakistan since the partition of a united India under the British Raj led to the creation of the two states in 1947. The Pakistani military has only backed away from that policy after India and Pakistan began a new peace process in January 2004.

The other important use of the jihad concept has indeed come from the Pakistani military, which has used it as a tool to motivate its troops facing a much larger foe, as India's military strength is considered to be three to four times that of Pakistan.

A NEW WORLD

The events following the New York terrorist attacks have exposed Pakistan to the realities of essentially a new world where support for militant causes is increasingly unacceptable. General Musharraf himself has often articulated his determination to root out groups such as Al Qaeda whose mastermind, Osama bin Laden, is widely believed to have been patronized by Pakistan, the United States and Saudi intelligence services in the 1980s at the height of the Afghanistan war.[3]

The General's latest measures such as ordering registration of 'madrassahs' are widely expected by Pakistani officials to reap further political and economic support from key international players such as the Bush administration and the governments of Britain and other European states.[4] In a related development in July 2005, the United States began shipments to Pakistan of F-16 fighter planes, whose delivery was suspended in 1990 owing to suspicion that Pakistan was producing nuclear weapons. These measures are seen widely in Pakistan as examples of active US support to the military and General Musharraf; they are also perceived to have little relevance to radically promoting the welfare of ordinary Pakistanis.

Pakistan had previously conducted its maiden nuclear tests in May 1998 and remained a non-signatory to such international treaties as the non-proliferation treaty and the comprehensive test ban treaty until 2005. But its emerging relationship with the United States, driven mainly by measures against Al Qaeda and the Taliban, led to the United States agreeing to a five-year military and economic assistance package worth about US$3 billion.

However, for critics of General Musharraf, his ties with the United States highlight a central paradox faced by Pakistan. On the one hand, the country under a military ruler remains distant from the prospect of becoming as representative a democracy as its south Asian peers such as India, Bangladesh and Sri Lanka. On the other hand, US backing for the General can only continue to bolster his position and that of the Pakistani military. To this extent, democracy in Pakistan seems even more distant.

A POLITICAL VOID AND CURBING MILITANCY

Pakistani politicians are quick to note that the country's lack of political development is likely to continue to undermine its journey towards stability and any hope of eventually reducing the influence of the Islamists. The main coalition of Islamic political groups known as the MMA (Muttehedah Majlis-e-Amal), a six-party coalition that scored its largest victory ever in the elections of 2002, continued to hold charge of the provincial government in the NWFP in 2005. It remained a key partner in the ruling coalition in another province – Baluchistan.

These two provinces, out of the four Pakistani provinces, are the key to fighting and curbing militancy. Both border Afghanistan and have a long history of close association with key members of Al Qaeda and the Taliban. It is in the NWFP that the Pakistani military has fought militants from the two groups in a rugged mountainous region since 2003.

Opposition politicians argue that the MMA has a chance of scoring another success in 2007, especially given that the leaders of Pakistan's two mainstream parties – the Pakistan People's Party (PPP) led by Benazir Bhutto, and the Pakistan Muslim League–Nawaz group, led by Nawaz Sharif – remain in exile. Mr Sharif was ousted by General Musharraf in a bloodless coup in 1999. He was subsequently exiled to Saudi Arabia. Ms Bhutto had left the country two years earlier. General Musharraf continues to refuse them the right to return. That has undermined the standing of the two parties that were once the main players on the turf of Pakistani politics.

In the absence of a clear and credible political challenge, the MMA's chances of dominating critical parts of Pakistan's political scene remain bright, in spite of General Musharraf's tough message. In the meantime, the General has tried to create a new ruling party, also known as the Pakistan Muslim League but built around the memory of the late Mr Muhammad Ali Jinnah, the founding father of the country. The effort appears to have badly faltered. The ruling party in its first three years in power was surrounded by criticism from the opposition. Party members were accused of winning their seats in parliament through manipulation of different types in various constituencies.[5] The MMA in municipal elections in August 2005 faced some setbacks in the NWFP, where candidates from other more mainstream opposition parties unexpectedly won some seats that earlier belonged to the MMA. However, this has not changed the character of the MMA's control over the province.

CONCLUSION

General Musharraf's promise notwithstanding, his success in beating militancy is unlikely to remain sustainable without a clear, robust and credible political strategy. The groups dedicated to militancy are bound to remain active in the absence of a political challenge from the mainstream parties.

If indeed the measure of General Musharraf's success remains numerical – that is, the number of suspected militants arrested – he is likely to impress the outside world. But if the measure is taken in terms of permanently curbing the militancy of Islamic groups from Pakistan, there are many reasons to remain sceptical, mainly driven by the country's history, the military's own standing and present-day trends. In the long run, unless the Pakistani military charts out a course for a return to a stable democracy, Pakistan's internal outlook will continue to face periodic political instability and uncertainty. As in a number of other countries ruled by military regimes, notwithstanding General Musharraf's personal appeal to world leaders, he will have to face the challenge of overseeing a smooth transition. Musharraf has survived three assassination attempts in the past six years. These underline a key challenge for Pakistan: if indeed his rule comes to an abrupt end, the General would leave Pakistan surrounded by a new environment of potential instability and uncertainty.

NOTES

1. 50000 copies of this school textbook were published in Urdu.
2. This despatch details the arrests in Pakistan subsequent to the arrest of Abu Faraj Farj Al Liby.
3. For an example of General Musharraf's view on this subject, see Musharraf (2005b).
4. Background interviews with Pakistani officials at the foreign and interior ministries in Islamabad, Pakistan, July/August 2005.
5. Interviews with various politicians from the MMA and the main opposition groups.

REFERENCES

Johnson, Jo and Farhan Bokhari (2005), Interview with General Musharraf in Army House, Rawalpindi, Pakistan, as reported in the *Financial Times*, 31 May, Punjab, www.ft.com, accessed October 2005.
Musharraf, Pervez (2005a), 'Address to Pakistanis', Pakistan Television, 21 July.
Musharraf, Pervez (2005b), 'We have broken Al Qaeda's back', interview with the *Financial Times*, UK, 31 May, www.ft.com, accessed October 2005.
Mutala-e-Pakistan [*Pakistan studies*] (2005), Punjab Textbook Board, Lahore, Pakistan, April.

Reuters news agency (2005a), 5 May.
Reuters news agency (2005b), 'Musharraf urges Pakistanis to choose progress', Lahore, 14 August.

8. Deconstructing Muslim terrorism

Pervez Hoodbhoy

In 2005 London joined that chain of cities – from New York to Mombassa, Madrid to Istanbul, Casablanca to Riyadh, Islamabad to Bali – whose ordinary citizens have suffered indiscriminate, violent and cruel assaults by Islamists. Terrorism is once again on centre stage, and no one doubts that such acts will return to prominence again and again. Ours may well be called the 'Century of Terror'.

Horrible, yes! Nevertheless it is time for the world to end its unreasonable fear and preoccupation with terrorism, put it into reasonable perspective, and compare it with other threats faced by human civilization. Homicides in the world's major cities, for example, add up to a yearly number far in excess of those killed in terrorist attacks, including those of 9/11. Traffic fatalities are several times that. This is not an argument to belittle the horror of terrorism and its consequences, but it is only by considering facts in totality that we can arrive at a measure of calmness and contemplate the way ahead.

EXORCISM WILL NOT WORK

Medieval exorcists believed that insanity could be cured by expelling evil spirits from those who were thought to be possessed. But this was a doubtful strategy; medieval 'doctors' may have derived some cruel satisfaction from their work, but very little real success. On the contrary, they vastly increased the numbers of mentally ill.

The US 'war on terror' is predicated on a similarly faulty assumption. It is now trapped inside a top that spins faster and faster while going nowhere. Bombed, hounded and evicted from former sanctuaries in Afghanistan, bin Laden's men – and countless others who share his goals – now repeatedly demonstrate that they are alive and well. Like angry hornets that have survived the destruction of their nest, they have spread far and wide. Ever since the 'coalition of the willing' formally declared a 'war on terror', major terrorist attacks have increased.

Instead of macho pumping, fighting terrorism needs a scientific approach. It must be recognized as a grave, but treatable, mental illness that must be dealt with by methods similar to those of scientific medicine. One must record the symptoms, examine the patient's history, ask the right questions, identify relevant environmental factors and then proceed with the cure.

WHY MUSLIM TERRORISM?

A Muslim typically responds to the news of an act of terror allegedly performed by his co-religionists with a knee-jerk denial of any Muslim involvement. But when this becomes untenable, he or she will insist that this act had nothing to do with Islam. Others will justify it as a befitting response to centuries of enslavement by the West, and more recently the US invasion of Iraq. Substantial sections of Muslim societies undeniably support terrorism and violence today. The 2003 Pew Global Survey found that solid majorities in several Muslim countries actually believe that Osama bin Laden can do 'the right thing regarding world affairs'. In 2005 another such survey in Pakistan found that over 50 per cent of the population consider bin Laden a hero.

Nevertheless, the recent rise of fundamentalist, neo-totalitarian Muslim movements that use terrorism is an aberration, not a norm, in Muslim history. Until a few years ago suicide bombings had been unheard of. Many believe that Al Qaeda is a mythical creation of the Americans to explain 9/11. While this is absurd, nevertheless it is true that groups like Al Qaeda did not exist three decades ago.

Many have sought to explain why the situation changed so dramatically. The Pipes-Lewis school, which is so popular in America today, regards Islam's current hostile relationship with the West as a consequence of Islam being fundamentally negative towards secular, democratic and pluralistic values. But even if Islam rejects such values, surely the relationship between the United States and conservative Arab countries, as well as Islamic dictators in many countries, have traditionally been much warmer than with most Muslim secular states. Tying terrorism with Islam's particular belief system is a tenuous proposition.

On the other side, some sympathetic analysts see Islamic terrorism and suicide bombings in terms of poverty, deprivation and lack of opportunity. These can certainly be important contributory factors. But the poor and desperate do not necessarily take up the gun. Hundreds of millions of impoverished Africans, as well as 200 million Dalit untouchables of India, are perfectly docile and free from violence.

Others have hypothesized that Islam is an extraordinarily violent religion. It is certainly true that Islam – like Christianity, Judaism, Hinduism or any other religion – can readily rally its adherents into making war. Indeed, every religion is about the finality of its truth and militant defence of its beliefs, and every religion is potentially violent. Christianity's bloody past, the fanatical zeal of Zionist settlers, and the Hindu zealots who massacred 2000 Muslims in the Indian state of Gujarat show the violence latent in any kind of blind belief. But, unless one can understand why and how mere potential for violence turns into real violence, this has no explanatory value.

The sea change in Muslim attitudes over the last few decades is entangled in a complex web of factors. But one can get the glimmerings of a genuine understanding by looking at history.

The Rise and Fall of Muslim Modernization

When new Muslim nation states emerged in the twentieth century after the end of the colonial period, not even one of their leaders was a fundamentalist. Turkey's Kemal Ataturk, Algeria's Ahmed Ben Bella, Indonesia's Sukarno, Pakistan's Muhammad Ali Jinnah, Egypt's Gamal Abdel Nasser and Iran's Mohammed Mosaddeq all sought to organize their societies on the basis of secular values. However, Muslim and Arab nationalism, part of a larger anti-colonial nationalist current across the Third World, included the desire to control and use national resources for domestic benefit.

The conflict with US and Western greed was inevitable. Indeed, the United States' foes during the 1950s and 1960s were secular nationalists, not fundamentalists. Mossadeq, who opposed Standard Oil's grab at Iran's oil resources, fell victim to a CIA coup. Sukarno, accused of being a communist, was removed by US intervention and a resulting bloodbath that consumed about 800 000 lives. Nasser, who had Islamic fundamentalists like Saiyyid Qutb publicly executed, fell foul of the United States and Britain after the Suez Crisis. On the other hand, until very recently, America's friends were the sheikhs of Saudi Arabia and the Gulf states, all of whom practised highly conservative forms of Islam but were friendly to Western oil companies.

Pressed from outside, corrupt and incompetent within, secular Muslim governments proved unable to defend national interests or deliver social justice. Failure after failure left a vacuum that Islamic religious movements grew to fill – in Iran, Pakistan and Sudan, to name a few. There was widespread anger, in both Muslim and non-Muslim countries, at outright US support for Israel's annexation of captured territories in the 1967 war and its settlement policies. The defeat of the secular PLO and its expulsion from Lebanon in 1982 paved the way for Hamas to dominate the Palestinian resistance. Nevertheless, there was no global terrorist movement as yet.

The Genesis of International Jihad

There may well have been no 9/11 but for 1979, the year of the Soviet invasion of Afghanistan. With Ronald Reagan as the rival presidential candidate, Jimmy Carter could not afford to appear soft on the Soviets. Officials like Richard

Perle, Assistant Secretary of Defense, immediately saw Afghanistan not as the locale of a harsh and dangerous conflict to be ended but as a place to teach the Russians a lesson. Such 'bleeders' became the most influential people in Washington (Ahmad and Barnet 1988; Ahmad 2000).

The bleeders soon organized and armed the Great Global Jihad, funded by Saudi Arabia, and executed by Pakistan. A powerful magnet for militant Sunni activists was created by the United States. The most hardened and ideologically dedicated men were sought on the logic that they would be the best fighters. Advertisements, paid for from CIA funds, were placed in newspapers and newsletters around the world offering inducements and motivations to join the jihad. American universities produced books for Afghan children that extolled the virtues of jihad and of killing communists. Readers browsing through book bazaars in Rawalpindi and Peshawar can, even today, find textbooks produced as part of the series underwritten by a USAID $50 million grant to the University of Nebraska in the 1980s (Davis 2002). These textbooks sought to counterbalance Marxism by creating enthusiasm in Islamic militancy. They exhorted Afghan children to 'pluck out the eyes of the Soviet enemy and cut off his legs'. Years after the books were first printed they were approved by the Taliban for use in madrassahs – a stamp of their ideological correctness – and they are still widely available in both Afghanistan and Pakistan.

At the international level, radical Islam went into overdrive as its superpower ally, the United States, funnelled support to the mujahidin. Ronald Reagan feted jihadist leaders on the White House lawn, and the US press lionized them. When Soviet troops withdrew from Afghanistan in the face of the US–Pakistani–Saudi–Egyptian alliance in 1988, a chapter of history seemed complete. But the costs of this victory revealed themselves over the course of the next decade. By the mid 1990s, it was clear that the victorious alliance had unleashed a dynamic beyond its control. After the Soviet Union collapsed, the United States walked away from an Afghanistan in shambles. Millions of Afghan people had fled into Pakistan, creating instability there. Then the Taliban emerged; Osama bin Laden and his Al Qaeda made Afghanistan their base. 11 September 2001, followed.

WHAT SUSTAINS TERRORISM?

Once set in motion, Islamic terrorism has been sustained by the following factors. The Palestinian–Israeli issue, with daily televised images of Palestinian suffering, together with unstinting US support for Israel, evoke anger and bitterness in Muslim populations around the world. This is by far the greatest single element that rallies Muslims against the United States. Each old reason gains new ferocity whenever, with America's nod, Israeli bulldozers plough into Palestinian homes and reduce towns to rubble. Other nationalist movements such as in Chechnya, Kashmir and the Philippines have turned increasingly towards Islam when denied political accommodation. Their impact is still largely local, but they add to the general feeling that Muslims are being specifically targeted.

George W. Bush once rhetorically asked, 'Why do they hate us?' After the Iraq war, that question has a ready answer for millions the world over. The daily televised bombardment of Baghdad with cruise missiles and bombs hailing down from the skies, smashed bodies and decapitated children, bombed-out hospitals, women and children shot dead at checkpoints policed by US Marines, and the burning of Iraq's priceless architectural and literary heritage have added to all older reasons.

America's war on Iraq, waged on the pretext of chasing WMD, was supposed to crush terrorism. Instead, 100 000 deaths later, Iraq has become a new fountainhead for terrorism and will remain so for the foreseeable future (Stein 2004, p. A16).[1] Here, Islamic groups have an opportunity to engage the United States in battle. It is one that uses asymmetric tactics and is popular because Muslims overwhelmingly believe that this war was about oil and supporting Israel. Moving away from its previous contention that the threat came only from Al Qaeda, the Pentagon now identifies the 'primary enemy' as 'extremist Sunni and Shia movements that exploit Islam for political ends' and that form part of a 'global web of enemy networks'.

Western media reporting often falls into absurdity by attributing all acts of terrorism to Al Qaeda. In fact, shadowy and strongly motivated but largely uncoordinated and unlinked with others, various different Islamic groups are responsible. These groups represent part of the popular sentiment in Muslim populations, a highly dangerous sign.

Poisoning Young Muslim Minds

The London bombings have again drawn attention not merely to the international networks that sustain terrorism (not only Muslim terrorism) but also to the role played in this by education. Children are not born terrorists. They need education first and training later to be converted into zealous suicide bombers.

Militant Islamic movements sustain themselves through relentless brainwashing. At least some Muslim states (for example, Pakistan and Saudi Arabia) have school curricula that explicitly call for jihad, denigrate other religions, and create a mindset eminently suited for recruitment into extremist organizations. Preachers in mosques, who have large audiences, openly call for violence. Centralization of religious authority, as in Egypt (under Al-Azhar University), has been imposed to prevent radical clerics, with large public access, from stoking the fires by issuing arbitrary 'fatwas'. In Pakistan, such an imposition, if attempted, would be bitterly fought.

In Pakistan the process of providing the 'right kind of education' began in 1976 with the national curriculum prepared by the Curriculum Wing of the Federal Ministry of Education, Government of Pakistan. The usefulness of having a national curriculum was soon recognized by General Zia-ul-Haq, an Islamic fundamentalist who hanged his benefactor, prime minister Zulfiqar Ali Bhutto, after staging a coup in 1977. In 1981 he decreed that henceforth Pakistani education was to be totally redefined and history rewritten according to his vision of Pakistan. Until then it can be said that, although Pakistan had been a predominantly military regime, it still adhered to the original idea of the founders that it should be a secular state.

All this changed in the early 1980s. From now on the struggle for Pakistan was no longer to be shown as a victorious struggle for a Muslim homeland. Instead, it was to be depicted as the movement for an Islamic state run according to Islamic law. Even if it conflicted with reality, the heroes of the Pakistan movement – Jinnah, Iqbal and Syed Ahmed Khan – were to be projected as Islamic heroes. Furthermore, all subjects, including the sciences, were to be speedily Islamized. The following excerpts from the Curriculum for classes K–V in primary schools, developed by the National Bureau of Curriculum and Textbooks, Federal Ministry of Education, in 1995 (with acknowledged international donor assistance from UNICEF, USAID, GTZ and the World Bank) states that on the completion of Class V, the child should be able to:

- 'acknowledge and identify forces that may be working against Pakistan'
- 'demonstrate by actions a belief in the fear of Allah'
- 'make speeches on Jehad and Shahadat' (Shahadat = martyrdom)
- 'understand Hindu–Muslim differences and the resultant need for Pakistan'
- 'acknowledge India's evil designs against Pakistan'
- 'be safe from rumour mongers who spread false news'
- 'visit police stations'
- 'collect pictures of policemen, soldiers, and National Guards'
- 'demonstrate respect for the leaders of Pakistan.'

(National Bureau of Curriculum and Textbooks 1995)

This curriculum remains in place today and it is unlikely to change, despite General Musharraf's call that all foreign students in Pakistan's madrassahs be expelled. Changing the curriculum is far more important than changing the kind of students who sit in class. Sadly, while many Pakistanis are aware that there is something wrong with the nature of their schooling, only a few have access to public documents such as those reproduced here, which expose the country to international shame, condemnation and ridicule.

Consider the impact of the national curriculum objectives on 12-year-old children in their last year of primary school. Instead of a future that is joyous and a peaceful country that offers hope to all, they are told that life is actually about battling invisible enemies. Fear is ever-present because beneath every stone lurks a venomous snake and Pakistan is under siege by sinister forces that the children must learn to acknowledge, identify and fight to death. What mental space can remain for children's innocence when they must learn to make speeches on jihad and martyrdom? And what scope exists for being tolerant and accepting of beliefs other than their own? What kind of people does the national curriculum seek to install as role models? They are not scholars and poets or scientists, or those who have struggled for the rights of others. Instead they are policemen, national guards and soldiers. The children must collect their pictures, revere them, perhaps kiss them. Their visits to police stations – where rapes, tortures and deaths in custody occur so routinely as to be unremarkable – are expected to imbue them with the spirit of humanism and patriotism. Is a greater perversion of human values really possible?

Some of the curriculum objectives present more than just a slight difficulty of implementation. To 'demonstrate by actions a belief in the fear of Allah' certainly left me stumped, but surely some wise reader can think of ways to grade a child on this. How it is possible to 'be safe from rumour mongers who spread false news' is also beyond my intelligence to answer. As for the requirement to 'demonstrate respect for the leaders of Pakistan', one presumes that on the morning of the 12 October 1999 coup a model student had to present evidence of respect for prime minister Nawaz Sharif, and in the evening for General Musharraf.

An incompetent, self-obsessed, corrupt and ideologically charged education bureaucracy today squarely blocks Pakistan's entry into the twenty-first century. Its future is to be made by those who cannot write a single straight sentence and for whom good education means passivity, blind obedience and indoctrination. A system blind to the requirements of pedagogy insists that Pakistani children learn in at least three languages – Urdu, English and Arabic – and often the mother tongue as well, which is usually different. This linguistic burden alone is sufficient to cripple children's minds. While there are no quick fixes to a problem that has compounded over five decades, not a moment should be lost in beginning the slow process of rehabilitation and reform of the education system. A country suffering from xenophobia and hatred for others harms primarily itself. Therefore, instead of being virulent and aggressive, Pakistani patriotism must be identified with civic responsibilities such as paying one's fair share of taxes, acceptance of

Pakistan's diversity of cultures and peoples, assurance of social justice, and preserving the environment.

Terrorism Versus Empire

The US has lost the sympathy it rightfully had after 9/11. An impenetrable narcissism prevents most Americans from learning that the world does not share their self-image of a generous, libertarian and humane people whose innocence was injured by a savage attack on its cities. Although the United States has fought 28 wars since 1945 and bombed 26 countries, it maintains 12 aircraft carrier groups that constantly prowl the oceans, stations a million soldiers over five continents, and keeps thousands of nuclear weapons. Nevertheless, a majority of Americans continue to believe that the United States seeks no more than self-defence. The re-election of George Bush and Tony Blair was a vote for a peremptory dismissal of world opinion and for contempt for international laws and treaties. Bush's appointment of John Bolton to the UN amounts to vicious sneering at the world body and all that it stands for.

Imperial America's master plan calls for redrawing national boundaries in the Muslim world wherever necessary, and for recalcitrant nations to be forcibly occupied until they lose the will to resist. After 9/11 there was no lack of spokespersons for the American Empire. In unabashedly imperial language, Zbigniew Brzezinski, who initiated the anti-Soviet jihad in Afghanistan, writes that the United States should seek to 'prevent collusion and maintain dependence among the vassals, keep tributaries pliant and protected, and to keep the barbarians from coming together' (Maynes 2000).

To keep the 'barbarians' at bay, Pentagon planners have been charged with the task of assuring US control over every part of the planet. Major (P) Ralph Peters, an officer responsible for conceptualizing future warfare in the Office of the Deputy Chief of Staff for Intelligence, is clear about why his country needs to fight (Peters 1997):

> We have entered an age of constant conflict.
>
> We are entering a new American century, in which we will become still wealthier, culturally more lethal, and increasingly powerful. We will excite hatreds without precedent.
>
> There will be no peace. At any given moment for the rest of our lifetimes, there will be multiple conflicts in mutating forms around the globe. The de facto role of the US armed forces will be to keep the world safe for our economy and open to our cultural assault. To those ends, we will do a fair amount of killing.

But this exercise of raw power, with a single-minded goal to subdue and subjugate, is now proving very costly in Iraq. Tragically, the world – Americans included – will pay, and pay again, for Washington's imperial adventures.

How US Policy Plays Out in Pakistan

Anti-US sentiment has translated directly into a vote for Pakistani Islamists. An alliance of religious parties, the MMA, successfully formed the government in two of Pakistan's four provinces in the provincial elections of 2002. It is firmly committed to the talibanization of Pakistan. Almost immediately upon assuming office, the new government ordered a ban on the playing of music in public transport, required public buses to stop dead at the time of the five daily prayers, and closed down video shops and cinema houses. Folk singers have been threatened, abducted and forbidden to sing in public. Cable television operators have seen their premises ransacked. Women without a hijab and a chaperone may not leave their homes; shops may not advertise the sale of ' sanitary pads or undergarments; hair-removing creams and lotions may not be sold; use of perfume and make-up will be banned; women will not be allowed to use male tailors; male doctors may not treat women patients; women guests at hotels are not allowed in the swimming pool; coeducation has been identified as a cause of fornication and is to be phased out; family planning is considered un-Islamic; and sale of contraceptives may soon be banned.

General Musharraf, caught between popular sentiment against the Iraqi war and his regime's heavy economic and political dependence on the United States, has so far walked a tightrope. In what appears to have been a characteristically thoughtless statement, Musharraf declared that Pakistan could very well be next on the US hit list. He had refused to take a strong stand on the Iraq war. Whether out of fear or hope of a reward, as a non-permanent member of the Security Council Pakistan refused to announce its outright opposition to Resolution 1441. It seems fairly certain that, if it had been forced to vote, Pakistan would have abstained.

Today, General Musharraf provides but one example of the difficulty that the United States faces as it sets about its messianic quest to change the world. The United States can scarcely afford representative democracy in most Islamic states. Although the stated objective in Iraq was claimed to be the establishment of a democratic state, it is difficult to imagine that any popularly elected government in Pakistan, Egypt, Syria, Jordan, Iran or Saudi Arabia would be friendly to the United States. Indeed, reviving monarchies and military dictatorships, backed up with awesome force, may be Washington's best bet. When a government sets itself up against the interests of the citizens it supposedly rules to protect, it is then that the legitimacy of that regime is most deeply corroded. Musharraf may have turned the macroeconomic indicators around, may have rehabilitated the international credibility of Pakistan and may even have contributed towards pulling India–Pakistan relations back from the brinkmanship of the 1990s. But none of these things is a sufficient precondition for ensuring domestic stability and the legitimacy of his regime. The groundswell of opposition increasingly comes from disaffected people who turn towards an Islamic leadership that claims to be less corrupt and more sympathetic to the needs of ordinary people. That groundswell carries with it Islamic militants whose quest for a pure world is not moderated by respect for the sanctity of life.

Although Islamists rail against the West, they are – and will remain – fundamentally a very weak force. They have no science – the strength behind modern civilization – and can never be capable of it. Irrespective of their numbers, they cannot have the awesome strength that springs from accepting the paradigm of reason and logic, respecting democratic institutions, allowing value systems to evolve, and boldly challenging dogma without being condemned as blasphemers. They cannot see why the West's success has anything to do with personal freedom and liberty, artistic and scientific creativity, the compulsive urge to innovate and experiment, and its universities.

Each blow inflicted by the United States has led Islamists to predict that the pain and humiliation will make all Muslims close ranks, forget old grudges, purge traitors and renegades from the ranks, and generate a collective rage great enough to take on the power of today's governing civilization. Each time they have been wrong. This inability to learn has led to self-defeating and self-harming terrorism. Islamic militant organizations have done far greater harm to Muslims, whose causes they claim to promote, than to those whom they battle against. They have yet to learn that fanatical acts can sting and provoke the US colossus but never seriously hurt it.

CONCLUSION: ANY REASON FOR HOPE?

Islamists are dangerous but weak. Faced with internal failure, manifest decline from a peak of greatness many centuries ago, and cultural dislocation in an age of globalization, many Muslim societies have turned inwards. This has had political consequences that favour Islamist movements, both in Muslim countries and in Europe.

Ultimately, the only way by which Muslim societies can become democratic, pluralistic and free from violent extremism is by going through their own struggles. It cannot be done – as the failure of the United States' efforts in Afghanistan and Iraq demonstrates – by imposing colonial rule. The US imperial agenda, and support for groups in Israel with fanatical beliefs, works towards slowing internal reform and even reversing it.

Is there any reason to believe that indigenous reform is possible? Islam is certainly as immutable as the Quran. But Muslims have changed and will continue to.

The Muslim country that offers the most hope for indigenous reform is a declared member of George Bush's axis-of-evil. The election of the arch-conservative Ahmadenijad over the relatively moderate Rafsanjani is admittedly a big setback and can be directly traced to US threats to attack Iran. Nevertheless it does not change the fact that Iran has the finest education system in the Muslim world, a population that is culturally more advanced and accepting of modernity than in Arab countries, and young people who abhor the Islamic theocracy that has ruled the country for over two decades. Even though the US refused to take notice of the fact, immediately after 9/11 nearly 40 000 Iranians came out into the streets in Tehran and lit candles in sympathy with the American people. Contrast that with celebrations held in countries like Pakistan that are declared US allies.

At least in the near future, the relationship between Muslims and the West is likely to continue its downward descent. Muslim terrorist groups will continue to recruit successfully as long as large numbers of Muslims feel that they are being unfairly targeted. Unless this changes and there is a perception that there is some measure of justice in world affairs, this trend must be considered irreversible. Moreover, static/declining economies will allow for an abundant supply of terrorist recruits. Unless mitigating economic strategies, skill development, job creation mechanisms and other ameliorating measures are seriously considered, the situation will deteriorate as Muslim populations expand.

NOTE

1. In late 2005 President Bush admitted that civilian casualties were about 30 000 (Jackson 2005). It is reasonable to assume that this is a gross underestimate, as civilian deaths in Iraq have not been properly recorded and the study quoted by Stein was an estimate based on a sample survey of the death rates.

REFERENCES

Ahmad, Eqbal (2000), *Confronting Empire: Interviews with David Barsamian*, Cambridge, MA: South End Press.
Ahmad, Eqbal and Richard J. Barnet (1988), 'Bloody games', *The New Yorker*, 11 April, reprinted in 'Articles by Eqbal Ahmad', B.T.S., www.bitsonline.net/eqbal/articles_by_eqbal_view2.asp, accessed January 2006.
Davis, Craig (2002), '"A" is for Allah, "J" is for jihad', *World Policy Journal*, XIX (1), 90–94.
Jackson, Derrick Z. (2005), 'Iraqi civilian deaths mount – and count', *Boston Globe*, 17 December, www.boston.com/news/globe/editorial_opinion/oped/articles/2005/12/17/iraqi_civilian_deaths_mount_and_count/, accessed January 2006.
Maynes, Charles William (2000), 'Two blasts against unilateralism', in Gwyn Prins (ed.), *Understanding Unilateralism in US Foreign Policy*, London: RIIA.

National Bureau of Curriculum and Textbooks, Federal Ministry of Education (1995), 'Curriculum for Class V', Islamabad.
Peters, Ralph (1997), *US War College Quarterly*, summer, http://carlisle-www.army. mil/usawc/Parameters/97summer/peters.htm, accessed October 2000.
Stein, Rob (2004), '100,000 Civilian Deaths Estimated in Iraq', *Washington Post*, 29 October, www.washingtonpost.com/wp-dyn/articles/A7967-2004Oct28.html, accessed October 2005.

9. The Indo-Pakistan peace process and the China factor

Asad Durrani

Wars are easier to plan and execute than peace. But then hardly any war has ever been executed as planned, and we, therefore, hardly ever make 'peace plans'. In due course, we will also give up chalking out 'road maps' to peace. Road maps lay down milestones and well-defined directions. Peace on the other hand is a process that evolves, never smoothly, and often taking an unchartered course. Like a sapling, it has to be constantly watched and tenderly nourished till it is firmly rooted. It is best planted when the ground is adequately prepared.

India and Pakistan took 50 years to prepare the ground for the peace presently in process. Some others, like Europe, took longer. Peace, after all, though a desirable objective, cannot be achieved just because we long for it. It is only when all other means, force included, have played their part that we find the right framework for durable peace. Having fought wars, sought external involvement, and even made some half-baked efforts to peacefully resolve our conflicts, we in the subcontinent were also prepared, nearly a decade ago, to make peace. The process started in 1997 before the two countries went overtly nuclear, but their well-known nuclear potential helped.

This chapter is an attempt to follow the evolution of the peace process between India and Pakistan, from its inception eight years ago to its present (as acclaimed in Islamabad and New Delhi) 'irreversible' state, and to assess its sustainability. It certainly has implications for the region and beyond. Here I will only discuss its impact on China's relationship with the two sub-continental powers.

THE PEACE PROCESS

The partition of British India in 1947 was accompanied by much heartache and bloodshed. But the issue that has been at the 'core' of Indo-Pakistan acrimony ever since is the Himalayan state of Jammu and Kashmir (or simply Kashmir), which borders India and Pakistan as well as China. Both countries laid claim to it. India referred the dispute to the UN Security Council after its army fought a brief war against local resistance groups and irregular forces from Pakistan. The UN-negotiated ceasefire resulted in the de facto division of the disputed territory. It was to be followed by a plebiscite under UN auspices to determine which of the two countries the majority of Kashmiris wished to join.

This UNSC resolution 47 (1948), reaffirmed by another resolution, 91 (1951), remains unimplemented. Pakistan, in the belief that the Muslim majority would vote in its favour, has striven for its implementation. India, on the other hand, since it was in possession of the larger and the better part of the disputed territory at the time of the ceasefire, was not too keen. More importantly, India believed in its ability to resist the risky course. It turned out to be a fair assessment. Yet despite many efforts by Pakistan, the last being its support to the insurgency in Indian-held Kashmir for the last 15 years, the plebiscite has not taken place. India in the meantime went ahead and declared Kashmir an integral part of the Indian Union.

Kashmir is indeed one of the longest running disputes in modern times. With the widely divergent interests of the two belligerents, prospects of a negotiated settlement were never good. With the passage of time, the domestic environments in the two countries have complicated even the start of a purposeful dialogue.

In Pakistan, Kashmir is a sentimental issue. Securing the right of self-determination for the people of Jammu and Kashmir is one of the national objectives. It is therefore very difficult for any Pakistani leadership to embark upon a structured dialogue with India that is not seen to be addressing the Kashmir issue seriously, if not urgently. India, on the other hand, having declared the disputed state as integral part of itself, cannot be seen to be renegotiating its status; not seriously, at least. The foreign secretaries' meeting of June 1997 found an ingenuous solution to circumvent this dilemma.

Evolution of the Concept

Their recipe, now famously known as the 'composite dialogue', was to form a number of 'working groups', eight in all, to discuss important bilateral issues more or less concurrently. Peace, security and Kashmir were to be dealt with at the level of the foreign secretaries. The other issues – such as trade, terrorism, drugs and some territorial disputes – could be addressed by relevant ministries or departments ('India, Pak firm on ending hostile propaganda' 1997). Pakistan could now claim that its core issue had been granted due status. And the Indian side could 'quietly' assure their 'hawks' that it would only discuss those aspects of the dispute that were of concern to India.

With the contentious issues segregated, by type as well as by the degree of their complexity, in theory the dialogue could start, even move forward, since some of the agenda points were likely to be settled without loss of time. But a clause in the joint statement (4.2) came in the way. The Pakistani side had a reservation. It feared that while the Indian interests, such as greater economic cooperation, could be addressed in short time, talks on Kashmir, owing to the complexity of the matter, would make little headway. There was, and still is, a fairly broadly based belief in Pakistan that, if the Kashmir question was not resolved before the rest of the issues, India would no longer be interested in settling it. According to clause 4.2 all issues were to be discussed in an 'integrated' manner.

This meant that progress on all subjects had to be in tandem. This sounded fine, but for one problem. If there were little or no movement on one issue, we would have to slow down on all the others. The favourable environment needed to deal with the more complex problems, and it would thus become contingent on progress in all areas. This was exactly the catch-22 situation we had set out to avoid.

The 'integrated' part was quietly dropped (but not from the official text). The process was now more like moving our disputes along parallel tracks and getting them out of the way as and when possible. No longer strictly 'composite', the dialogue retained the politically correct adjective. What we now had was in fact a 'multiple-track, multiple-speed' formula.

The evolution of this concept was purely a civilian sector enterprise but its logic would have appealed to a military strategist, too. When operating along multiple axes, forces that meet less resistance continue their momentum. That helps movement on other fronts. When the situation is right, some fronts are reinforced to effect the breakthrough needed to capture the main objective: in this case, durable peace in the subcontinent.

The Learning Phase

Good concepts, brilliant designs and even sound strategies have never been enough. For their success, we make certain assumptions and lay down conditions that must be fulfilled. It must be assumed, for example, that an agreement, no matter how favourable to one or the other side, is not to be touted as a unilateral victory. In this situation, eager to make political capital out of the accord, the Pakistani government exulted over for having made the Indians 'finally' agree to discuss Kashmir. The Indians reacted predictably and 'clarified' that the only aspect of Kashmir that they ever intended to discuss was Pakistan's support to the insurgency in Indian-held Kashmir. The composite dialogue, and along with it the peace process, were put on ice.

The following year, 1998, the arch-rivals brought their nuclear bombs out of the basement. The celebrations that followed in India and Pakistan, and not only on the streets, were accompanied by plenty of chest beating and bellicosity towards each other. Obviously, there were also concerns, both inside and outside the region: how would the two nascent nuclear powers adjust to the new, potentially dangerous, environment? At the very least, some measures were necessary to prevent a situation in which one or the other country could fire a nuclear weapon in panic or because it misread a signal such as a missile test by the other side. Undoubtedly, the new development provided the two countries with another chance to review their chronically tense relationship.

In February 1999 Atal Bihari Vajpaee, the Indian prime minister, undertook his famous bus journey to Lahore. The Lahore Declaration[1] that he signed on 21 February with his Pakistani counterpart, Nawaz Sharif, went beyond nuclear confidence-building measures and attempted to revive the peace process. The 'composite dialogue' once again formed the bedrock of the agreement. And once again it was shelved before it got a fair chance.

It is not clear whether India was the first to violate the spirit of Lahore when it failed to notify Pakistan of a routine missile test carried out soon after Vajpaee returned to Delhi. But the agreement was most certainly dead when in early May 1999 Pakistani-backed militia were found occupying the Kargil heights, in Northern Kashmir, on the Indian side of the Line of Control (LOC). They were withdrawn after two months of intense fighting and bilateral as well as multilateral haggling. Pakistan was held entirely responsible for the breach. Its excuse, that it was only pre-empting another Indian attempt to secure a foothold on the Pakistani side (the previous one, in 1988, resulted in Indian occupation of Siachen Glacier, further north), found no takers.

India–Pakistan relations suffered another setback when in October 1999 the Pakistani army chief, General Pervez Musharraf, took power in a bloodless military putsch. The Indians believed that the general was the architect of the Kargil misadventure and were unwilling to resume the peace process as long as he was in power. But when Musharraf was found firmly in the saddle, Vajpaee invited him to give 'peace another chance'. Musharraf, who had in the meantime assumed the office of president, visited India in July 2001 and met Vajpaee in what became known as the Agra Summit. No agreement was reached this time round.

In the aftermath of 9/11, events took a further dip. When the United States decided to invade Afghanistan to flush out Al Qaeda, the group suspected of orchestrating 9/11, it sought allies in the region. Pakistan was one of the countries asked. India argued that Pakistan was 'part of the problem' and therefore ill-suited to be a partner in the global 'war on terror'. It offered its own services instead. Pakistan all the same got the role, as it was better placed to assist directly. Already sulking for being upstaged by Pakistan, India mobilized for war when its parliament was attacked, on 13 December 2001, probably by members of a banned Pakistani militant group. For most of 2002, the armed forces of the two countries remained in a state of high alert. There were, however, good reasons that prevented this tension from escalating into even a limited war.

Some of these reasons are well known: the risk of nuclear conflagration was one. Because of that, third parties were primed to restrain the two sides before they went over the brink. Another, perhaps the more potent, constraint is less known. An all-out conventional war between the two countries was very likely to end in a stalemate. Since countries do not normally start wars without a reasonable chance of achieving a strategic objective, during the last three decades India and Pakistan have not taken their conflicts beyond building up their military presence on the borders and conducting skirmishes across the LOC.

India could still have initiated a war during 2002, either in frustration or in the belief that the US presence in the area would deny Pakistan its nuclear option. There were other implications to be worried about. With no constraints now on Pakistan's support to the insurgency in Kashmir, the Kashmir situation could become more intense and durable. More importantly, if the war did end without causing major damage to Pakistan, it would deprive India of a potent card that it had so far used to good effect: the threat of war.

Even though Pakistan has a reasonable chance of preventing India from achieving a decisive military victory, it is still sensitive to Indian war threats. Being the smaller country, its economic activity is more vulnerable to warlike tensions. After 30 years of high economic growth, it experienced its worst recession during the 1990s. Now that some recovery looked possible, significantly as an important ally of the United States, tension with India was an unwelcome development. Paradoxically, when the drums of war receded, both countries found that their threat cards had been played perhaps for the last time.

Indeed, Pakistan, too, had time and again threatened that, if India did not agree to settle the Kashmir problem, the region could blow up in a nuclear holocaust. In the absence of any desperate resolve in Pakistan to back up these threats, this card was fast losing its effectiveness. I believe that in 2002 India's threat of a conventional war, too, had run its course. Now that the two countries had manoeuvred each other into a deadlock, it was time to revive their on-again off-again peace process. The 2004 South Asian Association of Regional Cooperation (SAARC) Summit in Islamabad seemed to be the right moment. Before that, the stumbling blocks that had caused the failure at Agra had to be removed.

The very fact that the framework evolved in 1997 had survived nuclear tests, the Kargil episode, a military coup, 9/11 and the stand-off of 2002 proves that it was wisely conceived. One of its best features is that it can accommodate preferences of both the parties, and it can prevent concerns, even serious ones like Kashmir, from scuttling the process. In Agra this capacity was not used when the two sides insisted that their respective interests be recognized as '*the* core issue', namely Kashmir for Pakistan and cross-border infiltration for India. To resolve this conflict in the spirit of the original concept, all that was needed was to make both concerns part of the process.

Two extracts from the joint press statement of 6 January after the Indian Prime Minister Vajpaee had met General Musharraf to seal the agreement (Pakistan–India Joint Statement 2004) show how smoothly it could be done:

> President Musharraf 'reassured' Prime Minister Vajpaee that he would not permit 'territory under Pakistan's control' to be used to support terrorism in any manner.

> The two leaders are confident that the resumption of composite dialogue will lead to peaceful settlement of all bilateral issues, including Jammu & Kashmir, to the satisfaction of both sides. (Pakistan–India Joint Statement 2004)

Launching of the Process

The plan was now perfect, but to start the process some movement had to take place on the ground; for example, a round of meetings on mundane issues to show a good beginning. It had, however, been the thinking in some quarters that a gesture on Kashmir, even a symbolic one, might be the best way to kickstart the process. Kashmir after all was not only the 'core issue' for Pakistan but also a 'multi-corps' problem for India (having sucked in hundreds of thousands of Indian troops).

The gesture had to meet some essential criteria: it should be without prejudice to the declared Kashmir policies of India and Pakistan; it had to provide some hope that a resolution of the dispute was seriously sought; and it needed to sufficiently engage the Kashmiris to let the two countries work on their less intractable issues. A meeting of the Kashmiri leadership on both sides of the divide seemed to meet these criteria adequately. Ultimately it was decided to start a bus service between the two parts of Kashmir on 7 April 2005. The idea must have been that not only the leaders but also the divided families could be brought together. The bus was also bound to make a bigger and better all-round impact than meetings of a few individuals, who in any case were not expected to show immediate results. There was, however, a risk involved: if the odd bus was blown up by any of the many detractors of the peace process, at this nascent stage the peace process could suffer a serious setback.

Is it Sustainable?

Now that the bus has started running, fortunately without any untoward incident, and more buses are expected to follow, even if the odd one gets hit the process is likely to continue. There are a number of factors that support the present optimistic prognosis that the peace process is now 'irreversible'. Scepticism in Pakistan over the process is fairly broadly based, and of course there are a good number who oppose it. One also cannot ignore the proven ability of the Indian Ministry of External Affairs (the infamous 'South Block') to scuttle the process. The overwhelming sentiment in the region, however, remains supportive. The popular wave may not yet have taken over the process, but, backed by the business interests and because of our prolonged 'tension fatigue', it is likely to resist its reversal. A few caveats are still in order.

The design logic of the peace process is, rightly, based on the resolution of issues taking their natural course; a pace that is essentially slow, more so when we consider our poor track record and cautious bureaucratic cultures. Neither our peoples nor the political leadership are known for the patience needed to keep faith in a process that does not show tangible results on a regular basis. For a while it may be possible to keep them in good humour with political declarations and cultural exchanges, but very soon they will demand increased economic and trade benefits that we are not likely to accrue any time soon. I also have no idea how long we might take to resolve, if at all, our ever-worsening water disputes.

And indeed there is always the threat of sabotage, not only by the militants, who would find periods of no progress propitious for their activity, but also from any other quarters not in favour of India–Pakistan rapprochement. Some very brave statements have been made in the two capitals that acts of terror will not derail the process. There are reasons to believe that the leadership of both sides understand that the handle over peace should not be yielded to its detractors; however, some well-planned and well-timed acts of sabotage may set the process back.

Then there is the explosive issue of Kashmir. Though deftly handled lately, it will continue to need delicate care and patient treatment. Even if the two sides abide by the spirit of the 'composite dialogue', there may be problems. Pakistanis, for example, may become impatient because the 'favourable environment' that is supposed to help resolve the issue is taking too long to deliver results. Indians, on the other hand, might start getting nervous when the Muslim majority from their part of Kashmir finds greater affinity with their co-religionists in Pakistan.

The shape of the final settlement in Jammu and Kashmir, India and Pakistan have agreed, will emerge when the two countries have established friendlier relations. Though this is a wise decision, how the two would react if they suspected that the new trends in Kashmir were not compatible with their desires would be the 'acid test' of their commitment to the peace process.

These and many other difficulties and deficiencies notwithstanding, I believe that the peace process is sustainable. There will certainly be hiccups, interruptions, even setbacks. But, as in the last eight years, and that was only our learning period, we are not likely to abandon the path. The expected peace dividends, some of them already manifest though admittedly only in the psychological domain, will also prod us to keep at it. The other SAARC countries, which have blamed both India and Pakistan for the region not keeping pace with the rest of the world, also have a vested interest in the process, and China is now a new stakeholder.

THE ROLE OF CHINA

When the People's Republic of China was proclaimed on 1 October 1949, India and Pakistan were among the first countries to recognize it. During the first decade, until 1959, China's relations with India were exceptionally friendly. In the case of Pakistan, these relations were formally 'correct' because Pakistan had joined the Western military pacts in 1954 (Bhatty 1999, p. 16). Differences over Tibet and a border clash in 1962 badly strained Sino-Indian ties, a development that Pakistan exploited to its advantage, especially during and after its own war with India in 1965. In 1971 Pakistan facilitated a link between the United States and China that proved very useful to all three countries, especially to China whose relations with its ideological and strategic mentor, the Soviet Union, had collapsed.

China, however, is too big a country with too wise a people not to leave room for policy adjustments. The Chinese leadership was aware that, with its rising power, it would have to make many adjustments. During the Soviet occupation of Afghanistan, for example, it condemned the invasion and supported all efforts to end it, but without any apparent hostility towards Moscow or interrupting work on the construction of the Urumqi–Siberia railroad. Similarly, while playing the role of a low-profile balancer for India's smaller neighbours, it closed no door for a rapprochement with its big southern neighbour. According to Sawaran Singh (Ghulam Ali 2005), China played an important role in preserving Nepal's identity as a sovereign state, helped contain Indian influence in Nepal's internal affairs and promoted Nepali–Tibetan interdependence. In return, Nepal prevented any hostile activity against China from its soil. Singh's opinion on Sino-Bangladeshi relations, too, is widely accepted: 'Beijing has greatly facilitated Dhaka's assertions in recent years' (Ghulam Ali 2005), a process helped by improving Sino-Indian relations.

Some China watchers in the subcontinent, like Singh (in Ghulam Ali 2005) and Moonis Ahmar (2004, p. 40) believe that Sino-Indian relations were already on the mend when Rajiv Gandhi, the Indian prime minister, visited China in 1988. This is possible, but the visible turnaround came only after the end of the Cold War. The shift in US policy towards India and Pakistan was probably the main reason.

Post-Cold War

Bhatty (1999, p. 17) argues that Huntington's thesis about the 'clash of civilizations' (namely, that Confucian and Islamic civilizations are the main threat to the West) being a major influence on Chinese thinking has not yet been proven. The evidence for this is questionable. For example, when US policy tilted towards India and away from Pakistan after the collapse of the Soviet Union, China too stepped up its efforts to improve relations with India. The Chinese could not possibly replace the Soviets as India's major strategic partner, but they could at least prevent the formation of a powerful, potentially hostile, bloc in its neighbourhood.

China and India signed two border agreements, in 1993 and 1996, aimed at 'maintaining peace and tranquillity' and 'confidence building' along their line of actual control. The concept, later to be known as 'the Chinese Model', was to freeze bilateral conflicts till the atmosphere became right for a final settlement (Moonis Ahmar 2004, p. 40). China has often advised its close friend, Pakistan, to resolve the Kashmir problem bilaterally with India, and indeed the 'composite dialogue' formula may well have been inspired by the Chinese model. The last thing that China wanted was the United States to assume a role in Kashmir, an area uncomfortably close to its sensitive Xinjiang and Tibet regions. The eternal strife between its two nuclear-armed southern neighbours could have landed the Americans such a role. In the meantime, not India and Pakistan but some other factors have brought the United States uncomfortably close to Chinese borders.

I do not believe that the new great game in Central Asia is only, or even mainly, about oil and gas pipelines. But the initial interest of the United States in being a player in the area, when it was liberated from Moscow's formal control, was because of its huge hydrocarbon deposits. According to one estimate, by 2050 Central Asia could account for 80 per cent of the United States' oil supply (Zaman 2004, p. 85).

During the Clinton administration its Russo-centric Deputy Secretary of State, Strobe Talbott, was the leading advocate of 'playing the game together'; in other words, with the Russians. The United States was content with letting the multinationals ensure supply, if possible keeping countries like Iran out of the loop, without physically controlling the source. With Bush as president since 2001, a whole range of oil men and women, including Bush, Vice-President Cheney and (now) Secretary of State Rice, came to power. The policy towards the region became more aggressive owing to 'tempting prospects for energy development' (Zaman 2004, p. 87). The invasion of Afghanistan, duly sanctioned by the UN Security Council after the 9/11 attacks in New York and Washington, provided the United States with the opportunity it needed to establish military bases in Central Asia.

Two of these bases, Manas in Kyrgyzstan and Kulyab in Tajikistan, cause concern to China, especially because the developments there clearly indicate that the United States is present for the long haul. With the inauguration, in October 2003, of a Russian air base in Kant near Bishkek (Zaman 2004, p. 94), the situation became even more complex. It raised serious doubts about the future of the Shanghai Cooperation Organisation (SCO), which was created in 1995 at the initiative of China, with Russia, Kazakhstan, Kyrghistan, Tajikistan and (in 2001) Uzbekistan as its other members. Its original purpose – combating terrorism and Islamic extremism in Central, West and South Asian regions (Moonis Ahmar 2004, p. 44) – was now unlikely to be achieved except to the extent that it served US designs.

Most contemporary Sinologists do not attribute the thaw in China–India relations during the last decade and a half to any deliberate Chinese attempt to pre-empt a possible US-led encirclement. Pramit Mitra and Drew Thompson at the Centre of Strategic and International Studies in Washington believe that 'the real motivator ... is trade and commerce' (Mitra and Thompson 2005, p. 30). By a strange coincidence though, just when this warming-up period was reaching its culmination with Premier Wen Jiabo's visit to India in April 2005, another sensitive Chinese flank, the eastern one, erupted with suspected US encouragement.

On 14 April 2005 the BBC reported that Tokyo's decision to issue drilling rights in a disputed area of the East China Sea was for Beijing a 'serious provocation'. The Japanese foreign minister, however, signalled that he would take a 'tough line' in the ensuing talks with China. In the same news item, it was reported that there were violent protests in China over Japanese textbooks which critics said played down Japan's wartime brutality. The protests were also directed at Tokyo's bid for a permanent UN Security Council seat. *The Economist* of London, in its 13 April issue confirmed these developments.

In the historical context, irritants like these may not be entirely unexpected, even decisive, considering that in the meantime China has replaced the United States as the biggest export market for Japan (Raja Mohan 2005a). China will indeed not let this development, or for that matter renewed acrimony over the Taiwan question, distract it from the pursuit of economic development and regional stability. But it will certainly remain quietly engaged with the strategic environment in its own 'near abroad'.

China's regional environment can be summed up as follows. The US military presence in Central Asia seriously limits China's policy options in the area and its access to the region's mineral resources, in which China had invested. The recent commotion in Sino-Japanese relations will subside, but China cannot ignore the fact that Japan's defence budget is, in the meantime, the world's second largest, and the country may well have an active nuclear program. Given that China's three important eastern neighbours – Japan, Taiwan and South Korea – are allies of the United States, her 'East Policy' will continue to be containment through economic engagement. The real strategic space for China exists only in the south. The ASEAN countries will remain important economic partners and keep the sea lanes open for Chinese trade. But China's best bet to prevent the region from falling under US hegemony is its old and new friends on the subcontinent.

Of course it will not be easy. China's oldest and to date most dependable friend, Pakistan, has a US military presence on or close to its territory. India, with real political and economic potential to serve as a strategic partner, is itself being wooed by the world's sole surviving superpower, which can offer better terms in almost all fields: investments, technology and weaponry. Bangladesh is swamped by Western NGOs. Even in Nepal the United States is backing the fight against Maoist insurgency (Muni 2004, p. 87). But China still has a real chance to protect its interests in South Asia.

To start with, Pakistan will not support any policy directed against China's interests. The public sentiment is strongly pro-China and very anti-American. The United States is content with whatever help it can get against Al Qaeda, and is unlikely to suggest that Pakistan change its China policy, or for that matter pursue its desire that India and Pakistan give up plans to construct a pipeline from Iran.

How India, the lynchpin of China's sub-continental strategy, will shape its own China policy became apparent after the recent visit of the Chinese premier. For all practical purposes, the two countries have accepted the status quo on Tibet and Sikkim; they have frozen other boundary disputes; both being so heavily dependent on the import of oil and gas, they have also undertaken to cooperate on energy security and indeed to continue their rapidly expanding bilateral trade, which stood at US$13 billion in 2004 (Mitra and Thomson 2005). India is the only country with a favourable trade balance with China.

The assessment of the Chinese premier's visit to India in April 2005 by some experts is of great interest. According to Mitra and Thompson (2005, p. 33), 'Both India and China share the aspiration of a world order that is multi-polar and takes greater account of their role.' The authors also wonder whether India and China, individually or by mutual agreement, will spoil Washington's efforts to impose a pax Americana and isolate rogue regimes like Iran and Sudan because of their dependence on the import of energy from these countries. Joseph Nye, on the other hand, suggests that 'while both the US and India seek trade and good relations with India, both are wary of China's growing strength and should therefore improve their strategic relationship' (Nye 2005, p. A7).

Raja Mohan, formerly of Jawaharlal Nehru University, is of the opinion that after the visit by the Chinese premier there was a real chance that China and India would restore their historic cross-border routes and develop their frontier regions (Raja Mohan 2005b). It is Gwynne Dyer, however, who might have captured the zeitgeist. He posits that India and China have not fallen for the neo-con game plan and if India were to do so, it would destroy the fragile hopes of reconciliation with Pakistan (Dyer 2005, p. A8).

CONCLUSION

India values its ties with the United States and will seek to strengthen them. But it knows that it is the cross-Himalayan relationship that will bring durable benefits. The lesson from the days of a bipolar world divided between Russia and the United States is that India can have beneficial relations with more than one superpower. Now an emerging economic power in its own right, India can draw on this Cold War experience in handling both China and the United States. The same tactics will be quite helpful while dealing with China and the United States. In the process, if the regional environment can be improved, including relations with Pakistan, so much the better.

China can live with this Indian policy and believes that in the long term it stands to gain more than the United States, since the latter would be constrained by geography. China also benefits if the two largest and most powerful South Asian powers, India and Pakistan, keep their peace. That would deny the United States any excuse to intervene, and it might help revive an almost forgotten Sino-Indian-centric concept of a 'Southern Asia'. When this was first propounded nearly a decade ago, Pakistan remained unmoved, owing to its less than friendly relations with India. It may respond differently in the future.

For Pakistan, too, the overall environment is not unfavourable. It continues to be the United States' major non-NATO ally; its special relationship with China, though diluted, is still helpful; and it is set to gain from peace with India.

NOTE

1. The Lahore Declaration was released by the Indian Ministry of External Affairs on 21 February, 1999, www.nyu.edu/globalbeat/southasia/Lahore022299.html

REFERENCES

Bhatty, Maqbool Ahmed (1999), 'Pakistan's security and Sino-Pakistan relations', *Journal of the National Defence College*, Islamabad.

Dyer, Gwynne (2005), 'India and China are not falling for the neo-con game plan', *The Jordan Times*, reprinted in the *Daily Times*, Lahore, 15 April.

Ghulam Ali (2005), review of Singh, Sawaran (2003), *China–South Asia: Issues, Equations, Politics*, New Delhi: Lancer's Book, in *IPRI Journal* (Islamabad Policy Research Institute), V (1), http://ipripak.org/journal/winter2005/bookreview2. shtml accessed June 2005.

'India, Pak firm on ending hostile propaganda' (1997), *The Hindu*, 24 June.

Mitra, Pramit and Drew Thomson (2005), 'China and India: Rivals or Partners', *Far Eastern Economic Review*, 168 (4), 30–33.

Moonis Ahmar (2004), 'Pakistan, India, China triangle', *Margalla Papers*, National Defence College, Islamabad, 36–46.

Muni, S.D. (2004), *September 11: The Asian Giants Get Closer, Regional Security in Asia Pacific*, Bodmin, Cornwall: MPG Books.

Nye, Joseph (2005), 'An India–China axis?' *Daily Times*, Lahore, 17 April, www. dailytimes.com.pk/default.asp?page=story_17-4-2005_pg3_6, accessed June 2005.

Pakistan–India Joint Statement, 6 January 2004, www.un.int/pakistan/140104, accessed June 2005.

Raja Mohan, C. (2005a), 'India won't let Chinese shadow darken Koizumi visit', *Indian Express*, 27 April, www.indianexpress.com/archive_frame.php, accessed June 2005.

Raja Mohan, C. (2005b) 'From peace to Sino-Indian prosperity', *Daily Times*, 11 April, http://www.dailytimes.com.pk/default.asp?page=story_11-4-2005_pg3_5, accessed June 2005.

The Economist (London) (2005), 'Japan and its neighbours', 13 April, www.economist. com/agenda/displaystory.cfm?story_id=E1_PRVGGNP, accessed June 2005.

Zaman, Aly (2004), 'The American military presence in South Asia: motives and implications', *IPRI Journal*, 4 (2), Islamabad Policy Research Institute, http:// ipripak.org/journal/summer2004/theamerican.shtml, accessed June 2005.

10. South-east Asia's counter-terrorism dilemma

David Wright-Neville

A defining feature of the post-9/11 world has been counter-terrorism's emergence as an organizing principle of international politics (Steinberg 2002). Although not all states attach as much importance to fighting terrorism as the Bush administration does, under pressure from Washington and its allies and prodded by the United Nations there are very few states that have not been forced to make some adjustments to domestic and foreign policy structures to take account of the spread of terrorist networks.

In South-east Asia the quality and intensity of such counter-terrorism policies have been mixed. In a positive sense, the region has witnessed some important improvements in the regional states' ability to monitor and interrupt terrorist activity within their own borders, while at the same time enhancing bilateral counter-terrorism cooperation with their neighbours. However, both unilateral and bilateral initiatives have had to build from a low base and therefore there is still much that needs to be done. Moreover, the positive benefits generated by such initiatives have often been outweighed by a combination of domestic policy decisions of dubious quality as well as lingering intra-regional rivalries that militate against the establishment of a more effective counter-terrorism regime within South-east Asia.

At the domestic level, countries with long-running domestic insurgencies, such as Indonesia, the Philippines and Thailand, have struggled to balance the authoritarian implications of stronger counter-terrorism legislation against a desire to nurture their comparatively new and fragile democracies. Some governments, such as those of Indonesia and the Philippines, have managed this balance better than others. In countries such as Malaysia and Thailand the effectiveness of some counter-terrorism initiatives have been undermined by an instinctive urge by the state to capitalize on the fear of terrorism by paring back civil liberties and further limiting the scope for peaceful opposition to the government. Meanwhile, in other South-east Asian states, most notably the newer members of the Association of South East Asian Nations (ASEAN) such as Cambodia, Laos, Myanmar and Vietnam, terrorism still tends to be seen as a phenomenon only remotely connected to their own national interests. As a result, these states have committed themselves to a minimum level of policy adjustment, doing only what they have to in order to avoid the opprobrium of some of their neighbours or, more menacingly, the United States.

At the foreign policy level, the sudden significance of terrorism has provided ASEAN (as a group) with a fresh issue with which to try and revive the organization's waning importance. However, as will be discussed more fully below, the lack of enthusiasm displayed by newer members means that grandiose schemes for the development of initiatives such as a Concert of South-east Asian Powers (Ferguson 2004; Smith 2004) are unlikely to make the transition from rhetoric to reality. At the same time, the anticipated strategic impotence of ASEAN has rejuvenated US interest and prompted Washington to invest new energy into consolidating its bilateral relationships with the countries of the region. In particular, there has been a boost in the importance attached by US military and intelligence planners to Washington's relationship with Singapore – a long-time (albeit low-profile) supporter of a strong US military presence in the region. The establishment of deeper bilateral intelligence and security relationships with which to combat the threat posed by terrorism to the United States' global interests has even seen a revival of Washington's troubled relationships with Manila and Kuala Lumpur. In the latter case, the 2003 retirement of the irascible Malaysian Prime Minister Dr Mahathir Mohamad has helped smooth the process.

However, the impact of the 'war on terror' in South-east Asia, considered by some as a key battleground against international terrorism, has been ambiguous. Indeed, my argument in this chapter is that in the post-9/11 period, but especially since the tragedy of the 2002 Bali bombings and subsequent attacks in Indonesia, Thailand and the Philippines, regional counter-terrorism dynamics have entered a holding pattern. Hence, while it is true, as Tan and Ramakrishna (2004) point out, that counter-terrorism cooperation between regional states has improved (as borne out by the capture of senior terrorist leaders and the thwarting of several terrorist attacks) (del Puerto 2005), measured against the speed with which terrorist networks are spreading this cooperation remains at a dangerously embryonic level. Particularly problematic is the failure by South-east Asian states to calibrate their domestic and foreign counter-terrorism policies. For instance, while valuable in its own right, closer cooperation between Thailand and some of its ASEAN neighbours is unlikely to generate the returns needed to counter the increased threat of terrorism caused by the recent escalation of separatist tensions in southern Thailand. In other words, the benefits in countering terrorism that have accrued from closer regional counter-terrorism cooperation in the region are less than the costs measured in terms of the support generated for terrorist networks by poorly designed and implemented domestic policies.

In sum, isolated counter-terrorism successes aside, there is little prospect that intra-ASEAN cooperation will stymie the longer-term evolution and consolidation of regional terrorist networks. At the core of this atrophy is the resilience of concepts such as 'non-interference' which rest on an archaic notion of sovereignty that provides protection for individual governments from wider criticism and allows them to disregard the regional (and global) consequences for terrorism that flow from their own domestic insurgencies.

THE 'WAR ON TERROR' IN SOUTH-EAST ASIA

The types of non-conventional conflict that provide an environment within which terrorist networks thrive are especially evident in simmering violence in various Indonesian provinces, in the recent upsurge in violence in Muslim majority provinces in southern Thailand (Liow 2004a), and in the escalation of hostilities in the southern Philippines (Gloria 2005). Especially ominous is the ease with which terrorists appear to be internationalizing these once parochial conflicts (Liow 2004a; Liow 2004b; Fullbrook 2004; Davis 2002a).

At the same time, the lack of confidence that outside players such as Washington and Canberra have in South-east Asian states' ability to deal collectively with the spread of terrorist networks is implicit in their clear preference for bilateral cooperation with individual ASEAN members. In fact, a striking feature of the contemporary South-east Asian security landscape is the extent to which bilateral, or occasionally trilateral, initiatives involving the United States or Australia and one or two South-east Asian states have begun to spread across the region.

Recognition of the sensitivity of bilateral security cooperation partly explains the low-profile manner in which Washington has pursued most of its post-9/11 counter-terrorism initiatives in South-east Asia. Despite the region being seen in some US policy circles as among the world's most dangerous areas in terms of potential terrorist violence, Washington's approach to South-east Asia has been of a lower key than in other parts of the world. A brief military foray into the southern Philippines island of Basilan in early 2002 notwithstanding, Washington's preferred strategy has been to deepen bilateral cooperation with individual South-east Asian states through extensive transfers of financial, technical and military counter-terrorism assistance, while at the same time offering only rhetorical support for ASEAN's efforts in this area.

There is no doubt that for the Bush administration, as distinct from US intelligence and security circles, this emphasis on a bilateral strategy is yielding significant results. In a 2005 speech at the National Defense University, President Bush praised the work of several Asian allies:

We're more secure because Pakistani forces captured more than one hundred extremists across the country last year, including operatives who were plotting attacks against the United States ... We're more secure because the Philippines' new Anti-Terrorism Task Force has helped capture more than a dozen terrorist suspects – including seven members of al Qaeda and affiliated networks. (The White House 2005)

However, in the current environment where highly mobile groups of terrorists are evincing a greater capacity to involve themselves in parochial conflicts and inject into them a broader set of international grievances, it is far from clear that the strategy of compartmentalizing terrorist groups according to their dominant national status will produce viable long-term results. Indeed, absent from the up-beat prognoses offered on progress in the 'war on terror' from the Bush administration and its South-east Asian allies are any clues as to why, after almost five years of this strategy, new threats against local and Western targets in the region have continued to emerge. In a similar vein, we need to ask how the personnel gaps in groups such as Jemaah Islamiyah and the Abu Sayyaf Group (ASG) left by successful counter-terrorism operations have been filled easily through the promotion of younger but equally capable cadres drawn from across the region.

In short, in South-east Asia, as in much of the rest of the world, the effort to counter terrorism appears to have entered a holding pattern. This pattern includes a tendency to look at counter-terrorism overwhelmingly through a policing and paramilitary lens, seeing terrorism as essentially a security phenomenon and not the result of a more complex mixture of social, cultural and political forces. As a result, in conjunction with their South-east Asian partners, the major Western players (namely the United States and Australia) continue to focus overwhelmingly on the symptoms rather than the causes of the spread of terrorist violence. Hence, belying the ebullient puffery surrounding isolated victories such as the arrest of Jemaah Islamiyah's chief of operations Hambali, are a worrying set of developments including a suicide bombing outside Australia's Jakarta embassy, a dramatic escalation in the number of attacks against government and civilian targets in southern Thailand, the reconsolidation of the ASG and an extension of its capacity to strike outside the southern Philippine provinces and into Manila, and credible information pointing to the ability of different factions within Jemaah Islamiyah to circumvent counter-terrorism operations by reorganizing their order of battle and other operational protocols (International Crisis Group 2003).

In brief, without a reconsideration and recalibration of counter-terrorism policies – in a unilateral, bilateral and multilateral sense – terrorism risks becoming a more permanent and deadly feature of the South-east Asian regional landscape.

PROBLEMS AT THE LEVEL OF DOMESTIC POLITICS

Indonesia

Especially noteworthy in the South-east Asian context has been the revival of Washington's interest in the political machinations in Jakarta – a renewed focus that at the level of public diplomacy has been made easier by the consolidation of post-Suharto democratic institutions. However, despite Indonesia's impressive strides away from the excesses of the Suharto period, key elements of the political apparatus remain anchored in a culture hostile to the principles of democratic accountability and transparency. Especially evident in this regard has been the Indonesian military, which despite its retreat from an overt political role, retains many of the belligerent anti-democratic instincts that defined its character during Suharto's New Order (International Crisis Group 2004, pp. 13–16).

The renewed interest in the bilateral relationship with Jakarta reflects a decision made in Washington that Indonesia is critical to combating Jemaah Islamiyah and its different factions, which taken together constitute what at present is the only genuine Pan Malay terrorist network, stretching from the Philippines through Indonesia and Malaysia into southern Thailand. Although there is a tendency in some quarters to downplay the parochial interests that motivate the network's constituent parts, to exaggerate its overall cohesion and to overplay the significance of its links to Al Qaeda, it is generally agreed that a handful of Indonesians have and continue to play a critical coordinating role. Add to this the sheer demographic size and diversity of Indonesia's Muslim population, as well as the archipelago's numerous insurgencies and secessionist troubles, and it is not surprising that Jakarta now attracts so much attention from the Bush administration.

Although the burst of Indonesian legislative and operational activity unleashed by the terrorist attacks in Bali on 12 October 2002 suggested that Jakarta had been shaken from its lethargy and embraced the importance of bilateral counter-terrorism cooperation, both President Yudhoyono and his predecessor Megawati Sukarnoputri have struggled to balance a genuine desire to cooperate with Washington against widespread anti-US sentiment within the country (Smith 2005; Pew Research Centre 2005, Chapter 7). The resilience of a public mood hostile to the United States (and to a lesser degree Australia) has resulted in a counter-terrorism agenda that is evolving in fits and starts; periods of political atrophy are punctuated by frenetic but poorly targeted counter-terrorist activity in the period immediately after attacks such as those launched against Jakarta's Marriott Hotel and the Australian embassy. The problem with this type of policymaking is that productive bursts of bureaucratic energy are prone to dissipate rapidly once political interest fades or once extraneous political developments render tough policy decisions electorally difficult. This problem has been especially evident in the erratic way that Jakarta has dealt with Jemaah Islamiyah, the existence of which Jakarta still refuses to formally acknowledge, as well as Abu Bakar Ba'asyir, a Islamist cleric who the weight of evidence suggests held a senior leadership position in Jemaah Islamiyah in the period before and immediately after the attacks in Bali (Smith 2005; Bonner 2005).

Malaysia

As part of its wider counter-terrorism strategy in the region, Washington has also moved to put relations with Indonesia's neighbours on a new diplomatic footing. In the case of Malaysia it moved quickly to overcome irritations associated with the tenure of former Prime Minister Mahathir Mohamad and enhanced cooperation with the new administration of Abdullah Badawi. Until 9/11, Mahathir was regarded in Washington policy circles as a distant curiosity, an ageing autocrat whose self-image as the Third World's premier statesman was a reflection of a deluded sense of self-importance rather than an international political reality. The difficulties in dealing with Mahathir, especially his instinctive urge to turn Washington's overtures in the months after 9/11 to his own domestic political advantage, complicated early efforts to build a workable bilateral counter-terrorism relationship despite significant US gestures designed to satisfy Mahathir's ego – such as a decision to locate a US-funded regional counter-terrorism centre in Kuala Lumpur. Needless to say, few in Washington lamented Mahathir's retirement in late 2002 and since then bilateral counter-terrorism cooperation with Kuala Lumpur has improved significantly.

Even so, the assumption that Mahathir's departure would result in the rapid development of a trouble-free bilateral counter-terrorism relationship with Kuala Lumpur proved naive. During his long tenure as prime minister, Mahathir worked assiduously to cultivate a political culture modelled on his own idiosyncratic interpretation of international politics. After more than two decades as Malaysia's political leader, Mahathir's world view had struck deep roots within the Malaysian bureaucracy, and the United States is therefore still seen in many circles as a quasi-imperialistic power. To this end initiatives such as joint US–South-east Asian patrols of the strategically important Straits of Malacca, where container ships carrying oil are considered especially vulnerable to sea-based terrorist attacks, have foundered on regional objections engineered and fanned by Kuala Lumpur. (For a brief discussion of the limited military cooperation between Malaysia, Singapore and Indonesia that supplements US involvement, see Ali and Chen 2004.) To appease the Malaysian government and avoid prodding it towards a resumption of Mahathir's anti-American belligerence, Washington has deliberately downplayed criticisms of the Malaysian government's use of the terrorism issue to demonize its opposition and silence critics through its iron-fisted Internal Security Act. Yet while this might have temporarily placated some senior Malaysian officials, it has done little to improve Washington's image among ordinary Malaysians, many of whom take little notice of such nuanced diplomatic gestures but have been angered by the invasion of Iraq and what are perceived as other anti-Muslim actions, such as unwavering support for Israel and sabre-rattling against Iran and Syria.

The Philippines

During the early post-9/11 period Washington also seemed to have overcome its decade-long disappointment with Manila's decision in the early 1990s not to renew the US military's access leases on Clarke airfield and Subic Bay naval base. Indeed, in partnership with the Armed Forces of the Philippines the US military's first counter-terrorism deployment outside Afghanistan was to the southern Philippine island of Basilan, where ASG terrorists were holding two American missionaries among a group kidnapped from a hotel on the resort island of Palawan. Soon after this joint exercise, President Arroyo travelled to Washington with an extensive counter-terrorism wish list, which included an extensive array of new military hardware that Manila argued was necessary to enhance its ability to deal with groups such as the ASG.

However, Washington's eagerness to develop the bilateral counter-terrorism relationship was tempered by lingering suspicions about Manila's capacity to manage a high volume of expensive and complex equipment without it falling victim to corruption and inefficiencies within the Philippines security sector. Consequently, Washington balked at a unilateral transfer; its preference was for an arrangement whereby the US Pacific Command would play a major role in deciding the nature of counter-terrorism operations and the manner in which military assistance would be used.

In essence, Washington's proposal was for joint operations. However, a first step in this direction in the form of a more ambitious follow-up to the Basilan experiment was abandoned after public opposition and infighting among Manila's political elite. Soon after, intra-service rivalries within the armed forces contributed to a botched rescue attempt in which one of the US citizens held by the Abu Sayyaf Group was killed in crossfire (Gloria 2002). Since then, Washington has evinced little interest in the idea of joint operations. Instead, it has offered limited military and intelligence assistance to Manila and hoped for the best. However, with evidence emerging that the Jemaah Islamiyah and other groups, possibly linked to Al

Qaeda, have continued to consolidate a presence in the southern Philippines, a fresh attempt to forge an agreement that allows for a US military presence on the ground is not out of the question.

Thailand

Washington's relationship with Thailand has proven less complicated, partly because of a lower level of public hostility towards the United States and partly because the spread of terrorist violence in the south of the country has created widespread public support for Prime Minister Thaksin's efforts to build a deeper bilateral counter-terrorism relationship with Washington. Indeed, in August 2003 the United States had its most significant counter-terrorism success in partnership with Thailand when the intelligence and security services of both countries combined to capture Hambali.

However, this counter-terrorism success story occurred against the steady erosion of political freedoms by the government of Thaksin Shinawata (Human Rights Watch 2005). The government's belligerent disregard for the sensitivities of Thailand's Muslim minority appears to have set back a reconciliation process which from the 1980s until Thaksin's election in 2001 had all but addressed the alienation that had hitherto been the basis for support for secessionist groups such as the Pattani United Liberation Organisation (PULO) and Gerakan Mujahideen Islam Pattani (GMIP), the latter group having links to both al Qaeda and Jemaah Islamiyah (Davis 2002b). In fact, by the late 1990s PULO and its counterparts had lost their political character and degenerated into little more than organized crime gangs involved in drug smuggling and extortion rackets. It is for this reason that new groups, such as the GMIP, might have captured the political credibility that was once enjoyed by longer-standing secessionist organizations.

However, by 2002 there were signs that things were changing and that militant groups were recovering their momentum and were again poised to launch a credible insurgency. Since then, southern Thailand has seen large-scale rioting; systemic attacks against police stations, army garrisons, government offices and schools; and bombing attacks against bars and shopping malls, particularly in the provinces of Yala, Pattani, Narathiwat and Songkhla. Some of this might have been a response to the Thaksin government's use of extra-judicial killings to eliminate suspected drug traffickers, moves which undoubtedly impacted on and angered elements of Thailand's Muslim minority (Ganesan 2004).

The presence of powerful organized crime cartels and their links to one-time insurgents in southern Thailand necessarily complicates the counter-terrorism picture in this part of South-east Asia. Robbed progressively of the constituency that provided their early momentum, the political enthusiasm of even hardcore elements of separatist groups has gradually waned, and many have turned to organized crime. Their involvement in enterprises such as drug trafficking, illegal gambling and prostitution rings, blackmail and extortion is well documented. Responding to pressure from legitimate business interests in the south and eager to promote the image of a leader who is tough on crime, Thaksin's government has launched a concerted anti-crime campaign that has included a large number of extra-judicial disappearances and other initiatives of dubious merit. It is therefore possible that a significant degree of the violence that has occurred since 2002 is less terroristic than criminal in nature. That is to say, it is part of a campaign of retribution by organized crime syndicates, some of which may have links to PULO or any one of a number of other secessionist groups.

With an eye on the tourism industry, which has also had to deal with the devastating consequences of the Tsunami that struck the region in late 2004, the Thaksin government has been keen to blame crime gangs for much of the violence and to downplay the possibility that the area is witnessing a revival of the insurgency and a corresponding spread of terrorist violence. However, despite the confusion that still surrounds the issue, it seems likely that both crime gangs and terrorists are involved, perhaps on occasions operating in league with each other. Indeed, the involvement of former insurgents in crime cartels means that networks linking both groups already exist, and in the current atmosphere of general Muslim hostility towards Bangkok it is conceivable that such partnerships might have been consolidated.

Notable in this regard are rivalries between different elements of the Thai security apparatus and the ham-fisted manner in which Bangkok and its security forces have responded to even peaceful demonstrations by Muslim groups (Liow 2004a). The deaths of 85 men, 78 of whom suffocated while in detention following a demonstration in the town of Tak Bai in October 2004, is only the latest example of how the actions of the Thai authorities might be contributing to the revival of an attitudinal environment conducive to terrorist groups regaining the foothold they lost more than a decade ago (Levett 2004).

However, the possibility that the resurgence of violence in southern Thailand might have a criminal dimension is of no less concern. The types of social problems that breed crime can also foster terrorism. Accordingly, high unemployment, a growing law and order problem exacerbated rather than attenuated by the activities of the police and military, and a history where there are already cooperative links between violent secessionists and organized crime syndicates portends a dangerous future in which any terrorist network eager to tap into social anxieties could benefit from the operational networks and criminal links already enjoyed by the secessionists.

PROBLEMS AT THE MULTILATERAL LEVEL

Structural inadequacies at the multilateral level exist as a parallel obstacle to domestic problems in the establishment of a comprehensive counter-terrorism regime for South-east Asia as a whole. Specifically, the absence of a mature regional multilateral strategic framework capable of facilitating a proactive intelligence and security regime among South-east Asian states themselves threatens to seriously undermine counter-terrorism efforts in the region and, in so doing, will continue to impose substantial costs on outside powers such as the United States and Australia. These can be measured in terms of the financial costs and information gaps that are more likely to occur when there is an overwhelming reliance on bilateral rather than multilateral intelligence sharing and security cooperation. Indeed, the inability to forge closer cooperation between almost 30 separate regional intelligence and security agencies, each with core responsibilities in the area of counter-terrorism, looms as a major problem. The extent of the problem is made even clearer when we consider that many of these agencies are involved with inter-service rivalries even with national counterparts, let alone in their dealings across borders. Hence it is not surprising that ASEAN as an organization has achieved very little in this regard.

At a strategic level, ASEAN's strength has always rested in skills in the area of *conflict avoidance* rather than *conflict resolution*. Many of the internecine regional conflicts that threatened ASEAN's survival during its formative years remain largely unresolved (see for example Denoon and Colbert 1998–99; Henderson 1999), and, although issues such as overlapping maritime claims in the South China Sea, the Philippines' claim to Sabah and the treatment of respective Muslim and Chinese minorities no longer threaten ASEAN's existence, they do sustain subterranean intra-regional suspicions that militate against more open and productive exchanges on intelligence and security matters. For instance, ASEAN's failure to address and resolve these historically embedded rivalries militates against ASEAN states sharing with their neighbours any material that might inadvertently reveal the extent of both their human and signals intelligence capabilities. Not only would such revelations feed suspicions and stimulate inter-state antagonisms, but they would also risk an intelligence-related version of an arms race as different countries tried to steal a march on their neighbours.

There is nothing new in this suspicion – regular rhetorical commitments by ASEAN leaders to higher levels of multilateral security cooperation have almost always been tempered by recalcitrant intra-regional rivalries and suspicions. Indeed, the perpetuation of these suspicions is institutionally embedded in ASEAN's modus operandi, the dual principles of non-interference and consensus decision making, or the so-called 'ASEAN Way'. Calls to either eliminate or dilute these concepts to facilitate a more mature organizational culture have only succeeded in opening divisions and like the proposals mooted by Thailand's former foreign minister Dr Surin Pitsuwan in 1999, have fallen prey to the institutional atrophies they sought to redress ('Statement by His Excellency Dr Surin Pitsuwan' 1999). Hence, the very concepts that bring ASEAN members together lie at the core of the organization's failure to move forward on security issues in general and counter-terrorism in particular.

RECENT ASEAN SUMMITS: MUCH ADO ABOUT NOTHING

The pessimistic view of ASEAN's inability to deal with the threat posed by new forms of organized violence is not shared by all analysts. In particular, the ninth and tenth ASEAN Summits held respectively in Bali in 2003 and Vientiane in 2004 are seen by some as marking a concerted effort to rejuvenate the organization. They mark an important step on the road to a genuine security community that will adjust quickly to the threat posed by terrorist networks.

For regional optimists, the proclamation at the Bali Summit of ASEAN Concord II is especially important. The declaration charts a vision for the development of an integrated South-east Asian community through initiatives in the areas of security, economic and socio-cultural cooperation. As it relates to the specific field of security, Ferguson (2004) and Smith (2004) argue that ASEAN Concord II signifies a fresh determination by an expanded ASEAN to collectively address the security challenges posed by non-conventional threats such as terrorism and organized crime. However, Concord II also symbolizes ASEAN's attempts to deal with new economic challenges marked by the rise of China and India as competitors for both markets and investment capital, and new socio-cultural challenges in the form of the attitudinal consequences of globalization. Indeed, at first blush ASEAN Concord II, in its typically grandiose ASEAN-speak, contains a number of visionary statements that appear capable of removing the obstacles that have thus far impeded deeper levels of intelligence and security cooperation. Article 10 of the security portion of Concord II summarizes this vision in the following terms:

> The ASEAN Security Community shall fully utilize the existing institutions and mechanisms within ASEAN with a view to strengthening national and regional capacities to counter terrorism, drug trafficking, trafficking in persons and other transnational crimes; and shall work to ensure that the Southeast Asian Region remains free of all weapons of mass destruction. It shall enable ASEAN to demonstrate a greater capacity and responsibility of being the primary driving force of the ARF. (Association of South East Asian Nations 2003).

However, for a more nuanced appreciation of the significance of ASEAN Concord II for the dynamics of South-east Asian security, it is important that we look beneath the veneer of ASEAN speak. Article 10 contains the only reference to counter-terrorism cooperation in the entire document, and even then it lies buried within a more general discussion of transnational crime and other non-conventional security threats. The significance of counter-terrorism as an organizing principle for future South-east Asian security cooperation is further diluted by yet another affirmation of ASEAN's long-standing determination to rid South-east Asia of WMD, a principle that despite its obvious idealistic merits is nevertheless a relic of Cold War jostling in the region between external superpowers and the possibility that unilateral decisions by fellow ASEAN members to align themselves more closely with a major external power might impact on their own strategic well-being. To this extent ASEAN's stand on WMD, embodied formally in the Zone of Peace Freedom and Neutrality (ZOPFAN) agreement, reflected a desire by ASEAN members to use multilateral frameworks to regulate the behaviour of each other and through this influence the ability of external powers to shape regional politics. While this is consistent with middle and small power diplomacy more generally, and as such might conceivably provide the basis for the future development of a more comfortable set of regional norms, its repetition in Concord II points to the extent to which South-east Asian policymakers remain anchored in a Cold War mindset and still view security through a national rather than a regional lens.

More importantly, Concord II makes it clear that ASEAN's vision of a 'Concert of Southeast Asian Powers' must rest on its foundational principles of non-interference and the sanctity of domestic sovereignty – the very practices that have been used to stymie earlier similar visions. Indeed, it is possible to mount a credible argument that the principle of non-interference, especially the manner in which it has been used within intra-ASEAN diplomacy, is antithetical to the idea of a genuine security community. More immediately, however, the persistence of a jealous defence of national sovereignty will continue to deny ASEAN the institutional dexterity needed to adapt quickly and effectively to the threat posed by new security challenges, such as terrorism. Articles 2–4 of Concord II's vision of a Security Community evince clearly the resilience of these ASEAN core principles:

2. The ASEAN Security Community, recognizing the sovereign right of the member countries to pursue their individual foreign policies and defence arrangements and taking into account the strong interconnections among political, economic and social realities, subscribes to the principle of comprehensive security as having broad political, economic, social and cultural aspects in consonance with the ASEAN Vision 2020 rather than to a defence pact, military alliance or a joint foreign policy.

3. ASEAN shall continue to promote regional solidarity and cooperation. Member countries shall exercise their rights to lead their national existence free from outside interference in their internal affairs.
4. The ASEAN Security Community shall abide by the UN Charter and other principles of international law and uphold ASEAN's principles of non-interference, consensus-based decision-making, national and regional resilience, respect for national sovereignty, the renunciation of the threat or the use of force, and peaceful settlement of differences and disputes. (Association of South East Asian Nations 2003)

As Nicholas Khoo (2004) has pointed out, the security community vision as outlined in Concord II reflects very much the efforts of Indonesia to shape the regional environment in accordance with its own interpretation of South-east Asian and wider international political machinations. Indonesia's status as the largest member of the organization has conferred upon Jakarta a significant amount of influence within ASEAN, and the institutional atrophy that struck the organization in the late 1990s had as much to do with the national introversion that followed the fall of Suharto as it did with ASEAN's abject failure in the face of the regional economic crisis. The consolidation of a post-Suharto democracy in Indonesia has seen Jakarta re-emerge as an active player in South-east Asian regional diplomacy, but at the same time it has sought to shape regional security dynamics in accordance with its own national security concerns, especially as they relate to the numerous insurgencies that bedevil the archipelago. Hence, while Indonesia might find the ideal of a concert of South-east Asian powers an attractive intellectual construct, it seeks to balance this against its desire to minimize the capacity for external players to interfere in these domestic problems. However, as the problems posed by the spread of the Jemaah Islamiyah network from Indonesia into the rest of the region have shown, in the contemporary world it is becoming increasingly difficult to quarantine parochial disputes within the neatly demarcated borders of the nation state. To this end, there is an air of naive optimism about Concord II. ASEAN Concord II therefore is unlikely to develop into anything more than a blueprint for maintaining South-east Asia's strategic status quo. It reminds us that for most South-east Asian states the most significant threat to their security lurks not in the new generation of security challenges, but in the possibility that terrorism, crime or other phenomena might be used as an excuse to break the long-standing conventions of non-interference.

Looked at from this perspective, Concord II is a reaffirmation of a conventional notion of national political sovereignty in an era where global economic, political and social dynamics are rendering the concept increasingly redundant. Indonesia's support for Concord II evinces concerns about its territorial integrity in the wake of US (and Australian) support for the concept of pre-emptive warfare to counter (real or imagined) terrorist threats. This concern has been accentuated by the departure of East Timor and the loss of the islands of Sipadan and Ligitan to Malaysia after a ruling in 2002 by the International Court of Justice. In a similar vein, Bangkok's support for Concord II reflects its determination to deal with its respective secessionist problems in its own way and without the sort of critical comments from Malaysian politicians that followed the brutal repression of Muslim demonstrators in Tak Bai. Concord II also gives subtle voice to the concerns of some ASEAN members during Manila's 2002 decision to invite US military action against the Abu Sayyaf Group in Basilan, and it provides an institutional framework with which to chastise any member who might entertain such prospects in the future. In this sense ASEAN Concord II also provides an institutional framework for rejecting proposals such as that from the Commander of the US Navy's Pacific Command for joint US–ASEAN patrols of the Straits of Malacca referred to above. In a more general sense it also expresses the discomfort of a majority of states at the possibility that the unilateralist urges of the Bush administration – as expressed in the White House's belligerent disregard for international opinion over its invasion of Iraq – might one day see the United States entertain similar unilateralist action against suspected terrorist groups in South-east Asia. In short, ASEAN Concord II is little more than a rhetorical reminder that as an organization ASEAN continues to draw comfort from traditional notions of territorial sovereignty and political independence. Jones and Smith's (2002) observation that ASEAN has always operated 'primarily as a realist concert of powers, rather than a harmonious multilateral community' is especially apposite in the area of counter-terrorism cooperation.

CONCLUSION

Unfortunately, the ASEAN states' romantic attachment to the principles of non-interference and absolute sovereignty is unlikely to stimulate the types of regional cooperation required to deal more effectively with non-conventional threats to regional security. To be sure, intelligence and security cooperation on these issues has increased significantly in recent years, especially after the attacks in Bali on 12 October 2002. But these improvements have occurred from a very low base and the types of region-wide counter-terrorism protocols required for keeping in check highly mobile transnational terrorist groups such as Jemaah Islamiyah remain a distant possibility. Despite the heady rhetoric, the sacrosanct character of the principles of non-interference and consensus decision making within Concord II affords these increasingly redundant concepts a status they no longer deserve. Thus Concord II maintains those very obstructions that for the past decade have stymied ASEAN's institutional maturation.

At face value the ASEAN members' inability to produce more than recycled rhetorical flourishes on the desirability of a 'Concert of Nations' is a result of the instinctive refusal – especially by more reactive newer ASEAN members – to make the small sacrifices in sovereignty required to institutionalize the types of multilateral surveillance and intelligence-sharing systems required to pre-empt transnational security threats. Although the types of collaboration outlined in Concord II might lead to more official meetings between intelligence services and thereby add to regional confidence, it is unlikely that these exchanges will overcome the instinctive tendency to view security in conventional realist terms. In other words, as evinced by ASEAN Concord II, member states are likely to organize their security around traditional conceptions of sovereignty that posit neighbouring states, rather than non-state actors, as the only enduring threat to national security. As a result, South-east Asian policymakers will continue to disaggregate transnational terrorist networks into their constituent parts and focus overwhelmingly on local terrorist cells at the expense of coordinated region-wide counter-terrorism initiatives. At the same time, the principle of non-interference will continue to be used to rebuff offers of external assistance and occasional constructive criticism from fellow members. The ASEAN member's rejection of a US proposal to jointly patrol the strategically vital Straits of Malacca to protect oil tankers and other major prime targets against a terrorist strike is a case in point (Orsz g-Land 2005). The trend, therefore, is likely to continue along the path set in the wake of the Bali bombings with the framework counter-terrorism cooperation retaining its reactive character in the form of joint investigations and inquiries *after* a terrorist event rather than multilateral actions designed to interrupt attacks *before* they are launched.

REFERENCES

Ali, Mushahid and Jeffrey Chen (2004), 'Maritime security cooperation in the Malacca Straits: prospects and limits', *IDSS Commentaries*, 23/2004, June, pp. 1–3, www.ntu.edu.sg/idss/publications/Perspective/IDSS232004.pdf, accessed June 2005.

Association of South East Asian Nations (2003), Declaration of ASEAN Concord II (Bali Concord II), www.aseansec.org/15159.htm, accessed 8 November 2003.

Bonner, Raymond (2005), 'Radical cleric in Indonesia is acquitted of terrorism', *The New York Times*, 4 March, p. 16.

Davis, Anthony (2002a), 'Extremism exported: Hambali's Indonesian brand of holy war travels to the Philippines on the back of local Islamic groups', *Time Asia*, 1 April, www.time.com/time/asia/features/malay_terror/jemaah_islamiah.html, accessed 1 February 2003.

Davis, Anthony (2002b), 'The complexities of unrest in Southern Thailand', *Jane's Intelligence Review*, September, 17.

del Puerto, Luige A. (2005), 'Lenten terror threat over, says military: but PNP still on alert for Abu Sayyaf terror strike', *Philippine Daily Inquirer*, 26 March, www.inq7. net/globalnation/sec_new/2005/mar/26-01.htm, accessed 28 March 2005.

Denoon, David B.H. and Evelyn Colbert (1998–99), 'Challenges for the Association of Southeast Asian Nations', *Pacific Affairs*, 71 (4), 505–23.

Ferguson, James R. (2004), 'ASEAN Concord II: policy prospects for participant "Regional Development"', *Contemporary Southeast Asia*, 26 (3), 394.

Fullbrook, David (2004), 'Thailand: behind the Muslim insurgency', *International Herald Tribune*, 17 December, www.iht.com/articles/2004/12/16/opinion/edfull. html, accessed 20 December 2004.

Ganesan, N. (2004), 'Thaksin and the politics of domestic and regional consolidation in Thailand', *Contemporary Southeast Asia*, 26 (1), 31–2.

Gloria, Glenda M. (2002), 'The road to Sira Wai', *Newsbreak*, 8 July, www.inq7. net/nwsbrk/2002/jun/25/nbk_4-1.htm, accessed 5 March 2005.

Gloria, Glenda M. (2005), 'The AFP's "Hamburger Hill"', *Newsbreak*, 1 March, http://partners.inq7.net/newsbreak/istories/index.php?story_id=29068, accessed 5 March 2005.

Henderson, Jeannie (1999), *Reassessing ASEAN*, Adelphi Paper No. 328, London: Oxford University Press for the International Institute for Strategic Studies.

Human Rights Watch (2005), 'Elections amid government assault on rights', *Human Rights News*, 3 February, http://hrw.org/english/docs/2005/02/03/thaila10120.htm, accessed 20 February 2005.

International Crisis Group (2003), *Jemaah Islamiyah in Southeast Asia: Damaged but Still Dangerous*, Asia Report No. 63 Jakarta and Brussels, 26 August, pp. 1–60, www.crisisgroup.org/home/index.cfm?id=2959&l=1, accessed June 2005.

International Crisis Group (2004), *Indonesia: Rethinking Internal Security Strategy*, Asia Report No. 90, Jakarta and Brussels, 20 December, pp. 1–36, www.crisisgroup. org/home/index.cfm?id=2959&l=1, accessed June 2005.

Jones, David Martin and Mike Lawrence Smith (2002), 'From *Konfrontasi* to Disintegrasi: ASEAN and the rise of Islamism in Southeast Asia', *Studies in Conflict and Terrorism*, 25 (2), 346.

Khoo, Nicholas (2004), 'Constructing Southeast Asian security: the pitfalls of imagining a security community and the temptations of orthodoxy', *Cambridge Review of International Affairs*, 17 (1), 137–53.

Levett, Connie (2004), 'Fear mixes with anger in Thailand's seething south', *Sydney Morning Herald*, 30 October, 8.

Liow, Joseph Chinyong (2004a), 'The security situation in southern Thailand: toward an understanding of domestic and international dimensions', *Studies in Conflict and Terrorism*, 27 (6), 531–48.

Liow, Joseph Chinyong (2004b) 'Philippines blast toll rises to 15', *Sydney Morning Herald*, 14 December, 6.

Ország-Land, Thomas (2005), 'UN Launches Global Initiative to Defend Malacca Straits', *Jane's Terrorism and Security Monitor*, 25 January, http://jtsm.janes. com/public/jtsm/more_info.shtml, accessed June 2005.

Pew Research Centre (2005), *Trends 2005*, Washington DC: The Pew Research Centre.

Smith, Anthony L. (2004), 'ASEAN's Ninth Summit: solidifying regional cohesion, advancing external linkages', *Contemporary Southeast Asia*, 26 (3), 416–33.

Smith, Anthony L. (2005), 'The politics of negotiating the terrorist problem in Indonesia', *Studies in Conflict and Terrorism*, 28 (1), 33–44.

'Statement by His Excellency Dr Surin Pitsuwan, Minister of Foreign Affairs of the Kingdom of Thailand, at the 32nd ASEAN Ministerial Meeting, Singapore, 23 July' (1999), ASEAN Secretariat, www.aseansec.org/3836.htm, accessed 1 August 1999.

Steinberg, James (2002), 'Counter terrorism: a new organizing principle for American national security?', *Brookings Review*, 20 (3), 4–8.

Tan, Seng and Kumar Ramakrishna (2004), 'Interstate dynamics in Southeast Asia's war on terror', *SAIS Review*, 24 (1).

The White House (2005), 'President discusses war on terror: National Defense University – Fort Lesley J. McNair, 8 March 2005', www.whitehouse.gov/news/releases/2005/03/20050308-3.html, accessed 10 March 2005.

11. South-east Asian responses to arms and terror

K.S. Nathan

During the Cold War era (1947–91), South-east Asia as a sub-region of the international political system became entwined in the politics of ideological conflict and superpower rivalry. The end of ideological conflict at the global level inevitably impacted on the role, perceptions, influence and involvement of major, medium and small powers at the regional (Asia-Pacific) and sub-regional (South-east Asia/ASEAN) levels. With the decline of both internal and international communist movements and their sponsors, the focus shifted to issues related to governmental legitimacy, political and economic performance, human rights, and non-traditional threats to security – such as illegal migration, drug trafficking and environmental degradation. At the military/strategic level, low-intensity conflicts have persisted to this day, and will continue to persist in the form of ideological and religious groups that are discontented with the status quo. At the conventional level of military power, South-east Asian states are continuing to upgrade and accelerate arms purchases and modernize the military, to an extent that has raised concern as to whether they are engaged in an arms race.

The onset of the Asia financial crisis in mid-1997 exposed some of the structural weaknesses of the regional subsystem in terms of its capacity to manage and overcome financial chaos initiated by external forces such as currency speculators. The interventions of the International Monetary Fund to bail out the devastated economies of Thailand and Indonesia in particular, and nationalistic efforts at currency and capital controls such as those introduced by Malaysia, helped to stabilize the situation and to begin the process of economic recovery. The 2000 Chiang Mai Initiative on currency swap arrangements among ASEAN countries to avert, if not more effectively manage, the situation in the event of another major financial crisis is clearly indicative of a higher degree of regional concert and consciousness. In any event, the economic dislocations in the wake of the Asian financial crisis invariably impacted on the political and military dimensions as well. Most significantly, the downfall of the 32-year Suharto regime in Indonesia unleashed internal forces that attempted to fill the political vacuum in the post-Suharto period. ASEAN's attempts to stave off the financial crisis and to resolve the security situation arising from the East Timor Crisis in 1998–2000 were less than successful, thus pointing to institutional limitations in achieving regional solidarity over major economic, political and security issues. However, as the economies of South-east Asia began to recover from the financial crisis, state capability to speed up military modernization and enhance military power vis-à-vis neighbours again increased in line with long-term trends in the regional balance of power in ASEAN.

At the global level, the terrorist attacks on the World Trade Center in New York, the Pentagon (US Department of Defense) in Washington DC and in Pennsylvania on 9/11 compelled the new Bush administration to initiate major policy revisions in the direction of a more interventionist role in world affairs. This major change in US foreign policy has consequences for the post-9/11 strategic scenario in South-east Asia, particularly from the angle of mutual perceptions of security threats and the propriety of policy responses to the common threat of international terrorism. South-east Asian states have responded in different degrees to the threat of religious (Islamic) terrorism in the post-9/11 era – a subject discussed in this chapter.

ASEAN'S RESPONSE TO 9/11

ASEAN's response to 9/11 was predictable in the sense that a regional or collective response could not in any way contradict the global condemnation of terror at the level of international organization vis-à-vis the United Nations. ASEAN collectively condemned the terrorist attacks and pledged to work with the United Nations and also the United States in organizing a global coalition against terror. All ten ASEAN members (Brunei, Cambodia, Indonesia, Laos, Malaysia, Myanmar, the Philippines, Singapore, Thailand and Vietnam) endorsed various anti-terror measures at the 7th ASEAN Summit (Brunei, 2001) and the 8th ASEAN Summit (Phnom Penh, 2002). The Brunei Summit issued a strong statement that the 9/11 attack on the United States 'was a direct challenge to the attainment of peace, progress and prosperity of ASEAN and the realization of ASEAN Vision 2020' (ASEAN Secretariat 2002). The APEC Forum was another platform for ASEAN members to join forces with major global players like the United States, China and Japan to condemn terror. The members of both fora attempted to implement UN Security Council Resolution (UNSC) 1373, which was unanimously adopted on 28 September 2001.

Pursuant to UNSC Resolution 1373, the regional grouping held the ASEAN Ad Hoc Experts Group meeting in Bali, Indonesia, in January 2002 to implement the ASEAN Plan of Action to Combat Transnational Crime. Eight taskforces were established, aimed at combating (1) terrorism, (2) trafficking in persons, (3) arms smuggling, (4) sea piracy, (5) money laundering, (6) illicit drug trafficking, (7) international economic crime and (8) cyber crime. This Action Plan, formally adopted in May 2002, covered six strategic areas of collaboration: information exchange, legal issues, law enforcement measures, institutional capacity building, training and extra-regional cooperation. Each ASEAN member also agreed to establish a national anti-terrorism taskforce to facilitate cooperation with other members in the event of a terrorist attack, including the apprehension of suspects and the seizure of evidence ('ASEAN efforts to counter terrorism' 2002).

The 21-member APEC forum, a body normally dedicated to trade, endorsed its first major political statement in its 12-year history by declaring at its 9th Summit in Shanghai (20–21 October 2001) that terrorist acts were a profound threat to the peace, prosperity and security of all people, all faiths and all nations ('APEC unites against terrorism' 2001). Two weeks later, the ASEAN leaders issued a 'Joint Declaration on Joint Action to Counter Terrorism'. Despite these joint announcements, some ASEAN countries (for example, Malaysia, Singapore and the Philippines) have identified more closely than others with the US global anti-terror campaign. By early 2004, the United States had already sent 650 troops, including Special Forces to Manila, to provide anti-terrorism training to Philippine forces. There are official reports to suggest that this has been successful, with Abu Sayyaf guerrillas being killed or captured or having surrendered. The leader of this criminal gang, Abu Sabaya, also appears to have been killed by US–Philippine security forces, while the remaining 240 bandits are being pursued in Basilan and Jolo islands (*Straits Times* 2002d). In recognition of these achievements, at the 10th ASEAN Summit in Vientiane in November 2004, both ASEAN and APEC members endorsed the Philippines as head of the APEC counter-terrorism taskforce. The leaders also approved the role of Japan and Indonesia in the ASEAN Security Community Plan of Action on Counter-Terrorism (Romulo 2004). Under the auspices of the Thai and Australian governments, the ASEAN Regional Forum (ARF), the 23-member regional security consultative group, also held a workshop in April 2002 to discuss counter-terrorism. Malaysia took a further step by hosting the Special ASEAN Ministerial Meeting on Transnational Crime in May 2002, in furtherance of Resolution 1373. Three ASEAN members – Indonesia, the Philippines and Malaysia – underscored their determination to fight terror in the region by signing an Anti-Terrorism Pact on 7 May 2002 in Putra Jaya, Malaysia. Some of these measures could be interpreted as state-level responses to transnational threats, aimed at establishing a single Islamic state comprising these three nations. There is also a fear that Islamists will seek a new Asian base, now that they have been flushed out of Afghanistan. The tripartite pact is aimed at (1) targeting potential terrorist threats and (2) devising measures to tackle money laundering, smuggling, drug trafficking, hijacking, illegal trafficking of women and children, and piracy (*Straits Times* 2002b).

ASEAN members have since 9/11 given special prominence to the threat from Al Qaeda. This priority was justified by the simultaneous arrest of pro-Al Qaeda militants in Kuala Lumpur and Singapore. These militants had plans to bomb prominent sites in Singapore, including the embassies of the leading members of the anti-terror coalition, namely Australia, Britain and the United States. The Singapore government stated that high-value US commercial and strategic assets in Singapore were being targeted (Tan and Boutin 2001). Elsewhere in the region, the arrests of Islamic militants are continuing, despite the lack of consensus about an operable definition of terrorism. ASEAN members concur that the absence of agreement on definitions need not hold back collaboration on counter-terrorism (*Straits Times* 2002c). Thus cooperation has continued in order to defeat Jemaah Islamiyah (JI) in Singapore, KMM (Kumpulan Mujahideen Malaysia, later known in Malaysia as Kumpulan Militan Malaysia), the Laskar Jihad in Indonesia, and the Abu Sayyaf Group (ASG) in the southern Philippines. However, there have been serious limits to this cooperation, as the following section shows.

THE TRANSNATIONAL CHALLENGE OF RADICAL ISLAM

Radical Islam's transnational nature requires the formulation of regional strategies with a clear multilateral dimension. ASEAN has been moving in this direction since 9/11, although the efficacy of this multilateral approach is necessarily diluted by the rather strict adherence of member states to the principle of national sovereignty. A few years ago, Thai Foreign Minister Surin Pitsuwan attempted to circumvent this problem by proposing a formula for 'flexible engagement', but this was resisted by the majority. The objective was to build and strengthen ASEAN's capacity to tackle internal problems in member countries that posed a threat to regional security (Isaacson and Rubenstein 2002, p. 228). Only the Philippines supported Thailand; the other eight members, including the two Muslim-majority states (Malaysia and Indonesia), preferred to adhere strictly to the principle of non-interference. This division scuttled the prospect of a radically new approach to ASEAN regional cooperation. Responding to Osama bin Laden's Al Qaeda activities in South-east Asia requires heightened vigilance of a new order. But Malaysia, in particular, in response to the pressures and prospects of global Islamic revivalism since the 1970s, has adopted a lax immigration policy towards the Muslim world during the last decade. The space created by this official approach was quickly seized on by Islamic fundamentalist and radical groups, who were able to enter and leave Malaysia by escaping official scrutiny.

Eventually they were able to consolidate their activities to the point of setting up local cells with transnational agendas. As a result, from the early 1990s JI was able to set up regional *shura* (operational bases) in Malaysia and send at least 100 recruits to train in the use of firearms and explosives in Al Qaeda's Afghan training camps at Khalden, Derunta, Khost, Siddiq and Jihad Wal (Gunaratna 2002, p. 193). Rohan Gunaratna claims that the 13 people arrested in Singapore all reported to a regional *shura* in Kuala Lumpur, and that 'the units under the regional *shura* also mirror the world-wide Al Qaeda units in both structure and *modus* operandi' (ibid.).

The revelation that Malaysia was part of the Al Qaeda and JI network was undoubtedly discomforting to Putra Jaya. Malaysia has responded by strengthening the Internal Security Act to cover a wider scope of activity, and openly criticizing Indonesia's uncooperative attitude in dealing with Islamic militants seeking refuge in Indonesia and allegedly plotting against the Malaysian government (Tan 2004a, p. 27). The significance of the Malaysian and Singapore arrests of JI suspects lies in the profile of the detainees:

> the common denominator among those arrested is neither poverty nor lack of education but a shared religious ideology that depicts the United States as the enemy of Islam and a belief that Allah will reward them for waging a global *Jihad*. (Gunaratna 2002, p. 193)

An additional problem of combating Al Qaeda-linked JI terrorism in South-east Asia is the fact that its 'compartmentalized, loose-knit network means that breaking up individual cells may only have a limited effect on the operation of other groups or the network as a whole' (Corera 2001, p. 82) According to Corera, 'the only way to disrupt Al-Qaeda is either by infiltrating its core – almost impossible since at the centre is a highly committed, ideological group – or by destroying the entire leadership' (ibid.). He notes that counter-terrorism strategies are compounded by the existence of 'a vast pool of potential supporters, unhappy with the economic and social dysfunction of their nations, alienated by globalization and modernization, and humiliated by American power' (ibid.). These conclusions are hard to contradict. Yet, as the following sections demonstrate, the individual ASEAN member nations all have distinctive ways of addressing terror.

GLOBAL AND REGIONAL TERROR: THE MALAYSIAN APPROACH

For Malaysia and other ASEAN members, cooperation with the United States should not be confined to the military dimension, as the root causes of terrorism are multiple and do not lie in religious compulsions alone. Malaysia concurred with the view presented by Sultan Hassanal Bolkiah on the US–ASEAN Accord to Combat Global Terror, emphasizing that terrorism could not be wiped out with military might alone. It was also necessary to remove the frustration and resentment that made people join or associate with groups that promoted terrorism. Economic factors are very important in US–ASEAN cooperation against terrorism, hence trade and economic issues must be high on the agenda of the multifaceted relationship that Washington has with the region (*Straits Times* 2002e).

The effectiveness of regional cooperation is governed by national security perceptions and the pressures of domestic politics and interests. In the case of Malaysia, a fundamental concern of national security managers in the wake of 9/11 is containing Islamic extremism within its borders. The government moved swiftly to arrest and detain over 70 suspected militants as a pre-emptive measure. The Bali bombings on 12 October 2002 help to explain why such timely intervention was necessary. While Australia and the United States posit an external dimension to the doctrine of pre-emption, Malaysia, and arguably Singapore as well, emphasize its internal importance. The risk is that this pre-emptive strategy could restrict the scope of legitimate action taken by civil society to curb governmental abuse. Yet national security policy managers would, perhaps rightfully, assert that protection of the freedom and liberties of the overwhelming majority of the public should take priority over the freedom and fundamental liberties of the few who, given the opportunity, might deprive the whole society of its freedom to live free of terror.

The impact of counter-terror action by Malaysia can also be viewed in terms of the spillover effects in other spheres of the country's multiethnic mosaic. Apart from its value in putting terror-inclined religious militants out of action, the Internal Security Act enables the government to deal with other types of 'extremists'. These include racial, ideological, language, cultural and political advocates whose agendas and actions are deemed to be prejudicial to inter-ethnic harmony, social stability and national unity. The government claims, on the basis of a proven track record, that Malaysia's success as a multiethnic and 'Islamic' nation is the direct result of the ruling National Front Coalition's far-sighted policies based on moderation in all spheres of life. Communism as a radical ideology was defeated by this multi-pronged comprehensive approach to development and stability – a strategy that is now being challenged by Islamic radicalism, militancy and extremism. Indeed, post-9/11, the Mahathir administration (1981–2003) was emboldened to take stern measures to restore the 'status quo' in the religious sphere – adhere strictly to constitutional provisions for Islam as the official religion and arrest the downslide towards the creation of an 'Islamic State'. If tough measures were not taken now, when the atmosphere was politically conducive, Dr Mahathir's ruling party, the United Malays National Organization (UMNO), and his Barisan Nasional

(BN) government, were painfully aware that the opposition Parti Islam's (PAS) progress towards the 'Islamic State' was tantamount to the progressive defeat of the secular-oriented UMNO/BN government in the near future.

Indeed, the agenda of the Islamic state in Malaysia has thrown up innumerable opportunities for Islamists of different orientations from near and far to link up and consolidate their cherished goal of setting up an Islamic Nation, encompassing southern Thailand, Malaysia, Singapore, Indonesia and the southern Philippines. The point of coherence in the ASEAN region for this grandiose design is JI, whose operational structures in Malaysia, Singapore, Indonesia and the Philippines have been seriously disrupted by governmental anti-terror action. The regional Al Qaeda operatives (JI and KMM or Kumpulan Militan Malaysia, initially known as Kumpulan Mujahideen Malaysia) have thus far failed in their attempt 'to destroy the precarious work of post-colonial nation building in Southeast Asia with an Islamic arrangement ...' (Jones and Smith 2003, p. 162). Other than the arms heist carried out by the deviant religious sect Al-Ma'unah in Perak, Malaysia, in July 2000, the country has been relatively safe from religious terrorists. This is largely due to pre-emptive action and police and intelligence cooperation with ASEAN neighbours through, for example, Malaysia's Five Power Defence Arrangements (FPDA) with Singapore, Australia, New Zealand and Britain, and with the United States through the bilateral US–Malaysia Anti-Terrorism Pact signed in May 2002.

Malaysia's anti-terror strategy includes domestic measures aimed at re-vamping Islamic religious education with the aim of removing the underlying causes of militancy. Specifically, the government has begun monitoring the curriculum content of private Islamic schools (Sekolah Agama Rakyat or SARs) run by the opposition party PAS. Dr Mahathir claimed that these schools are the breeding grounds of anti-government sentiment and religious militancy. Of late, the government has cut funding to these schools, forcing many to close down or be taken over by the state. Additionally, it can be argued that the introduction of English as the medium of instruction for mathematics and science subjects in primary and secondary schools, beginning in 2003, is yet another strategy aimed at secularizing education, while obliging particularly Malay/Muslim students to pursue knowledge that can better ensure their economic competitiveness and success. An independent Malaysian think tank, the Malaysian Strategic and Research Centre (MSRC), has suggested that 'privately run religious schools are a breeding ground for future Muslim terrorists, and should be revamped and placed under strict government control' (*Straits Times* 2003). MSRC director, Abdul Razak Baginda, claimed that the PAS-aligned Sekolah Agama Rakyats (SARs) 'have become centres for extremism, anti-development and intolerance towards other religions' (ibid.).[1]

Malaysia, despite being a key advocate for ASEAN regionalism, has also strengthened bilateral ties with the Bush administration. In May 2002, Prime Minister Mahathir visited the United States and had summit-level talks with President Bush. Dr Mahathir, himself an exponent of realpolitik, used the visit to stimulate US economic, political and military engagement in South-east Asia in the full knowledge that only the US superpower has the wherewithal to launch and sustain a multi-pronged offensive against international terrorists out to destroy national and regional stability. The United States, for its part, was very impressed with 'the extent to which Malaysia is a cooperating partner in the global war on terrorism', said Defense Secretary Donald Rumsfeld prior to Dr Mahathir's visit (*New Straits Times* 2002). These warmer Malaysian–US ties in the immediate aftermath of 9/11 symbolized mutual interests in countering religious terror.

At the same time, certain domestic compulsions also lay at the root of Mahathir's desire to align himself more closely with the United States. While his detractors have argued that Mahathir was using the global anti-terror campaign to silence political foes at home, especially PAS, and to divert attention from detained populist leader Anwar Ibrahim, the prime minister claimed that certain Malaysian Muslims had obtained training in firearms and weaponry from Afghanistan, and if unchecked would pursue their cause of establishing an Islamic state by overthrowing the present elected government by force and violence if necessary. In the light of perceived threats to domestic stability, the Malaysian leader was even prepared to strengthen security cooperation with a superpower he had often criticized for being overbearing in its foreign policy. Accordingly, on 14 May 2002, a US–Malaysia Anti-Terrorism Pact was concluded in Washington DC. The primary areas of cooperation were defence, banking, intelligence sharing, border control, transportation and law enforcement (*Straits Times* 2002c). Given Dr Mahathir's full support of the global anti-terror campaign, Malaysia is now regarded by the United States as a 'friendly Muslim nation'. Mahathir even proposed a definition of terrorism at the Organization of the Islamic Conference (OIC) meeting in Kuala Lumpur (April 2002) that won US approval but was rejected by the 57 OIC members (*Straits Times* 2002a). Mahathir suggested that anyone using violence against civilians, regardless of whether the perpetrator is an individual or a state, is a terrorist.

Confronting Islamic extremism within Malaysia also necessitated a review of the political strategy of the UMNO-led government under Dr Mahathir and, since 31 October 2003, under the stewardship of Malaysia's fifth prime minister, Abdullah Badawi. While Mahathir was quite successful in re-engineering UMNO to strengthen its appeal to the younger generation of Malays and to reverse the setbacks of the 2004 general election, Abdullah Badawi has taken a new approach to political Islam in Malaysia. This new strategy has been labelled 'Islam Hadhari' or civilizational/progressive Islam. His three-fold strategy of Islamic governance (1) advocates an inclusive framework that recognizes and respects religious tolerance and coexistence in a highly pluralistic society; (2) recognizes secularism to the extent that politics and religion are kept separate; and (3) promotes socioeconomic progress in the context of modernization and globalization (Nathan 2004, p. 12). Through this revitalized, highly pragmatic and modernist approach, Abdullah hopes to stem the tide of Islamic fundamentalism and political extremism bordering on violence and terrorism spawned by the allegiance of a small fringe Malaysian Muslim group to extremist dogma.

GLOBAL AND REGIONAL TERROR: THE SINGAPORE APPROACH

The city state of Singapore, given its highly strategic location and its maritime vulnerabilities, continues to be vigilant while also projecting itself as the only ASEAN member that shares an identity of interests with the United States in the global and regional anti-terror campaign. Singapore's national interests, security and survival depend significantly on the availability of a regional and global environment that ensures freedom of navigation, safety of the sea lanes of communication (SLOCs), and a stable balance of power maintained either by a single superpower or by a concert of powers. Singapore's membership of ASEAN is seen to be contributing towards this goal as this indigenous regional organization demonstrates a growing capability for political empowerment in international relations. Ensuring sea-lane security, including combating piracy and terrorism, is an integral component of Singapore's national security policy, as the 651-square-kilometre republic's economic and consequently political survival is at stake (Collins 2003, p. 113).

In this context, besides engaging in regional cooperation, possession of adequate military power vis-à-vis such transnational challenges and likely conventional threats from neighbours is viewed by the city state as a *sine qua non* of national survival. The promotion of free trade, leading arguably to the establishment of an ASEAN economic community, is undoubtedly a complementary objective behind creating a 'security community' in which economic interests can be better advanced for national survival, while traditional and non-traditional threats can be more effectively addressed in a collective manner. For the island republic's Deputy Prime Minister and Coordinating Minister for Security and Defence, Dr Tony Tan, maritime security is paramount, suggesting that it might even be necessary to engage foreign, especially US, assistance in policing the pirate-infested Straits of Malacca. Pointedly, Tan observed that greater sophistication and possible overlap with maritime terrorism make increasing piracy attacks in the region a worrying trend. Singapore is particularly concerned about terrorist attacks being planned and launched against US vessels in Singapore and other maritime targets in the region (*Today* 2004).

Singapore detained 37 JI suspects in 2002 and 2003. The Home Affairs Minister, Wong Kan Seng, claimed that these arrests have significantly disrupted the JI cells in Singapore while dismantling JI's operational capability. The Republic's police and intelligence forces work closely with neighbours such as Malaysia, Thailand and Indonesia in pre-empting terrorist activity. Singapore was among the first in ASEAN to sign the Convention for the Suppression of the Financing of Terrorism in December 2001, which was followed by its endorsement of all UN resolutions on counter-terrorism. The government's White Paper issued in January 2003 enunciated a concrete, multidimensional strategy including financial, military, security, psychological, educational and strategic measures to combat the post-9/11 threat of international terrorism. Progress in this newly formulated approach was underscored by the Minister for Home Affairs, Wong Kan Seng, in his address to the intelligence services. He noted that terrorist plots against the city state have been disrupted, JI and MILF networks were crippled, and key operatives including those who received terrorist training in Afghanistan, Kashmir and Mindanao have been neutralized and no longer pose a threat to national security. More importantly, he emphasized that Singapore had evolved a counter-terrorism strategy that went beyond physical security and included the establishment of a religious rehabilitation program and counselling for JI and MILF members (Wong Kan Seng 2005).

Given the rich resources of the Singapore republic, it is not surprising that the JI terrorist threat has been significantly reduced. If there is lingering concern over the prospect of JI attacks on the republic, its anxiety stems from perceptions as to how well the war against terror is being pursued in countries in its immediate vicinity, namely Indonesia and Malaysia.

GLOBAL AND REGIONAL TERROR: THE INDONESIAN APPROACH

Indonesia's response to terrorism in the post-9/11 era has been marked by a high degree of ambiguity stemming from its political system, its ethnic geography, its position as the largest Muslim country in the world, and its own socio-political priorities. As one analyst put it, 'the fact that Islam is such an important force in Indonesian politics inhibits Indonesia's anti-terrorist struggle' (Weatherbee et al. 2005, p. 161). Prior to the Bali bombings of October 2002, which killed over 200 people, mostly Australians, the government of

President Megawati Sukarnoputri took the view that Al Qaeda operatives and its JI associates in the country did not pose a serious terrorist threat to national security, and hence did not merit greater attention than other pressing socioeconomic concerns. The reluctance on the part of the authorities to act against groups that preached violence and hatred has not only emboldened these militants but also weakened the hand of Jakarta vis-à-vis the stronger measures taken by its ASEAN neighbours, especially Singapore, Malaysia, the Philippines and Thailand. President Megawati's rather weak leadership, reflected in part by her reliance on coalition support from Muslim parties, inevitably produced the twin effects of Indonesia's incapacity to cooperate more vigorously with its neighbours and, at the external level, to join forces with the United States and its Western allies in the global war on terror (Tan and Ramakrishna 2002, p. 238).

The extent of involvement of JI leader and mentor, Abu Bakar Bashir, in the 2002 Bali blasts remains a matter of concern, despite legal proceedings resulting in his arrest in mid-2003 and conviction for treason. In March 2005 Bashir was sentenced to three years in prison for conspiring to overthrow the Megawati administration and for his complicity in the 2002 Bali blasts. As a weak president, Megawati Sukarnoputri, constrained significantly by her Vice-President Hamzah Haz (whose fundamentalist Islamic inclinations have stood in the way of effective counter-terror action to root out militant JI), could only settle for overt announcements that she was committed to the global war on terror. The US military campaign that ousted the Taliban in Afghanistan, the US-led war in Iraq that toppled President Saddam Hussein and Washington's pro-Israeli sympathies vis-à-vis the Palestinians limited her ability to speak in favour of concerted anti-terror action with her ASEAN neighbours, let alone engage in closer bilateral cooperation with the United States in the manner evidenced by Manila and Singapore. Only after the Bali attack and the J.W. Marriott bombing in Jakarta was Megawati arguably emboldened to work more closely with the United States and her ASEAN neighbours, officially acknowledging for the first time the presence of JI and Al Qaeda terrorists in Indonesia.

The election of Susilo Bambang Yudhoyono as Indonesia's president, succeeding Megawati in 2004, does augur well for the 'war on terror'. His previous role in the Indonesian military and his generally friendly attitude to the United States and the West would suggest that he is prepared to take stronger measures against terrorist suspects lurking within Indonesian borders. However, in view of the multitudinous problems facing any government in a country with a population of over 250 million and whose legal and administrative systems are weak and corruption-ridden, even a determined leader like Yudhoyono is unlikely to overcome earlier baggage that has resulted in weak institutions and poor governance. By early 2005, over 150 militants had been detained during the previous three years, but the authorities have been reluctant to link them to Al Qaeda or JI. Among the militant entities that may or may not be connected to Al Qaeda and JI but which favour a fundamentalist Islamic order in the republic are Laskar Jihad (disbanded immediately after the Bali blasts), Islamic Defenders Front (FPI), the Islamic Youth Movement (GPI) and Laskar Jundallah (a hard-line Islamic group committed to imposing Shariah law in Indonesia). Their activities have ranged from attacks on massage parlours, bars, karaoke lounges and gambling dens in Jakarta to street protests against the United States for its invasions of Afghanistan and Iraq and its stewardship of the global war on terror. They have also orchestrated the communal/religious violence in Sulawesi and Malukus from 2000 to 2002 (Holt 2004).

While the Yudhoyono government has indicated its willingness to ban JI (a move that would bring relief to its ASEAN neighbours involved in the anti-terror campaign, as well as foreign governments, especially the United States) it is unclear whether Jakarta has the political courage to incur the wrath of other non-JI Muslim extremists or activists mentioned above, who would still prefer Indonesia to be an Islamic State (Jihad Watch 2005).

GLOBAL AND REGIONAL TERROR: THE PHILIPPINE APPROACH

A major factor influencing Manila's approach to the 'war on terror' is its close security relationship with the United States. President Gloria Arroyo has taken a broader strategic perspective on how anti-terror cooperation within ASEAN, and with foreign powers, impacts on Philippine domestic and national interests. In terms of maintaining a wider Asia-Pacific strategic balance, Manila appreciates the continued influence and involvement of the United States in the region, especially in the context of the rising presence of China. The Philippines have had many testy encounters with Beijing over competing territorial claims in the South China Sea. Manila, like other ASEAN powers, is equally apprehensive about China's growing economic and political hegemony in South-east Asia in the decades ahead. Hence the need to maintain a balance of power via ASEAN and the regional engagement of major external powers such as the United States, Japan, India, Australia and also Russia and the European Union.

For President Gloria Arroya, the 9/11 terrorist attacks furnished a valuable strategic opportunity to combat militancy at home, especially in the Muslim south, and to expand security cooperation abroad, in particular with the United States. Pressing for solidarity with the United States means that Manila could benefit from the extra attention and funding for economic development and resources badly needed for upgrading training and other facilities for the Philippine Armed Forces. The strategic opportunity afforded to Arroyo by 9/11 has been succinctly stated by Abuza (2003, p. 203): (1) to revitalize the bilateral security relationship with the United States; (2) to defeat the Muslim insurgency in the south and to negotiate political compromises with groups prepared to abandon violence; (3) to eliminate terrorist bases and any form of shelter for Al Qaeda-type operatives on Philippine soil; and (4) to consolidate her position in domestic politics.

The renewed US–Philippine security cooperation, in addition to the 1998 Visiting Forces Agreement, enabled the stationing of 1300 troops, including 160 Special Forces, whose job was not only to train Philippine personnel in anti-terror operations but also, if necessary (although not openly stated), to engage in direct combat against the Abu Sayyaf and other rebels under the doctrine of self-defence. This joint effort was named Balikatan (shoulder-to-shoulder) exercises. Efforts by Arroyo to negotiate political settlements with other rebel groups such as the Moro National Liberation Front (MNLF) and its offshoot, the Moro Islamic Liberation Front (MILF), have thus far proved inconclusive. These complications aside, President Arroyo's endorsement of the US-led 'war on terror' is reflective of a broad measure of support by the ASEAN states for counter-terrorism operations in the post-9/11 context. ASEAN leaders still operate on state-based notions of national security and are loath to endorse the activities of transnational forces, especially when they espouse violence as an instrument for changing the status quo. Yet, when public sentiment is expressed in very strong terms on international issues, such as the taking of Philippine nationals as hostages in conflict-ridden Iraq, democracies find themselves in comprising situations, despite formal commitments by way of security alliances with external powers.

President Gloria Arroyo withdrew the small Philippine contingent of 51 peacekeepers from Iraq to the dismay of her key ally, the United States. This was a decision she felt would not only strengthen her political position at home but also appear to be in agreement with regional public opinion that US involvement in Iraq is not an integral part of the global 'war on terror'. There were also domestic constraints on Manila's support for the US action in Iraq, stemming from the presence of over 1.5 million Filipinos working in the Middle East, of whom 4000 are based in Iraq. Despite this apparent setback in US–Philippine relations, Manila is fully committed to the battle against transnational extremist Islam and secessionist tendencies in the Muslim south. The ongoing activities of Philippine terrorists ensure that Manila will not resile from that position. For example, on 14 February 2005 three bombing incidents occurred in three areas: Davao, General Santos in the south, and the Makati financial district of Manila. The Abu Sayyaf (literally, 'Bearer of the Sword'), which claimed responsibility for this recent wave of terrorism, is regarded by Manila and Washington as having links with Al Qaeda (*The Economist* 2005). Thus bilateral cooperation with the United States and regional cooperation within ASEAN, besides domestic socioeconomic reforms, are viewed as indispensable components for upholding national security and regional stability.

GLOBAL AND REGIONAL TERROR: THE THAI APPROACH

For Thailand under the leadership of Thaksin Shinawatra, the Muslim problem in the south was considered peripheral to the pursuit of core national interests, which ostensibly were, and are, shaped by the predominant Buddhist culture. The leadership in Bangkok has viewed the Muslim problem in the south as an aberration. Despite rising Muslim unrest in the post-9/11 era, the rebellion is approached and being managed as a military/security problem, and not one that requires a more sophisticated approach of managing ethno-religious plurality in the southern provinces. For the Thai ruling elite, the central security objective is maintaining independence, sovereignty and territorial integrity (Wattanayagorn 1998, p. 436). Such a conceptual approach inevitably incorporates the notion that the rebellious groups, including Muslim insurgents, will be targeted in the interests of national security. Thaksin's overwhelming military response to suppress Muslim rebels conforms to this time-tested method of maintaining public order and security in modern Thailand.

Since 9/11 the Muslim south has appeared more restive than ever. It has been more willing to reveal the influence and impact of transnational political Islam on its political consciousness and willingness to assert its autonomy and demands for independence against Bangkok. Bangkok's political and military leaderships were surprisingly slow in reacting to President Bush's call to close ranks in the fight against international terror. Bangkok's ambivalent attitude in part stemmed from the lack of US sympathy for Thailand's economic miseries during the 1997 Asian financial crisis. Bangkok was also in denial mode about reports that Al Qaeda and JI operatives were transiting its borders and using its territory to plot attacks against Western interests, including the bombing of a Bali night club that Western tourists were known to patronize. The lack of urgency in responding to intelligence reports on terrorists using Thai territory as a transit or rendezvous point was revealed in October 2002 when Thaksin dismissed CNN and *Washington Post* reports of Al Qaeda operations in Thailand. Specifically, both media reported that an Al Qaeda operative, Riduan Isamuddin or Hambali, convened a meeting in Thailand in January 2002 and took the decision to switch from 'hard' to 'soft' targets such as bars, night clubs and cafés in the region, including Western diplomatic targets (Ramakrishna and Tan 2003, p. 184). However, since the Bali bombings the Thai government has changed its attitude. Its intelligence services have provided assistance, leading to the arrest on 16 May 2003 of a Singapore-based JI operative, Arifin bin Ali, and the arrest by US authorities of an Al Qaeda operative, Mohammed Mansour Jabarah, on his way from Thailand to the United Arab Emirates. Thai intelligence and police authorities began to awaken to the grim reality that the predominantly Buddhist kingdom was host to terrorist activities following the arrest in June 2003 of two Thai Muslims who confessed to JI membership, as well as plotting attacks on embassies and tourist sites in Thailand (Weatherbee et al. 2005, p. 164).

Despite these developments, the Thaksin government has yet to formulate a clear-cut strategy for dealing with the three known Thai-Muslim rebel groups: the Pattani United Liberation Organization (PULO), the National Revolutionary Front or Barisan Revolusi Nasional (BRN) and the Pattani Islamic Warrior Movement or Gerakan Mujahideen Islam Pattani (GMIP). Among the growing incidences of Muslim unrest in 2004, the Tak Bai incident of 25 October 2004 stands out as an ugly sore in Thai–Muslim relations. Nearly 80 Muslims died from suffocation during military custody following arrests made during a protest held in the Muslim fasting month of Ramadan. The protest was apparently in response to a series of alleged police brutalities against suspected criminals and terrorists culminating in April 2004 when as many as 112 people were killed in clashes between security forces and Islamic militants who attacked more than a dozen security posts in three southern provinces (Nathan 2005, p. 36).

IS THERE AN ARMS RACES IN SOUTH-EAST ASIA?

The global 'war on terror' has come at a difficult time for the nations of South-east Asia. The balance of power in the region is being reformulated. To a considerable extent this is being driven by the economic growth and modernization of the South-east Asian economies. The expanded availability of financial and trained manpower resources is making this possible; at the same time, the military power in this region is being shaped to address real as well as perceived threats and challenges to national security. While it is arguable that the military strengths of most South-east Asian countries in the 1970s were at a rudimentary stage of development (with the possible exception of Thailand and Vietnam owing to external inputs into the Vietnam War), this trend has certainly been reversed through a conscious and consistent program of military modernization. South-east Asian leaders, like their counterparts elsewhere, are fully cognisant of the various elements that cumulatively combine to produce national power and security. Among these elements, military modernization to boost national capability and deterrence vis-à-vis neighbours is currently a key element in national security thinking and formulation in the ASEAN region.

What is behind the military modernization and the accelerated arms purchases by the ASEAN states? First, persistent bilateral tensions between any two regional states provides the rationale to maintain a military capability to boost deterrence. This scenario pertains to the Malaysia–Singapore relationship where Singapore in particular is concerned about the possibility, even if remote, of its larger northern neighbour entertaining predatory territorial ambitions arising from historical circumstances and colonial baggage. Singapore's purchase of state-of-the-art weaponry hardly goes unnoticed in Putra Jaya. Singapore currently has the most powerful airforce in ASEAN. As Gray notes in his seminal study of the arms race phenomenon, four conditions must be met to conclusively establish the existence of an arms race: (1) there must be two or more parties conscious of their antagonism; (2) they must structure their armed forces relative to those of other participants, with a view to deterrence; (3) they must compete in terms of quantity (personnel and weapons) and/or quality (men, weapons, organization, doctrine and deployment); and (4) there must be rapid increases in quality and/or improvements in the quantity of capabilities (Gray 1971, p. 41). To some degree, all four conditions apply to South-east Asia, although Andrew Tan's notion of 'arms racing' rather than a full-fledged arms race may be a more appropriate description of the current trends (Tan 2004b, p. 37).

Second, it is beyond question now that changes – perceived as well as actual – in the global and regional balance of power also drive arms acquisitions and military modernization. For Malaysia, the end of the armed struggle against local communists and the demise of the Cold War necessitated a reformulation of military doctrine from counter-insurgency warfare to an emphasis on building conventional forces, particularly vis-à-vis maritime threats to national security. This scenario of military development applies equally to other ASEAN countries with extended coastlines and maritime interests, such as Indonesia, the Philippines, Thailand and Vietnam. Nevertheless, the capacity to develop, expand and modernize the armed forces has varied according to national budgetary resources available. The Philippines, Indonesia, Vietnam and Myanmar have all been hamstrung by limited resources, while more impressive economic growth and better governmental capacity has enabled Singapore, Malaysia and Thailand to purchase high-tech weapons.

Third, the maritime zone encompassing the littoral states of ASEAN furnishes an area of concord as well as discord. Cooperation for joint exploitation of the natural and living resources of the South China Sea in which several states have overlapping claims – Malaysia, Vietnam, the Philippines,

Brunei, and also China and Taiwan – would necessarily entail the benign use of their respective military capabilities to address common threats such as piracy, smuggling, drug trafficking, environmental pollution and terrorism. Yet the reality of a conflict of national interests cannot be overlooked, so that each country has found it increasingly necessary to define as well as defend its own maritime interests. Additionally, as the realists would argue, a state's military power and prowess contribute towards enhancing national prestige in the community of nations. Through the possession of deterrent power, states in the Morgenthauian sense feel that they promote dialogue and negotiation to ensure desired outcomes. In adopting this approach they might very well be encouraging an interactive arms build-up in the region but, from their perspective, this is not an intended but rather a consequential development.

Fourth, all states, as actors in the international system, are affected by technological progress and the military sphere that we now call RMA (Revolution in Military Affairs). The RMA factor could well be generated by the major arms producers but, as technology is borderless in the era of globalization, technological innovation can either be bought from outside or be generated from inside a nation state. In the post-Cold War era, the breakdown of old supplier networks means that the supply-side control of recipients through arms transfers has become less feasible (Mussington 1994, p. 36). The corollary to this development is the creation of new supply networks for both hi-tech and medium-grade weaponry at relatively low cost, thus facilitating the process of regional arms modernization. The RMA factor has been operative since the early 1990s and has contributed to the upgrading of regional armed forces at all levels, including the use of satellites for advanced command and control and precision-guided munitions (Huxley and Willett 1999, p. 66). On the other hand, Huxley and Willett remind us that the low-level security problems of South-east Asia have less need for RMA-based armed forces (ibid.). This is likely to constrain any regional full-blown arms race, especially when advanced weaponry must be imported owing to the limited technological sophistication intrinsic to the region.

On balance, the nature and pattern of arms acquisitions exemplified by the 10-member ASEAN bloc do not necessarily point in the direction of an arms race. This is due primarily to the availability of non-violent conflict resolution mechanisms that the regional body has cherished and developed since the 1976 Bali Treaty. Table 11.1, which shows defence expenditures as a percentage of GDP in the region, bears this out – defence expenditure is relatively low except for Singapore. Brunei's high defence expenditure in 1985 was directly related to gaining independence from Britain in 1984, while Vietnam's disproportionately high expenditure ratio can be explained by its military occupation of Cambodia (1978–90), also a spin-off from the

Table 11.1 Defence expenditures of ASEAN countries (% of GDP)

	1985	2001	2003
Indonesia	2.8	3.8	3.7
Malaysia	3.8	3.8	3.6
Singapore	6.0	5.1	5.2
Thailand	4.0	1.7	1.5
Philippines	1.4	1.6	2.1
Vietnam	19.4	7.2	7.1
Myanmar	5.0	5.0	5.0
Laos	7.1	0.9	0.8
Cambodia	n.a.	2.5	2.5
Brunei	8.0	5.5	5.2

Source: The Military Balance 2003–2004 (2003, p. 337).

Vietnam War. It can be argued in the language of constructivism that habits of consultation have now been sufficiently developed to negate war as an instrument of national policy.

CONCLUSION

Any objective evaluation of the progress, success or failure to date of ASEAN's anti-terror strategies must be premised on the consideration that terrorism alone does not inform the entire agenda, perspective and priorities of the regional security approaches adopted by members of ASEAN. In addition to the increased threat of global terrorism, South-east Asia faces many other security challenges, many of them unrelated to 9/11. These challenges are an offshoot of expanding globalization and economic integration. The end of the Cold War has further complicated the regional security scenario by leaving in its wake an ideological power vacuum which the superpower, the United States, has been obliged to fill through its doctrines of globalization and, now, after 9/11, counter-terrorism. South-east Asian security approaches, strategies, policies and responses are invariably intertwined with the pressures emanating from this unipolarity.

Second, other non-traditional security threats also occupy the minds and energies of regional statesmen – such as piracy, illegal migration, drugs, religious militancy and environmental pollution. As noted by Tan and Boutin (2001, p. 5), 'globalization too has resulted in new security threats to communities and individuals that are transnational in character and are increasingly defined in social and economic terms'.

Third, the global coalition against terror is likely to be difficult to sustain over any length of time. New developments can, and are likely to, supersede the global 'war on terror'. By early 2004 it was already evident that many coalition partners such as Germany and other EU members were dragging their feet. European priorities have increasingly diverged from those of the United States. In South-east Asia the regional priorities are also different, despite the protracted 'war on terror'. As the London-based International Institute for Strategic Studies has observed:

> the U.S. faces an enormous challenge in keeping allies and newfound friends focused on a war that may appear to conform to a purely American agenda ... The transatlantic differences in threat perceptions prevalent before September 11 began to return in early 2002, as some European capitals appeared to relax counter-terrorism postures while the U.S. remained on high alert. (*Strategic Survey* 2002, p. 7)

Fourth, regional security in the twenty-first century (including the global war on terror) will increasingly be affected by the issue of leadership transition. Political transition in South-east Asia is ongoing, with personality-driven systems being progressively replaced by institutional mechanisms for the transfer of power, especially in non-communist states such as the Philippines and Indonesia. In Malaysia the process of leadership change has already taken place with Mahathir's 22-year tenure giving way to that of his deputy, Abdullah Badawi. This change is something of a test case as to whether power has been institutionalized to enable a smooth political transition to a younger generation of leaders. It also tests the sustainability of the Malay-dominant power-sharing formula that has defined Malaysia since its foundation. Any major political failure in these areas could trigger a range of threats to domestic and regional security.

Fifth, international terrorists might develop strategies to focus on penetrating 'failed states' or 'failing states' in Asia. States with 'receptive' Islamic populations such as Malaysia might be especially appealing to religious militants. So far, however, there has been no evidence to suggest that terrorism has been able to significantly alter the political status quo, let alone topple regional governments.

Sixth, the arms race phenomenon in South-east Asia will continue but remain muted by the emergence of a growing sense of regional consciousness and empowerment and the preference to resolve bilateral and multilateral disputes within the framework of the Treaty of Amity and Cooperation (TAC) or the ASEAN Concord I, endorsed at Bali in 1976. ASEAN Concord II of

2003 symbolizes further progress towards the creation of a regional 'security community'.[2] Most important of all, however, the regional security scenario in the first decade of the twenty-first century will remain one characterized by American strategic preponderance, more by default than by design. Alternative regional and global actors will remain relatively weak. The rise of China is unlikely to change this, given that its political interest will be matched by countervailing power from the United States, Russia, Japan and India. Rather, China's economic power will encourage regional bilateral and multilateral business arrangements. The Chiang Mai Initiative of May 2000 represents one such bold effort to take measures to avert another Asian financial crisis by linking together the foreign exchange reserves of 13 countries (ASEAN +3; that is, China, Japan and South Korea); the net value of this pool is about US$1 trillion (Cheng 2001, p. 437).

Finally, ASEAN as a regional institution, and the ARF as a broader security process, will continue to face major constraints in their ability to respond swiftly to acts of terrorism in South-east Asia for the following reasons: (1) the regional borders are porous and difficult to control; (2) cross-border and intra-regional trade will grow, but much of this will operate outside normal financial channels and escape government surveillance; (3) widespread criminal activity and drug trafficking have the capacity to facilitate the undetected movement of terrorists; and (4) large supplies of indigenously produced and imported weapons are available in South-east Asia (Frost et al. 2003). These factors are likely to increase the regional clout of the United States, provided that it remains willing to define, energize and underpin the security architecture of South-east Asia well into the new millennium.

NOTES

1. There are more than 500 SARs or privately run religious schools nationwide with 126 000 students. The government has already begun relocating over 70 000 students from such schools to national schools. Students have until 6 February 2003 to move out of SARs.
2. Indeed, the most recent example of how bilateral territorial and resource disputes can be settled by negotiation and compromise, and not by force, is afforded by the agreement by Malaysia and Singapore to resolve the two-year problem over land reclamation works undertaken by Singapore in the Johor Straits, which Malaysia claims has affected shipping, navigation and the economic livelihood of fishermen, and causes damage to the marine environment (*Straits Times* 2005).

REFERENCES

Abuza, Zachary (2003), *Militant Islam in Southeast Asia: Crucible of Terror*, London: Lynne Rienner Publishers.

'APEC Unites Against Terrorism' (2001), BBC News, 21 October, www.bbc.co.uk/ hi/english/world/asiapacific/mewsid_1611000/1611674, accessed April 2005.

'ASEAN efforts to counter terrorism' (2002), paper prepared for the UN Counter-Terrorism Committee, www.aseansec.org/14396.htm, accessed April 2005.

ASEAN Secretariat (2002), 'ASEAN way of fighting terrorism', Jakarta, www. aseansec.org/12776.htm, accessed April 2005.

Cheng, Joseph Y.S. (2001), 'Sino-ASEAN relations in the early twenty-first century', *Contemporary Southeast Asia*, 23 (3), 420–51.

Collins, Alan (2003), *Security and Southeast Asia: Domestic, Regional, and Global Issues*, Singapore: Institute of Southeast Asian Studies.

Corera, Gordon (2001), 'Inside the terror network', in Jenny Baxter and Malcolm Downing (eds), *The Day that Shook the World: Understanding September 11th*, London: BBC News.

Frost, Frank, Ann Rann and Andrew Chin (2003), 'Terrorism in Southeast Asia', Department of the Parliamentary Library, Parliament of Australia, Canberra, 7 January, www.aph.gov.au/library/intguide/FAD/sea.htm, accessed April 2005.

Gray, Colin S. (1971), 'The arms race phenomenon', *World Politics*, 24 (1), 39–79.

Gunaratna, Rohan (2002), *Inside Al Qaeda: Global Network of Terror*, London: C. Hurst & Co.

Holt, Andrew (2004), 'Indonesia and the global war on terrorism: Jakarta's mediocre response to terror', *Terrorism Monitor*, 2 (2), www.jamestown.org/publications_ details.php?volume_id=400&issue_id=2904&article_id=23507, accessed April 2005.

Huxley, Tim and Susan Willett (1999), *Arming East Asia*. Adelphi Paper No. 329, London: International Institute for Strategic Studies.

Isaacson, Jason F. and Colin Rubenstein (eds) (2002), *Islam in Asia: Changing Political Realities*, London: Transaction Publishers.

Jihad Watch (2005), 'Indonesia will outlaw Jemaah Islamiyah, anti terror chief says', 21 March, www.jihadwatch.org/archives/005437.php, accessed April 2005.

Jones, David Martin and Mike Lawrence Smith (2003), 'Southeast Asia and the war against terrorism: the rise of Islamism and the challenge to the surveillance state', in Uwe Johannen, Alan Smith and James Gomez (eds), *September 11 and Political Freedom: Asian Perspectives*, Singapore: Select Publishing Pte. Ltd.

Mussington, David (1994), *Understanding Contemporary International Arms Transfers*. Adelphi Paper 291. London: International Institute for Strategic Studies, September.

Nathan, K.S. (2004), 'Abdullah's burdens of victory', *The Straits Times,* 29 March, 12.

Nathan, K.S. (2005), 'Malaysia: political outlook', in *Regional Outlook: Southeast Asia 2005–2006*, Singapore: Institute of Southeast Asian Studies.

New Straits Times (2002), Kuala Lumpur, 4 May W1.

Ramakrishna, Kumar and Tan See Seng (eds) (2003), *After Bali: the Threat of Terrorism in Southeast Asia*, Singapore: Institute of Defence & Strategic Studies, Nanyang Technological University and World Scientific Publishing Co. Pte. Ltd.

Romulo, Alberto G. (2004), '10th ASEAN Summit ensures economic growth in a secure and humane environment', Statement of Romulo, Philippine Secretary of Foreign Affairs, 9 December, www.dfa.gov.ph/archive/speech/romulo/10thasean. htm, accessed April 2005.

Straits Times (2002a), 3 April, A7.

Straits Times (2002b), '3-way pact to tackle terrorism', 8 May, 1.

Straits Times (2002c), 'ASEAN building united front against terror', 21 May, 6.

Straits Times (2002d), 'Officials adamant: Abu Sabaya is dead', 26 June, A5.

Straits Times (2002e), 30 July, 1.

Straits Times (2003), 14 and 17 January, A9.

Straits Times (2005), 27 April, 1, H2.

Strategic Survey 2001/2002 (2002), London: The International Institute for Strategic Studies.

Tan, Andrew (2004a), *Security Perspectives of the Malay Archipelago: Security Linkages in the Second Front in the War on Terrorism*, Cheltenham, UK and Nothampton, MA, USA: Edward Elgar.

Tan, Andrew (2004b), *Force Modernisation Trends in Southeast Asia*, IDSS Working Paper No. 59, Singapore: Institute of Strategic and Defence Studies, Nanyang Technological University, January.

Tan, Andrew T.H. and Kenneth Boutin (eds) (2001), 'Non-traditional security issues in Southeast Asia', Singapore: Select Publishing (for Institute of Defence and Strategic Studies).

Tan, Andrew and Kumar Ramakrishna (eds) (2002), *The New Terrorism: Anatomy, Trends and Counter-strategies*, Singapore: Eastern Universities Press.

The Economist (2005), 19 February, 33.

The Military Balance 2003–2004 (2003), London: Oxford University Press for International Institute for Strategic Studies (IISS), October.

Today (2004), Singapore, 21 May, 6.

Wattanayagorn, Panitan (1998), 'The elite's shifting conceptions of security', in Muthiah Alagappa (ed.), *Asian Security Practice: Material and Ideational Influences*, Stanford, CA, US: Stanford University Press.

Weatherbee, Donald et al. (2005), *International Relations in Southeast Asia: the Struggle for Autonomy*, New York: Rowman & Littlefield Publishers.

Wong Kan Seng (2005), 'Singapore Government media release', speech by the Minister for Home Affairs, at the Intelligence Service Department (ISD) Promotion Ceremony, Meritus Mandarin Hotel, 18 April, http://app.sprinter.gov.sg/data/pr/20050418990.htm, accessed April 2005.

12. Progress and setbacks in Philippine–US security relations

Noel M. Morada

The withdrawal of the Philippine contingent in Iraq in July 2004 became an important turning point in Philippine–US security relations. Primarily, it highlighted the limited capabilities of the Philippine government in sustaining its support for the US-led war in Iraq in the face of domestic clamour for saving the life of an overseas Filipino worker kidnapped by terrorists. In a way, the Angelo de la Cruz saga that caused a strain in the relationship between Manila and Washington pointed to the clash between state and human security interests, which competed to define or redefine the national security interest of the Philippines in the context of its security alliance with the United States. This chapter examines the progress and setbacks in the two countries' security relations in the aftermath of the withdrawal of the Philippine humanitarian contingent from Iraq. What follows is an overview of Philippine–US security relations since 9/11.

PHILIPPINE–US SECURITY RELATIONS SINCE 9/11: GAINS, DOMESTIC POLITICS AND POLICY IMPLICATIONS

The Philippines had become an important pillar – and even a battlefront to some extent – in the US-led war against international terrorism in Southeast Asia. The revitalized bilateral security alliance between Manila and Washington has benefited both parties, albeit in different ways. The Armed Forces of the Philippines (AFP) gained much from the military aid and training provided by the United States. In 2003 the Philippines became a major non-NATO ally of the United States, which opened up opportunities for easy access to American military logistics support for the AFP. For its part, the United States also gained from the security alliance through a mutual logistics support agreement (MLSA) in 2002 – an accord that enhances its posture in the region in the fight against international terrorism.

Beyond the material and strategic benefits of the alliance, the closer security relationship between the two allies has had a number of implications for the Philippines' domestic politics and policies in the fight against terrorism at home and abroad. First, increased American military assistance improved the AFP's morale and capabilities vis-à-vis Islamist secessionist rebel groups, particularly the notorious Abu Sayyaf group (ASG) and the Moro Islamic Liberation Front (MILF). The alliance also enhanced the government's political leverage in dealing with communist and Islamist rebels with the inclusion of the ASG and the New People's Army (NPA, the armed wing of the Communist Party of the Philippines) in the United States' list of terrorist organizations. The MILF, however, has not been declared a terrorist organization, even though there have been reports about its links with Al Qaeda and Jemaah Islamiyah (JI). Ironically, the Philippine government had opposed labelling the MILF a terrorist organization in order not to undermine ongoing peace efforts. The Arroyo government had signed interim peace agreements with the MILF in May 2002 and continues to explore peace negotiations with the Islamist rebel group. On one hand, by opposing the inclusion of the MILF in the list of foreign terrorist organizations, the Philippine government gained a 'carrot' to persuade MILF leaders to enter into formal peace negotiations, which resumed in early 2003. On the other hand, the inclusion of the NPA in the list of foreign terrorist organizations enabled the government to pressure the communist insurgents to go back to the negotiating table even as their funds were frozen ('Terrorist tag on Philippine communist may spur peace talks: military' 2002). However, the communist rebels remain defiant and to date the listing of the CPP/NPA as a foreign terrorist organization continues to be a stumbling block to progress in peace talks between the government and the communist rebels.

There are also some downsides to the revitalized security alliance between the two countries. One is that the 'patron' role of the United States has become an object of criticism for some Filipino nationalist politicians and even some military officers who see the dangers of growing dependence on the Americans by the AFP in dealing with an essentially home-grown terrorist threat. In particular, the joint military exercises between Filipino and US troops have been criticized as unconstitutional and undermining Philippine sovereignty. Some Filipino politicians, non-government organizations and media people expressed opposition to allowing US troops in the combat zone, which could lead to them getting indirectly involved in the AFP's military operations against the Islamist terrorist groups in the country. Opposition legislators questioned the legality of US troop deployments in Mindanao and the wisdom of holding joint military exercises in that part of the country, as they worry about the Philippines becoming another Vietnam, especially if communist or Islamist insurgents begin attacking US forces. There is concern that, in this way, the United States could be drawn into an essentially domestic conflict.

Meanwhile, US military assistance to the Philippines appeared to have created a 'rift' within the AFP, to which the failed mutiny in July 2003 could be partly attributed. The mutinous junior officers accused top AFP officials of corruption and of staging bombings in Mindanao to get more US military assistance. While public opinion at the time was somewhat sympathetic to the grievances of the rebel soldiers, it did not support the unconstitutional means employed by them ('55% in Survey says soldiers' reasons for mutiny valid' 2003). Even the Feliciano Fact-Finding Commission, which investigated the failed mutiny and concluded that the July 2003 rebellion was an attempt to overthrow the government of President Macapagal-Arroyo, recognized that the incident was rooted in corruption and the politicization of the military (Avendaño 2003). Clearly, the US patron role has resulted in domestic tensions not only within the military but also in civil–military relations. These are the unintended consequences of closer security cooperation between the two countries.

The revived security alliance between the Philippines and the United States also had implications for the country's relations with ASEAN and the rest of the international community. At the regional level, Philippine support for the US campaign against international terrorism had to be weighed against the collective ASEAN position on the issue. Essentially, the ASEAN stance called for policy coordination and collective action, rather than unilateralism, in dealing with international terrorism. Unlike the more military-oriented approach of the United States, the Philippines agreed with the collective position of ASEAN that adopted a more comprehensive approach to the issue. While recognizing the need for US military assistance in containing the threat posed by the ASG and the MILF in the Philippines, the Macapagal-Arroyo administration repeatedly underscored the social-economic roots of terrorism in South-east Asian countries. To some extent, the need to anchor the Philippines' policy with ASEAN's position also serves a strategic purpose. Implicitly, the Philippine government is wary of US unilateralism, and its membership of ASEAN serves as a 'balancer' in this regard. On the other hand, ASEAN's regional perspective and collective position on terrorism has also constrained the Philippines' support for the United States, albeit with good reason. For one thing, the country needed the help of ASEAN members – in particular, Brunei and Malaysia – in the search for a negotiated peace settlement with the MILF.

Beyond South-east Asia, the revitalized security alliance with the United States became a springboard for the Philippines to project itself as an important member of the coalition of the willing in the fight against international terrorism. This was demonstrated in Macapagal-Arroyo's support for the US-led invasion of Iraq in March 2003, despite the unpopularity of that decision at home. The Philippine government also campaigned hard in 2003 for a non-permanent seat on the UN Security Council, which it was able to secure with the support of the United States and its allies. The Philippines' increasing role in global security, though modest, also facilitated the unanimous election, in 2004, of the Philippines to chair the anti-terror taskforce of Asia Pacific Economic Cooperation (APEC) during its summit in Chile.

PAINS AND STRAINS FROM THE IRAQ WITHDRAWAL: TAKING STOCK OF THE SECURITY ALLIANCE

Less than a month after she was proclaimed winner of the May 2004 presidential elections, President Macapagal-Arroyo faced a major political crisis following the kidnapping of an overseas Filipino worker in Iraq, Angelo de la Cruz. The terrorist kidnappers demanded that she pull out the 51-person Philippine humanitarian contingent in Iraq or face the consequences of de la Cruz's beheading. The political risk at home was certainly high if Manila refused to give in to the demands of the kidnappers. The beheading of de la Cruz could have been a rallying point for the followers of defeated presidential aspirant and movie actor Fernando Poe Jr. It would have been exploited by other anti-Arroyo forces in the country (including potential military coup plotters), thus undermining the government's political survival. With more than 4000 Filipino workers in Iraq and about 1.5 million in the Middle East, Angelo de la Cruz became an instant icon of many poor Filipinos who were willing to take risks even in war-torn Iraq in order to work and send money back home (estimated at US$6–7 billion a year). It is against this backdrop that Mrs Arroyo decided to withdraw the Philippine humanitarian contingent from Iraq. The president stated categorically that she made no apologies for that decision amid strong disappointment on the part of the United States and harsh criticism by the Australian government (Sy 2004a; 2004b). The kidnappers later released de la Cruz and public opinion, at least in Manila, was fully supportive of Macapagal-Arroyo's decision ('72% of Metro approve of Arroyo's decision: survey' 2004). Without a doubt, a serious political crisis that threatened the survival of the Philippine government was averted. Even so, there were some domestic criticisms of the government's decision that focused on concerns about the Philippines' international image and credibility as a reliable ally in the fight against international terrorism, which allegedly has been tarnished by 'giving in' to the demands of the terrorists.

In November 2004 two other Filipino workers were kidnapped separately in Afghanistan and Iraq. Angelito Nayan, a diplomat working for the United Nations in Kabul, was kidnapped with two other UN workers for three weeks and later released by their captors. Roberto Tarongoy, an accountant working for a US company, was kidnapped a week after Nayan and was held captive in Iraq for eight months. The kidnappers of Tarongoy reportedly demanded US$12 million in exchange for his release. On these two cases the Philippine government strictly imposed a news blackout in order not to jeopardize ongoing negotiations with the kidnappers even as it underscored a no-ransom policy. Meanwhile, the United States was careful in making statements about these two cases, so as not to exacerbate the situation and thereby aggravate further its already strained relations with the Philippines following the de la Cruz saga. Both countries at this time were quietly patching up their rift even as their leaders were preparing to meet at the APEC summit in Chile at the end of the month.

The Angelo de la Cruz saga no doubt forced the Philippine government to rethink its unequivocal support for the US-led war in Iraq, as it had clearly put at risk the lives of many Filipino overseas workers in the Middle East. In fact, as early as April 2004, President Macapagal-Arroyo had called for a review of the government's policy on Iraq (particularly the deployment of humanitarian troops in that country) following the kidnapping and subsequent release of an unidentified Filipino truck driver ('GMA to review policy on Iraq' 2004). Consequently, the foreign affairs department announced that Philippine participation in the reconstruction of Iraq will be conducted within the framework of the UN's Security Council resolution 1546, and only after elections were held in that country. It also stressed that no deployment of Philippine troops will take place in the near future (Sy 2004d). The Philippine government also banned the deployment of Filipino workers in Iraq notwithstanding calls by the United States to partially lift the ban. Even so, Filipino workers continue to enter Iraq illegally to work in US military camps and for private US companies. Apparently, there is no consensus within the Macapagal-Arroyo government on banning Filipino workers in Iraq, as some officials recommend their partial deployment only in areas where their security could be guaranteed (Sy 2004e).

The fall-out in Philippine–US relations resulting from the withdrawal of the humanitarian contingent in Iraq also forced the Macapagal-Arroyo government to re-examine its strategic alliance with the United States. Having been removed from the 'coalition of the willing' and warned of serious repercussions in bilateral relations (Katigbak 2004a; 2004b), Philippine defence and security officials raised the need to review the country's policy towards the United States (Labog-Javellana and Burgonio 2004). While reiterating its commitment to the fight against international terrorism – and stressing that the Philippines did not regret supporting the US invasion of Iraq (Calica 2004) – the Philippine government started to underscore its policy of continuing to assist the United States in its Iraq campaign 'within the capabilities' of the country. This signalled the importance of giving priority to the safety and welfare of overseas Filipino workers in Iraq in defining the extent of support the Philippine government would give to the United States in the fight against terrorism abroad. The apparent silence of US officials on this policy was interpreted in some quarters of the Philippines as an indication that Washington understood the dilemma faced by the Macapagal-Arroyo government, particularly in having to protect overseas Filipino workers in the Middle East. In fact, when Defense Secretary Donald Rumsfeld commented that the Philippines' weakness was 'provocative', many politicians in the Philippines were quick to point out that the withdrawal of 51 Filipino troops was very small compared with the 4000 Filipino civilians still working in Iraq, who are part of the estimated 1.5 million overseas Filipino workers in the Middle East.

The strain in the relationship between Manila and Washington prompted the former to explore opportunities for expanding Philippine–China security relations as the Macapagal-Arroyo government began playing the 'China card'. This was primarily triggered by strong reactions from some politicians in the Philippine legislature to criticisms by US officials of Manila's decision to withdraw its humanitarian contingent in Iraq. Some of them called for re-examination of the country's foreign policy, which was seen as being too biased in favour of the United States (Roncesvalles 2004). Playing the 'China card', therefore, is anchored to the belief that it is in the best interest of the Philippines to pursue a more independent foreign policy and that it should not be dictated primarily by US security interests. During her visit to China in early September 2004, President Macapagal-Arroyo stressed that the People's Republic of China (PRC) would play a key role in the Philippines' economic and security interests in the future, and that it is in the national interest of the country to boost bilateral relations with Beijing. A deal was struck between the two countries for a joint seismic mapping of oil reserves in the Spratlys and an agreement to boost bilateral defence cooperation. In March 2005, during a visit by Foreign Secretary Romulo to Beijing to mark the thirtieth anniversary of Philippine–China relations, some US$1.2 million worth of military assistance was promised by China to the Philippines. The military assistance will be in the form of military equipment, including engineering hardware. In late April 2005, during a visit to Manila by Chinese President Hu Jintao, Philippine Defense Secretary Avelino Cruz announced that Manila and Beijing are exploring the possibility of forging military ties, particularly in the area of maritime security and disaster coordination. The two countries are also expected to discuss the possibility of joint sea border patrols and even joint military exercises (Alave 2005). At another important meeting, in Kuala Lumpur on 11 December 2005, the Chinese Premier Wen Jiabao said that the China–Philippine relationship was 'showing a pleasing momentum'. Philippine President Arroyo reciprocated by describing the relationship as having entered a 'golden age' (Embassy of the People's Republic of China 2005).

Macapagal-Arroyo, however, was careful in playing the 'China card' and stressed that expanding defence ties with Beijing did not mean that the Philippines was renouncing its mutual defence treaty with the United States ('China to play key role in Philippines economic, security future' 2004). Even so, the United States appears to be wary of new Philippine–China security relations, coming as they did immediately after the withdrawal of Filipino troops from Iraq. US Chargé d'Affaires Joseph Mussomeli reportedly warned Manila that its bilateral relations with Washington could face further erosion if there are additional setbacks in bilateral ties. In particular, the United States is worried that a joint exploration agreement between China and the Philippines concerning the South China Sea, even if driven by China's need to diversify its energy sources, would enhance the PRC's naval projection in the area more permanently (Simon 2004). During a visit to China by Defense Secretary Avelino Cruz in November 2004, some retired Philippine military officials were quoted in the local press as saying that the United States was not happy with the way the Philippine government is actively courting Beijing, and that Washington apparently did not see the trip of President Macapagal-Arroyo in September as simply wooing Chinese support for her ten-point government agenda (Esguerra 2004). Japan was also worried about improvement in Philippine–China security relations. It began to explore defence cooperation with Manila for the first time, in February 2005. A six-member team of Japanese officials from the foreign ministry and the defence agency visited Manila to explore areas of defence cooperation, including counter-terrorism ('RP, Japan hold talks on defense cooperation' 2005). In May 2005, Japanese Defense Agency Chief Yoshinori Ono pushed for stronger security ties with the Philippines, particularly in those areas where China and the Philippines are attempting to establish closer defence ties. Ono was the first Japanese defence chief to visit the Philippines, at the heels of a visit by Chinese President Hu Jintao ('Japanese Defense Chief offers to boost security ties with RP' 2005). In January 2006, Japan's Senior Vice Minister for Foreign Affairs was in Manila to open the 'Philippines–Japan Friendship Year' to celebrate the special 'peer-to-peer' bond that had developed between the two countries (Embassy of Japan 2006).

SECURITY SECTOR REFORM AND GOVERNANCE ISSUES: US CONCERNS AND RESPONSES

Notwithstanding the rift in their bilateral relations following the withdrawal of Philippine troops from Iraq, the military alliance between Manila and Washington essentially remains intact. For one thing, joint military exercises between the two countries are still very much in order, even as counter-terrorism training in central Mindanao took place throughout the second half of 2004 (Pareño 2004). For his part, US Ambassador to the Philippines Francis Ricciardone acknowledged that, although the two allies had serious disagreements, both recognized that they had 'very important security relations' and 'very important common interests' and that it is in their mutual interest to rebuild their bilateral ties (Sy 2004c). US President George Bush echoed this to President Macapagal-Arroyo following his election victory in November 2004 and during the APEC meeting in Chile later in the same month.

An important concern for the United States is the reform of the AFP, particularly the problem of corruption in the military. The corruption scandal in the AFP that broke out in early October 2004, which involved senior military officials, has seriously affected the morale of the defence establishment (Alipala 2004). In an effort to contain the destabilizing effects of the scandal, President Macapagal-Arroyo ordered court martial proceedings against Major General Carlos Garcia, a former military comptroller, for corruption on the basis of unexplained wealth. His aide, Colonel George Rabusa, was relieved of his post as operations officer of the AFP's Central Command in Cebu City amid investigations into his unexplained wealth. More recently, the crackdown on corruption in the military went into high gear as the office of the Ombudsman filed perjury charges against, and ordered the forfeiture of some P11.2 million worth of questionable assets belonging to retired AFP Chief of Staff Lisandro Abadia (Porcala 2004). New AFP Chief General Efren Abu was tasked by President Macapagal-Arroyo to ensure transparency in the court martial proceedings against Garcia. She also ordered the AFP to 'civilianize' its comptrollership function and revamp the board of directors of the AFP Savings and Loans Association, Inc. (AFPSLAI). She also named civilians to replace retired military generals holding five key posts in the Department of National Defense (Villanueva 2004b). Prior to his retirement as AFP chief in October, General Narciso Abaya ordered the closure of five commercial subsidiaries of the AFP's Retirement and Separation Benefits System (RSBS) to prevent them from siphoning off millions of pesos from soldiers' pension and other benefits. RSBS has been the object of criticism by many soldiers in the military and has been a major source of corruption in the AFP. The Department of National Defense is contemplating a new civilian-run pension fund for soldiers, given the failure of the RSBS to meet their financial needs ('5 subsidiaries of military pension fund closed' 2004). For his part, AFP Chief, General Efren Abu, abolished the practice of funds 'conversion', which has been a source of corruption in the military establishment (Guinto 2004).

The United States had expressed satisfaction over efforts of the Macapagal-Arroyo government to weed out corruption in the AFP (Sy 2004f; Dumlao 2004). Nonetheless, the United States is keenly monitoring its military aid to the Philippines, including strict inventory control over equipment. Some 30 helicopters from the United States are due for delivery between the last quarter of 2004 and the first quarter of 2005. In October 2004 the US Senate appropriations committee approved an increase in military financing assistance to the Philippines in 2005, from US$30 million to US$55 million, as requested by the Bush administration. The US Senate committee added an extra US$25 million owing to strong lobbying by the Philippine embassy in Washington and the committee's concern over terrorist activities in South-east Asia. The United States has pledged more than US$300 million in total assistance to the AFP for five years from 2002, primarily for equipment and training.

However, early in 2005, the Bush administration recommended a 30 per cent reduction in America's aid package to the Philippines for fiscal year 2006, from US$124 million to US$87.8 million. The White House justified the reduction by an assessment that the Philippines had 'more or less contained the terror group JI in Mindanao' (Ilustre 2005, p. 1). The justification for the aid reduction, however, contradicts statements made by some US embassy officials in Manila – they believe that JI and other terrorist groups continue to pose a serious threat to the Philippines. For instance, US Chargé d'Affaires Joseph Mussomeli even described Mindanao as the 'next Afghanistan' because of the growing factions within JI and MILF and the increasing threat of the Abu Sayyaf. He even hinted at the possibility that the US government would include the MILF in the list of international terrorist organizations, although he also stressed that Washington continues to support ongoing peace negotiations between the Philippines government and the MILF (Lee-Brago 2005). During a visit to Manila in early May 2005, US Deputy Secretary of State Robert Zoellick recognized that, while progress was being made to contain regional terrorism, Mindanao remains in a 'dangerous situation' – although it was not, in his view, in danger of becoming another Afghanistan (Avendaño 2005). Zoellick also pointed out that Washington wants the Arroyo administration to put in place more effective fiscal reforms and anti-corruption measures before the Philippines can tap into the US$1 billion Millennium Challenge Account (MCA), a special US aid fund set up by the Bush administration (Cabacungan 2005). During his visit to Manila in December 2005, US Director of National Intelligence John Negroponte again expressed the United States' continuing concern over the use of Mindanao as a sanctuary for JI terrorists and urged the Arroyo government to pass an anti-terrorism law (Pamintuan 2005).

Notwithstanding the foregoing issues, joint military exercises continued throughout 2004, specifically in the area of counter-terrorism. Following the tsunami disaster in South-east Asia in December 2004, a number of scheduled military exercises were cancelled as US forces were involved in relief operations. Some 28 joint military exercises were apparently conducted during 2005 in different parts of the Philippines, most of which focused on counter-narcotics operations. Military cooperation will continue over the next five years under the Philippine Defense Reform Program, an upshot of the Joint Defense Assessment (JDA) conducted by the AFP and the US Pacific Command in 2003. The JDA report identified a wide range of weaknesses in the AFP's operational capabilities, such as ground mobility, air assault capability, intelligence, communications equipment and civic action. Apart from improving equipment, the Philippine military needs to reform its organization and structure in order to integrate operations and intelligence. More damagingly than by inadequate resources and funding, the AFP's effectiveness has been undermined by perceptions of widespread corruption within its ranks.

Beyond security sector reform, the United States is concerned with the political and economic reforms needed in the Philippines, particularly those related to increasing revenues. Fiscal reforms have not progressed significantly. The implications of these problems for the long-term political stability of the Philippines are serious concerns for the United States, as it cannot afford to have a weak ally in the fight against international terrorism in the region. There is no doubt that the Philippine government faces serious economic challenges that could undermine the political stability of the country. The fiscal crisis threatens to constrain economic growth and induce capital flight. During her inauguration, President Macapagal-Arroyo laid down a ten-point legacy program within her six-year term that includes balancing the budget through effective revenue collection and spending, and attaining peace in Mindanao. Of these, the most pressing is balancing the budget by improving revenue collection, given the chronic fiscal deficit that now runs close to P200 billion (or US$3.57 billion). A group of economics professors from the University of the Philippines have warned that the country will be facing a serious financial crisis in the next two to three years if the Macapagal-Arroyo government fails to arrest the growing public debt, which stood at P3.36 trillion by the third quarter of 2004 and has doubled since the 1997 Asian financial crisis. It now stands at approximately 130 per cent of the country's GDP (Villanueva 2004b). The Macapagal-Arroyo government has taken the warning seriously and proposed new tax measures to deal with the current fiscal crisis, even as it launched austerity measures to curb unnecessary public expenditures. Legislators were pressed to cut their government appropriations for local projects (that is, pork barrelling) as the media pointed to them as a source of corruption and waste of government resources. Some economists and former finance officials, however, insist that the Philippines is still far from having an Argentina-type financial crisis because the country continues to have accelerating economic growth, with increased earnings from exports averaging US$36 billion per year ('RP far from Argentina-style financial crisis, says ex-cabinet man' 2004).

Economic reform is seen as necessary, but the factional debates persist about the speed and direction of change.

National politicians continue to debate the best approach in handling the deficit problem, either via new taxes or by improving revenue collection. Some local politicians who will be affected by the proposed reduction in internal revenue and pork barrel allotments remain opposed to these proposals. In the meantime, international credit-rating agencies have downgraded the rating of the Philippines owing to concerns over the snail pace of fiscal reforms (Ferriols and Villanueva 2004). This was aimed at pressuring the Philippine legislature to pass the tax measures needed to arrest the growing budget deficit of the national government. Failure on the part of the government to address its fiscal problem will have serious implications not only for the country's economic and political reforms but also for the ongoing military reforms in the AFP, whose credibility and integrity have been tarnished by the corruption scandal. Altogether, these could undermine the political stability of the Philippines.

CONCLUSION

The withdrawal of the Philippine humanitarian contingent in Iraq following the kidnapping of a Filipino worker demonstrates the precariousness of the Philippine–US security alliance, especially in the face of competing national interests of the Philippines. On one hand, the security alliance had effectively benefited and improved the capability of the AFP in dealing with terrorist threats at home. On the other hand, the human security interests of thousands of Filipino overseas workers in Iraq and millions elsewhere in the Middle East appeared to clash with the national security of the country, which was narrowly premised on a strong security alliance with the United States following the tragic events of 9/11. Ironically, in the end it was the very political survival of the Philippine government, which has been a staunch supporter of the United States in the war against international terrorism, that was at stake. Such a 'weakness' of the state has led to a re-examination of Philippine policy towards supporting the US-led war in Iraq, in particular, and in relying solely on the revived security alliance with the United States, in general, as the anchor of Manila's defence and security policies. That the Philippines is an important pillar in the US war against terrorism in South-east Asia remains unchanged, notwithstanding the fall-out from the Philippines' withdrawal from Iraq. No doubt, it is still in the long-term strategic interest of both countries to maintain a strong security alliance. However, it ought to be based on realistic expectations and deeper appreciation of the capabilities and limitations of each partner in the alliance. The pains and strains in Philippine–US relations that resulted from the Angelo de la Cruz saga illustrate clearly that, ultimately, domestic politics still determines what is the national security interest of states.

REFERENCES

'5 subsidiaries of military pension fund closed' (2004), *The Philippine Star*, 7 October.

'55% in survey says soldiers' reasons for mutiny valid' (2003), Inquirer News Service, 26 September, www.inq7.net/nat/2003/sep/26/nat_1-1.htm, accessed September 2003.

'72% of Metro approve of Arroyo's decision: survey' (2002), Inquirer News Service, 22 July.

Alave, Kristine L. (2005), 'RP and China to explore possible military ties', *BusinessWorld Online*, 28 April, accessed May 2005.

Alipala, Julie (2004), 'Troops' morale down, military officers admit', Inquirer News Service, 21 October, accessed May 2005.

Avendaño, Christine O. (2003), 'Oakwood mutiny a power grab, probe concludes', Inquirer News Service, 18 October, www.inq7.net/nat/2003/oct/18/nat_2-1.htm, accessed October 2003.

Avendaño, Christine (2005), 'Mindanao still "a dangerous situation", says US official', Inquirer News Service, 6 May.

Cabacungan, Gil C. (2005), 'US ties reforms, anti-corruption measure to aid', Inquirer News Service, 6 May.

Calica, Aurea (2004), 'DFA chief: RP has no regrets about Iraq', *The Philippine Star*, 19 September, www.newsflash.org/2004/02/hl/hl101027.htm.

'China to play key role in Philippines economic, security future' (2004), *The Philippine Star*, 7 September.

Dumlao, Artemio (2004), 'US happy with RP tack vs. corruption', *The Philippine Star*, 24 October.

Embassy of Japan (2006), 'Manila, Philippines, 11 January', www.ph.emb-japan.go.jp/pressreleases/2006/01-06.htm, accessed January 2006.

Embassy of the People's Republic of China (2005), 'Manila, Philippines', http://ph.chineseembassy.org/eng/xwdt/t230054.htm, accessed January 2006.

Esguerra, Christian (2004), 'RP courting more US displeasure with China visit', Inquirer News Service, 8 November.

Ferriols, Des and Marichu Villanueva (2004), 'Moody's warns RP of credit rating downgrade', *The Philippine Star*, 11 November.

'GMA to review policy on Iraq' (2004), *The Philippine Star*, 14 April.

Guinto, Joel Francis (2004), 'Abu outlaws "conversion", military practice considered source of corruption', Inquirer News Service, 26 November, http://news.inq7.net/breaking/index.php?index=1&story_id=19353.

Ilustre, Jennie L. (2005), 'Bush slashes aid to RP by a third to $87 M', *Malaya*, 7 March, www.malaya.com.ph/mar07/news1.htm.

'Japanese defense chief offers to boost security ties with RP', Agence France Presse, 2 May.

Katigbak, Jose (2004a), 'US warns of pullout repercussions', *BusinessWorld Online*, 16 July.

Katigbak, Jose (2004b), 'US: RP no longer part of the coalition', *The Philippine Star*,

6 August.

Labog-Javellana, Juliet and T.J. Burgonio (2004), 'RP to review its US policy', Inquirer News Service with Agence France Presse, 24 July.

Lee-Brago, Pia (2005), 'Mindanao could be next Afghanistan – US diplomat', *The Philippine Star*, 11 April.

Pamintuan, Anna Marie (2005), 'US Intel Director: JI terrorists using RP as sanctuary', 8 December, Philippine Headline News Online, www.newsflash.org/2004/02/hl/hl103309.htm, accessed 21 January 2006.

Pareño, Roel (2004), 'US counterterror training starts', *The Philippine Star*, 26 July.

Porcala, Delon (2004), 'Ex-AFP chief faces perjury raps, forfeiture of P11-M assets', *The Philippine Star*, 1 December.

Roncesvalles, Carina (2004), 'Senate panel to file motions vs strong policy bias towards US', *BusinessWorld Online*, www.bworldonline.com/BW030606/today.php, 23 September.

'RP far from Argentina-style financial crisis, says ex-cabinet man' (2004), *BusinessWorld Online*, www.bworldonline.com/BW030606/today.php, 20 September.

'RP, Japan hold talks on defense cooperation' (2005), Inquirer News Service and Agence France-Presse, 10 February.

Simon, Sheldon W. (2004), 'Philippines withdraws from Iraq and JI strikes again', *Comparative Connections*, Pacific Forum CSIS, 3rd Quarter, US–Southeast Asia Relations, www.csis.org/pacfor/cc/0403Qus_asean.html.

Sy, Marvin (2004a), 'Iraqi, US officials say RP set bad precedent', Inquirer News Service, 20 July.

Sy, Marvin (2004b), 'Australia blames RP for new terror threat', *The Philippine Star*, 26 July.

Sy, Marvin (2004c) 'RP, US vow stronger ties', *The Philippine Star*, 10 August.

Sy, Marvin (2004d), 'Albert insists no troop return to Iraq', *The Philippine Star*, 13 August.

Sy, Marvin (2004e), 'DFA chief: ban on OFW deployment in Iraq stays', *The Philippine Star*, 8 September.

Sy, Marvin (2004f), 'US lauds RP handling of Garcia case', *The Philippine Star*, 19 October.

'Terrorist tag on Philippine communist may spur peace talks: military' (2002), Agence France-Presse, 11 August.

Villanueva, Marichu (2004a), 'GMA revamps AFPSLAI, DND', *The Philippine Star*, 1 December.

Villanueva, Marichu (2004b), 'GMA admits RP in fiscal crisis', *The Philippine Star*, 24 August.

13. Counter-terrorism legislation in the Philippines[1]

Charles G.L. Donnelly

Since the bombings in Bali in 2002, Australian and US regional officials have routinely described the Philippines as the weakest link in the fight against Jemaah Islamiyah (JI) and affiliated terror groups in South-east Asia. The Philippines, unlike Indonesia, Malaysia, Thailand and Singapore, has not enacted an anti-terrorism or internal security law in the post-9/11 regional environment. Senior US diplomats to the Philippines sparked controversy in April and May 2005 by describing the southern Philippine island of Mindanao as potentially the 'next Afghanistan' and a 'doormat for terrorists'. These comments, based on US intelligence assertions (US Embassy in Manila 2005; Diaz 2005), were domestically unpopular and sparked recriminations within the capital and beyond. In Manila, an official press statement was released from the presidential palace, stating 'we hope this unfortunate incident is not repeated', in relation to the comment made by the US Chargé d'Affaires, Joseph Mussomeli (Department of Foreign Affairs 2005). In Mindanao, Mayor Muslimin Sema symbolically burnt a US flag to protest against the 'doormat' remarks of outgoing US Ambassador to the Philippines Francis Ricciardonne. This domestic backlash revealed Muslim Mindanao as a major fault line in the US–Philippine relationship and highlighted the political sensitivities involved in Manila's handling of Islamic terrorism and secessionism in the south.

The bombing of the Super Ferry in Manila Bay on 26 February 2004, perpetrated by the Abu Sayyaf Group (ASG), caused approximately 130 casualties (US Department of State 2005, p. 38), underscoring the serious nature of terrorism in the Philippines. Globally, this was the fourth-largest attack since 9/11. Regionally, it was the second most deadly attack since Bali and overall the most damaging terror strike in the history of Philippine and maritime history. Promoting fear and panic, the bombing revealed a reconsolidated and revitalized ASG, now capable of sowing seeds of terror and violence into the administrative heart of the country. Striking again one year later in metropolitan Manila, General Santos and Davao, the ASG coordinated a series of explosions on Valentine's Day 2005, killing 12 and injuring over 100 people. Later that month, President Gloria Macapagal-Arroyo announced that the passage of numerous anti-terror bills filed intermittently since the Rizal Day bombings of 2000[2] was urgent, claiming that it would 'add teeth' to her country's fight against terrorism. With one atrocity after another, many local and international observers of terrorism had come to the conclusion that South-east Asia is a key battleground in the global 'war on terror', thus establishing the deeply rooted insurgency in Mindanao as its front line.

This chapter analyses the implications for the Philippines' fragile liberal democracy of a potent new counter-terrorism bill, which is about to be enacted; it is a bill that boosts coercive executive power at the expense of judicial review. Critics of the bill have described it as 'draconian'. Philippine efforts to enact anti-terrorism legislation go to the heart of the international debate as to how the liberal democratic states can address the threat of terrorism without violating constitutional order and reducing responses to barbarism. This chapter describes the political context in which the Consolidated Anti-Terrorism Bill has arisen, outlines the substantive and contentious aspects of the document, and assesses the implications of such legislation on the situation in Mindanao and elsewhere in the Philippines.

THE IMPACT OF BALI ON MINDANAO

The 'Moro'[3] rebellion of the southern Philippines is one of South-east Asia's longest running insurgencies and among the most difficult to understand. The contemporary conflict had its beginnings in the 1970s. Led by separatist intellectuals who created the Moro National Liberation Front (MNLF), the minority Muslim population of Mindanao took up arms and waged war against the dictatorial and martial law regime of President Ferdinand Marcos. By 1976 the fighting had taken 120 000 lives and had displaced over 300 000 people. Embedded in this postcolonial conflict was a far deeper history of Muslim resentment against foreign colonial rule by Spain (1565–1899) and the United States (1899–1941, 1945–47).

When the air strikes of 9/11 penetrated US sovereignty, President Arroyo phoned President Bush that day and stated that 'the Philippines stands behind him and is ready to do what needs to be done' (Zabriskie 2002, p. 18). Declaring its former colony its 'staunchest ally', in early 2002 Washington designated Mindanao the second front in its 'war on terror' after the Afghanistan campaign (US Embassy in Manila 2002). By October 2003 President Bush had made the Philippines a 'major non-NATO ally', promising unprecedented military aid. This decision elevated the Philippines to a position in US foreign policy unrivalled since its suspension of the US Clarke airfield and Subic Bay naval base leases in the early 1990s. The readiness of the Philippines to fight terrorism is further exemplified by its leadership of the APEC anti-terrorism taskforce.

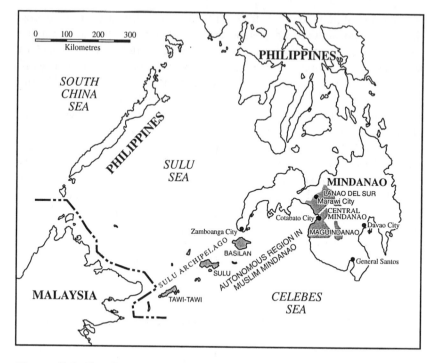

Figure 13.1: Sketch of the southern Philippines

Before 9/11 the Philippines received an annual US military commitment of $1.9 million (Berrigan and Hartung 2005). In 2005 it was the top Asian country and the fourth in the world in terms of US military aid, receiving no less than US$115 million in 2003, up from $38 million in 2001 (Conde 2005, p. 3).

In January 2002 approximately 660 US military personnel were deployed against the 250-strong ASG for the purposes of rescuing hostages and undertaking counter-insurgency operations against the ASG in Basilan island, located in the Sulu Archipelago (see Figure 13.1). Considered locally as more of a criminal bandit group than a legitimate secessionist entity, the ASG continues to be pursued militarily. The ASG was the first Philippine group to be designated a 'foreign terrorist organization' by the US Department of State in 1997. Although its original aim was to create an independent Islamic state based on the Shariah (Islamic law), it facilitated criminality and profiteering from violence. Boasting tenuous links to Al Qaeda and established links with JI, the ASG weaves Islamic jihadism into its disguise. The main methods employed by the group are indiscriminate bombings, kidnap for ransom, murder and piracy. In a critique of its ability to profit from kidnap for ransom and heinous crime, Eric Guiterrez (2003, pp. 146) effectively encapsulated the ASG as 'entrepreneurs of violence'.

In relation to the broader field of Muslim or 'Moro' secessionism, the 12 500-strong Moro Islamic Liberation Front (MILF) hailing from Central Mindanao is now the principal revolutionary movement in the Philippines. The MILF declared itself a rival faction to the MNLF in 1984 to 'underscore Islam as the rallying point of the Bangsamoro struggle' (Mastura 1985, p. 17). Peace talks between the MILF and Manila commenced in 1997 and entered a decisive phase in April 2005. Malaysia acted as host and third-party facilitator for the talks, sidelining the United States Institute of Peace. The peace talks covered issues of concept, territory and resources, but failed to address the issue of governance. The MILF put forward four options for the future structure of government for Muslim Mindanao: federal state, commonwealth, association of free states and independence. Under the first three options the MILF would maintain ties with Manila based on the principle of self-determination. However, under the fourth, albeit an unlikely prospect, all ties would be severed. The single strategy that MILF has rejected is that adopted by the MNLF, which in 1996 signed a final peace agreement with Manila leading to their accommodation within the Autonomous Region in Muslim Mindanao (ARMM). The ARMM (see Figure 13.1) was created to help resolve the Moro insurgency and foster economic development in Muslim Mindanao, comprising the provinces of Sulu, Tawi-Tawi, Maguindanao, Lanao del Sur and Basilan and the city of Marawi. Leadership and administrative issues have marred the ARMM. In the view of the MILF, autonomy is a dirty word and the ARMM has been a dismal failure.

If the attacks of 9/11 exposed the international tentacles of the Al Qaeda network then the attacks in Bali revealed Jema'ah Islamiyah as one of Al Qaeda's most active and lethal regional affiliates. Investigations by Australian and Singaporean authorities following the 2002 bombings in Bali also revealed that JI members were using Mindanao as a refuge, transit post and training camp. Investigations into the bombings in Bali in October 2005 have confirmed these links. The statements of detained JI members confirmed long-held beliefs that Al Qaeda and JI operatives had been using MILF-controlled areas as a 'military academy' since 1994. Both groups have been building on ties forged in the International Islamic Brigade during the Afghan–Soviet War (Jones 2005, p. 6; ICG 2004). Owing to the porous nature of Mindanao's borders and the inadequate border control, penetration of MILF camps has simply been a matter of reaching Central Mindanao and arranging transportation through an intermediary.

To counteract mounting pressure, the MILF leadership has responded by condemning all major terror strikes since 9/11 as 'un-Islamic'. This action also serves to deflect any criticism of suspected operational and training links between it, Al Qaeda and JI. In relation to the ASG, the MILF has condemned it as a separate and unaligned organization. What remains unclear is whether the MILF leadership denied these links because of changes in the security environment or whether they simply lacked any organizational control over their subordinate commanders, who had these active connections with the ASG and JI (ICG 2004). MILF Chairman, Al-Haj Murad Ebrahim, rejects both of these assertions, declaring that an open-door policy existed for all visitors to MILF camps prior to 9/11 and Bali. While conceding that visitors to his camps were sometimes trained in weapons proficiency, Chairman Ebrahim reiterates that backyard military training of private militias is a common practice in Muslim Mindanao also performed by legitimate government interests, such as private political families aligned to the administration, as well as illegitimate interests, such as gun-running and drug syndicates. Despite these links on the ground between the MILF and the ASG and JI, the official position of the MILF that rejects these connections allows it to be seen as an organization that is willing to negotiate with Manila. This, in turn, has meant that, in contrast to the ASG, the MILF has not been declared by either the United States or the Philippine government to be a terrorist organization.

Subsequent to the Bali attack, both Australian and US government officials continue to impress on the Philippines that the rebellion in the south not only is a threat to regional stability but also hampers any attempt to generate a suitable foreign investment climate for mineral-rich Mindanao.[4] The response of Manila has been twofold: first, to clamp down on the ASG militarily, and second to step up the peace process with the MILF. Utilizing evidence of its connections with JI as a trump card, Manila has obtained concessions from the MILF. In May 2005 the MILF held their first ever 'open' general assembly in front of nearly 500 000 people in the town of Sultan Kudarat, Maguindanao province. MILF Chairman Ebrahim announced to this record audience that the MILF had decided to undertake imminent clearing operations against JI members who were determined to remain 'high-value targets' to the Philippine military.[5]

If the doors of the MILF camps had been wide open for penetration by foreign terrorists before the Bali bombings, they were now metaphorically shut. Whether they remain locked and impenetrable remains another question. While concessions were being made in the south, however, powerful new counter-terror laws were being debated in the north.

THE CONSOLIDATED ANTI-TERRORISM BILL

In May 2005 debate commenced on the Consolidated House Bill, known by its short title as the 'Anti-Terrorism Act of 2005', at the Committee level of the House of Representatives in the Philippine Congress. Introduced by the Committee on Justice and the Committee on Foreign Affairs, this bill merges no less than ten anti-terrorism bills. These bills had been filed intermittently since the Rizal Day bombings of December 2000 and the Davao City bombings of March and April 2003.[6] The 30 December 2000 bombings claimed 22 dead and were linked to MILF operatives. The Consolidated House Bill defines terrorism, establishes institutional mechanisms to prevent and suppress it, and provides penalties for terrorism and related purposes. The 32 sections of the bill are extremely broad in scope and retributive in their mode of justice. No provision for a sunset or expiry clause is included. If the bill is passed, the institutionally weak and habitually corrupt Philippine state will be afforded unprecedented and unfettered power.

Under the 1987 Constitution of the Philippines, judicial determination of probable cause is required before an arrest warrant can be issued. The presumption of innocence exists and the accused are informed of the charges against them and have the right to counsel. In court they have right to confront witnesses, present evidence and appeal against convictions before an independent jury. No such rights will exist for persons deemed to be terrorists under the pending bill.

Terrorism is defined as:

> the premeditated, threatened, actual use of violence, force, or by any other means of destruction perpetrated against person/s, property/ies, or the environment, with the intention of creating or sowing a state of danger, panic, fear, or chaos to the general public, group of persons or particular person, or of coercing or intimidating the government to do or abstain from doing an act. (Anti-Terrorism Act of 2005, Section 3)

Under this wide, vague and ambiguous definition, law enforcers are granted unbridled discretion in interpreting terrorist acts. The all-encompassing nature of the definition is likely to encourage arbitrary and erratic arrests and convictions. It is unclear whether the arresting officer, the Anti-Terrorism Council created by the Act or the Court[7] will determine intent. Because a legislative vacuum exists, the demarcation of terrorism from criminal activities is difficult. Arrests could be influenced by wider political pressures and the beliefs and assumptions of law enforcers.

Despite numerous attempts over a number of years there is still no internationally accepted definition of the 'abstract noun – "terrorism"' (Allen 2002, p. 157). The political rhetoric of President Bush pitting 'freedom-loving' people against the 'axis of evil' effectively polarizes public opinion. This crude reduction of the multifaceted and complex struggle against acts of violence perpetrated by non-state actors sustains the conflict. At the same time, initiatives by Washington since 9/11 to label the MILF a 'foreign terrorist organization' have been stopped by Manila. Bids by the Bush administration to persuade Manila to lift 'shoot to kill' restrictions on US combat personnel in the southern Philippines were also rejected. Each attempt was met with hefty domestic and political opposition demonstrating both the intent and the capacity of Philippine democracy to counter undue external interference. The Philippine government has been compelled to curb US interests in the global war against terror in at least this regard. However, this does not in any way make the impending anti-terrorist legislation any more acceptable by the standards of any liberal, democratic society.

The penalties provided in the bill are retributive. They sanction prison sentences from life to six months and fines ranging from P10 million (US$194 287) down to P50 000 (US$971). Under Section 4, 'Terrorism: How Committed', and Section 7, 'Acts that Facilitate, Contribute to or Promote Terrorism' any attack resulting in loss of life earns life imprisonment and the maximum fine. This amounts to a sizeable sum, considering that the minimum daily wage for non-agricultural workers around Manila is US$5.36 and the lowest minimum wage for agricultural workers in the Autonomous Region in Muslim Mindanao is US$2.64 (US Department of State 2004).

From its first reading in the House of Representatives in May 2005 to its third and final reading in April 2006, two major changes were made to the Bill that effectively watered down its most severe provisions. The first change involved limitation of the maximum period of detention from 15 days to 36 hours. The second alteration involved suspension of the death penalty as the maximum sanction. This latter change derived from President Arroyo's decision to place a moratorium on the death penalty under Article 7, Section 19 of the 1987 Constitution of the Philippines. The moratorium does not however prevent the courts from imposing the death penalty. For abolition to legislatively occur, both houses of Congress must repeal the death penalty law. House of Representatives Minority Leader Francis Escudero insisted that President Arroyo was only placing the moratorium to survive a major political crisis arising from her improperly calling an electoral official during the 2004 presidential ballot and her husband's complicity in an illegal gambling racket (Cabacungan Jr. and Avendaño 2006). In response to these criticisms President Arroyo certified repeal of Republic Act 7659 (the Death Penalty Law) as 'urgent'.

Capital punishment in the Philippines has had an ambiguous past, considering that 85 per cent of the population of 84 million are Catholics. Within Asia, the Philippines holds the dubious distinction of being the only country to eliminate, reinstate and then suspend, the death penalty. Abolished by virtue of the 1987 Philippine Constitution, the death penalty was reinstated in 1994 under the Ramos administration, although actual executions did not start until 1999. Seven people were executed that year. Observance of the Christian Jubilee of 2000 by President Joseph Estrada ushered in a de facto moratorium on capital punishment. Similarly opposed to the death penalty, Gloria Macapagal-Arroyo, the newly appointed President, commuted 18 death sentences in 2001. However, her position changed following 9/11 when, in order to 'strike fear into the hearts of criminals', capital punishment was reinstated (Tagayuna 2004). A presidential moratorium enacted in March 2006 again changed this position.

The defining feature of the bill is the establishment of institutional mechanisms to avoid guarantees associated with the criminal process. Under Section 24 an administrative body, the Anti-Terrorism Council, is commissioned by the executive branch of government to be the 'central policy-making, coordinating, supervising and monitoring body of the government on all matters of domestic and international terrorism' (Anti-Terrorism Act of 2005, Section 24). The Chairperson of the Council is the Executive Secretary. The Vice-Chairperson is the National Security Advisor. Other members include the Secretaries of Foreign Affairs, Justice, National Defense, the Interior and Local Government; the Presidential Adviser on the Peace Process; Director General of the National Intelligence Coordinating Agency; Chairperson of the National Commission on Indigenous Peoples; Executive Director, Office on Muslim Affairs; Chairman, Commission on Human Rights; a representative recommended by the Minority in Congress; and any others personally designated by the President.

If approved by the Secretary of Justice, the Anti-Terrorism Council has the sole power in determining which individuals and organizations are unlawful. On the other hand, the Secretary of Justice cannot overturn a decision of the Council. This can be interpreted as a violation of due process. There is no evidence of due process in the determination and criminalization of a terrorist organization. In its present design, nor does the Council include a judge or member of the judiciary within its ranks.

The Anti-Terrorism Council is afforded unbridled discretion in defining and prosecuting acts of terrorism. By invoking this administrative process, the Philippine government is avoiding the normal guarantees associated with the criminal process in much the same way as the military tribunals of detainees in Guantanamo Bay have attempted to insulate the executive of the US Government and their national security cases from scrutiny by the courts. The 29 June 2006 US Supreme Court ruling of *Hamdan* v *Rumsfeld* (2006), established that President George W. Bush had overstepped his powers and breached the Geneva Convention by setting up special war crime tribunals for 'war on terror' suspects. This type of administrative body invites excesses and abuses and with the benefit of hindsight it is almost always considered a mistake (Cole 2003, p. 3). In the context of the Philippines where just 15 of the estimated 15 million families control most of the country's resources and capacities, this is even more the case.

Means for the prevention and suppression of terrorism form the bulk of the bill. Membership of a terrorist organization is deemed unlawful, as is participation, facilitation, possessing property for purposes of terrorism and threatening or inciting terrorism. Included in the anti-terrorism provisions are citizen's arrest, warrant-less arrest, a 36 hour period of warrant-less detention, surveillance and interception of communication, the power of inquiry, and the authority to freeze bank accounts.

Membership of a terrorist organization is deemed unlawful under Section 9. It carries a sentence of between six and 12 years, unless the accused can show he or she had no knowledge of the organization's activities and immediately withdraws from it (Anti-Terrorism Act of 2005, Section 9). In this sense, the Anti-Terrorism Act of 2005 is a Bill of Attainder, as it abridges due process by punishing individuals or members of a proscribed terrorist organization without a judicial trial. This contravenes the 1987 Philippine Constitution's Bill of Rights (Section 22, Article III).

It is deemed unlawful to incite others to terrorism 'by means of speeches, proclamations, writings, emblems, banners or other representations *tending* to incite others to terrorism' under Section 6 (author's emphasis added). 'Inciting to Terrorism' receives a prison sentence of between six·and 12 years and a fine of P5 million (US$97 143). The vagueness of the term 'tending' is problematic and could conceivably lead to government campaigns against legitimate criticism and voices of dissent, should an inhospitable political climate take root. The cronyism and martial law era of President Marcos (1972–86) and the economic plunder of President Estrada (1998–2001) were illustrative of political mismanagement and the pervasive corruption it gave rise to. Both these administrations ended in populist revolt, which resulted in the People Power I and II Revolutions of 1986 and 2001 respectively.

Acts that facilitate, contribute to or promote terrorism carry life imprisonment if the terrorist act results in loss of life, under Section 7. Establishing, maintaining or serving as a contact with an individual or group who is pursuing terrorism; arranging or assisting two or more people who are meeting to support or further terrorism; participating or providing training facilities to terrorists – all carry a life sentence (Anti-Terrorism Act of 2005, Section 7). In other words, guilt by association and the perpetration of terrorism are one and the same. Groups like the ASG have managed to evade capture because they have support within the community. The level of power conferred to the state as a consequence of the bill could conceivably lead to the imprisonment and even life imprisonment for community members deemed guilty by association. State power of this type is prone to abuse and could incite further terrorism, primarily because the bill lacks any judicial checks and balances. Only in Subsection 2 must the state prove intent and knowledge of the accused in instances where arranging or assisting in the meeting of two or more persons was done for the purposes of terrorism.

Any peace officer or citizen may, under Section 14, without warrant, detain a suspect for committing or attempting to commit a terrorist act, provided that there is 'reasonable ground' to do so. This replaces the 'personal knowledge' standard under the extant Rules of Court (Section B). Under this Section of the new bill a citizen or law enforcer does not require direct personal knowledge that a terrorist act has been committed, provided that there is 'reasonable ground' to detain the suspect (Anti-Terrorism Act of 2005, Section 14). Legislative freedom of this type has the capacity to provoke communal tensions in areas where distrust already prevails.

Article 125 of the Revised Penal Code that presently governs the Philippines states that the maximum period for warrantless detention is 36 hours (Anti-Terrorism Act of 2005, Section 14). Under the pending bill this period can increase if the person arrested without warrant demands a preliminary investigation and consents to it in writing in the presence of his or her counsel (Albano and Tubianosa 2006, p. 2).

In the view of Philippine human rights groups, forced confessions, police brutality and torture usually occur in the first couple of days of detention. The most prominent human rights group in Manila, the Task Force Detainees of the Philippines (TFDP), have recorded 146 incidents of torture inside jails and safe houses since the Arroyo administration came to power in 2001 (Task Force 2005a). TFDP investigations revealed that torture usually occurs in the early days of detention, generally before charges have been filed. Despite ratifying the UN Convention Against Torture and Resolution 2003/37, stating that freedom from torture is a non-negotiable right, there is still no Philippine law against it. Police brutality, including instances of torture, remains an 'open secret' in Philippine civil society.

The Anti-Money Laundering Act of 2001 is subsumed into the bill under Section 18, meaning that the Anti-Terrorism Council has the power to inquire into and freeze bank accounts for a period not exceeding 90 days (Anti-Terrorism Act of 2005). To repeal the decision of the Council the purported owner is given three days notice to justify their position. If they are unable to do so the court has power to dissolve the account. A fine of between P50 000 (US$971) and P100 000 (US$1942) is also applicable.

A wide range of wire-tapping possibilities is provided for government officials under Section 19 of the new bill. This intrusion into individual privacy is bolstered by the relaxation of the laws that govern the process by which a witness is produced and the need to justify police surveillance of, and intrusion into, the life of a citizen. Providers of telephone, internet, banking and other services must comply with the demands of the authorities or face a sentence of not less than six months and not more than six years (Anti-Terrorism Act of 2005, Section 19).

Making false threats about acts of terrorism (Section 10) and failing to disclose acts of terrorism (Section 11) carry a sentence of between six and 12 years with a fine between P50 000 (US$971) and P100 000 (US$1942). Fines between P10 000 (US$194) and P500 000 (US$9714) and a sentence of eight to 12 years are imposed in order to deter corrupt public officers from assisting terrorists in jail breaks, or officers whose negligence results in a terrorist's escape (Section 12).

President Macapagal-Arroyo appealed for the swift passage of the Consolidated Anti-Terrorism Bill, as part of her 25 July 2005 state of the nation address, claiming it would 'protect rather than subvert' and 'enhance rather than weaken' the rights and liberties threatened by terrorism (Macapagal-Arroyo 2005). Protests coinciding with meetings on the substantive and contentious aspects of the bill suggested otherwise. Opposition groups protesting outside Congress on 1 August 2005, declared that the bill was being railroaded in exchange for the US government's continued support, adding that the real threat to democracy in the country was the 'bankruptcy of elite rule' upheld by the President (AKBAYAN and Alliance of Progressive Labor 2005). On 6 April 2006 an overwhelming majority of the chamber passed the Anti Terrorism Act of 2005 under House Bill 4839, 116 to 28, on its third and final reading. The measure now awaits plenary debates in the upper house as Senate Bill 2187. To become law, the bill must pass its second and third readings in the Senate. If passed, the bill will be reconciled with the lower house version before it is signed by the president and becomes law. It is expected that the Anti Terrorism Act of 2005 will face further scrutiny in the 24-seat Philippine Senate controlled by the opposition bloc in order to safeguard against potential human rights abuses (Senate of the Philippines 2006).

NATIONAL IDENTIFICATION SCHEME

In addition to pushing forward the Consolidated Anti-Terrorist Bill of May 2005, in February 2005 President Macapagal-Arroyo insisted on the urgency of implementing a national identification system. On 13 April 2005 she signed Executive Order No. 420, called the 'harmonisation of government ID numbers', which authorized the implementation of such a scheme. The order was initially implemented at the local level and took effect in June. The order mandates government agencies to synchronize existing ID systems from various government departments such as the National Statistics Office, the Land Transportation Authority and the Commission on Elections. Under the system a unique number is assigned to every citizen, which will improve the government's capacity to monitor terrorism by cross-referencing data. The synchronized ID scheme includes personal and biometric details such as home address, sex, photo ID, signature, date of birth, place of birth, marital status, names, height, weight, tax identification numbers, prints of both index fingers and both thumbs, and any prominent distinguishing features (Remollino

2005). The scheme is designed to complement the Consolidated House Bill by making it easier for law-enforcement agencies to track terrorists.

This is not the first time that the Philippine government has sought to introduce an effective national ID scheme. Former Philippine President Fidel Ramos issued Administrative Order 308 in 1996 to create a national computerized ID system. Opponents contended that it was unconstitutional. In 1998 the Supreme Court of the Philippines dismissed it as unlawful, adding that such a system had 'the power to compile a devastating dossier against unsuspecting citizens' (Dalangin-Fernandez 2005). President Macapagal-Arroyo's signing of Executive Order 420 has effectively circumvented these legal obstacles and created, by default, a national ID system that did not have the approval of Congress, but that was nevertheless easier to administer, more cost effective and less invasive than the original proposal. In April 2006 the Supreme Court of the Philippines found the proposal constitutionally valid (Cabacungan Jr. 2006, p. 1). Critics of the move towards this type of security assert that it is part of a global infrastructure accommodating mass surveillance.

THE IMPLICATIONS OF THE NEW LAW

The Anti-Terrorism Bill has not yet been passed, yet it is worth asking what implications might it have if it became law? In particular, how might such an Act impact on the social and political situation in Mindanao? In the view of Michael Ignatieff (2005, p. 61) the tendency of liberal democracies to overreact in times of mass fear introduces a process whereby their institutional framework is twisted to strengthen secret government at the expense of adversarial review, a process that fuels the loss of liberty, especially among marginalized sectors of the community. These concerns have special relevance to the Philippines, where poor governance has already had a negative impact on those without wealth and resources. If enacted the bill is likely to impact most heavily on the already marginalized five-million-strong Muslim minority, who are predominantly concentrated in the Sulu Archipelago and Central Mindanao. The Philippines is not the first society in which the minority Muslims have been most affected by new anti-terrorist legislation: the Prevention of Terrorism Act in India provides another example of the asymmetrical impact of 9/11 on Muslims (Vicziany 2003, pp. 258–9). The bill's provisions will strengthen the already powerful hand of the secret service, police and military by setting aside judicial review in favour of a powerful Anti-Terrorism Council. Given the high levels of corruption in these organs of the state, the new laws will enhance popular perceptions that official justice is beyond the reach of ordinary citizens in the Philippines. The following parts of this section consider the impact of the Anti-Terrorism Bill in the context of corruption in the Philippines, the history of torture and the failings of the prison system, the poverty of Mindanao and the proliferation of small arms trading.

Corruption in the Philippines

Systemic corruption plagues the Philippines. Global surveys consistently rank the Philippines among the lowest in the world in terms of transparency and adherence to the rule of law (ADB 2005, p. 19). Consequently, a 'justifiable' public perception of corruption in the executive, judicial and legislative branches of government remains high (US Department of State 2004). Corruption is also cited as one of the main reasons that the Armed Forces of the Philippines are ineffective in dealing with domestic and regional terrorists. In June 2003 nearly 300 disgruntled soldiers seized the Oakwood serviced apartments in the heart of the Makati business centre, demanding reforms and accusing their superiors of mismanaging funds and supplies and selling guns and ammunition to the ASG and MILF. Quashed after 18 hours, the incident exposed the extent of graft and corruption in the military. Terrorists and insurgent groups in the Philippines openly proclaim that the armed forces and the national police are their two most important sources of weaponry (Heijmans et al. 2004, p. 297).

Two further scandals broke in June 2005, revealing the Philippines as habitually corrupt. In June 2005 the Garcillano tapes surfaced and exposed President Macapagal-Arroyo as improperly communicating with an electoral officer during the May 2004 presidential ballot, which she won by only 900 000 votes. Opposition parties called for her resignation. The electoral fraud scandal was compounded, later that month, by the *jueteng* or gambling payola scandal implicating the president's son and brother-in-law, both congressmen, in receiving proceeds from illegal gambling. Eleven cabinet members resigned and protestors took to the streets in scenes reminiscent of the People Power Revolutions of 1986 and 2001. As the president's approval rating plummeted, impeachment proceedings were filed moments before Macapagal-Arroyo gave her annual state of the nation address to Congress on 25 July. To deflect mounting pressure on her legitimacy as president, Macapagal-Arroyo devoted a third of her annual address to the 'great debate on Charter Change' as the best way to reform the Philippine political system, which has become a 'hindrance to progress' (Macapagal-Arroyo 2005). Constitutional change, proposed Macapagal-Arroyo, should take the form of a federal Westminster type of parliamentary structure led by a prime minister, replacing the existing fractious unitary US type of presidential system. By September 2005 impeachment proceedings against Macapagal-Arroyo were dropped owing to inadequate congressional support. Peace talks between the MILF and the government resumed in Malaysia soon after. For the MILF the contemporary debate on constitutional change was fortuitous, considering the failure of the April 2005 talks with central government to resolve governance arrangements. The call for 'Charter Change' plays into the hands of the MILF with its demands for significant decentralization.

Torture, Illegal Extractions and the Failings of the Prison System

Despite serious failings in governance, the Philippine state remains pre-occupied with reclaiming its former status as Washington's 'staunchest ally' in the US-led 'war on terror' by passing the anti-terror bill. With the potential to be politically effective in the short term, this strategy fails to recognize and address the root causes or conditions that lead to and perpetuate extremism. The Task Force Detainees of the Philippines suggest that the existing state of lawlessness will merely become institutionalized by the enactment of the bill. They predict that communal tensions will be aggravated and that the sense of injustice in the Autonomous Region in Muslim Mindanao will increase. Two important sets of annual reports produced by the US Department of State substantiate the assertion that the bill will exacerbate violence and lawlessness in the Philippines.

The *2004 Country Reports on Terrorism* verify that corruption, low morale, inadequate salaries, recruitment and retention difficulties and lack of effective cooperation between police and prosecutors all hamper effective law enforcement and criminal justice in the Philippines (US Department of State 2005, p. 39). The *2004 Country Reports on Human Rights Practices* provide specific examples of unlawful police practice, overcrowding in the prison system and other undesirable aspects of the Philippine legal system:

> Some elements of the security services were responsible for arbitrary, unlawful, and in some cases, extrajudicial killings; disappearances; torture; and arbitrary arrest and detention. The physical abuse of suspects and detainees remained a problem, as did police, prosecutorial, and judicial corruption. As in the past years the constitutionally mandated Commission on Human Rights described the PNP (Philippine National Police) as the worst abuser of human rights. Police and local government leaders at times appeared to sanction extrajudicial killings and vigilantism as expedient means of fighting crime and terrorism. (US Department of State 2004)

In fighting criminal organizations, security forces are also known to resort to 'salvaging' or summary executions. Various local government officials in Mindanao condone this practice as necessary and justifiable. The Mayor of Davao City, tough-talking Rodrigo Duterte, is one such voice. Duterte allegedly backs vigilante groups to conduct extrajudicial slayings. In his municipality alone, 67 suspected criminals were 'salvaged' between January and August 2004, according to the TFDP.

Torture remains an ingrained part of the arrest and detention process, according to the TFDP, despite the Constitution's prohibition of this. Common forms of abuse include beatings, threats with guns, suffocation with cellophane, strangulation, solitary confinement and psychological or mental torture (Task Force 2005b). Omar Ramalan, a 50-year-old former MNLF combatant, was illegally detained for 15 days as a suspect of the January 2005 bombing in Parang, Maguindanao. Stripped naked, blindfolded and hog-tied in a secluded room, Ramalan was electrocuted, fed dirty food and mauled until he lost consciousness (Asian Human Rights Commission 2004). Given this inhospitable culture of violence, it is not surprising that moderate citizens are reluctant to speak out as they fear swift reprisals from police, soldiers or vigilante groups.

Prisons in the Philippines are generally harsh and lack infrastructure. In metropolitan Manila, for instance, jails operate at 323 per cent of their capacity (US Department of State 2004). In 2004 the campaign against illegal drugs led to further overcrowding. In provincial jails, prisoners often have to resort to sleeping in turns. Wardens sometimes permit wives and children to move in with inmates to help feed prisoners. Sanitation and a slow judicial system are likewise problematic. Corruption among guards demanding payments from prisoners for food, the use of amenities or to avoid beatings has been reported. Despite the horrors of prison life, security remains slack and corrupt guards often connive at facilitating escapes. In 2004 some 115 prisoners escaped; 61 were recaptured and 54 remained at large. It is predicted that the enactment of the Anti-Terrorism Bill will aggravate this already fragile prison system, especially in Muslim Mindanao, for it is safe to assume that many more detentions and lengthy arrests will follow.

The Economic Backwardness of Mindanao

Poor governance in the Philippines is fuelled by the concentration of power in the hands of some 15 feudal families that have ruled the country for a very long time. The gap between the impoverished and the super-rich grows ever wider. Poverty is abundant in the archipelago nation comprised of 7100 islands and islets: 33 per cent of families live in poverty, while a staggering 46 per cent of Filipinos live below the poverty line, earning merely US$2 a day. Exacerbating national poverty is the high level of national debt. By the end of 2003, total debt for the Philippines was US$60 billion: the external debt to GDP ratio was 70 per cent and 30 per cent of the national budget was required to service the foreign debt (Abinales 2004).

Things are worse in the provinces: the Autonomous Region in Muslim Mindanao (ARMM) is ranked at the bottom of the country's 17 administrative regions, using conventional socioeconomic indicators. Proclaimed on 1 August 1989 through the Republic Act No. 6734, the ARMM presently comprises the five provinces of Maguindanao, Lanao del Sur, Sulu, Tawi-Tawi and Basilan and the city of Marawi (see Figure 13.1). The ARMM provinces have a total population of 2 873 232; 89.17 per cent are Muslim. The ARMM represents 4 per cent of Philippine territory and 3.5 per cent of the Philippine population. Development needs are greatest in the conflict-affected and battle-prone provinces of Maguindanao, Basilan and Jolo. Access to basic social services remains an enormous problem. Extreme poverty, conflict and historical disadvantage underpin the disparity in health and education between ARMM and the rest of the country's provinces.

In the ARMM the incidence of poverty is 63 per cent, almost double the national average. Average per capita income is also the lowest in the Philippines at less than US$1 per day (USAID 2005). Life expectancy for women is a mere 59.3 years and for men 55.5 years; both are ten years below national averages. Infant mortality, at 63 deaths per 1000 live births, is higher than the national average. Net primary and secondary school enrolment rates, at 82 and 39 per cent respectively, are 14 and 33 percentage points lower than the national average (World Bank 2003, p. 17). Educational indicators for the ARMM show the lowest levels of basic literacy and the highest school dropout rates for the Philippines (Sorza 2005). These indicators suggest that any serious and sustainable attempt to address the causes and effect of terrorism in Mindanao will require better prospects for human development.

Under the leadership of incumbent ARMM Governor Zaldy Ampatuan, new anti-poverty projects have been pledged but little evidence yet exists on the ground of any amelioration of socioeconomic conditions. The attempted ambush in July 2006 of Maguindanao Governor Andal Ampatuan, the father of ARMM Governor Zaldy Ampatuan, has led to an outbreak of fighting between his clan's private armies and the rebel forces of the MILF (Abinales 2006). The superimposition of the Anti-terrorism Act on this type of internecine conflict between unaligned Muslin groups could conceivably lead to a renewal of violence. It is likely that popular support for the banditry and terrorism of the ASG and other rebel groups will persist in genuinely depressed Muslim communities of Mindanao in the face of a corrupt regime of wealthy families in far-off Manila.

The Proliferation of Small Arms, the ASG and the MILF

The proliferation of small arms is also problematic. In Mindanao, over 70 per cent of the population owns one or more guns. Handguns can be purchased for as little as US$15 and machineguns from around US$375 (Amnesty International 2005). Oxfam found that 78 per cent of all violent deaths were carried out with military-style weapons (*Small Arms Survey* 2003, p. 138). In the ASG stronghold of Basilan, for instance, weapons outnumber people. This precludes any weaponry held by legitimate government forces (Torres 2001, p. 170). The inventory of the ASG and MILF is dominated by Philippines state-issue small arms. According to MILF spokesperson, Eid Kabalu, local sources are plentiful while buying from external sources is 'long, expensive and risky' (Heijmans et al. 2004, p. 300). On this basis, the post-9/11 transfer of 30 000 M-16 rifles by the United States to the Armed Forces of the Philippines is counterproductive. Any serious attempt to fight terrorism in the Philippines requires programs aimed at reducing gun trafficking and creating weapon-free zones in the ARMM provinces where the local insurgent groups are strongest.

Since its first attack in 1991, the ASG has displayed an uncanny ability to evade capture, then regroup and re-strike in the wake of military offensives. One Australian academic recognized as early as 1995 that a recurring tactic of the group was to launch counter-diversionary assaults when hard-pressed by the military (Turner 1995, p. 6). The planting and detonation of bombs on the Super Ferry 14-passenger ferry in Manila Bay during 26 February 2004 and on a bus in Metro Manila on 14 February 2004 suggests that the ASG is extending its localized hand of terror into the capital in retaliation for scaled-up operations against it.

Since early 2005 thousands of government forces have been tracking down the ASG in the Sulu province. Human rights activists have complained that the Philippine military have illegally detained citizens, burnt houses, displaced residents and shelled villages suspected of being ASG strongholds (US Department of State 2004). Armed Forces Chief, General Efren Abu, announced in May 2005 that most ASG leaders had moved to Central Mindanao in order to avoid government forces; yet local communities in Sulu had suffered the full brunt of the anti-terror campaign in the previous months.

A significant bounty system, operated by the US Department of State through its Rewards for Justice program, aims to round up key ASG leaders. A payment of US$1 million was made to three Filipino informants for the attempted capture of ASG leader Hamsiraji Sali, who was killed in the process (US Department of State 2005, p. 38). In June 2005 seven ASG members received 12 death sentences each for their involvement in abduction, beheadings and rape during an attack on Basilan in 2001 (Inquirer News Service 2005). The risk is that the new Philippine counter-terror law will lift the bar for the ASG and other extremists, and reprisals and counter-reprisals will escalate.

Through attacks on central Manila causing mass casualties and insecurity, the ASG appears to be challenging the moral and political certitude of the Philippine government. By revealing its hand in this manner, the ASG is provoking the Philippine government into a heavy-handed response. As an extremist group the ASG seeks three ends. First, it wishes to polarize public opinion against the moderate voices of Islam in Mindanao. Second, it seeks to destabilize and overshadow the peace process between the MILF and the government of the Philippines. Third, it is hoping to directly threaten Philippine liberal democracy by indulging in *la politique du pire* – literally the politics of the worst. The strategy of the group since 9/11 has been aimed at provoking Manila into indiscriminate acts of atrocity in response to its own acts of violence. In turn, state reprisals in the heightened security environment have acted as a recruiting mechanism for the group. Evidence from the US State Department (2004) demonstrates that in pursuing its goals the ASG has had no trouble in recruiting teenagers and children to fight, run errands, spy and undertake criminal activities.

The response of the MILF to the Anti-Terrorism Bill has been very different, partly because it has not yet been declared a terrorist organization. The Arroyo administration has effectively thwarted US attempts to brand the group a 'foreign terrorist organization', realising that to do so would irrevocably break down the peace process with the MILF. According to the Center for Moro Law and Policy Concerns, however, Muslims in Mindanao fear that if passed, the bill will escalate harassment and vilification of their communities, aggravate criminal tensions and potentially fracture the MILF. Officially the MILF does not acknowledge Philippine government laws because as a revolutionary group it considers itself to be outside the national political and legal system. At the same time, the leadership of the MILF is keen to retain the option of negotiating a peace settlement with Manila and also keep at bay the younger, more radical elements within its own party organization. It has been suggested that there is a growing ideological attraction among the younger, local MILF members to the ideas espoused by Al Qaeda and JI. If passed, the new anti-terror bill runs the risk of strengthening the hand of these Al Qaeda/JI sympathizers and simultaneously undermining the position of the MILF moderates, who will have difficulty retaining control of the movement if the corrupt and corrosive apparatus of the state begins to racket up the level of surveillance and violence against ordinary citizens and its own more moderate spokespersons. Given this, the MILF unofficially continues to work with lobby groups and the media to oppose the bill.[6]

CONCLUSION

The Philippines faces many problems in its fight against terrorism. The labelling of the Philippines as the weakest link in the regional 'war on terror' by Australian and US officials in the aftermath of the bombings in Bali is based on three considerations: first, the unrelenting terrorism of the ASG;

second, evidence of collaboration between JI and the MILF; and third, the absence of 'a law defining and codifying terrorist acts, and restrictions on gathering evidence [that] hinder the building of effective terrorism cases' (US Department of State 2005, p. 39). In the view of Washington and its regional allies, a counter-terrorism law will strengthen the Philippines, the so-called weakest link in the region. But will it?

In this chapter I argue that the new anti-terror bill cannot deliver the results expected of it unless domestic governance improves at the same time. There is no sign, however, that any attempt is being made to address the wider question of why regions like the ARMM wish to secede from the Philippines. It is suggested here that domestic stability hinges critically on addressing mass poverty, corruption, and lack of transparency and adherence to the rule of law. These are the most serious weak links in the Philippines' fight against terrorism. Condaleezza Rice, the US Secretary of State, recently noted the urgency of promoting democracy in the fight for global stability. As Mendelsohn comments (Chapter 4), Rice's insight seriously questions the appropriateness of the anti-terrorist laws that have been introduced into various Asian countries since 9/11. By giving unfettered power to an already institutionally weak and habitually corrupt Philippine state, the Consolidated House Bill will increase the legitimate grievances of an economically marginalized minority community. The inevitable result of increased police and military power and corruption will be greater communal tensions in an already conflict-prone area. The only group likely to benefit from such an outcome is the banned ASG, which bases its strategy on creating an unremitting war between the weak and marginalized citizens of the Philippines and the state.

NOTES

1. This chapter is based on interviews with the executive director of the Task Force Detainees of the Philippines (TFDP) and the director of the Center for Moro Law and Policy Concern and fieldwork in Manila and Cotabato City in early 2002.
2. The Rizal Day bombings of 30 December 2000 in metropolitan Manila resulted in 22 casualties and approximately 100 injuries. Rizal Day is a national holiday in the Philippines commemorating the 1896 execution of José Rizal, the country's pro-independence national hero who was put to death under the Spanish colonial administration for his role in the Philippine Revolution. The masterminds of the Rizal Day bombings were reputedly Islamic militants from JI and the Moro National Liberation Front. One of the blasts exploded about 100 metres from the US Embassy.
3. 'Moro' is a pejorative term that was applied to all the Muslim populations of South-east Asia by Portuguese and Spanish conquerors in the early sixteenth century with scant regard for linguistic and political differences. Some 13 ethnolinguistic groups adopted Islam as a way of life in Mindanao when Arab and Indian Muslim traders, as well as Muslim preachers, arrived on the shores of the Sulu Archipelago and Mindanao in the twelfth century. The three largest are the Maguindanaoan (people of the flooded plain) of the Cotabato provinces, the Maranaw (people of the lake) of the two Lanao provinces and the Tausug (people of the current) of the Sulu Archipelago. Muslim separatist intellectuals reactivated the term as an

all-encompassing identity for their struggle against the oppressive dictatorship of President Marcos in the early 1970s (McKenna 1998, pp. 80–81).
4. The Philippines has the second-highest gold endowments and third-highest copper deposits in the world. Mindanao accounts for 80 per cent of the total national deposits of gold, copper and nickel (Ilagan-Bian 2003).
5. Information based on a telephone interview with the Center for Moro Law and Policy Concerns, Cotabato City, Philippines, from Melbourne, Australia (Task Force 2005b).
6. The Davao City bombings of 4 March and 2 April 2003, respectively targeted at its main airport and seaport, caused 36 casualties and injured nearly 200 people. The MILF were held responsible by local authorities but charges were dropped in late 2004 for lack of evidence.
7. In early 2006 Philippine courts faced a backlog of no fewer than 800 000 cases (USAID 2006). Given the backlog of Philippine courts it is not uncommon for inmates, correctly or falsely accused, to wait years for a trial.

REFERENCES

Abinales, Patricio N. (2004), 'Deeper into the quagmire', *Asian Analysis*, December, www.aseanfocus.com/asiananalysis/article.cfm?articleID=802, accessed September 2005.

Abinales, Patricio N. (2006), 'From the margins: the end of an experiment', *MindaNews*, 18 July, http://mindanews.com/index.php?option=com_content&task=blogcategor y&id=48&Itemid=117, accessed July 2006.

ADB (Asian Development Bank) (2005), *Philippines: Private Assessment Sector*, Manila: ADB, February, pp. 1–96, www.adb.org/PHCO/Private-Sector-draft.pdf, accessed June 2005.

AKBAYAN and Alliance of Progressive Labor (2005), 'Terror bill strengthens GMA hands against critics', *Manila Independent Media Collective*, 8 August, http://manila.indymedia.org/?action=newswire&parentview=5141, accessed August 2005.

Albano, Noel and Diony Tubianosa (2006), 'House passes anti-terrorism bill on 3rd and final reading', House of Representatives press release, 5 April, www.congress.gov.ph/press/details.php?pressid=1200, accessed June 2006.

Allen, R. (2002), 'Terrorism and truth', *Alternative Law Journal*, 27 (4), 155–98.

Amnesty International (2005), *USA Supplies Small Arms to the Philippines*, www.web.amnesty.org/web/web.nsf/print/6258D7FD7F7a9d1d80256d40004ff45c, accessed May 2005.

Anti-Terrorism Act of 2005, Republic of the Philippines, House of Representatives, Quezon City, Metro Manila, Thirteenth Congress, First Regular Session, Introduced by the Committee on Justice and Foreign Affairs, 'An Act Defining Terrorism, Establishing Institutional Mechanisms to Prevent and Suppress its Commission, Providing Penalties Therefore and for Other Purposes', Draft as of 4 May 2005, www.privacyinternational.org/article.shtml?cmd%5B347%5D=x-347-224693, accessed June 2005.

Asian Human Rights Commission (2004), 'A torture victim Omar Ramalan filed five criminal charges against the military personnel who tortured him', 23 February, www.ahrchk.net/ua/mainfile.php/2004/624/, accessed May 2005.

Berrigan, Frida and William D. Hartung (2005), 'US weapons at war 2005: promoting freedom or fuelling conflict: US military aid and transfers since September 11', A World Policy Institute Special Report by the Arms Trade Resource Center, June, www.worldpolicy.org/projects/arms/reports/wawjune2005.html#10, accessed August 2005.

Cabacungan, Gil C. (2006), 'Palace orders implementation of ID system', Inq7, 21 April, http://news.inq7.net/nation/index.php?index=1&story_id=732221, accessed April 2006.

Cabacungan, Gil C. and Christine O. Avendaño (2006), 'Legal experts: Arroyo ignoring SC, Congress: President set to endorse bill ending death penalty', *Inq7*, 18 April, http://news.inq7.net/nation/index.php?index=1&story_id=72867, accessed June 2006.

Cole, David D. (2003), 'The new McCarthyism: repeating history in the war on terrorism', *Harvard Civil Rights–Civil Liberties Law Review*, 38, 1–30, www.law. harvard.edu/students/orgs/crcl/vol38_1/cole.pdf, accessed May 2005.

Conde, Carlos (2005), 'Corruption troubles Philippine military', *International Herald Tribune*, 26 May, www.iht.com/articles/2005/05/25/news/phils.php, accessed June 2005.

Dalangin-Fernandez, Lira (2005), 'Arroyo backs national ID system', Inq7, 24 May, http://beta.inq7.net/top/index.php?index=1&story_id=27929, accessed May 2005.

Department of Foreign Affairs (2005), 'Statement of the Honourable Ignacio Bunye Press Secretary', Malacañang, 13 April, www.dfa.gov.ph/archive/speech/romulo/ josephmussomeli.htm, accessed May and June 2005.

Diaz, Patricio P. (2005), 'Knee jerking for truth', *MindaNews,* 17 May, 3 (435), www. mindanews.com/2005/05/17vws-diaz.html, accessed May 2005.

Guiterrez, Eric (2003), 'From Ilaga to Abu Sayyaf: new entrepreneurs in violence and their impact on local politics in Mindanao', *Philippine Political Science Journal*, 24 (47), 145–76.

Hamdan v Rumsfeld (2006), Cornell Law School, Legal Information Institute, Supreme Court Collection, No. 05-184, 415 F. 3d 33, reversed and remanded, www.law. cornell.edu/supct/html/05-184.ZS.html, accessed July 2006.

Heijmans, Annelies, Nicola Simmonds and Hans van de Veen (eds) (2004), *Searching for Peace in Asia Pacific: an Overview of Conflict Prevention and Peacebuilding Activities*, Boulder and London: Lynne Rienner.

ICG (International Crisis Group) (2004), 'Southern Philippines backgrounder: terrorism and the peace process', *Asia Report No. 80*, 13 July, www.crisisgroup. org/home/index.cfm?id=2863&1=1, accessed May 2005.

Ignatieff, Michael (2005), *The Lesser Evil: Political Ethics in the Age of Terror*, Edinburgh: Edinburgh University Press.

Ilagan-Bian, Joji (2003), 'Waking up a giant: revitalising mining in Mindanao', *Philippine Daily Inquirer*, 11 August, www.mindanao.org/min~one//0308/11.htm, accessed June 2005.

Inquirer News Service (2005), '7 Abu Sayyaf men get 12 death sentences each', 23 June, http://news.inq7.net/regions/index.php?index=1&story_id=41169, accessed June 2005.

Jones, Sidney (2005), 'Terrorism and "radical Islam" in Indonesia', in Marika Vicziany and David Wright-Neville (eds), *Terrorism and Islam in Indonesia: Myths and Realities*, Annual Indonesia Lecture Series No. 26, Monash Asia Institute, Clayton.

Macapagal-Arroyo, Gloria (2005), 'State of the Nation Address', 26 July, *ABS-CBN Interactive*, www.abs-cbnnews.com/storypage.aspx?StoryId=11357, accessed August 2005.

Mastura, Datu Michael O. (1985), *The Crisis of the MNLF Leadership and the Dilemma of the Muslim Autonomy Movement, Collected Papers of the Conference on the Tripoli Agreement: Problems and Prospects*, 13–14 September, Manila: International Studies Institute, University of the Philippines.

McKenna, Thomas M. (1998), *Muslim Rulers and Rebels: Everyday Politics and Armed Separatism in the Southern Philippines,* California: University of California Press.

Remollino, Alexander Martin (2005), 'Arroyo gov't pushing ID system amid snowballing opposition', *Bulatlat*, 5 (4), www.bulatlat.net/news/5-4/5-4-IDsystem.html, accessed June 2005.

Senate of the Philippines (2006), 'Arrest of 5 Estrada supporters dampens Senate's interest in enacting anti-terrorism law', press release, 28 May, www.senate.gov.ph/press_release/2006/0528_pimentel2.asp, accessed July 2006.

Small Arms Survey 2003: Development Denied (2003), a project of the Graduate Institute of International Studies, Geneva, Oxford: Oxford University Press.

Sorza, Rexcel (2005), 'Women in Mindanao ... key to development', *Islam Online*, 16 June, www.islam-online.net/English/News/2005-06/16/article02.shtml, accessed June 2005.

Tagayuna, Airlie (2004), 'Capital punishment in the Philippines', *Journal of the Southeast Asian Studies Student Association*, 5 (1), www.hawaii.edu/cseas/pubs/explore/v5/vol5no1.html, accessed June 2005.

Task Force Detainees of the Philippines (2005a), 'TFDP condemns military action in Bagong Diwa, calls for justice for those who were unjustly killed', press statement, 18 March, www.tfdp.org/resources/ps_20050318.htm, accessed May 2005.

Task Force Detainees of the Philippines (2005b), telephone interview with Dr. Aurora Parong, 30 May, Melbourne, Australia.

Torres, Jose (2001), *Into the Mountain: Hostaged by the Abu Sayyaf*, Quezon City: Claretian Publications.

Turner, Mark (1995), 'Terrorism and secession in the southern Philippines: the rise of the Abu Sayyaf', *Contemporary Southeast Asia*, 17 (1), 1–19.

US Department of State (2004), *2004 Country Reports on Human Rights Practices*, released by the Bureau of Democracy, Human Rights, and Labor, 28 February, www.state.gov/g/drl/rls/hrrpt/2004/41657.htm, accessed June 2005.

US Department of State (2005), *2004 Country Reports on Terrorism*, released by the Office of the Coordinator for Counterterrorism, 14 April, www.state.gov/s/ct/rls/c14813.htm, accessed May 2005.

US Embassy in Manila (2002), 'Ambassador's remarks at the 58th anniversary of Leyte landing, Oct. 28', MacArthur Landing National Memorial Park, 20 October, http://philippines.usembassy.gov/wwwham05.html, accessed July 2006.

US Embassy in Manila (2005), 'US remains "very strong supporter of the peace process" in southern Philippines', transcript of interview with Chargé d'Affaires Joseph Mussomeli on SBS-TV Australia, http://usembassy.state.gov/posts/rp1/wwwhr533.html, accessed June 2005.

USAID (2005), 'Philippine's budget summary: the development challenge', www.usaid.gov/policy/budget/cbj2006/ane/ph.html, accessed June 2005.

USAID (2006), 'Suggested remarks of Robert E. Wuertz, chief, USAID/OEDG, nationwide awareness campaign on the ADR Act of 2004 and its impact on the construction industry discovery suites', Ortigas Center, Pasig City, 26 April, http://ph.gov/documents/newsroom/speeches/aprilspeech0306.pdf, accessed June 2006.

Vicziany, Marika (2003), 'State responses to Islamic terrorism in western China and their impact on South Asia', *Contemporary South Asia*, 12 (2), 243–62.

World Bank (2003), *Human Development for Peace and Prosperity in the Autonomous Region in Muslim Mindanao*, Manila: The World Bank, November, 1–108, www.wds.worldbank.org/servlet/WDSContentServer/WDSP/IB/2004/02/11/000112742_20040211174102/Rendered/PDF/2759310paper.pdf, accessed June 2005.

Zabriskie, Phil (2002), 'Interview with the President: to sacrifice and to suffer', *Time (Asia)*, 28 January, 18.

14. Issues in South Asian terrorism

S.D. Muni

South Asia, as it exists today, has been experiencing terrorism since the late 1940s and the 1950s. It was then understood differently from what is being articulated today. Simply put, terrorism is the conscious use of terror for advancing political goals. In this sense, it is inherent in any conflict, but then a conflict is much more than the use of terror. In common understanding, the state is spared from the charge of terrorism because it has the right (perhaps the sole right and legitimacy) to use force and violence against its own citizens. No one has so far sat down seriously to define the rational and permissible levels of violence by the state in the name of maintaining social order. As such, most of the excessive, irrational and even illegal use of force and violence by the state goes unquestioned. Conversely, the use of force and violence by non-state actors is conveniently labelled 'terrorism'.

This was not the case before the events of 9/11 and the unleashing of a global 'war on terror' in retaliation for the events of 9/11. Conflicts, even terrorism-generating ones, were then understood using different concepts such as rebellions and revolutions, freedom and independence struggles, ethnic and religious insurgencies, proxy, asymmetric and unequal conflicts and so on. The post-9/11 understanding of terrorism has erased most of these distinctions. All violence against the state now is terrorism. According to the United States, there are only two broad categories of terrorism: global and regional or local. For the United States, global terrorism is the real challenge and this terrorism is seen to be spearheaded by Islamic extremism. The rest are all small conflicts that can be managed regionally or locally, or so it is assumed.

SELF-SERVING DEFINITIONS OF TERRORISM

This all-pervasive thrust of the US definition of terrorism has served to distort the reality of raging conflicts in various regions of the world (Varadjaran 2005).[1] South Asia is no exception to this. Looked at from the US perspective, terrorism there represents both the 'global' and the 'regional' streams. Islamic jihad is unleashing its fire in Pakistan (in its areas bordering with Afghanistan) and the Kashmir region of India. But a large part of South Asia is under regional, ethnic and ideological conflicts that generate terrorism. The ethnic and regional insurgencies in India's north-east, the Tamil–Sinhalese ethnic conflict in Sri Lanka and the Maoists, left-extremist rebellion in Nepal and parts of India may be mentioned as examples of the latter category. However, it is misleading to follow the US categorization strictly. The United States is often hesitant, for political and strategic reasons, to consider the jihadi extremist forces in India's Kashmir as part of global Islamic extremism. This is not simply because Kashmir is seen as a political and territorial dispute between India and Pakistan but also because, by doing so, it would have to question Pakistan's deep involvement in terrorism in Kashmir and India, and thus strain its strategic alliance with Pakistan in the global 'war on terror'. India has attempted to produce a substantial body of substantial evidence to show that Al Qaeda and other extremist jihadi groups have direct connections with those active in Kashmir. This has brought about a softening in the US position on India's concern for terrorism, leading to some pressure on Pakistan to curb 'cross-border' terrorism against India and also to recognize some of the other Indian terrorist groups like the Peoples War Group (PWG) and the United Liberation Front of Assam (ULFA) as terrorist organizations. But in the US scheme of priorities the violence in Kashmir and also by other terrorist groups falls into a different category from the violence of Al Qaeda and Islamic jihad. The United States has added some of the Pakistan-based jihadi groups to the list of 'foreign terrorist organizations' – like Jaish Mohammad, Lashkar-e-Toiba and Harkatul Mujahedeen – which are active in India's Kashmir. But this has been done primarily because of their connections with Al Qaeda and opposition to General Musharraf's collaboration with the US war on global terrorism.

Further, is it really proper to describe the non-Islamic terrorism in South Asia as local terrorism, ignoring the trans-border linkages and implications of involved terrorist groups? Terrorism is a global phenomenon where information networks, financial institutions and transactions, ethnic and religious linkages, travel and transport facilities, ideological affinities, and the underworld of arms transactions and training all play an important part in propping up terrorist groups. Making a narrowly based tactical and notional differentiation between one terrorist group and another is a reflection of strategic and foreign policy priorities. In South Asia, even the non-jihadi terrorist groups have a reasonably spread-out structure of networks and linkages. Defining them as localized groups would be misleading in some respects. For instance, the Maoists of Nepal are known to have been inspired and supported by Peru's *Shin Pet*. They have also established a regional network with other left-extremist groups in South Asia called CCOMPOSA (Coordinating Committee of Maoist Parties and Organisations of South Asia). They also have connections with other extremist groups in the neighbouring countries – for example with the Liberation Tigers of Tamil Eelam (LTTE) of Sri Lanka and the United Liberation Front of Assam (ULFA), Bodo Liberation Tigers (BLTs) and KLO (Kamtapur Liberation Organisation) in India's north-east (Ramana 2005). Now there are reports of the LTTE training the Nepali Maoists and teaching them about suicide terrorism. Similarly, the LTTE of Sri Lanka has established linkages with the PWG in India and some of the other north-east groups. The LTTE's links with these groups are conditioned partly by the LTTE's commercial interests and partly by tactical political considerations to keep India under pressure. The LTTE's worldwide connections are well known. Links between the LTTE and Al Qaeda have been reported occasionally in the media, and also their links with some of the Pakistan-based jihadi groups like Hizbul Mujaheedin. Therefore, this distinction between 'global' and 'local' terrorism and terrorist groups is meaningless. The United States includes the LTTE in its list of terrorist organizations, but there are many other South Asian and Indian terrorist groups that do not find any mention in this list.

The US differentiated approach to terrorism in South Asia is reflected in other ways also. Look at the contrast between Sri Lanka and Nepal. While the United States treats the LTTE as a foreign terrorist group, it is fully backing negotiations between the LTTE and the Sri Lankan government under Norway's third-party facilitation. The United States has directly encouraged Colombo to talk to the LTTE. However, in Nepal the US approach to the Maoists is quite explicitly militarist. How can one explain these differences in US strategies on terror? A careful look at the broader framework of the US approach to terrorism suggests that, under the umbrella of the global 'war on terror', the United States is consolidating its strategic presence in Asia and elsewhere. South Asia cannot be an exception in this respect. Here individual countries and regimes are facilitating the US presence in Asia in return for their own survival, as in the cases of Nepal and Pakistan, and for short-term economic and politico-strategic advantages, as with Sri Lanka and India.

THE QUESTION OF ROOT CAUSES

The thrust of post-9/11 approaches to countering terrorism does recognize the notional importance of root causes of terrorism, but does not give adequate importance to it in immediate and concrete policies. But in South Asia some of the countries and leaders are acutely aware of the significance of root causes. Striking a strong dissenting note in the prevailing dominant understanding of terrorism, Sri Lanka's President Chandrika Kumaratunga said:

Someone once said, 'A hope betrayed transforms itself into bombs'. I would add that 'perceived injustice, if allowed to continue unresolved, would also transform itself, first into despair and then into violence'. In today's context the demand for the rectification of injustice is with acts of violence, which by itself raises issues of ethics in terrorist violence.

... At this point it would be useful to remind ourselves that it is not terrorism nor terrorists that divided Ireland nor caused the Israel–Palestinian problem 50 odd years ago. They did not impose white rule in South Africa, nor did the terrorists overthrow the duly elected government of Salvador Allende in Chile.

The terrorists did not separate India and Pakistan and create the tragedy of Kashmir as a buffer zone. To come closer home, neither did the LTTE nor the armed Tamil militants create the circumstances for the marginalisation of the minority communities of Sri Lanka.

Violence – social, political or physical – perpetrated by the State or the agents of the State, against other States or its own peoples is the womb of terrorism, humiliation its cradle and continued revenge by the State, becomes the mother's milk and nourishment for terrorism. (Kumaratunga 2002)

Other South Asian leaders have also referred to the root causes and the importance of addressing them in the fight against terrorism, but not so explicitly and courageously. In India, the new UPA government that came to power in April 2004 emphasized the necessity of talking to some of the extremist groups, like the Naxalites, for resolving the problem. It also deviated from the previous government's policy of ending cross-border terrorism as a precondition for talks and a peace process with Pakistan. General Musharraf of Pakistan has also been drawing attention to problems such as the lack of education in rural areas as a source of religious extremism, and the United States is helping him financially in creating a better infrastructure of educational facilities.

From the perspective of the grass-root realities of terrorism in South Asia, the basis of the menace has to be seen at three levels, namely the internal, the regional and the global.

Internal Causes

Internally, the state is one of the important culprits in South Asia in creating conditions that lead to the expression of protest and dissent through violence. Two aspects of the state may be underlined here. One is that the character of the South Asian state has undergone a serious change, from being secular to being sectarian. Even the Pakistan of Jinnah's vision was a secular state, despite its rationale for being established as a homeland for Muslims. Sri Lanka, Nepal and Bangladesh have all drifted from being secular states to being sectarian states based on religious and ethnic (Sinhala, in the case of Sri Lanka) identity. Even in the case of India, irrespective of the secular thrust of the Constitution, the rise of sectarian forces is clearly evident and such forces are playing an increasingly dominant role in political and social matters. This drift of the state towards a sectarian identity has disturbed the internal social balance and political harmony. It has marginalized minorities (religious, social, cultural and regional), driving them to a state of desperation and generating violence in the clash of perceived or real interests between the dominant majorities and neglected minorities. This has also eroded democratic space for the resolution of conflicts, irrespective of the broad contours of the political system and electoral processes.

The second aspect of the South Asian situation is poor governance by the state, where problems of poverty and underdevelopment have been allowed to persist in the interests of the dominant sections. It is not surprising, therefore, that the movements of the Maoists in Nepal and India have arisen through the mobilization of poor and deprived sections of society. At the root of many of the movements for autonomy lies a sense of deprivation and discrimination. The state has almost been ruthless in ignoring and suppressing the early protests from such deprived sections of society. Where actions have been initiated they have been delayed and have been inadequate. There is no disputing the fact that one of the major factors behind the rise of militancy in India's Jammu and Kashmir states, as well as the north-east region, is poverty and bad governance. This is notwithstanding the fact that political manipulations and the imperatives of a power struggle have often resulted in the rise and expansion of extremism of one type or another. This also applies to the rise of the Madrassah culture and jihadi extremism in Pakistan.

While the state is a major culprit in creating the conditions that give rise to forces that have taken to terrorism, it is not the only one. The blame must be shared by the insurgency movements and their respective leaderships in South Asia. They have developed strong material and political stakes in enlarging and perpetuating such movements and even making them violent. Huge resources have been amassed through looting, extractions, contributions from the diaspora, drug trafficking, money laundering and so on by some of these movements. Such resources have facilitated the rise in the level of violence by these movements on the one hand and deterred their leadership from bringing violence to an end on the other. The LTTE presents a typical example in this respect (*The Hindu* 2005).[2] The role of money as a motivation behind the activities of some of the arrested jihadi operators in India has also come out clearly in their confessions.

Regional Causes

Besides the internal roots of terrorism there is an important regional dimension to this violence in South Asia. The states have sponsored, encouraged and exploited terrorism as an instrument of their respective strategic policies against each other. The implications of Pakistan-sponsored cross-border terrorism against India are quite well known. Bangladesh has encouraged and sheltered many of India's extremist groups from the north-east. India has been blamed for encouraging and supporting Tamil militancy in Sri Lanka during its initial years, particularly before July 1987, in pursuance of its strategic policy. Bhutan has experienced tensions on account of suspected support from Nepal for the Nepali uprising in Southern Bhutan, and India has been unhappy with the Bhutanese authorities being soft on ULFA and BLT militants using Bhutanese territory for shelter, sanctuary and training purposes.

There are obviously complex and diverse dimensions to each of these problems. The point is that terrorism has an important inter-state aspect in South Asia. It is because of the entanglement of terrorism with conscious state policy that no regional cooperation has been possible in dealing with the challenge of terrorism. At the regional level the question of terrorism was raised at the very first SAARC summit in 1985, and soon in 1987 all the countries agreed to adopt a SAARC convention on the suppression of terrorism. However, there was no political will in implementing this convention, as that would have interfered with the strategic policy of using terrorism as an instrument to pressurize neighbouring countries. It is unfortunate that even with the evidence of possible networking among terrorist groups in South Asia – such as the coordination among the Maoist groups and the LTTE's links with the Maoists and India's north-east extremists, as mentioned above – the states in South Asia have not become serious in advancing mutual cooperation in collectively meeting the challenge. There are instances of limited bilateral cooperation in this regard, but that is certainly far less than what is needed and is possible (Muni 2003).

International Causes

South Asian terrorism has received further impetus and support from international sources. Ideologically, the post-Cold War emphasis on concepts like the erosion of state sovereignty, respect for human rights and self-determination have provided moral support to insurgency and autonomy movements of various shades. The events of 9/11 have eroded these values somewhat, but moral justification will continue to be extended in favour of them. The flow of resources to the Tamil, jihadi and Kashmiri insurgencies has originated through the international diaspora of these ethnic groups. The money collected has flowed through official, as well as underground, banking channels. These groups have secured their weapons through the international networks of arms dealers and they have used a global network of information and communication to spread the rationale of their respective causes, mobilize support and even coordinate specific operations. The growth of the global terrorism 'industry' in many ways reflects the negative side of globalization.

RESPONSES TO TERRORISM

The Use of Force[3]

In responding to the challenge of terrorism, the South Asian states have shown a strong inclination towards the use of force and a rather feeble use of other strategies, including political accommodation and poverty alleviation. Resorting to the use of force comes naturally and out of urgency as terrorism loudly announces the precipitation of a security crisis. Force is often the first and most immediate response because all other responses need patience, planning and a longer gestation time. Terrorism puts the credibility and legitimacy of the state to the test and calls for an urgent and fitting response. The use of force is also a reflex action of what the state knows best. Moreover, it is convenient. In all the terrorism-generating conflicts in South Asia, the use of force has been, continues to be and perhaps will remain a dominant form of response.

But this has not yielded the desired result except in a very few cases, like the Punjab in India (Sahni 2006). Even here, the success story of combating terrorism in the Punjab is not entirely due to the use of force, as political action, particularly the holding of elections and an agreement between the central government and the local Punjabi leadership (Rajiv–Longewal Agreement), also played a very important role in ending the insurgency. What the Punjab case brings out clearly is that the use of force starts becoming effective only when it is employed as a well-planned and carefully calibrated comprehensive strategy that includes political and constitutional accommodation, as well as developmental incentives. Ruthless and unplanned use of force may in fact strengthen terrorist forces, reinforce insurgencies and erode the credibility of the state. Of this there are several examples: in Jammu and Kashmir; tribal insurgencies in India's north-east; the growing popularity of the Maoists in Nepal after the Romeo (1995) and Kilo Sierra (1998) operations; and Tamil resistance to the Sri Lankan state after the pogrom of July 1983 and 'Operation Liberation' (April–May 1987).

The important factor that is often missed is the adequacy and appropriateness of the force structure to be used in countering terrorism. The nature of the insurgency, the terrain, clearly defined objectives and targets, effective coordination and so on are the critical inputs that should be carefully assessed in planning the use of force. But such efforts are made rarely, if at all. In the absence of such planning, the use of force has either become counter-productive or failed, as is evident in most of the cases cited. The ultimate goal of the use of force cannot be the elimination of terrorism but crippling the capabilities of the terrorists so as to force them to come to the negotiating table. Terrorism cannot be eliminated unless its root causes are properly addressed.

The use of force also needs political/legal provisions, in the form of special acts and powers for the armed forces. In all the South Asian countries, such special provisions have been enacted. Some of these provisions have raised strong protests due to their abuse; for example, the Armed Forces Special Powers Act in India's north-east (the Manipur agitation during 2004). The legislative provisions for combating terrorism curb freedom for ordinary citizens and make the armed forces less accountable. The Royal Nepal Army (RNA) has often insisted on the imposition of emergency laws before launching its anti-Maoist operations. The RNA spokesperson, Brigadier General Deepak Gurung, justified King Gyanendra's action of taking power on 1 February 2005 and the imposition of emergency rule in the following words:

> Now we can solely go after the Maoists in a single minded manner without having to worry what's going to happen on the streets, people's agitation. We can solely direct our resources and energy towards them. Definitely, we can deal with the Maoists in a decisive manner. Our main aim will be to force them to come to talks. (*Indian Express* 2005)

The consequences of the un- or ill-planned use of force have been many and diverse in South Asia. The worst of these has been the huge backlash of innocent deaths and human rights violations, for which the states are answerable, though there may be no accountability for the terrorists. However, since the terrorists are seeking international recognition and support, they are also brought under the scrutiny of the international and national human rights organizations and movements. Innocent people are killed, women raped and children orphaned by the indiscriminate use of force. Most of the South Asian states have set up national human rights commissions, generally under international pressures. Nepal was forced in April 2005 to allow UN Human Rights Commission monitoring of its social situation. Violations of human rights have brutalized societies, created trauma and psycho-sociological distortions and pushed social harmony backwards by years and decades.

The use of force as a terrorism-combating strategy also carries enormous economic costs. The defence burden has grown in the countries facing the menace of terrorism, and this has affected smaller countries more than bigger ones like India. In Nepal and Sri Lanka the increased defence burden has been at the cost of the economic and social sectors, as resources have had to be diverted. Some assistance is provided to meet the demands of these sectors but it is seldom adequate. Pakistan presents us with a unique experience in this respect because fighting terrorism in collaboration with the United States has helped it to secure economic support, manage its debt burden, raise resources for selected social development activities (like education and health) and even attract investments. In Nepal and Sri Lanka the intensification of conflict has hampered economic activities like trade and commerce, production and agriculture. It has also harmed tourist inflows that are so critical for economic activity. Internal war zones have been adversely affected with regard to the flow of food and agricultural products from production centres to the markets. The long-term costs are often not calculated properly, because such costs also include the destruction of economic infrastructure such as roads, power projects, schools, administrative buildings and so on by the terrorists.

As for its political consequences, the military approach has tended to strengthen and legitimize autocratic systems and authoritarian power structures. In Sri Lanka during the early 1980s, Tamil insurgency facilitated constitutional changes that concentrated power in the hands of the president. In the case of Pakistan and Nepal it is obvious that undemocratic military rule and an autocratic monarchy have succeeded in consolidating a hold on their respective societies. The King of Nepal even dared to concentrate more powers in his hands in the name of combating Maoist terrorism. In Pakistan, General Musharraf's role in combating the Taliban and Al Qaeda has helped him to diffuse pressure for a fully democratic and civilian political structure.

Political and Constitutional Accommodation

It was mentioned earlier that, together with the use of force, the South Asian states have responded to terrorism-generating conflicts with offers of political and constitutional accommodation, but the latter strategy has not been dominant as a whole at the regional level. The two South Asian countries that have had recourse to political and constitutional accommodation towards insurgencies and terrorism are India and Sri Lanka. An obvious reason behind this could be that both have always been democratic countries and therefore more susceptible to popular accountability.

India's strategy of political and constitutional accommodation facilitated conflict resolution in at least three insurgency situations. They were the Tamil identity crisis during the early 1960s, which was diffused by evolving the three-language formula, and the Punjab and Mizo insurgencies, where the offer of power sharing at the provincial level and use of constitutional resilience played a positive role in resolving the conflicts. The trappings of a political approach in Jammu and Kashmir were also evident when, in the September 2002 elections, the defeat of the central government's ally, the National Conference, was accepted as a positive development towards turning the corner in the terrorism-affected state. The constitutional question of autonomy is still very critical in Kashmir, and some real accommodation will have to be made of the Kashmiri aspirations in this regard if the situation there is to be stabilized.

Unlike in India, in Sri Lanka an additional factor behind a sustained political approach has been the state's realization that it cannot militarily subdue the LTTE. However, the Sri Lankan government has lacked sincerity in engaging seriously on political and constitutional issues to resolve the Tamil grievances. This lack of sincerity in accommodating Tamil aspirations is a consequence of internal politics, both within the Sinhala mainstream political parties and in the Tamil groups. The Sinhala competitive politics have not allowed the ruling party, particularly the Sri Lanka Freedom Party (SLFP), to show accommodation towards the Tamils. Earlier the United Progressive Alliance had blocked President Kumaratunga's efforts in this direction. Now even an ally of the SLFP, the Janatha Vimukthi Peramuna (JVP), is doing so and reflecting its ethnic prejudices. The JVP has withdrawn from the ruling coalition government on the issue of President Kumaratunga working out a joint mechanism with the LTTE for dealing with the tsunami disaster of December 2004. The LTTE has also been equally guilty in not agreeing to the political and constitutional process. It wants to keep its option of a separate state and sole representation of the Tamil community intact.

In Nepal the demand for a new constitution to be framed by an elected Constituent Assembly is central to the resolution of the Maoist insurgency. But the King cannot accept this because any new constitution will erode the status of the monarchy in Nepal. The Maoist insurgency is linked to the demand for restructuring the Nepali state, and its present incumbents are averse to permitting any drastic alteration of the existing power balance among communities and social groups.

International Collaboration

There is an unavoidable external dimension to the challenge of terrorism in South Asia, primarily owing to the integrated nature of the region – unnatural borders, socioeconomic contiguities and cultural identities across these borders – and also because globalization has played a significant role in the spread of terrorism. No internal conflict is truly internal. There is now an international resolve to fight the forces of terrorism, particularly after 9/11, as reflected in a number of UN Resolutions such as 1373 of September 2001 and 1430, 1438, 1440 and 1450 of October–December 2002.

In meeting the challenge of terrorism in South Asia the external dimension impinges at three levels: bilateral, regional and international. The importance of bilateral cooperation in responding to terrorism is highlighted by the cross-border nature of terrorism and its spillover, dictated by the geo-strategic structure of the region and the conscious, strategic use of conflicts and insurgencies in one country by a neighbour. Almost all the South Asian countries are victims, as well as culprits, of cross-border terrorism in relation to their neighbours at one time or another.

Bilateral collaboration

The most striking example of bilateral cooperation in combating terrorism has been Bhutan carrying out military operations against Indian insurgent groups within its borders in December 2003. Another example in this category is Myanmar's 'Golden Bird' operations in 1995, which were coordinated with India to flush out Naga insurgents who were operating along the Indo-Myanmar border. India also extended this type of cooperation to Sri Lanka when it sent the Indian Peace Keeping Force (IPKF) to fight the LTTE and to help the Sri Lankan government in the implementation of the 1987 agreement on resolving the Tamil issue. However, the prospects for such bilateral cooperation between India and Bangladesh in containing the activities of the India's north-east insurgents do not look promising.

These contrasting cases underline the fact that, for close bilateral cooperation in dealing with terrorism militarily, either of two preconditions is essential. One is that the level of political and strategic understanding between the cooperating countries should be of a very high order; and second, the neighbouring country cooperating with the terrorism-afflicted country should see such cooperation as being in its own interests. Let us illustrate this point with the example of Bhutan–Indian cooperation in combating terrorism. Close treaty-bound political and strategic understanding has existed between India and Bhutan for a long time. However, Bhutan has had its own constraints on sovereignty and force capability. This impeded its undertaking of a terrorism-combating operation for nearly six or seven years. It came forward to extend the required cooperation only when it realized that the Indian insurgents were not going to be persuaded by anything less than the use of force to vacate sanctuaries. And further, the continuation of such sanctuaries in Bhutanese territory was becoming a serious threat to Bhutan's own security interests (Hussain 2006).

Multilateral collaboration

Since close political and strategic understanding does not exist among all the South Asian countries, it may be unrealistic to expect any meaningful cooperation at the regional level in combating terrorism. The SAARC Convention on Suppression of Terrorism was first concluded in 1987. But the lack of political will among the member countries did not allow this convention to be ratified by all the members. The convention was taken up for reinforcement at the Kathmandu SAARC Summit in 2002. However, as long as a lack of political will persists and as long as member countries continue to use terrorism and internal conflicts in neighbouring countries to further their own security and strategic interests, it may not be possible to have even a normal level of regional cooperation. The South Asian regional geo-strategic structure is such that the basic thrust of cooperation in the field of combating terrorism, including sharing of intelligence and curbing of illegal financial and arms transactions among the regional terrorist groups, has to be implemented bilaterally.

There have been very significant developments in India–Pakistan relations as a result of General Musharraf's visit to India in April 2004. The two traditionally adversarial neighbours have committed themselves to ensuring that terrorism will not be allowed to disrupt their nascent peace process. If such understanding gathers strength and momentum, the prospects for a regional approach in responding to terrorism will improve considerably.

International initiatives

At the extra-regional level, the role of the international community in conflict resolution and dealing with terrorism has been significantly enhanced over the past decade. In particular, the spread of globalization, the emergence of the unipolar world order and the cascading impact of 9/11 have combined to make the 'suppression of terrorism' into a priority for global security. Several UN Resolutions and regional commitments may be recalled, including those related to financial flows, arms supplies and drug trafficking involving terrorist organizations and insurgencies. South Asian countries have been considerably benefited by these international efforts.

An important multilateral initiative that is gathering momentum is the emergence of developmental assistance donors as peacemakers. International donors are coordinating their efforts – through the offer of financial initiatives, diplomatic engagement and political persuasion – to bring the conflicting parties to the negotiating table. The offer and denial of assistance, both financial and military, is being used to nudge the conflicting parties towards a peace process. The sponsors of such a process are also defining the parameters. Leadership and guidance is generally provided by the United States, with active support from Japan and the European Union. In South Asia, Sri Lanka and Nepal have become direct targets of the donors' peace-making initiatives.

In the Sri Lankan case this started with the Oslo Declaration issued on 25 November 2002, after a conference of several government representatives from the Asia-Pacific region, North America and Europe. Representatives of both the Sri Lankan government and the LTTE were present at this conference. The Oslo Declaration identified the basic requirements of a 'lasting peace' in Sri Lanka and proposed a donors' conference to focus on 'longer-term financial assistance and ... efforts at donor co-ordination'.[4] This was followed by two conferences: in Washington in April 2003 and Tokyo in June 2003. The Tokyo declaration promised, over a period of four years from 2003 to 2006, 'a cumulative estimated amount in excess of US$4.5bn'. This assistance was 'closely linked to substantial and parallel progress in the peace process towards the fulfilment of the objectives agreed upon by the parties in Oslo'.

The international community took upon itself to 'monitor and review' progress in the peace process.[5] However, this assistance has not yet started flowing. Political priorities are distorting reconstruction of the conflict-prone areas. The economic incentives have not changed political positions and terrorist violence persists in Sri Lanka, even under the LTTE–Sri Lankan government ceasefire.

Third-party mediation

Third parties have also emerged in the conflict resolution process, through direct mediation or indirect facilitation. Offers of a third-party role in conflict resolution have been numerous, from non-state actors, states and international organizations, particularly the United Nations. Conflicts in Kashmir, Nepal and Sri Lanka have been targeted for this. However, there is only one active third-party role being played in a terrorism-generating South Asian conflict – in Sri Lanka. Norway, acting as a facilitator since 2000, initiated a peace process between the LTTE and the Sri Lankan government. Its most spectacular achievement so far has been the ceasefire since February 2002, which has held despite its fragility and frequent breaches. The tsunami disaster that struck Sri Lanka in December 2004 has brought the promise of economic assistance for rehabilitation and reconstruction, worth US$2 billion. The management of the flow of this assistance, which was mutually agreed to in July 2005, has further strengthened Norway's efforts to bring the two warring sides to work together for the larger good of the Sri Lankan people.

The involvement of the international community in general, and the role of third parties in particular, in conflict resolution is fraught with many questions. The most important are related to the stakes and interests, as also to the objectivity and neutrality, of the third party in resolving a given conflict. These stakes and interests are often defined in terms of the universal values of peace, stability and development, which may look suspect in the eyes of one or other of the parties involved in the conflict

The third-party role is vulnerable to the charges of intervention and partiality at any stage when one side or another finds this role to be not in its narrowly defined self-interest. If a great power is involved as a third party or is backing a third party, the questions of sovereignty and 'favouritism' are raised. Norway has come under such attacks in Sri Lanka from diverse quarters, including from President Kumaratunga as well as the ruling coalition partner the JVP. The United States and General Musharraf have come under heavy criticism in Pakistan for their anti-terror coalition against the Taliban and Al Qaeda. The third-party involvement, when not based on a broader political consensus, tends to divide political opinions. This weakens the state's political will to fight terrorism. As a consequence it also helps the terrorist organizations to gain legitimacy and mobilize internal and countervailing international support in the name of preserving 'genuine' national interests. However, in a situation of stalemated conflict the prospects of a third party making a constructive contribution are promising, provided that such a role is defined and pursued after careful planning and with the support of a broader consensus among the parties involved.

NOTES

1. Some of the glaring adverse implications of the US definition of terrorism and its global 'war on terror' for the protection of human rights have been meticulously identified and analysed by Professor Kalliopi K. Koufa, the UN Special Rapporteur for Terrorism and Human Rights, in her report for the UN Sub-commission for Protection and Promotion of Human Rights.
2. There are reports that the LTTE is collecting huge sums of money from London through their control of Hindu temples.
3. The following section draws heavily on S.D. Muni's contribution in Muni (ed.) (2006).
4. The text of the Oslo Declaration has been made available by the Sri Lankan High Commission in India.
5. The text of the Tokyo Declaration, 10 June 2003, has been made available by the Sri Lankan High Commission in India.

REFERENCES

Hussain, Wasbir (2006 forthcoming), in S.D. Muni (ed.), *Responding to Terrorism in South Asia*, RCSS Colombo Project, New Delhi: Manohar Publishers.
Indian Express (2005), New Delhi, 6 February.
Kumaratunga, Chandrika Bandaranaike (2002), Address of the President of Sri Lanka at the 11th SAARC Summit in Kathmandu, Nepal, 5 January, RSS (National News Agency), Nepal, www.rss.com.np/saarc/state_sri.html, accessed July 2005.
Muni, S.D. (2003), 'Terrorism and inter-state relations in South Asia', in Sridhar K. Khatri and Gert W. Kueck (eds), *Terrorism in South Asia□Impact on Development and Democratic Process*, New Delhi: Shipra Publications.
Muni, S.D. (ed.) (2006), *Responding to Terrorism in South Asia*, RCSS Colombo Project, New Delhi: Manohar Publishers.
Ramana, P.V. (2005), 'The Maoist web: an overview', paper presented at the Workshop on the Naxalite Movement, Observer Research Foundation, Chennai, India, 28–29 January.
Sahni, Ajai (2006 forthcoming), in S.D. Muni (ed.), *Responding to Terrorism in South Asia*, RCSS Colombo Project, New Delhi: Manohar Publishers.
The Hindu (2005), 11 July.
Varadarajan, Siddharth (2005), 'Playing on fear from Godhara to Guantanamao', *The Hindu* (New Delhi), 13 June, www.thehindu.com/2005/06/13/stories/2005061301641000.htm.

15. Missile proliferation in India and Pakistan

Ben Sheppard

In this chapter I will assess the ramifications of missile proliferation by India and Pakistan in South Asia. Discussion will first analyse the missile capabilities of both these nations and whether these developments constitute an arms race. This is followed by an analysis of the impact of missile proliferation on regional stability. The concluding section proposes the need for a short-range nuclear forces treaty as a confidence-building measure. Since the early 1990s New Delhi and Islamabad have steadily augmented their aircraft-based nuclear deterrence with land- and sea-missile-based platforms. Outside the original five declared nuclear states of China, the United Kingdom, the United States, Russia and France they have developed one of the most sophisticated missile programs. Although both have ballistic missiles capable of delivering a nuclear warhead, their development programs have taken two different paths. India has been more reliant on internal research and development through cultivating an indigenous missile program and incorporating technology from its own space program. Pakistan, by contrast, has relied very much on external support from North Korea, China and to a lesser extent Iran.

CAPABILITIES

Pakistan

The remarkable aspect of Pakistan's missile capabilities is not so much the weapon systems it has at its disposal, as the relatively short time it has taken Islamabad to procure advanced missiles through its extensive foreign connections, notably from China and North Korea. India's first test of the Agni missile in 1989, coupled with the US block on the delivery of F-16 aircraft to Pakistan in 1990, led Islamabad to conclude that missiles were the most effective means to counter New Delhi's nuclear weapons development and conventional superiority. At the time of the 1989 Agni launch, Pakistan's missile arsenal comprised only the Hatf I (80 km range) and Hatf II (300 km

231

range), which lacked guidance and control functions and were not nuclear capable (Binkley 1994, p. 85). The Hatf I has since been improved with the successful launch of the Hatf IA in February 2000. The Hatf I and II sounding (small) rocket technology based on three decades of experience in this area provided Pakistan with the foundation to develop a credible nuclear force based on missiles to strike key Indian targets. However, this goal has only been achieved with significant foreign assistance.

Today, there are two main ballistic missile programs in Pakistan: first, the North Korean-based Ghauri missiles (the 1500 km range Ghauri I, the 2300 km range Ghauri II and the 3000 km range Ghauri III); and second, the Chinese-based Shaheen systems (the 750 km range Shaheen I, the 2500 km range Shaheen II and possibly a 3000 km range Shaheen III).

The North Korean connection goes back to the early 1990s, culminating in a visit by Prime Minister Benazir Bhutto to Pyongyang in December 1993 to secure North Korea's help in developing ballistic missiles (Sheppard 2000). With India further improving Agni, Pakistan sought to extend its missile capability beyond the 280 km range of the nuclear-capable M-11 (CSS-7/DF-11) missile it had received from China in 1992. The confirmation that Pakistan had received and was developing North Korean-based missiles was the test by Islamabad of the 1500 km range Ghauri I (Hatf V) missile in 1998, followed by the Ghauri II/Hatf VI (2300 km range) in 1999. This marked a dramatic development for Pakistan's strategic capability as it far exceeded its previous missile delivery range of 280 km offered by the M-11.

The liquid fuel Ghauri missiles are based on North Korea's 1500 km range Nodong-1 missile. The Nodong-1 technology has also been exported to Iran where Tehran has further developed and inducted the missile as the Shahab-3 (Lennox 2003). Flight data from Iran's Shahab 3 testing program is likely to have been fed back into the Ghauri and Nodong programs in Pakistan. While North Korea provided Pakistan with its first medium-range missiles, China's contribution enabled Pakistan to induct a proven missile delivery system and a technology base.

A key development in augmenting Pakistan's program came in 1992, when China delivered around 30 280 km range M-11 (CSS-7/DF-11) missiles, which were capable of carrying a nuclear warhead. Chinese assistance, in other words, predated North Korean support to Pakistan's missile program. Around the same time China provided a demonstrated nuclear weapon design to be married with a ballistic missile (Albright 1993).[1] China's assistance to Pakistan has been primarily based on the desire to maintain a balance between India and Pakistan by helping Islamabad develop a minimum nuclear deterrent sufficient to deter India, but not so extensive that it threatens New Delhi. To enable Pakistan to indigenously develop solid-fuel ballistic missiles, Beijing has assisted Islamabad with the development of the Shaheen missile series.

Solid-fuel Shaheens have the advantage over liquid fuel Ghauris, because they can be more quickly prepared for launching. Liquid fuel missiles have to receive their fuel prior to firing, while solid-fuelled missiles are manufactured with their fuel in place. The 750 km range Shaheen I (Hatf IV), the first of the Shaheen series, was successfully flight tested in April 1999 and reported to have entered serial production in mid-1998 (Farooq 1998a),[2] although it was not officially announced to be in service until early 2003, when it was formally handed over to Pakistan's Strategic Force Command. The Shaheen II (Hatf VI) was first displayed at the Pakistan Day military parade in Islamabad in March 2000, and was exhibited alongside the Shaheen I at the Pakistan Defence exhibition in November 2000. In March 2004 the Shaheen II was successfully flight tested to a range of 2000 km although it has a reported maximum range of 2500 km.

Although China provided an off-the-shelf, short-range nuclear capability with the transfer of the M-11 280 km range missiles in 1992, prior to Bhutto's visit to North Korea the following year, North Korean assistance was *more* extensive. It provided Pakistan with longer-range nuclear-capable missiles (1500 km range) than China's technology transfers. It also provided a manufacturing base to indigenously produce the Nodong, renamed as the Pakistani Ghauri I. The fact that the flight testing and induction of the Ghauri systems occurred before the Shaheen systems means that potential the of the Shaheen program over the Ghauri platforms has yet to be demonstrated. Complementing Pakistan's ballistic missiles is its cruise missile program. In August 2005 Pakistan successfully tested the nation's first cruise missile – the Babur Hatf VII, with a reported range of 500 km. Pakistan claims it is capable of carrying nuclear and conventional warheads, and that it can be fired from submarines, ships and aircraft. The Babur missile is likely to be in response to India's Brahmos cruise missile, which is discussed in the following section. Although there is not much publicly available material on the capabilities and future development of Babur, its testing does suggest a major strategic development for Pakistan to diversify and enhance its nuclear capability.

India

Research into ballistic missiles began in the 1960s under the Defence Research and Development Organisation (DRDO). In July 1983 India created the Integrated Guided Missile Development Program (IGMDP) with the aim of developing an indigenous missile infrastructure. The IGMDP's first indigenously developed missile was the Prithvi (meaning 'Earth'). There are three variants: a battlefield support version for the Indian Army with a range of 150 km, referred to as the SS-150; a medium-range missile of 250 km (SS-250) for the India Airforce; and a boosted liquid propellant version with a range of

350 km (SS-350) (Sawhney 1996, p. 28). Although all versions of the Prithvi are nuclear capable (ibid.), the ballistic missile nuclear role is more likely to be the preserve of the Agni series.

There are perhaps four variants of Agni with ranges of 700 km (Agni I), 2500 km (Agni II), 3500–4000 km (Agni III) and 5000 km (Agni IV). In addition to these there are the Surya ICBMs. There is very little information publicly available on the Surya (meaning 'Sun'). There could be two Suryas: Surya I (6000 km) and Surya II (8000 km). Although it is not known for certain what range the Agnis III and IV and Suryas can cover, India is technologically capable of developing missiles with a range of 8000 km (Sheppard 2002). This gives India's missile capability a 3000 km reach beyond any missile capability possessed by Pakistan.

The Agni program had its first launch in 1989 with what was then called the Agni I, later referred to as a 'technology demonstrator'. The induction of the Agni (meaning 'Fire') into India's nuclear doctrine was held up in the early to mid-1990s by successive governments' reluctance to order further tests of the missile in the face of international pressure not to develop longer-range missile capacities. This attitude changed with the coming to power of Atal Vajpayee and his nationalist Bharatiya Janata Party (BJP) in 1998. The April 1999 launch of the 2500 km range Agni II heralded the resumption of the Agni flight-testing program and was shortly followed by the announcement that the Agni II was ready to be 'mass produced' ('Defence official says Agni ballistic missiles can be mass produced' 1999). With a range of 2500 km, India had suddenly developed a missile that could strike cities in southern China. A handful of Agni IIs are believed to have entered service by early 2001. To develop a shorter-range version of the Agni missile specifically for Pakistan, India flight tested the 700 km range Agni I in January 2002. Beyond the Agni III lies the Agni IV with a range of 5500 km. The Agni IV may well utilize the same Indian Space Research Organisation's (ISRO) technology as the Surya ICBM program. The Agni IV and the Surya ICBM series could be derived from the successful conversion of the Polar Satellite Launch Vehicle (PSLV) as a missile, or they could incorporate the ISRO ambitious rocket technology from the Geosynchroneous Satellite Launch Vehicle (GSLV) program.

The propulsion systems for all the Agni variants receive important technical data from ISRO's satellite launch vehicle (SLV) launchers. Throughout India's ballistic missile program development the IGMDP has integrated valuable propulsion technology from the ISRO.

In addition to the land-based Agni and Prithvi delivery systems, India is developing sea-launched nuclear-armed missiles: the PJ-10 BrahMos, the Dhanush and the Sagarika missiles. The 50–300 km range BrahMos PJ-10 cruise missile, although currently being developed for a conventional role, is likely to be developed into a nuclear-armed air- or ship-launched cruise missile. The BrahMos was first successfully tested in June 2001 and had its sixth test in November 2004. Initial production will focus on the anti-ship variants carrying a high-explosive warhead, before the land attack version equipped with a nuclear warhead is developed. It may not be until around 2006 that a nuclear land attack version delivered by sea or air (based on the PJ-10) is under development, assuming that the government decides to proceed with this.[3] BrahMos is a joint development initiative by the Indian and Russian companies, Brahmaputra–Moscow Pvt. Machinostroyeniye. Russia manufactures the airframe and engine.

The nuclear version of BrahMos may have a reduced range of 150 km to enable a larger payload capacity of 450 kg to accommodate a nuclear warhead. BrahMos could be deployed on the Akula-class submarine should Russia lease these to India, or the indigenously developed advanced technology vessel (ATV). This latter submarine may be completed by 2007. It may be operational by the end of the decade if the existing developmental problems are overcome. A ship-launched version named Dhanush, based on the Prithvi SS-250, is currently in development and might be fitted to future destroyers and frigates, or to the new nuclear-powered ATV submarine as a submarine-launched ballistic missile (SLBM). The first Dhanush test in April 2000 failed after about 30 seconds of flight. Owing to the technological problems in developing this version, it is reported that India is seeking Israeli assistance to overcome 'technological hurdles' to enable its deployment as an SLBM (Bedi 2003). In November 2004 India successfully tested the Dhanush. In addition to the above sea-based platforms there is the Sagarika missile program. No other missile under development in India has been the subject of such intense debate and discussion, with considerable confusion and little clarity (Roy-Chadhury 2005a). While it is generally agreed that a sea-based missile called Sagarika is under development by the DRDO, there is very little accurate information publicly available about its capability or development progress.

AN ARMS RACE OR ARMS CRAWL?

The rapid development and operation of the ballistic missiles outlined above could be seen as an arms race between India and Pakistan. While rapid progress was made in the early years in increasing the range of the missiles on both sides, neither side has been concerned about matching the opponent's capabilities missile by missile or aircraft by aircraft. Rather, both India and Pakistan have sought to develop a credible minimum nuclear deterrent. Neither side has expressed an interest in silo-based missile systems ready to launch within a short period of time akin to the US–Soviet Union stance of the Cold War. Instead, both India and Pakistan have kept storage facilities for warheads and delivery systems at separate physical locations in times of peace. In effect, this reduces the capacity of both India and Pakistan to effect an instant strike against the other. Finally, both India and Pakistan now possess missiles with sufficient range to strike deep into each other's territory and thus have no need to develop missiles beyond the 3000 km mark vis-à-vis each other.

Despite this, India has been developing the Agni II and Agni III to have the ability to deliver a nuclear warhead deep inside Chinese territory. While the shorter-range Agni I is Pakistan specific, the operational Agni II and the Agni III that is under development are intended for the China sphere. The intention of the longer range Agni missiles is summed up by Raja Mohan, former Strategic Affairs Editor of *The Hindu* newspaper and the India correspondent for *Jane's Defence Weekly*, who noted after the first Agni II flight test:

> India has been dying to get this [Agni II] capability vis-à-vis China. For India it is now being able to look at China in the eye to say we are equal now. The central element of this long-range missile for India is about gaining parity with the Chinese, parity not in numbers of missiles, but we have the ability to deliver nuclear weapons on to China and thereby gain a credible deterrence against China. That is the real political significance of Agni II. (Raja Mohan, 1999)

While Pakistan may at a later date test-fire and induct the 3000 km range Ghauri III, the Shaheen II and Ghauri II missiles with ranges of 2000–2000 km could be the longest-range missiles to be developed. In the longer term Islamabad is likely to consolidate the capabilities of the Ghauri and Shaheen series. It may well be that the Ghauri series will be retired, leaving the Shaheen missiles as the main staple for its strategic nuclear forces. Compared with liquid-fuel missiles like India's Prithvis and Pakistan's Ghauri I and II, Pakistan's solid-fuelled Shaheen I and Hatf IV are easier to maintain once deployed in the field, and are relatively easy to move, thus making them simpler to hide and shelter from a pre-emptive attack.

India's missile program is likely to continue developing its land- and sea-based capabilities on both the cruise and ballistic missile fronts. While India has maintained the pace of testing the Prithvi and the Agni I and II missiles in recent years, it is revealing that there has been a delay in the testing of the Agni III. The 3500 km range missile has been ready to flight test since 2004, but its first test launch in July 2006 was unsuccessful, with the second stage reportedly failing to seperate. The test had been held back owing to political considerations, with India not wishing to court international opposition. In particular, Indian Prime Minister Manmohan Singh's Congress government has made strenuous efforts to improve relations with China. Although strategically the Agni III could not pose a significant threat to China in view of

Beijing's superior nuclear capability (for a comprehensive account of China's ballistic missile capability versus India's, see Lennox 2003), testing the Agni III could send the wrong signal, undermining improving Sino-Indian relations (Roy-Chadhury 2005b). Manmohan Singh's government has established a strategic dialogue with China that considers wide-ranging issues including political, nuclear and energy needs. If India were to test the Agni III, it is unlikely it would be launched to its maximum range. It may instead be flight tested to 1500 km and then it may be publicly announced that the missile can fly further. Although the testing of the Agni III has been held up, the Congress government has shown no signs of slowing down other missile programs. For instance, in October and November 2004 India tested the BrahMos, Dhanush and Prithvi III missiles.

Islamabad is unlikely to be concerned about the Agni III missile, given that its range is too long to pose a threat to Pakistan. Agni III is intended as a nuclear deterrent against other neighbouring regional powers like China. For the first decade of the twenty-first century the greatest development in India's missile program is likely to be the operation capability of nuclear-armed ship and submarine-launched missiles: the PJ-10 BrahMos and possibly the Dhanush, should the technical difficulties be overcome. Certainly India desires a sea-based nuclear weapons capability to form part of a 'sufficient and survivable' minimum nuclear deterrent that entails a triad of aircraft, mobile land-based missiles and sea-based assets. The question is whether this will take the form of cruise or ballistic missiles, or both. Given the advancement of the PJ-10, India is likely to achieve a sea-based nuclear-tipped cruise missile capability. The Dhanush needs to resolve some serious technological issues before becoming operational. The rationale behind India's commitment to developing the naval component of its nuclear force can be gleaned from Navy Chief, Admiral Arun Prakash, who revealed in October 2004 that 'logic demands that as a nuclear weapon power India must acquire a deterrent and the most important part of the nuclear triad is sea based' (Bedi 2004).[4] He went on to note that the Indian navy's cruise missiles, such as the Russian Novatar 3M54E1 Klub-N and the BrahMos, could be converted to carry nuclear warheads if the government insisted. Although Pakistan may be concerned about India's naval nuclear developments, it has started to respond to these developments with the testing of the Babur cruise missile. However, it lags behind India in developing and possessing suitable sea-based platforms to compete with New Delhi in this area. Pakistan is likely to rely on its land-based missile systems, knowing that in particular its Shaheen systems are based on proven Chinese nuclear weapons technology, while continuing to build on its cruise missile capability. Unlike India, Pakistan, through purchasing Chinese technology, has acquired a nuclear warhead and missile delivery system that as a package has been successfully tested. This provides some comfort to Pakistan, despite the elaboration of India's nuclear triad.

STRATEGIC STABILITY

As India and Pakistan continue to develop and induct nuclear capable ballistic missiles, the maturity of their nuclear deterrent arguably warrants the initiation of possible arms control and reduction measures. The ongoing operationalization of nuclear-capable ballistic missiles heightens concerns about an inadvertent nuclear war occurring through miscommunication and misperception during a period of heightened tension – a risk that could be lowered without significantly affecting the current nuclear parity by eliminating short-range nuclear and conventionally armed ballistic missiles on both sides.

Consequences for Regional Stability

During the 1990s India and Pakistan made significant inroads into procuring nuclear-capable ballistic missiles through a combination of internal developments and external procurements. This led to a shift in the nuclear posture of both countries from aircraft-based to missile-based nuclear deterrence as the backbone of their nuclear capabilities. However, this development has arguably led to a greater risk of an inadvertent nuclear confrontation during a crisis or conflict.

During the 2001–02 crisis, when both countries deployed significant forces along their borders,[5] Indian forces reportedly moved Prithvi missiles forward to positions along the border, providing New Delhi with the option of launching their missiles within a short period of time. The possession of short-range missiles by India and Pakistan could arguably pose serious problems in the event of a major crisis or conflict. The main concern is that during a conventional conflict the deployment of short-range conventionally armed missiles will create a risk that the other side will judge that the missiles are armed with nuclear heads. Dinshaw Mistry, Director of Asian Studies, University of Cincinnati, observes that

> ambiguity arises because one side may deploy/use these systems for conventional missions, but the other side will easily misperceive their deployment for a strategic nuclear move, and would launch military strikes on these systems or related targets which could greatly complicate a crisis. (Mistry 2003)

The prospect of either side launching a pre-emptive nuclear attack is aggravated by Pakistan's declaration that it will be the first to launch a nuclear strike if necessary. Islamabad's refusal to follow India's decision to adopt a policy of 'no first use' is due to Pakistan's concerns that such a stance would restore Indian conventional superiority (Farooq 1998b). Pakistan views its nuclear capability as a means to compensate for the nation's conventional forces imbalance with India. Should India direct its land forces to cross into Pakistan, New Delhi would be justified in fearing Pakistan might be tempted to launch a pre-emptive nuclear strike if Islamabad perceived its national survival to be critically under threat. India, on the other hand, readily concedes that it can give up the 'first-strike option' because it has sufficient military and other resources to survive a first-strike attack and launch a response. At the same time, in renouncing the first-strike option, India gains considerable political prestige in global forums for appearing to be a more reasonable player.

According to Ganguly and Harrison (2004) the presence of nuclear weapons in South Asia may have actually made Pakistan less fearful of India's conventional military forces. They argue that New Delhi is more reluctant in the nuclear age to execute large-scale conventional operations for fear of escalating a nuclear conflict. Pakistan, in turn, has used this reluctance to conduct and support low-intensity conflict in Kashmir in an attempt to change the status quo, knowing that India is unlikely to launch a large-scale conventional attack. Instead it will only resort to punitive strikes as it did during the Kargil crisis in 1999.[6]

As a comparison the United States during the Cold War used nuclear weapons as a means to compensate for their conventional forces inferiority, and therefore were not interested in using military force to upset the status quo. Conversely, Ganguly and Harrison (2004) believe it is partly because Pakistan has recognized that India is less willing to launch full-scale military operations against Pakistan that Islamabad has become more deeply involved in the Kashmir insurgency since 1989. The nuclear dimension, while deterring to some degree conventional war between the two countries, may have provided Pakistan with the perception of an escalation ceiling under which it can operate by conducting low-intensity conflict in Kashmir, knowing that India is reluctant to escalate to full-scale conventional conflict. Despite the new nuclear balance in South Asia, one concern is the nuclear signalling employed by India and Pakistan during a period of high tension. Nuclear signalling is designed to publicly enhance deterrence or emphasize resolve. This can happen through various means: public statements or silences; the issue of provocative or inflammatory statements and subsequent denials or clarifications; relative action or inaction on various issues. All these means were used by both countries during the heightened tensions of 2001–02 to send 'signals' on nuclear as well as conventional matters (Roy-Chadhury 2004).

Whether or not one country intends to send a message of intent or resolve to another, events like missile tests and recalling diplomats can imply a certain stance or position of intent to escalate or de-escalate a conflict. Effective nuclear signalling requires an awareness of how actions taken by politicians and the military could convey various messages to the other side. Such an awareness would ensure that a country conveys the message it intends, thereby reducing misunderstandings. Rahul Roy-Chadhury has made a detailed analysis of the challenges of India's and Pakistan's nuclear signalling during the 2001–02 crisis and the lessons for stability. During this period one of the earliest casualties was the official channel of communication between the two countries. The diplomatic missions were reduced, leaving insufficient means by which perceptions and intentions on both sides could be sorted out. This led to an increased dependence on public diplomacy and rhetoric as the dominant channel of bilateral communication, a less reliable way of contact and one that opened the way for misperceptions and miscalculations that in turn could heighten the crisis.

A wide range of signals was employed from ballistic missile flight tests and public speeches through to military manoeuvres and press briefings. These signals were not clear or readily discernible; indeed, the opposite was the norm, with signals from New Delhi and Islamabad appearing confusing and ambiguous (Roy-Chadhury 2004). For instance, during the period December 2001 to May 2002, comments from Prime Minister Vajpayee, Defence Minister George Fernandes and Indian Chief of Army Staff (COAS) General Padmanabhan, together with the Agni I missile flight test, sent mixed signals to Pakistan. While Vajpayee refused to comment on Musharraf's statement to a German newspaper that Islamabad 'threatened' to employ nuclear weapons against India, General Padmanabhan stated that India would strike back 'severely' at Pakistan in retaliation for such an action. However, hours later Defence Minister George Fernandes publicly repudiated the 'uncalled for concerns' caused by the army chief (Roy-Chadhury 2004). Despite efforts by Vajpayee and Fernandes to play down comments on the use of nuclear weapons, India then tested the Pakistani-specific 700 km range Agni I missile. Although the Indian Ministry of External Affairs stated after the Agni I launch that the test was 'not directed against any country', considerable publicity was given to the range of the missile – 700 km – with the implicit signal that it was, quite clearly, a Pakistani-specific nuclear-capable missile.

Given the security concerns surrounding the Indo-subcontinent, additional risk reduction measures need to be considered, including an arms control system for ballistic missiles that could serve as a significant confidence-building measure.

A Short-range Nuclear Forces (SNF) Treaty for South Asia?

One possible risk reduction measure that India and Pakistan could adopt is a South Asian version of the US–Soviet Union Intermediate-range Nuclear Force (INF) Treaty. Signed by Washington and Moscow in 1987, the INF Treaty led to the eradication of all nuclear-armed ground-launched ballistic and cruise missiles with ranges of between 500 and 5500 km and their infrastructure.

By May 1991, 846 longer- and shorter-range US INF missile systems and 1846 Soviet INF missile systems, including the modernized US Pershing II and Soviet SS-20 missiles, had been dismantled. With India and Pakistan possessing short-range missiles capable of delivering either a nuclear or a conventional payload when deployed, neither side can ascertain from normal reconnaissance whether the other has armed their short-range missiles with conventional or nuclear warheads. Although one side may deploy short-range missiles for the conventional role, the other could misinterpret the deployment as possibly containing a nuclear warhead, thus misreading the intent (signal) and causing it in turn to heighten its nuclear strike readiness. This would inadvertently escalate tensions. The Prithvi missiles, for instance, have been factored into the Indian defence plan for a conventional role, but they can also be armed with a nuclear warhead (Sawhney 1996). Indian military commanders view the Prithvi SS-150 as an extension of their artillery capability by increasing their range from 40 km to around 100 or 200 km, depending on the variant of Prithvi used (Sawhney 1997).[7]

To remove this ambiguity and the potential for escalation, Islamabad and New Delhi could consider eliminating from their arsenals all missiles with ranges of 500 km and under. This would leave only land-based missiles with a range over 500 km that would be primarily employed for the nuclear and not the conventional role. The 500 km range cut-off would not include India's Pakistan-specific Agni I. However, it is very unlikely that either India or Pakistan would use their longer-range missiles to extend their artillery range or other conventional roles in view of the inaccuracy of the missiles and the poor return of employing such an expensive platform compared with other more efficient means of delivering conventional munitions, for instance, aircraft (for a detailed discussion on the value of ballistic missiles compared with using aircraft to deploy conventional munitions, see Harvey 1992).

An agreement in the form of a Short-range Nuclear Forces (SNF) Treaty could include India's Prithvi missile series and Pakistan's 280 km range M-11, Hatf II and Hatf III. It could also cover any ground-launched cruise missiles that may be inducted in the future, for instance, a ground-launched version of India's BrahMos PJ-10 or Pakistan's Babur. The main advantage of such a treaty is its capacity to reduce the possibility of an accidental nuclear war occurring through miscommunications or misperceptions about the deployment of conventionally armed short-range missiles to forward positions. Dinshaw Mistry has noted the value of such a treaty. He also acknowledged the difficulty of persuading the military and scientific establishments in both India and Pakistan to accept such a treaty, but argued that it could be done with a combination of the right incentives. A modest treaty of the kind proposed would be significant if only because it would be the first ever such accord between India and Pakistan – no major arms control treaties have been signed, or even seriously discussed, at a high level between the two nations beyond confidence-building measures, such as the 1999 Lahore Accord,[8] hotlines and the missile test notification process.

A treaty of the kind proposed would not adversely alter the current nuclear balance in South Asia, which is sufficient to meet the minimal nuclear deterrence needs of India and Pakistan. Both states already possess a credible medium-range nuclear-tipped missile force and aircraft delivery capability. What is needed, however, is a political environment of greater trust so that the mindset of the military and scientific communities can also begin to change. To take the discussions beyond the Lahore Accord requires that the question of missile control be de-linked from other political issues. It is important to note that the 1997 Washington Summit, where the INF Treaty between the United States and the USSR was signed, required decades of arms control discussions before this particular measure was agreed on. Previous Cold War agreements had only managed to cap existing capabilities and technologies; for instance, the Anti-Ballistic Missile Treaty in 1972, and the Strategic Arms Limitation Treaty (SALT) – both I and II. Although discussions for the first Strategic Arms Reduction Treaty (START) began in the early 1980s, START I was not signed until 1991. India and Pakistan have a long way to go. So far, they have only adopted limited confidence-building measures in their nuclear relationship. At the same time the long history of the original INF holds lessons for India and Pakistan – lessons that could accelerate the process of reaching an accord.

The ratification of an SNF treaty by India and Pakistan would require an unprecedented level of trust and transparency. As with the INF, a South Asian version would need a comprehensive verification regime and cooperative monitoring entailing on-site inspection provisions, inspections of closed-down facilities, short-notice inspections of declared sites and inspections to observe the elimination of the missile systems. For the United States and the USSR, the INF treaty was for its time the most comprehensive verification regime agreed upon by the Cold War foes. Certainly the INF provides a useful model for South Asia, in particular by stressing the need for continuous monitoring of the portals and perimeters of short-range missile production facilities. These are highly contentious issues for India and Pakistan.

As a starting point a debate is needed about an SNF treaty to create the preconditions for a landmark agreement. Once such a debate begins, other treaties could be added to the discussions, including the Fissile Material Cut-off Treaty (FMCT) and the Comprehensive Test Ban Treaty (CTBT). Neither of these internationally established accords has yet been signed by Pakistan or India.

The inclusion of cooperative monitoring as part of an SNF agreement could further reduce the dangers posed by accidents, inadvertent decisions and faulty intelligence. Cooperative monitoring entails representatives of both sides (usually from the armed forces) jointly observing sites, production facilities and other areas agreed on in a treaty to ensure compliance. Such monitoring could conceivably cover the entire gamut of a country's nuclear weapons infrastructure from production facilities to storage sites, launch sites and test sites. However, as Ganguly and Biringer (2001) point out there are two caveats to cooperative monitoring. First, both countries will have to decide on the extent to which these mechanisms can reduce nuclear danger without compromising national security. Second, none of these mechanisms can contribute nuclear stability by themselves. They will have to be embedded in political, organizational and institutional routines and agreements to ensure that they help allay fears, concerns and misgivings. This could include confidence-building measures in the economic, cultural and political arenas to provide a favourable atmosphere of trust and openness for agreements in the military sphere. The improvement in India–Pakistan relations in 2005 contributes to this with the proposed $4 billion Iran–Pakistan–India natural gas pipeline and the opening of the Srinagar–Muzaffarabad bus route. This is the first service to span divided Kashmir in nearly 60 years.

Despite the difficulties of ratifying significant arms control measures in India and Pakistan, the maturity of their nuclear weapons programs and the development of advanced delivery systems require serious consideration of arms control and reduction measures. The confidence-building measures undertaken to date provide a foundation for more complex agreements. It took the United States and the USSR until the late 1960s, around 15 years into the nuclear arms race, before they seriously began discussing arms control measures. This only came about because both sides believed they had sufficient resources and determination to keep up with each other in the nuclear arms race and that neither side could hope to achieve or maintain a meaningful position of superiority. This led to the 1972 Anti-Ballistic Missile (ABM) Treaty and the Strategic Arms Limitation Treaty (SALT I) interim accord in the early 1970s. With India and Pakistan not pursuing an arms race but more of an arms crawl through their adoption of a minimum nuclear deterrent, they have now reached a similar threshold. Once both countries recognize this, they can embark on the long and arduous road of serious arms negotiations.

The difficulty of India and Pakistan agreeing to such a treaty is made clear by the drawn-out process the two states have encountered in formally agreeing on nuclear confidence-building measures to reduce the risk of inadvertent nuclear war. In late 2004 it was hoped that Islamabad and New Delhi would officially agree on the parameters for a pre-notification of ballistic missile tests, codifying the informal agreement evolved from the June 1999 Lahore Accord. It was not until October 2005, six years after Lahore, that both countries finally agreed on the specific terms and signed the agreement on the pre-notification of ballistic missile tests. Prior to October 2005 the two countries abided by the Lahore Accord, which required an advance notification system whereby they informed each other and also other neighbouring countries about their ballistic missile tests to prevent misunderstandings and misinterpretations. The difficulty and time it took for India and Pakistan to sign this confidence-building measure highlights the long way the two have to go to develop comprehensive arms control and disarmament measures. There has been some progress on other nuclear confidence-building measures like upgrading the existing hotline between the directors of general military operations (DGMO) and the establishment of a dedicated and secure hotline between the two foreign secretaries. These hotlines are intended to prevent misunderstanding and reduce risks relevant to nuclear issues. It is hoped that the periodic expert-level meetings to discuss, review and monitor the implementation of nuclear confidence-building measures, as called for by the Lahore Memorandum of Understanding or the Lahore Accord (1999), will eventually lead to more substantial agreements.

CONCLUSION

The 2001–02 crisis illustrated all too clearly the propensity of India and Pakistan to become embroiled in a crisis that could lead to open conflict and with it the risk of escalation to a nuclear level. The poor nuclear signalling employed in the past, the use of short-range missiles for both the conventional and nuclear roles, the dissatisfaction with the status quo regarding Kashmir, and Pakistan's willingness to conduct low-intensity conflict in the Indian-controlled region of Kashmir collectively add to the negative variables that determine stability in South Asia.

However, there is not an arms race but an arms crawl between the two missile powers. Neither side is likely to adopt a launch-on-warning strategy, but instead they hold their missiles and warheads at separate locations during peacetime. India will develop and achieve its nuclear triad of sea-, land- and air-launched nuclear weapon delivery systems and platforms. But these are more qualitative than quantitative developments as India looks to augment its credible minimum nuclear deterrent. Pakistan recognizes that most of these developments, for instance the Agni III, are not suited for being directed against it, but rather fulfil India's desire to project its capability beyond Pakistan (for example, to China).

The balance of nuclear power achieved in the early 2000s has created a climate that is suitable for embarking on significant arms control and reduction measures; for instance, an SNF proposal. However, it is the political conditions of trust and willingness that have yet some way to go. As with the Cold

War superpowers, it may take some years before there are the right political conditions for both countries to embark on significant confidence-building measures. The difficulty Islamabad and New Delhi had in signing the missile test notification regime agreed to in principle at the 1999 Lahore summit is testimony to the long way ahead to achieve arms reductions measures. But, if the experience of the superpowers during the Cold War is anything to go by, India and Pakistan stand a good chance of eventually adopting such measures. The improvement in relations in 2005 is a major step towards this.

NOTES

1. The Chinese design was proven at China's fourth nuclear weapons test in 1966 at Lop Nor. It involved the detonation of a warhead carried across China on a missile.
2. Dr Mubrik told *JDW*: 'The NDC has started serial production of the 700 km range Shaheen I missile although it has not been tested yet.'
3. Publicly the Indian government has not stated that it will develop a nuclear version of the land attack version of the PJ-10, but the capability exists for India to pursue this option as part of its nuclear triad requirements to retain a credible minimum nuclear deterrent.
4. Admiral Arun Prakash's comment is a rare insight into the thinking behind the sea-based nuclear component, but dovetails into the overall strategic direction of India's nuclear development for a survivable minimum nuclear deterrent.
5. There were ten months of tension on the subcontinent in 2002 as Indian and Pakistani troops faced each other at several locations along the border. There were massive deployments along the Line of Control (LOC), the de facto border with Kashmir. This followed the crisis created by the December 2001 attack by Islamic extremists on India's parliament.
6. The Kargil conflict took place in May–July 1999, when Pakistani forces and Kashmiri militants were detected on top of the Kargil ridges. During this period India launched air strikes in Indian-administered Kashmir for the first time in 20 years.
7. Sawhney formerly commanded the 333rd Missile Brigade, which operates the Prithivi missile.
8. The Lahore Accord was signed by the prime ministers of India and Pakistan on 21 February 1999 and identified areas in which the two countries agreed to work together to bring greater peace and security to the subcontinent, including confidence-building measures to reduce the risk of nuclear and conventional military confrontation.

REFERENCES

Albright, David (1993), 'India and Pakistan's nuclear arms race: out of the closet but not in the street', *Arms Control Today*, 23 (5), 13.

Bedi, Rahul (2003), 'India courts missile help from Israel', *Jane's Defence Weekly*, 1 October, jdw.com website 26 September 2003, accessed February 2005.

Bedi, Rahul (2004), 'Admiral Arun Prakash – Indian Chief of Naval Staff', *Jane's Defence Weekly*, 3 November, jdw.janes.com, accessed February 2005.

Binkley, Cameron (1994), 'Pakistan's ballistic missile development: the sword of Islam', in William C. Potter and Harlan W. Jencks (eds), *The International Missile Bazaar: The New Suppliers' Network*, Boulder: Westview.

'Defence official says Agni ballistic missiles can be mass produced' (1999), *BBC Survey of World Broadcasts* (FE/3230 A3), 19 May .

Farooq, Umer (1998a), 'Pakistan needs up to 70 nuclear warheads', *Jane's Defence Weekly*, 10 June, 3.

Farooq, Umer (1998b), 'Islamabad rejects "no-first-use" pact for nuclear weapons', *Jane's Defence Weekly*, 22 July, 15.

Ganguly, Sumit and Kent L. Biringer (2001), 'Nuclear stability in South Asia', *Asian Survey*, 41 (6), 907–24.

Ganguly, Sumit and R.H. Harrison (2004), 'India and Pakistan: bargaining in the shadow of nuclear war', *The Journal of Strategic Studies*, 27 (3), 479–507.

Harvey, John (1992), 'Regional ballistic missiles and advanced strike aircraft: comparing military effectiveness', *International Security*, 17 (2), 41–83.

Lennox, Duncan (2003), *Jane's Strategic Weapon Systems*, Issue 38, Coulsdon: Jane's Information Group, pp. 133–4.

Mistry, Dinshaw (2003), interview by the author, August.

Mohan, Raja (1999), interview by the author, April.

Roy-Chadhury, Rahul (2004), *Nuclear Doctrine, Declaratory Policy and Escalation Control*, Henry Stimson Centre, www.stimson.org.southasia, accessed February 2005.

Roy-Chadhury, Rahul (2005a), 'India and Pakistan nuclear-related programs and aspirations at sea', unpublished paper, London: International Institute for Strategic Studies.

Roy-Chadhury, Rahul (2005b), interview by the author February.

Sawhney, Pravin (1996), 'Standing alone: India's nuclear imperative', *Jane's International Defence Review*, November, 25–8.

Sawhney, Pravin (1997), interview by the author, February.

Sheppard, Ben (2000), 'India and Pakistan: a tale of two processes', in Ben Sheppard (ed.), *Jane's Special Report: Ballistic Missile Proliferation*, Coulsdon: Jane's Information Group, pp. 115–23.

Sheppard, Ben (2002), 'Ballistic missiles: complicating the nuclear quagmire', in D.R. SarDesai and C.G. Thomas Raju (eds), *Nuclear India in the Twenty-First Century*, London: Palgrave Macmillan, pp. 189–210.

16. The role of Russian industry in the Asian arms race

Carlo Kopp

Post-Soviet Russia remains the single largest supplier of high-technology weapons to India and the People's Republic of China. Russia's industry, now decentralized and increasingly privatized, retains significant capabilities for the design, development and manufacture of advanced combat aircraft, warships, submarines, guided missiles, radars, electronic warfare equipment and other military systems. Much of this technology matches or exceeds the capabilities of equivalent systems currently in the operational service of the United States, its allies in the Asia Pacific and the European Union. As a result, the strategic balance in the Asia Pacific and Indian Ocean is changing, as India and China progressively acquire advanced and often long-range weapons systems with capabilities that clearly challenge many systems operated by Japan, Singapore, Taiwan, South Korea, Australia and the United States.

RUSSIA'S DEFENCE INDUSTRY

The current involvement of Russia's industrial base in modern arms supply to Asia has its origins during the Cold War period, when the Soviet Union was the principal supplier of modern weapons to communist-aligned nations and some non-aligned nations in Asia. The evolution of Soviet industry during the Cold War period, from the late 1940s until the collapse of the Soviet Union in 1991, is pivotal to appreciating the current capabilities of Russian industry and its relationship with its clients in Asia.

At the end of World War II the Soviet Union possessed a large and diverse arms industry, but one which lacked design and development capabilities competitive against leading Western nations, especially the United States, the United Kingdom and Germany. Typical Soviet designs from this period were unique, but uncompetitive compared with Western equivalents.[1]

The immediate post-war period was one in which Soviet industry embarked on a large-scale effort to reverse engineer or emulate as much Western technology as could be absorbed. British, United States and especially German weapons technology were reverse engineered, or used to define new indigenous Soviet designs (Hyland and Gill 1998; Kopp 2005; Nowarra 1993).

The post-war period of technology infusion by Soviet industry allowed the Soviet military to rapidly close the gap between NATO and Soviet military capabilities. It was followed by two decades of largely original design and evolution of existing weapons. The pattern of absorbing new technology from Western nations, and then evolving and developing new products independently, is a recurring theme in Soviet and now Russian industry.

The second period of rapid technological advancement in Soviet industry occurred during the 1970s, largely as a consequence of concerns arising from adverse combat experience in Vietnam and the Middle East, where Soviet weapons were decisively defeated in combat, and access to captured US weapons technology. Stockpiles of US weapons technology were accessible in South Vietnam and later in Iran, and thus state-of-the-art Western technology could be yet again infused into the Soviet technology base (Kopp 2004b).

At the time the Soviet Union collapsed, Soviet industry was mass-producing a generation of weapons technology that largely matched or outperformed in-service Western equivalents, comprising a wide range of uniquely Soviet designs and a number of designs influenced by or derived from Western designs. The United States, however, possessed an unassailable lead and de facto monopoly in two key areas of technology: stealth technology to defeat radar surveillance, and advanced digital computing technology to automate and network weapon systems and weapons. This technological dichotomy remains to date, as neither Russian nor Western industries have been funded on the required scale to introduce significantly new basic technologies, although access to commercial computing technology has allowed Russia to close much of the gap in computing technologies.

In some specific categories, Soviet weapons clearly outperformed their Western counterparts. Soviet anti-shipping cruise missiles were a generation ahead of US and EU designs. Soviet supercavitating high-speed torpedoes remain unmatched by the United States and European Union. Soviet long-range surface-to-air and anti-ballistic missile systems match or outperform US equivalents. The generation of highly agile close combat air-to-air missiles introduced by the Soviets during the 1990s remained unmatched in the West until a decade later, the same being true of advanced helmet-mounted sights for fighter aircraft (Kopp 1997a, 1997b, 1997c, 1998, 2000b, 2003a, 2003b, 2003c, 2003d).

The collapse of the Soviet Union was a calamity for the Soviet military industrial complex, tightly integrated into the centrally planned economy and distributed widely across the federated Soviet republics. Until 1991 Soviet industry was assured high-volume production orders for new products and lucrative orders for spares parts, equipment overhauls and mid-life upgrades.

With the Soviet armed forces, the Warsaw pact nations, Soviet-aligned client states and many non-aligned states as established clients, the Soviet Union directly challenged US and EU industries in production volumes and military exports ('Soviet military power' 1987, 1988, 1989).

Unlike Western industries, where design bureaus are integral with manufacturing plants operated by government or private industry, the Soviet system separated research and development from production, using a network of research establishments, design offices termed OKBs, and production plants, all scattered geographically across the Soviet Union. As a result, design and development expertise was physically separated from production facilities; good examples were the Sukhoi bureau sited in Moscow, with manufacturing plants located in Irkut and Komsomolsk na Amure; the Ilyushin bureau, relying on a plant in Tashkent, Uzbekistan; and the Antonov bureau and plant in the Ukraine.

The rapid and large-scale reduction in the size of the Russian military, in comparison with the Soviet military machine, resulted in a de facto collapse of orders for new equipment by the Russian military and a significant reduction in the volume of orders for equipment overhauls and spare parts. While many export clients remained, the end of the Cold War also resulted in the end of generous military and financial aid packages by the United States and the Soviet Union in the Third World, which in turn severely damaged the volume of export business for the industry.

The three most significant results of the changed environment faced by Russian industry were thus a large-scale shift to export business over domestic production, large-scale privatization and consolidation of many defence industry entities, and the virtually complete removal of Soviet era restrictions on which technologies could be exported and which could not. Hard limits on exportable weapons technology largely vanished during the 1990s, as a result of which products exported by Russian industry today are frequently more advanced than equivalents in the Russian military service ('National security of the Asian Pacific region countries and export of Russian arms' 1997).

Concurrently, Russian industry gained virtually unlimited access to Western technologies, which were commercially available, especially in the key areas of computing technology and software tools for design automation and software development. This coincided in the West with the large-scale availability of high-performance open software tools, providing Russian industry with unrestricted access to many tools previously unavailable, at zero cost. The 1990s thus became another period of Western technology infusion into the Russian industry base, largely nullifying the asymmetric advantage in computing technology held by the West before 1991.

By the mid-1990s Russian industry was actively involved in marketing upper-tier Russian weapons technology globally, competing directly with US, Israeli and EU manufacturers. Many upper-tier Russian weapons on offer were based on previously classified design concepts created before 1991, for which launch customers were sought to cover development costs.

While new production Russian military hardware constitutes a large fraction of export sales, refurbished former Soviet inventory equipment is also on offer and has been exported extensively. Equipment manufactured during the late 1980s typically saw little use after 1991, as a result of which Russia retains a significant stockpile of mothballed hardware that has incurred little usage-related wear and tear since its manufacture. In practical terms, a weapon system built in 1990 and supplied in 2005 refurbished will be in 'as new' condition.

Collaborative development programs and technology transfer schemes have also materialized in recent years, concurrently with new technology upgrade packages for Soviet-era export weapons. The most notable of these collaborative arrangements are with India for the BrahMos/Yakhont supersonic cruise missile and the unique Novator R-172 long-range air-to-air missile, the latter designed to destroy surveillance aircraft from ranges outside the cover of protective fighter escorts.

There are few Russian military technology products today that are not available for export. As of January 2005, even refurbished and upgraded Tu-160 Blackjack, Tu-95MS Bear H and Tu-22M3 Backfire C strategic bombers were publicly advocated as export products (Pronina 2005; Novosti 2005).

RUSSIAN WEAPON EXPORTS IN ASIA

The large-scale downsizing and restructuring of Russia's defence industries after 1991 resulted in a major export drive by the state arms export agency, *Rosvooruzheniye*, an umbrella entity formed to market Russian military technology. Two key markets were targeted: the Middle East and Asia. While Middle Eastern sales have not been prominent in numbers, exports to Asia in many key categories have exceeded Soviet-era performance.

The collapse of centralized state-controlled planning and privatization of the industry saw the growth of very rapid and aggressive competition between Russian manufacturers, typified by companies selling different Russian products to the same client or variants of the same product to different clients. This was a by-product of the decentralized manufacturing model employed during the Soviet era, where multiple geographically and organizationally separate entities often produced variants of the same equipment.[2]

Rosvooruzheniye, later renamed *Rosoboronexport*, actively marketed the full spectrum of Russian military technology, but to date the most successful areas in export sales have been combat aircraft, guided missiles, submarines and warships. Conversely, exports of armoured vehicles, tanks, helicopters and especially surface-to-air missile and air defence systems have not been as successful as during the Soviet era.

A factor in the diminished export performance of Russian air defence weapons has with little doubt been the poor performance of the Iraqi and Serbian air defence systems during the 1990s and the 2003 invasion of Iraq. These were mostly equipped with S-75, S-125 and 9M9 surface-to-air missile systems, which faced the technologically and operationally superior US and British air power. The failure of essentially obsolete 1970s supplied technology Soviet air defence weapons in Iraqi and Serbian service was no surprise. What is surprising is that state-of-the-art and vastly more capable weapons such as the S-300PMU, S-400 and S-300V have suffered in the wider market as a result of the failure of 1960s generation products (Zaloga 1989, 1997).

The dynamic of Russian military sales in Asia post-1991 is best characterized by cycles of 'tit-for-tat' purchases, usually of identical or similar weapons systems. This dynamic has been most prominent between China and India, especially in purchases of combat aircraft, guided missiles, warships and submarines, both newly built and refurbished (Kopp 1998, 2000a, 2000b, 2003a, 2003d, 2004a, 2004b).

What is strategically significant is that the types of equipment now being exported, especially to China and India, are qualitatively very different from the types exported during the Cold War period (Kopp 1998, 2000b, 2003a, 2003d, 2004a, 2004b). As is evident from the composition of equipment fleets exported during the Cold War, the Soviet leadership concentrated on supplying weapons with a limited range and thus strategic reach. This restriction vanished during the 1990s, and export clients are now acquiring weapons with strategic reach. In practical terms the weapons that provided the Soviet Union with much of its non-nuclear strategic punch during the 1980s are now being exported, resulting specifically in both China and India acquiring non-nuclear strategic capabilities approaching that of the Soviet Union in its latter years.

Sukhoi SU-27/30/34

There is no doubt that the most successful Russian export product over the last decade is the Sukhoi T-10/Su-27 Flanker family of long-range fighters, licence-built now in India and China, and ordered by Indonesia, Malaysia and Vietnam. This family of high-performance fighter aircraft was developed to defeat the US Boeing F-15 Eagle fighter, which remains to date the highest performance Western fighter to be widely exported (Kopp 1998, 2003a, 2003d, 2004g).

Sukhoi's T-10, while a uniquely Soviet design, exploits many design features pioneered in the US F-14, F-15 and F-16 to produce the most agile design in its class. Built to win control of the air in the NATO theatre, as well as to intercept

US strategic bombers, the Sukhoi Su-27/30 has the greatest internal fuel capacity, and combat radius and the largest radar antenna, missile payload and installed thrust of any third-generation fighter. Advanced Su-27 derivatives, such as the Su-30, Su-35 and Su-37 demonstrator, were the first production fighters to incorporate thrust-vectoring engines for low-speed agility (Kopp 1998, 2003a, 2003d, 2004g; Novichkov 1996).

The only Western combat aircraft that is not challenged by the latest Su-30/35 variants is the stealthy US F-22A, currently in early production and not available in significant numbers until 2010 or later. While the European Rafale and Eurofighter can match the agility of the Sukhoi, they are much smaller and cannot match its range or weapon payload (Kopp 1998, 2003a, 2003d).

The first client for Sukhoi fighters in Asia was China, which ordered an initial batch of the basic Su-27SK in 1992. By 1996, licensed assembly of 200 Su-27s by Shenyang was negotiated; Chinese-built models were designated the J-11. Subsequently, China's air force ordered additional Su-27 fighters and an advanced dual-seat fighter bomber variant, armed with smart weapons, designated the Su-30MKK. The Chinese navy then ordered additional Su-30MK2s, equipped with anti-shipping weapons (Kopp 1998, 2003a, 2003d, 2004f, 2004g; Novichkov and Morocco 1998; 'National security of the Asian pacific region countries and export of Russian arms' 1997; Nemets and Torda 2002c).

Russian sources speculate that China's total in Su-27 and Su-30 aircraft could exceed 500. For comparison, the current US air force fleet of equivalent F-15C and F-15E fighters is 600 aircraft.

India responded to China's initial purchase of Su-27SK fighters by ordering the Su-30MKI, a much more advanced fighter bomber variant that incorporated many features trailed in the Su-37 demonstrator and some European avionics. While initial aircraft were delivered directly, 150 are being built by Hindustan, for a planned fleet size of 180 aircraft. This number is very close to the circa 200 equivalent F-15E aircraft now flown by the US air force (Kopp 1998, 2003a, 2003d, 2004g; Velikovich and Barrie 1998).

More recently, Malaysia has ordered a batch of 18 Su-30MKM, a similar configuration to the Indian Su-30MKI, following an earlier order of the smaller MiG-29N. Vietnam has ordered a small number of Su-30MKV, similar to the Chinese Su-30MKK. Indonesia negotiated a purchase of 12 Su-30KI prior to the economic collapse, suspended the order, but last year took delivery of two Su-27SK and two Su-30MK fighters, with a publicly stated intention to acquire if possible 48 in total (Kopp 2003a, 2003d, 2004g).

The Su-34 Fullback strike fighter is expected to enter production before the end of the decade, and exports to Asia are expected. This aircraft is much larger than the equivalent US F-15E and is designed primarily as a precision bomber (Kopp 2004e).

The deployment of hundreds of Sukhoi fighters in Asia represents the single greatest qualitative change in the relative balance of power in this region since the influx of early Soviet fighters during the 1950s. The Sukhois have a combat radius of circa 700 nautical miles, therefore nations operating them gain an ability to project air power, armed with smart weapons, to a distance without precedent.

Air–Air Missiles and Guided Bombs

Russia has exported a wide range of air-to-air and air-to-surface guided missiles since 1991, primarily to arm Sukhoi fighters, but also to arm existing fleets of the much smaller MiG-29 Fulcrum fighters. Many of these missiles match or outperform Western equivalents operated by US-aligned nations in the region.

The most widely exported air-to-air missiles are the medium- and long-range Vympel R-27 (AA-10 Alamo) series and the short-range Vympel R-73/74 (AA-11 Archer), primarily to arm the Su-27/30 and MiG-29. More recently, the active radar-guided medium-range Vympel R-77 (AA-12 Adder) has been supplied to India and China. This missile is a credible equivalent of the US Raytheon AIM-120 AMRAAM, the primary armament of US-supplied fighters in the region. Advanced ramjet powered variants of the R-77 remain in development.

Long-range air-to-air missiles, designed to destroy intelligence, surveillance and reconnaissance aircraft such as the US E-3 AWACS or the Australian Wedgetail from outside the protective cover of defending fighter escorts, have also appeared in the market. India is negotiating the collaborative final development and production of the Novator R-172 missile, which has a range of 200 nautical miles. China has acquired the shorter-ranging Zvezda Kh-31 (AS-17 Krypton) and may produce this weapon. It is not known whether the 160 nautical mile range Vympel R-37, offered by the manufacturer for advanced Sukhoi fighters, will be acquired in the region (Kopp 1997b, 1997c, 1997d, 2003a, 2003d).

Standoff and anti-radar missiles have also been exported. The Kh-31 acquired by China is available in anti-radar variants. It is used to destroy ground-based radars and is functionally equivalent to the US AGM-88 HARM. However, it offers more range. Variants of the Kh-59 standoff missile have been supplied to China for the Su-30MKK, and an anti-ship variant, the Kh-59MK2, for the Su-30MKK (Kopp 2004b).

The KAB-500/1500 family of smart bombs have been exported to China and India, including a bunker-busting variant of the PLA-AF. These weapons are available with optional television/radio-link, laser and Glonass satellite guidance packages, making them functionally equivalent to the widely used

US GBU-15, Paveway II/III and JDAM smart bombs (Kopp 2004b; Fisher 2003).

In practical terms, Russian missiles and guided bombs exported since 1991 provide their users with direct equivalents of all the high-technology weapons used by the West in conflicts since 1991.

Cruise Missiles

The Soviets fielded the most diverse collection of cruise missiles globally during the latter part of the Cold War. While most of these were designed to destroy shipping, a good number were land attack missiles. After 1991, many of these hitherto restricted weapon types appeared in the global market.

To date anti-shipping cruise missiles have been the most successful exports. The Zvezda 3M-24/Kh-35 Uran (SS-N-25 Switchblade/AS-20 Kayak) is a very close equivalent of the US Harpoon missile, the most widely used Western type in this class. It has been acquired by India and China for surface warships and publicly discussed for use on the Il-38 and Tu-142 (Kopp 2000b, 2004h, 2005).

The largest anti-shipping cruise missile sold is the 4.5 tonne supersonic Raduga 3M-80 Moskit (SS-N-22 Sunburn) supplied to China for its new 956 Sovremenniy class destroyers. India has acquired the competing 2.5 tonne supersonic NPO Mashinostroyenia P-800/3M-55/Kh-61 Oniks/Yakhont (SS-N-26), to be co-developed in a joint venture company as the BrahMos and built in India. The BrahMos will be carried by a range of aircraft, warships and submarines and launched from mobile coastal batteries. Both of these weapons are considered exceptionally difficult to destroy, given their high speed, and will defeat most shipboard defensive systems. There are no comparable Western missiles (Kopp 2000b, 2004h, 2005).

Both China and India have also acquired Novator's 3M-54 Club (SS-N-27) family of anti-shipping cruise missiles. Three variants are notable. The 3M-54E1 and 3M-14E resemble anti-shipping and land attack variants of the US RGM/BGM-109 Tomahawk respectively. The unique 3M-54E adds potency by employing a rocket-propelled warhead section, which flies at Mach 2.7, to destroy the target warship, once the missile has acquired its target. The 3M-54/3M-14 missiles have been intentionally limited to a range of 160 nautical miles to comply with international agreements on proliferation. Variants of these missiles are available for submarine launch, surface warships, or launch from aircraft (Kopp 2000b, 2004h, 2005; Fisher 2004a, 2004b, 2005).

Anti-shipping and anti-radar variants of the supersonic Zvezda Kh-31 (AS-17 Krypton) series, the Kh-31A and Kh-31P, have been marketed and China is claimed to have licensed this missile as the YJ-91. China is also known to have acquired the Raduga Kh-59 family of missiles. The unique anti-shipping Kh-59MK2 is being built for the PLA Navy Su-30MK2 fighter, and the television-guided Kh-59M Ovod (AS-18 Kazoo) for the PLA Air Force Su-30MKK fighter (Fisher 2004a, 2004b, Kopp 2004b, 2004h).

The prospect of Tu-22M3 Backfire bombers being exported to China and India raises the likelihood of the large supersonic Raduga Kh-22 Burya (AS-4 Kitchen) family of missiles being exported. The Kh-22 weights circa 6 tonnes at launch, flies at speeds between Mach 3.5 and 4.5, and is available in land attack, anti-shipping and anti-radar variants. Its closest Western equivalent was the British Blue Steel missile, carried by the V-bomber fleet during the 1960s. Like other supersonic missiles it is considered very difficult to intercept (Kopp 2000b, 2004b, 2004h).

Reports have emerged that China has acquired tooling for the Raduga Kh-65 (AS-15 Kent), a non-nuclear variant of the Kh-55/RKV-500 cruise missile carried by the Russian Air Force Tu-95MS Bear, and may have illegally acquired six examples of the Kh-55 from the Ukraine ('Ukraine admits Iran, China missile sale', 2005). This missile is a direct equivalent of the AGM-86C/D cruise missiles carried by the US B-52H and used extensively in Iraq. Video footage released in 2002 also showed a Chinese H-6H Badger prototype carrying dummy missiles which resembled the Kh-65 (Fisher 2004a, 2004b, Kopp 2004a, 2004f, 2004h).[3]

Aerial-Refuelling Tankers And Airlifters

Aerial-refuelling tanker aircraft form the backbone of modern air forces, as they provide additional range and persistence. They are considered vital 'force multipliers' in combat. The US-led bombing campaigns in Vietnam, Iraq and Serbia were largely dependent on the number of available tanker aircraft.

The Soviets used obsolete Myasischev M-4 bombers until the 1980s, when they were replaced by the Ilyushin Il-78 Midas tanker, a derivative of the well-established Il-76 Candid airlifter. The Il-78 is fitted with three UPAZ-1A Sakhalin aerial-refuelling pods. The aircraft has no direct Western equivalent, but provides similar capability to the widely used Boeing KC-135 Stratotanker and Boeing 707 aircraft.

India recently acquired six Il-78MKI tankers from TAPO in Uzbekistan, and reports have emerged of China negotiating a purchase of six Il-78MKK tankers ('IAF requires tankers to fulfill su-30's potential' 1997; Fisher 2004a, 2004b; Kopp 2004a, 2004g).[4]

While these are modest numbers by Western standards, the growing emphasis on long-range combat espoused by the IAF and PLA-AF indicates that additional purchases are very likely in the future. For China to fully support its fleet of Sukhoi fighters, at least 100 Il-78 tankers would be required.

China is currently negotiating a purchase of 30 Il-76MD Candid airlifters, equivalent to but larger than the US C-141B Starlifter. China already operates 20 earlier Il-76 variants, India 25.

Surveillance and Patrol Aircraft

Aircraft equipped to perform intelligence, surveillance and reconnaissance (ISR) roles have provided a decisive advantage to Western nations since the 1960s. The most critical category are airborne early warning and control (AEW&C) aircraft, which employ large radars, secondary radars and passive surveillance equipment to track aircraft and cruise missiles at all altitudes to ranges in excess of 240 nautical miles.

The most widely used upper-tier AEW&C system is the Boeing E-3 AWACS, introduced during the late 1970s and flown by the United States, NATO, France, the United Kingdom and Saudi Arabia. The Soviet equivalent was the Beriev A-50 Mainstay, based on the Il-78M airframe and equipped with an NPO Vega Shmel surveillance radar. It was introduced in 1984 and between 16 and 20 are known to be in service ('Soviet military power' 1987, 1988, 1989).

During the late 1990s China negotiated a purchase of Beriev A-50 airframes, to be equipped with the state-of-the-art Israeli Elta Phalcon phased-array surveillance radar ('Beijing to acquire AEW capability' 1997). Phased-array radars are attractive as they are very effective at detecting small targets, especially cruise missiles and aircraft with applied stealth measures. This radar was bid for the Australian AEW&C requirement and is a generation ahead of the APY-1 and APY-2 radars carried by the US E-3 AWACS and the Shmel carried by the Russian A-50. In July 2000 the United States pressured Israel into abandoning the project. China has since then proceeded with an indigenous program, also based on the A-50 airframe and a phased-array radar. Photographs showing prototypes of this aircraft in flight and of a radar ground test facility have been circulating on Internet sites since early 2004 (Novichkov and Taverna 1997; Kopp 2004a, 2004f, 2004h).

India exploited the collapse of the Chinese project in Israel, and contracted Elta to supply several A-50I systems equipped with a variant of the same radar. These will be delivered in the latter part of this decade (Kopp 2003a).

The importance of A-50 exports to India and China should not be understated. These nations will be fielding AEW&C aircraft with phased-array radars at least five years before the United States fields its planned E-10 MC2A AEW&C variant equipped with a radar using comparable technology.

China has also acquired the Signal Stavropol Topol E ground-based jamming design to defeat the APS-145 radar on the E-2C AEW&C aircraft flown by Taiwan and the US Navy (Fisher 2003).

Russia has also actively marketed anti-submarine and maritime patrol aircraft. India's navy acquired both the Ilyushin Il-38 May, comparable to the US Lockheed P-3 Orion, and the unique Tu-142M Bear F during the 1980s. The latter is the largest and longest-ranging maritime surveillance aircraft in existence, and is a derivative of the Tu-95 Bear strategic bomber. India's Bears were to be subjected to an extensive avionics upgrade by Leninets, based on the Russian navy Tu-142MN package, fitting the aircraft to carry the Sea Dragon avionic suite and eight anti-shipping cruise missiles. These are expected to be the BrahMos or Kh-35 Uran. This project now appears to be in difficulty, with the prospect of an Israeli upgrade package replacing the Leninets design ('The naval air arm' 2005; Kopp 2005).

Strategic Bombers

Russia's current fleet of strategic bombers is a legacy of the Soviet Dalnaya Aviatsia Voenno Vozdushnykh Sil (DA-VVS), comprising the Tupolev Tu-95MS Bear H, the Tupolev Tu-22M3 Backfire C and the Tupolev Tu-160 Blackjack. All three of these bombers remained in production well into the 1990s, despite the Tu-95 being a contemporary of the 1950s Boeing B-52 bomber (Mason and Taylor 1986; 'Soviet military power' 1987, 1988, 1989).

China has had a long-standing interest in acquiring newer and longer-ranging bombers, as its existing reverse-engineered H-6 Badger is not considered competitive (Nemets and Torda 2002a; Kopp 2004f). While arming Badgers with modern cruise missiles makes them viable, it does not improve their limited combat reach of less than 1500 nautical miles. There are claims that China sought Tu-22M3 Backfires in 1993 but was rebuffed. In 2004 the PLA air force leadership declared a fundamental change in doctrine, whereby strategic bombers would be introduced, and Tupolev aircraft were cited (Kopp 2004c, 2004d, 2004i).

Until the late 1990s none of the Tupolev bombers were cleared for export, despite the Russian air force lacking the budget to fly them at useful annual rates. The first evidence of a policy change in Russia was the announcement that the Indian navy would be leasing several Tu-22M3 Backfires while their Tu-142 Bears were being upgraded in Russia. The status of this arrangement is unclear now. By January 2005 evidence of a policy change towards China appeared, with the chief of staff of the Russian air force publicly advocating the sale of surplus Backfires and Bears to China (Pronina 2005; Novosti 2005). More recent reports support this shift and claim the Tu-160 is also on offer (Ping Kuo Jih Pao 2005).[5]

Introduced initially in the early 1970s, the supersonic swing-wing Backfire is the mainstay of the Russian strategic strike force and naval air arm. Late models of the Backfire compare closely to the US Rockwell B-1B Lancer bomber, although the Backfire is smaller and with a combat radius of approximately 2500 nautical miles. Armed with a range of cruise missiles and bombs, the Backfire is highly effective in striking land targets or interdicting shipping.

The larger Tu-95 Bear was also used for strategic strike and maritime interdiction by the Soviets, and has a useful combat radius of approximately 4500 nautical miles, making it a true intercontinental strike aircraft. The newest Russian bomber, the Tu-160 Blackjack, is a direct equivalent of the US B-1B, but considerably larger.

Given the late production dates and low accrued usage of the Russian air force inventory of Backfires and Bears, refurbished export aircraft could have a useful service life well past 2030.

Air Defence and Anti-Ballistic Weapons

Air defence weapons, encompassing surface-to-air missile systems, anti-aircraft artillery and supporting radar systems, were a high-volume export during the Soviet era. First- and second-generation weapons, such as the S-75 (SA-2 Guideline), S-125 (SA-2 Goa), S-200 (SA-5 Gammon), ZRK Kub (SA-6), ZRK Romb (SA-8), 9M31 (SA-9 Gaskin), 9M37 Buk (SA-11 Gadfly), 9M36 (SA-13 Gopher), ZSU-23-4P Shilka and supporting P-12, P-15 and P-35 family radars produced only limited success when new, and were effectively annihilated in combat with Western-equipped forces from the early 1990s. Upper-tier Soviet air defence weapons, specifically the S-300PMU (SA-10 Grumble) and S-300V (SA-12 Giant/Gladiator) families of weapons, were never exported, despite their demonstrably high effectiveness against most Western combat aircraft (Zaloga 1989, 1997; Kopp 1995, 2003b, 2003c, 2004j).

The Almaz S-300PMU family of missiles are Soviet equivalents of the US Patriot. Post-Soviet variants, such as the S-300PMU-2 and S-400 Triumf, match or outperform the Patriot in a range of key parameters. The Antey S-300V and later S-300VM are unique weapons, and the largest in their class, while also the only fully mobile dual-role long-range air defence and anti-ballistic missile systems in service. The S-300VM has been repeatedly bid against advanced Patriot models and the Israeli Green Pine/Arrow anti-ballistic missile system.

India has been involved in negotiations with Russia over the S-300V/VM system since the mid-1990s, but it remains unclear whether this system will be acquired.

China acquired its first S-300PMU-1 systems during the mid-1990s, and has since acquired several batteries of this capable system, remaining the single largest export customer for these missiles (Fisher 2004a, 2004b; Nemets and Torda 2002b).

Surface Combatants and Aircraft Carriers

The Soviets were a major exporter of surface warships during the Cold War, exporting Osa-I and II fast missile boats, Natya- and Yevgeniya-class minesweepers, Polnochniy-class landing ships, Pauk-II anti-submarine corvettes. Tarantul missile corvettes and Kashin II class destroyers. India was the single largest client for Soviet warships, although much of China's inventory were evolved derivatives of earlier Soviet designs ('The surface fleet' 2005).

After 1991, Russian industry aggressively marketed new and refurbished Voenno-Morskiy Flot inventory. China soon ordered the 7000-tonne Project 956 Sovremenniy-class destroyer, with its battery of eight 3M-80 Sunburn missiles, arguably the most heavily armed surface warship in operational use. The first pair of Sovremenniys were followed by an order in 2002 for an additional pair of enhanced 956EM vessels, claimed to be armed with newer Yakhont missiles (Fisher 2002a, 2004b; Nemets and Torda 2002e, 2002f).

India's largest surface combatants are the Kashin II vessels, ordered before 1991. Since then India acquired three Project 1135.6 Krivak III frigates, including the 3M-54 missile system. India has long operated aircraft carriers, using surplus Royal Navy vessels and imported Sea Harrier strike aircraft. After long-running negotiations, India announced in 2004 that the 45 000-tonne Project 1143 series aircraft carrier Admiral Gorshkov would be acquired, essentially for the cost of a refit, with an air wing comprising 16 MiG-29K fighters and a mix of Kamov Ka-28 anti-submarine and Ka-31 airborne early warning and control helicopters ('The surface fleet' 2005). While only half the size of US Nimitz-class supercarriers, the Gorshkov has approximately twice the displacement of existing Indian navy carriers. The Soviets developed two derivatives of the Sukhoi Su-27 for these vessels, the Su-33 and Su-33UB (Kopp 2003a, 2003d).

China has had a long-standing interest in aircraft carriers, but has not acquired any functional vessels to date. The former Soviet Varyag was acquired from the Ukraine as a hulk in 2002 and remains moored at Dalian. The vessel may yet become a template for a reverse-engineered indigenous carrier; its suitability for the naval variants of China's primary fighter, the Su-27/30, should not be overlooked (Fisher 2002b; Nemets 2002a).

Submarines

The Soviets supplied large numbers of diesel-electric submarines to Asian nations during the Cold War, and much of China's existing fleet consist of reversed-engineered derivatives of early Soviet designs.

India is now retiring its remaining Type Project 641 Foxtrots and introducing new-build Project 877EKM Kilo-class boats, ordered during the mid-1980s, with a planned total of ten boats. The most recent vessels delivered are fitted with the 3M-54 missile system, which will be retrofitted to all boats during refits. India's indigenous advanced technology vessel, five of which are planned, is believed to draw heavily on the Project 971 Akula and planned Project 885 Severodvinsk nuclear-powered class attack submarines ('The submarine arm' 2005).

China acquired a pair of Project 877EKM Kilo-class boats in 1996, and later ordered two more improved and stretched Project 636 Kilo boats, claimed to be also armed with the 3M-54 system. More recently, another eight boats were ordered. There was intensive public speculation during the late 1990s that China may acquire surplus Russian Project 971 Akula and Project 949A Oscar II nuclear-powered submarines; however, there is no evidence this has progressed to an agreement (Fisher 2004a, 2005; Nemets 2002b).

THE IMPACT OF POST-1991 EXPORTS

It is often argued that the supply of the most advanced Russian weapons technology represents incremental 'modernization' of existing equipment inventories. This misrepresents at the most fundamental level the qualitative changes in military capability we are now observing in Asia, especially in China and India.

During the Cold War the Soviets were highly selective in the choice of equipment exported outside the Warsaw Pact. While many types of equipment were ostensibly identical to types in Soviet and allied Warsaw Pact service, export models were often supplied in configurations no longer used or 'dumbed down' by the removal of more sensitive subsystems. A good example would be fighter aircraft supplied with inferior radars and missiles.

Another key aspect of Cold War-era exports was the absence of upper-tier Soviet systems in the export market, specifically the Su-27 fighter, the Tu-95 Bear, Tu-22M Backfire and Tu-160 Blackjack bombers, the Il-78 Midas tanker, the A-50 Mainstay AEW&C aircraft, and the S-300PMU and S-300V strategic air defence systems. These weapons were the backbone of Soviet conventional power projection capabilities in Europe and the Far East, and were jealously guarded ('Soviet military power' 1987, 1988, 1989).

With increased exposure since 1991, publicly available data on late-generation Soviet weapon systems supports the technical analysis in the 1980s editions of the US DoD 'Soviet Military Power' assessment quite convincingly ('Soviet military power' 1987, 1988, 1989). Upper-tier Soviet weapons generally matched or outperformed their Western counterparts, the latter being expected to comprise the bulk of Western military inventories for at least the next two decades. The very same Russian weapons are now being exported in large numbers, and often with technological improvements commensurate with 15 years of further development. With funding provided by arms sales to China and India, and with less rigid post-Cold War Western technology controls, many Russian weapon designs have evolved well beyond what was expected of them during the 1980s.

In strategic terms, China and India are now developing the type of conventional strategic power projection capabilities that Western analysts expected the Soviet Union to operate post-1990 in the European theatre. Perhaps the best example is provided by China's plans to deploy up to 500 advanced Sukhoi fighters, a number that rivals the existing US fleet of 600 equivalent F-15 fighters.

This will have profound long-term strategic implications for the United States, but also for Japan, South Korea, Taiwan, Singapore and Australia, all of whom will be presented with a military technological environment not unlike that which the United States and its NATO allies expected to face in a now historically projected post-1990 Cold War environment.

Intensive competition within Russia's increasingly privatized and decentralized arms industry has been pivotal to the influx of Russian weapons technology into the Asian market, exploiting very effectively the enormous established base of Soviet-era technology in this region. The now well-established trend to license and manufacture upper-tier Russian weapons, or engage in cooperative development of stalled advanced weapons in development, represents a technology transfer out of Russia that has no precedent since the late 1950s (Nemets and Torda 2002a, 2002c, 2002d, 2002j, 2002h).

This presents the prospect of China, and to a lesser extent India, becoming 'virtual' peer competitors to the European Union and in many areas of technology to the United States. Gaps in indigenous technological capabilities will be plugged with Russian and, on a lesser scale, European and Israeli technology. The prospect of advanced EU military technologies, especially sensors, being exported to China adds a major strategic dimension to the capabilities provided by Russian technology.

The developing long-term strategic picture in Asia is thus one of China and India becoming regional military superpowers, lacking the global reach and strategic depth of the United States, but capable of projecting formidable military power across the region, largely by virtue of unlimited access to post-Cold War Russian weapons technology.

NOTES

1. Perhaps the best comparison for this period lies in combat aircraft, the most demanding sector of 1940s industry. Frontline combat aircraft like the Yakovlev Yak-9, Lavochkin La-7, Ilyushin Il-2, Ilyushin Il-4, Tupolev Tu-2, Tupolev TB-7 and Petlyakov Pe-2 were in technological terms closest to Western designs of the early 1940s period, and typically uncompetitive. Soviet forces frequently relied on mass in combat, to offset inferior capabilities, a philosophy that persisted until the 1970s.
2. Perhaps the best example is KNAAPO selling Sukhoi fighters to China, while its sister plant, IAPO/Irkut, is selling variants of the same design to India.
3. China's intense interest in manufacturing modern long-range cruise missiles should not be surprising, as such weapons allow even uncompetitive combat aircraft to launch at targets from ranges in excess of 800 kilometres, minimizing exposure to opposing defences. As China now has an immense manufacturing base with controlled labour costs, cruise missiles could be mass produced at unit costs well below those in the United States or European Union, permitting large war stocks to be built up. Possession of examples of the Russian Raduga Kh-55 cruise missile would permit reverse engineering of key components, such as fuel-efficient small turbofan engines and the terrain contour-matching guidance package, while providing a mature and tested airframe design to copy.
4. Uzbekistan, like other central Asian former Soviet republics, retains considerable manufacturing infrastructure built during the Soviet era. In general, former Soviet republics present genuine risks in proliferation, as often large stockpiles of Soviet-era weapons remain available, and manufacturing capabilities exist. As these nations progressively drift outside the control of Moscow, there will be an increasing frequency of proliferation events, as such technology is exported, legally or illegally. The recent instance of Kh-55 strategic cruise missiles being supplied from the Ukraine to Iran and China is a case in point ('Ukraine admits Iran, China missile sale', 2005).
5. Hitherto Russian export policy has always excluded strategic weapons such as long-range bombers and ballistic missiles, as these not only had the potential to be used against Russia but also would reduce Russia's relative strategic standing on the global scene if used by other nations. The increasingly close military export relationship with China and India and sustained budgetary pressures have evidently overwhelmed objections by more cautious Russian strategists, leading to a reversal of the position on strategic bomber aircraft. It is unclear whether this precedent will open the door for the export of ballistic missiles and ballistic missile submarines.

REFERENCES

'Beijing to acquire AEW capability' (1997), *Jane's Defence Weekly*, 27 (22), 23.

Fisher R.D. (2002a), 'China buys new Russian destroyers', *China Brief*, 2 (3), The Jamestown Foundation, 31 January, www.jamestown.org/publications_details. php?volume_id=18&issue_id=643&article_id=4609, accessed January 2005.

Fisher R.D. (2002b), 'China's carrier of chance', *China Brief*, 2 (6), The Jamestown Foundation, 14 March, www.jamestown.org/publications_details.php?volume_ id=18&issue_id=646&article_id=4621, accessed January 2005.

Fisher R.D. (2003), 'New developments in Russia–China military relations: a report on the August 19–23 2003 Moscow Aerospace Salon (MAKS)', U.S.–China Economic and Security Review Commission, contracted research paper, August, www.uscc. gov/researchpapers/2000_2003/reports/mairl.htm, accessed January 2005.

Fisher R.D. (2004a), 'The impact of foreign weapons and technology on the moderization of China's People's Liberation Army', report for the U.S.–China Economic and

Security Review Commission, January, www.uscc.gov/researchpapers/2004/04fisher_report/04_01_01fisherrepot.htm, accessed January 2005.

Fisher R.D. (2004b), 'Report on the 5th Airshow China, Zhuhai, PRC, November 1–7, 2004', International Assessment and Strategy Center, 13 December, www.strategycenter.net/research/pubID.54/pub_detail.asp, accessed January 2005.

Fisher R.D. (2005), 'Developing US–Chinese nuclear naval competition in Asia', International Assessment and Strategy Center, 16 January, www.strategycenter.net/research/pubID.60/pub_detail.asp, accessed January 2005.

Hyland Gary and Anton Gill (1998), *Last Talons of the Eagle*, London: Headline Book Publishing.

'IAF requires tankers to fulfill Su-30's potential' (1997), *Jane's Defence Weekly*, 27 (23), 32.

Kopp, Carlo (1995), '76N6 Clam Shell acquisition radar revealed', *Australian Aviation*, May, 40, www.ausairpower.net/region.html, accessed January 2005.

Kopp, Carlo (1997a), 'Benchmarking the wider regional threat', *Australian Aviation*, December, 26–8, www.ausairpower.net/TE-Gen-4-AAM-97.html accessed January 2006.

Kopp, Carlo (1997b), 'Fourth generation AAMs & Rafael's Python 4', *Australian Aviation*, 127, April, 41–5, www.ausairpower.net/TE-Gen-4-AAM-97.html, accessed January 2006.

Kopp, Carlo (1997c), 'Fourth generation AAMs – Matra-BAe AIM-132 ASRAAM', *Australian Aviation*, 134, November, 36–8, www.ausairpower.net/asraam.pdf, accessed January 2006.

Kopp, Carlo (1998), 'Replacing the RAAF F/A-18 Hornet fighter: strategic, operational and technical issues', Submission to the Minister for Defence, May, www.ausairpower.net/strategy.html, accessed January 2005.

Kopp, Carlo (2000a), 'A future force structure for the Australian Defence Force – a response to the Green Paper', Submission to the Minister for Defence, 30 August, www.ausairpower.net/strategy.html, accessed January 2005.

Kopp, Carlo (2000b), 'Sunburns, Yakhonts, Alfas and the region', *Australian Aviation*, 165, September, 34–8, www.ausairpower.net/region.html, accessed January 2005.

Kopp, Carlo (2003a), 'Asia's advanced Flankers', *Australian Aviation*, 197, August, 26–30, www.ausairpower.net/region.html, accessed January 2005.

Kopp, Carlo (2003b), 'Asia's new SAMs Pt.1', *Australian Aviation*, 199, October, 46–50, www.ausairpower.net/region.html, accessed January 2005.

Kopp, Carlo (2003c), 'Asia's new SAMs Pt.2', *Australian Aviation*, 200, November, 30–34, www.ausairpower.net/region.html, accessed January 2005.

Kopp, Carlo (2003d), 'Su-30 vs RAAF alternatives', *Australian Aviation*, 198, September, 33–8, www.ausairpower.net/region.html, accessed January 2005.

Kopp, Carlo (2004a), '2010+ regional futures', *Defence Today*, September, www.ausairpower.net/region.html, accessed January 2005.

Kopp, Carlo (2004b), 'Asia's advanced precision guided munitions', *Australian Aviation*, 207, July, 31–5, www.ausairpower.net/region.html, accessed January 2005.

Kopp, Carlo (2004c), 'Backfires and the PLA-AF's new "Strategic Air Force"', International Assessment and Strategy Center, 22 September, www.strategycenter.net/research/pubID.5/pub_detail.asp, accessed January 2005.

Kopp, Carlo (2004d), 'Backfires for China?', *Australian Aviation*, 209, September, 40–44, www.ausairpower.net/region.html, accessed January 2005.

Kopp, Carlo (2004e), 'Sukhoi's fullback', *Australian Aviation*, 211, November, 41–5, www.ausairpower.net/region.html, accessed January 2005.

Kopp, Carlo (2004f), 'The sleeping giant awakens', *Australian Aviation*, 208, August, 50–54, www.ausairpower.net/region.html, accessed January 2005.

Kopp, Carlo (2004g), '2014: the regional balance of air power', *Asia Pacific Defence Reporter*, 30 (2), 21–5.

Kopp, Carlo (2004h), 'SEA 4000 – facing a hostile threat environment', *Asia Pacific Defence Reporter*, 30 (5), 31–2.

Kopp, Carlo (2004i), 'Backfires approaching', *Asia Pacific Defence Reporter*, 30 (7), 33–5.

Kopp, Carlo (2004j), 'Russia's impressive S-300 SAM systems', *Asia Pacific Defence Reporter*, 30 (8), 38–42.

Kopp, Carlo (2005), 'Asia's bears', *Australian Aviation*, unpublished draft.

Mason, R.A. and J.W.R. Taylor (1986), *Aircraft, Strategy and Operations of the Soviet Air Force*, London: Jane's Publishing Company.

'National security of the Asian Pacific region countries and export of Russian arms' (1997), *Russia's Aerospace News*, 2 (1), ITAR-TASS.

Nemets, Alexander (2002a), 'Aircraft carrier for PLA Navy', *NewsMax*, www.newsmax.com/archives/articles/2002/9/22/204248.shtml, Monday, 23 September, accessed January 2005.

Nemets, Alexander (2002b), 'PLA Navy obtains new-generation submarines', *NewsMax*, www.newsmax.com/archives/articles/2002/11/21/13404.shtml, 21 November, accessed January 2005.

Nemets, Alexander and Thomas Torda (2002a), 'China's guochanhua (reverse engineering)', *NewsMax*, www.newsmax.com/archives/articles/2002/6/13/24549. shtml, 13 June, accessed January 2005.

Nemets, Alexander and Thomas Torda (2002b), 'China's multi-level air defense network', *NewsMax.com*, http://www.newsmax.com/archives/articles/2002/7/8/165529. shtml, Tuesday, 9 July accessed January 2005.

Nemets, Alexander and Thomas Torda (2002c), 'Most recent trends in the development of the Chinese aviation industry and their strategic implications', *NewsMax*, www. newsmax.com/archives/articles/2002/5/1/192524.shtml, 2 May, accessed January 2005.

Nemets, Alexander and Thomas Torda (2002d), 'New great leap forward in Chinese–Russian military and defense technology cooperation?', *NewsMax*, www.newsmax. com/archives/articles/2002/7/3/013724.shtml, 3 July, accessed January 2005.

Nemets, Alexander and Thomas Torda (2002e), 'PLA Navy: from "green water" to "blue water" Part I', *NewsMax*, www.newsmax.com/archives/articles/2002/7/25/161633. shtml, 26 July, accessed January 2005.

Nemets, Alexander and Thomas Torda (2002f), 'PLA Navy: from "green water" to "blue water" Part II', *NewsMax*, www.newsmax.com/archives/articles/2002/7/30/141937. shtml, 30 July, accessed January 2005.

Nemets, Alexander and Thomas Torda (2002j), 'Russia suffers while arming China, Part 1', *NewsMax*, www.newsmax.com/archives/articles/2002/1/24/134056.shtml, Thursday, 24 January, accessed January 2005.

Nemets, Alexander and Thomas Torda (2002h), 'Russia suffers while arming China, Part 2', *NewsMax*, www.newsmax.com/archives/articles/2002/1/26/232016.shtml, 27 January, accessed January 2005.

Novichkov, N. (1996), 'Sukhoi set to exploit thrust vector control', *Aviation Week & Space Technology*, 26 August, 146 (36), 55.

Novichkov, N. and J.D. Morocco (1998), 'Russia alters arms export strategy for Southeast Asia', *Aviation Week & Space Technology*, 148 (8), 31.

Novichkov, N. and M.A. Taverna (1997), 'Russia, Israel plan A-50 ...', *Aviation Week & Space Technology*, 23 June, 27–50.

Novosti (2005), 'Russia might sell strategic bombers to China', news report, 14 January, accessed January 2005.

Nowarra, Heinz (1993), *German Guided Missiles*, Atlgen, Philadelphia PA: Schiffer Military/Aviation History.

Ping Kuo Jih Pao (Apple Daily) (2005), 'Russia wants to sell China sophisticated weapons', http://appledaily.atnext.com, FBIS, translated text, 19 March, accessed March 2005.

Pronina, Lyuba (2005), 'Air Force to offer strategic bombers to China', *The Moscow Times*, www.themoscowtimes.com/, 14 January, accessed January 2005.

'Soviet military power' (1987), Department of Defense, United States Government Printing Office, Washington DC, www.fas.org/irp/dia/product/smp_index.htm, accessed January 2005.

'Soviet military power: an assessment of the threat' (1988), Department of Defense, United States Government Printing Office, Washington DC, www.fas.org/irp/dia/product/smp_index.htm, accessed January 2005.

'Soviet military power: prospects for change' (1989), Department of Defense, United States Government Printing Office, Washington DC, www.fas.org/irp/dia/product/smp_index.htm, accessed January 2005.

'The naval air arm' (2005), *Bharat Rakshak*, www.bharat-rakshak.com/NAVY/Air-Arm.html, accessed January 2005.

'The submarine arm' (2005), *Bharat Rakshak*, www.bharat-rakshak.com/NAVY/Submarine.html, accessed January 2005.

'The surface fleet' (2005), *Bharat Rakshak*, www.bharat-rakshak.com/NAVY/Surface.html, accessed January 2005.

'Ukraine admits Iran, China missile sale' (2005), from correspondents in Kiev, 19 March, *The Australian*.

Velikovich, A. and D. Barrie (1998), 'India's avionics indecision holds back second batch of Su-30s', *Flight International*, 29 April, 16.

Zaloga, Steven J. (1989), 'Soviet air defence missiles – design, development and tactics', London: Jane's Defence Data, 26–352.

Zaloga, Steven J. (1997), 'Future trends in air defence missiles', *Journal of Electronic Defence*, October, 23–5.

17. China, the United States and National Missile Defence: an Australian perspective

Kim C. Beazley

Four years ago the Royal Australian Navy outlined the central features of an Australian government-endorsed maritime doctrine. It identified Australia's enduring strategic interests. The first of these was 'Avoidance of destabilising strategic competition developing between the United States, China and Japan as the power relationships between these evolve and change' (Beazley 2003, p. 37). No part of Australian strategic doctrine or policy imagines that Australia has more than a marginal influence on the outlooks of these three powers. The navy's statement, however, reflects a real and deeper interest. In the aftermath of the Cold War the focus of global politics has shifted to the northern Indian Ocean and western littoral of the Pacific. During the Cold War, Australia chose to engage itself with the core of the global balance of power by hosting significant and jointly controlled facilities with the United States on Australian soil. These were major intelligence-gathering, early warning and communication assets of the latter. Relationships developed through those facilities, and broader military collaboration left Australia deeply embedded in the American position globally and regionally. As the quotation above indicates, Australia also has evolved a direct interest in the interplay of US policy with local powers. Therefore, as US nuclear strategy has changed to incorporate more deeply within it defence against ballistic missile attack, Australia has been drawn inexorably into the debate about the United States' National Missile Defence (NMD) despite its minimal influence.

The development of 'destabilising strategic competition' is at least a possibility as the United States moves to establish a system of NMD. The possibility of an offensive/defensive arms race occurring in the north-western Pacific, across the Taiwan Straits, the Sino-Indian border and perhaps ultimately the South China Sea complicates the fraught elements in the politics of the region. The consensus among Europeans, Russians and Chinese in opposing President George W. Bush's announced withdrawal from the Anti-Ballistic Missile Treaty in December 2001 and the development of NMD

266

concealed a deep divergence of motivation and interest between these players. For the Europeans and Russians the issue was not strategic but political. For the European powers, jealous of American pre-eminence, it was politics pure and simple. For Russia, an effective US NMD capability of the limited kind now contemplated would not pose a strategic problem because its own nuclear capabilities remained sufficient to overwhelm any credible US NMD system. The demeanour of the Russian president was mild sorrow rather than anger: 'I fail to understand this insistence [on bilateral withdrawal from the ABM treaty] given our position, which was fairly flexible' (Putin quoted by Huisken 2002, p. 93).

But for China it was, and remains, different. China's concerns about the US NMD are profoundly strategic. Chinese strategists are concerned that even a limited US NMD would erode China's capacity to confidently deter a US nuclear strike on China, and thus lay China open to the threat of nuclear blackmail in the case of confrontation with the United States, most especially over Taiwan.

The probability of a Chinese response to these possibilities has been well acknowledged in the US foreign policy community. A US National Intelligence Estimate released the month of President Bush's declaration suggested that the number of Chinese warheads on intercontinental ballistic missiles might be increased fourfold in response (Mutahir, 2002, p. 21). Dean A. Wilkening of Stanford's Center for International Security and Cooperation, writing earlier, suggested that the proposed Alaskan NMD system 'would pose a serious threat to [China's] deterrent against the US'. Its future size would be 'affected by the presence of US missile defences'. He estimated that China might ultimately have up to 190 warheads; a force of 25 NMD interceptors would therefore degrade Chinese missile retaliation by 20 per cent. Wilkening insisted that 'A defence system in Alaska would therefore have to be limited to 20 interceptors for it to appear relatively unthreatening to China' (Wilkening 2000, pp. 41–2). At the time of President Bush's announcement, Senator Joseph Biden, then Chairman of the Senate Foreign Relations Committee, suggested the initiative was a serious error and would provoke interactive nuclear escalation in Asia (Huisken 2002, p. 90).

The purpose of this chapter is to consider the political and strategic consequences of these developments and to advocate a structured strategic dialogue between the United States and China to mitigate them. Before doing so I intend to examine the Australian response to the US NMD initiative. This is not because NMD is a more important issue for Australia than it is for other Asian-Pacific allies and friends of the United States. Japan and South Korea are intimately drawn into US NMD calculations, as is Taiwan. What distinguishes the Australian case is that Australia, alone among friends/allies, in what might be termed the southern tier of the US Pacific-extended deterrence system, has embraced the concept. At the same time, using the Australian government's own definition of its strategic interests, it has something to lose if NMD exacerbates an arms race and increases tensions in the Pacific area. Given Australia's intimacy with the US strategic deterrent, the issue of America's NMD provides an interesting brief case study.

AUSTRALIA'S RESPONSE TO THE US NMD PROPOSALS

In 2003 the Howard government committed Australia to support the US NMD program. What this means in practical terms is not entirely clear. No additional resources have been devoted to the task. Treasurer Peter Costello stated, 'If we judge that the programme is workable and that Australia can make a contribution then we would sit down and we would look at it in financial terms, but that's a long way down the track, this hasn't been developed' (Evans 2004).

Foreign Minister Downer has been similarly opaque by stating

> What we are looking at at this stage is that in all likelihood ... we don't know the answer to that question yet ... but in all likelihood our involvement will be in the research development and science and technology ... it could be. That is certainly a possibility. After all, you know we are speaking hypothetically here. Again, I'm not trying to be evasive about this. I hope I am giving the impression it is very much a work in progress. (Evans 2004)

Despite these ambiguities, the Australian government's position has been sufficiently clear to worry some neighbouring countries. In the opinion of Indonesian Foreign Minister Wirajuda, Australian involvement in the NMD program could undermine regional security efforts and spark an arms race: 'We have been working very hard, including with Australia and other partners, within the ASEAN regional forum process. This NMD defence program is not compatible with what we are doing. It is not helpful' (Davidson 2003).

It is impossible to avoid the conclusion that what the Australian government has said has been primarily for a domestic audience in a domestic political debate: an announcement pitching the government's credentials as unique devotees of the Australian–US alliance. Whatever doubts the Australian opposition has voiced over NMD, these have been portrayed as being based on a simplistic anti-Americanism rather than any real concern for Australian strategic policies. This is not the first time that the Howard government has been prepared to see Australia damaged in the region to score a domestic political point.

The real situation is more complex. In fact, entirely as a result of the efforts of the Hawke and Keating governments, Australia has been actively engaged in research on ballistic missile defences (BMD) and hosts sensor systems on which the architecture of some form of Australian BMD could be based. However, as far as the American NMD is concerned, the Australian contribution to such a system is modest. As Professor Ball has noted, in recent years the Australian government has tried to undermine the credibility of the Australian Labor Party opposition, which opposes NMD by 'Inflating the role of the relay ground station' (at Pine Gap) (McDonald 2001).

The relay ground station (RGS) at Pine Gap is a product of the previous Labor governments' determination to ensure a continued Australian role in satellite-based infra-red detection of rocket launches and similar activity that technology had threatened to eliminate.

The RGS at Pine Gap is not irreplaceable in the US system. Over time it is probable that the space-based infrared system (SBIRS) architecture will see information cross-linked by satellite to the US command centre. The Australian ground station could then be part of the redundant components of the system. As the SBIRS becomes more capable, information from the RGS passing into the Australian system would be a vital first warning for Australia of missile attack. The United States could at some point get its information from elsewhere.

It was not always thus. The Labor governments of the 1980s and 1990s opposed President Reagan's Strategic Defense Initiative (SDI).[1] They believed SDI was potentially deeply destabilizing to the nuclear balance. They were, however, highly supportive of the facility associated with the US early warning system – the DSP satellite[2] ground station at Nurrungar on the site of the Woomera rocket range in South Australia. Its early warning function, which approximately doubled the warning time of the North American DEWS radar system, was seen as essential in allowing a US president to reflect on possibly false warnings of attack. Though the United States agreed to exclude the joint facilities from SDI research, the Australian government recognized that knowledge was indivisible. As the Minister for Defence said in September 1987, 'Any data collected at the Australian sites has not been collected for the purpose of SDI research but specifically to support the early warning function of the DSP. Any other use to which the data may be put is quite incidental' (*House Hansard* 1987, p. 660).

From then until the late 1990s Nurrungar was one of three ground stations globally that were vital to the functioning of the early warning system. The Labor government approach shifted to one of collaboration with BMD research under two influences. The first was the belief that the system could directly serve direct Australian defence purposes. The second was that a surge in ballistic and cruise missile capabilities regionally and further afield created requirements for the defence of forward deployed allied forces and sometimes the defence of regional states under attack – a justification for theatre missile defences (TMD).[3] An interpretation of the Anti-Ballistic Missile Treaty (ABMT) of 2001 allowed the development of ground- and maritime-based interception systems without placing the signatory in breach.

The belief that the system could serve Australian defence interests directly was a product of the Labor government's experience with implementing party policy on the basis that Australia needed to have full knowledge of, and consent to, activities at the joint facilities. This meant a much larger number of Australian personnel operating the facilities and, in the case of Nurrungar, Australian officers commanding at least half the shifts. Had the doomsday button been pressed the chances were that it would have been an Australian RAAF squadron leader who alerted the US President. Familiarity with the potential of the system caused the Australian government to negotiate a data link to Canberra. Knowledge spread among defence planners of the value of the system to Australia's regional environment. Hence the reluctance of the Labor government to see the system disappear from Australia when, in 1999, the DSP system and Nurrungar were shut down. The presence of the RGS at Pine Gap was potentially more valuable to Australia than it was to the United States.

The value of the system in warning and perhaps cueing a response in a TMD context elsewhere was demonstrated during the Kuwait War. As the Defence Minister Robert Ray told the Australian Senate,

> During the Gulf war the DSP detected the launch of Iraqi scud missiles and gave warning to coalition forces and to civilian populations in Israel and Saudi Arabia. The DSP's superb performance during that conflict confirms the flexibility and the continued relevance of a system which was designed primarily to produce early warning of missile attack against the US and its friends and allies. (*Senate Hansard* 1991, p. 2374)

This caused the government to think further afield. Foreign Minister Gareth Evans told the Senate in May 1993:

> At the regional level, Nurrungar may yet have a further significant role. Australia may conceivably come to rely more than ever on this facility if a ballistic missile threat were to develop in our neighbourhood. On the other hand, the early warning capabilities of Nurrungar offer possibilities for new orders of cooperation with direct benefit to our neighbours' own security. The monitoring of arms control agreements, the discouraging of ballistic missile proliferation, the probabilities for defence of cities against missile attack and opportunities for new forms of regional cooperation are all on our agenda in the post Cold War era. (*Senate Hansard* 1993, p. 248)

Critical to the Australian government's collaboration with BMD was the collapse of the US SDI organization in the Ballistic Missile Defence Office (BMDO) in May 1993. To the Australian government this signalled a US intention to conduct research and development and deployment in the context of the ABMT. According to Minister Ray:

> Cooperation with the BMDO will contribute to DSTO efforts in developing familiarity with space systems and research, and in key technology areas relevant to the ADF [Australian Defence Forces] such as command, control and communications; information technologies; and surveillance technologies. [The Defence White Paper] highlights the importance for the ADF of technologies in these areas in the next 15 years. They relate to ADF interests in areas such as advanced defences for its combat forces and command, control and surveillance capabilities. Cooperation will also allow Australia, as a US ally, to share with the BMDO expertise to meet Australian needs, thus advancing our interests in strengthening global security, including cooperation in defence against ballistic missiles. (*Senate Hansard* 1995, p. 125)

Professor Ball (2001, p. 14) maintains that among the research projects associated with the DSP system was the tracking of aircraft in the region. The only substantial experiment in the BMD context thus far was approved during the period of the Keating government but conducted in August 1997 after its fall. The experiment combined the capabilities of the DSP system with the indigenous 'Jindalee over-the-horizon radar system'.[4] The system tracked launches of Terrier anti-ship missiles off the north-west coast of Western Australia (ibid).

The combination of the two systems with new AEW aircraft, and the possible acquisition in the next decade of an AEGIS system capable destroyer, would give a substantial TMD capability to the ADF if Standard Missile Block 3 missiles were acquired with it. Such a development would be a logical extension of previous Australian policy and has nothing to do with US-based NMD.

The Australian government has speculated on the capacity of North Korean missiles to hit Australia, citing the test of a three-stage rocket in 1998. Despite some literature projecting what might be missile capabilities in North Korea, China, Iran and India to hit targets in southern Australia in the future (Fruhling 2003), it is difficult to conceive of those states extending the range of ICBMs and IRBMs beyond that required to deal with their immediate neighbourhoods and the United States. No matter how closely aligned Australia is to the United States, it is difficult to see these nuclear powers and potential powers targeting major Australian population centres while trying to develop a capability against the United States (Swaine and Runyon 2002). What major national interest would these nations be serving by targeting Australia, even assuming that Australia retains such close diplomatic and defence ties with the United States?

Certainly there is nothing in Australian government planning that indicates it sees any credible threat that might require a response. The Howard government's position is not internationally strategic; rather it is driven by more narrow domestic, political considerations that play on the ongoing perceptions of regional insecurity among the Australian populace. At the same time, the north-west Pacific region contains most of Australia's major trading partners, while in South and South-east Asia lies the region of direct strategic significance to Australia. Given this, the manner in which the Australian government manages the nuclear relationships among these multiple parties and with the United States is of direct security and economic relevance to Australia.

CHINA'S RESPONSE TO US NMD PROPOSALS

In public presentations, US administration officials are upbeat about contemporary Chinese responses to the United States' development of NMD. Kerry Kartchner told an Australian audience in 2004: 'We have taken steps to assure China and Russia that our modest defences are not directed against them. My assessment is that they recognise that' (Barker 2004, p. 61). It is true that since December 2001, when President Bush announced his government's intention to develop NMD, Chinese responses have been muted. In the lead-up to the decision, as its likelihood increased with a succession of pronouncements by President Bush, the shift in the debate in the United States after the 1998 North Korean test and the report of the Rumsfeld Commission in 1998, Chinese assertions were much more strident (Huisken 2002). At that time, clear lines of Chinese thinking were exposed. After one of President Bush's speeches in May 2001, the Xinhua News Agency reported: 'Analysts said the US plan to build a missile defence system will not only spark a new arms race and create a proliferation of weapons of mass destruction but also threaten world peace and security in the 21st century' ('Bush: US must move beyond constraints of ABM', 2001).

The logic of China's concerns goes like this. Without a robust submarine-based missile capability, China's small and vulnerable arsenal of land-based ICBMs could be substantially destroyed by the United States in a first strike. An effective limited NMD capability could provide the United States with a higher level of confidence that any surviving Chinese missiles not destroyed in a US first strike could be destroyed by it after China launches them. This would make a US first strike less unthinkable than it would otherwise have been, and this in turn would undermine Chinese confidence that the United States would not contemplate first resort to nuclear weapons. .

China is also concerned about US Theatre Missile Defence (TMD) plans. Those concerns are based more on the possibility that effective TMD might neutralize Chinese short- and medium-range missile capabilities against Taiwan and to a lesser extent Japan. Michael Swaine and Loren Runyon have summarized Chinese objections from the extensive literature on them. They range from the military strategic to the political:

> TMD could force China to dramatically increase the size and sophistication of its Intermediate Range Ballistic Missiles (IRBM) arsenal and adopt a robust limited nuclear deterrence doctrine oriented toward WMD war-fighting. TMD would undermine regional and global arms control efforts reversing those processes designed to reduce nuclear stockpiles and Multiple Independently Targetable Reentry Vehicle (MIRVed) warheads. It could weaken China's support for the Comprehensive Test Ban Treaty (CTBT), the missile transfer control regime and the Fissile Material Cut-Off Treaty (FMCT). Transfer of TMD-related technologies to Taiwan would violate the Missile Technology Control Regime (MTCR) established in 1987. TMD-technology sales to Taiwan are an interference in China's internal affairs violating her sovereignty and weakening US–China relations. Such moves would recreate a de facto US–Taiwan military alliance, lead to an arms race and give Taiwan technologies to build offensive missiles. It would limit the capacity of China to exert political pressure in its own backyard. By providing a protective shield in northeast Asia for American interests, TMD might encourage Japan to develop a nuclear sword against China. (Swaine and Runyon 2002, pp. 57–8)

The TMD questions receive more attention than the NMD questions. They are charged with the daily politics of Taiwan issues. Strategically they are less significant than the NMD question. China has very large small-range ballistic missile (SRBM) and medium-range ballistic missile (MRBM) capabilities targeted against Taiwan. They are conceived in a conventional context and are plugged into a quality production line that can be cranked up to overwhelm TMD capabilities. They are only part of an array of conventional options for placing pressure on Taiwan. NMD is of a different order, both technologically and strategically. It will not have escaped Chinese notice that press reports during the time of the Clinton administration about the United States' highly sensitive nuclear targeting plans suggested China was back on the list after an absence of 20 years (Huisken 2002, p. 95).

Should the region worry about China's concerns about US NMD plans? There is an argument that we should. While it is hard to argue that missile defences are, in principle, destabilizing, China's concerns about US NMD plans threaten to add a destabilizing element to the US–China relationship. That relationship is already one of the most important, uncertain and potentially dangerous in the world today, as China's growing power meets US global pre-eminence. Any issue that lowers the chances of the United States and China being able to develop a durable and stable modus vivendi is important. As Alan Romberg and Adam Hartman (2003) have argued:

> Missile defence affects the strategic balance of vital interests for both nations because it cuts to the heart of what future relations will be all about. Handled well,

it could consolidate the current [improving] trend. Handled badly, it could be the fundamental driver of a downward turn in what may be the US's most important bilateral relationship in the 21st century.

As pointed out earlier, since President Bush's December 2001 announcement, the temperature of the public presentations by Chinese officials on the US NMD has cooled. The more circumspect attitude by China may reflect the fatalistic view among other critics as the United States seemed determined on its course. A number of matters may influence Chinese thinking, at least in the short term.

The first is that extracting the debate on NMD from BMD generally is not easy. Quite clearly, conventional forces, both regional and forward deployed US forces, will develop the capacity to defend themselves from ballistic and cruise missile attacks by both active and passive means. In the region there are now some 3000 such missiles, with the numbers and delivery systems in the hands of individual states growing exponentially (Ball 2003, p. 22). As the United States has gone to war over Kuwait and Iraq, derivatives of the Patriot interception system in both conflicts have been diverted to regional countries for BMD. China deploys a limited BMD capacity itself. Since the 1980s TMD capabilities have been an essential element of the protection of US carrier battle groups and general naval activities through the AEGIS system of tracking missile threats and cueing responses.

The sensor, tracking and interceptor systems for ballistic missile defence may be useful for TMD, NMD and point defence. Developing a special regime for NMD is not easy. North Korea's antics with missile tests over Japan, testing the capacity to develop a small ICBM force and admitting to a nuclear program, add veracity to the US claim that it has a rogue state focus to its NMD program, while making it difficult to criticize BMD cooperation between the United States and Japan and South Korea.

The latter consideration may influence a more general reading of the United States' strategic situation. In the decade or so since the end of the Cold War the United States has found itself, its relationships and its interests increasingly the focus of potentially hostile state and non-state actors. Breaches of agreements on non-proliferation of chemical, biological and nuclear (CBN) materials, and missile technology transfers encouraged overtly or covertly by states to those actors, have become an increasing focus of the American intelligence community and its allies and friends. The understanding of security officials around the globe has been expanded by the experience of the 9/11 atrocities in New York and the plethora of terrorist attacks since. The Chinese have been genuinely sympathetic and helpful in dealing with these problems, identifying a few of their own in the process. US withdrawal from the ABMT and the NMD announcements coming hard on the heels of these events have not fallen into an atmosphere conducive to strident criticism.

A further factor in the Chinese response may have been the substantial change in the high-profile elements of US defence strategy after 9/11. A close reading of the American Quadrennial Defence Review Report (Department of Defense 2001), written before but published after 9/11, suggests that an internal debate among US policymakers about whether China was a strategic competitor or partner resolved that it was. China is not mentioned in this report as an adversary. However, the description of asymmetrical warfare and sea denial tactics and strategies that a new capability-based approach to US defence planning is required to counter, appears to be a mirror image of what US planners know of the developing Chinese military doctrine. Rather than address the capabilities of an equivalent power, the United States seeks out strategies of weaker actors who intend to deny it access to an area of interest. In seeking to defeat such strategies, the open ocean, 'blue water' characteristic of US forward deployment is replaced by a focus on 'green water' littoral tasks. Of particular interest was a new geographic definition of the Asian littoral. One of the areas from which hostile domination is to be precluded is the East Asian littoral. This is defined as the region extending from the south of Japan through Australia to the Bay of Bengal. It scoops up Taiwan and the south-east Asian littoral on the way through (Department of Defense 2001, p. 1).

But for the events of 9/11, the combination of the withdrawal from the ABMT, the new defence strategy and a hardening of administration attitudes on Taiwan might have seen the US–China relationship drawn more closely to the type of adversary status that existed in the US–Soviet relationship during the Cold War. However, with the US focus drawn to the type of asymmetrical military challenge presented by hostile non-state actors, the significance of this changed defence strategy was submerged from public view. Indeed, far from seeking points of disagreement, the US–China relationship over the last two years has been marked by a new collaborative tone that contradicts previous predictions by the Bush administration of China's emerging strategic competitiveness.

In its initial response to the war in Afghanistan, China acquiesced, largely without complaint, to the emergence of US bases in parts of the former Soviet Union, on China's western borders. The United States has actively engaged China in seeking a resolution to the seemingly intractable problems posed by North Korea's nuclear efforts. The Chinese government has attempted to be helpful in defusing the dangerous possibilities of an Indo-Pakistan conflict. As the United States has delved more deeply into the illicit trade in nuclear and missile materials, and as fears of the capabilities of 'rogue states' and terrorist organizations have grown, China has looked more carefully at its own participation in technological transfers to third parties. China's strategy has reflected the tougher climate facing all nuclear states today in limiting the consequences of the arms trade.

Recognizing the considerable benefits from cooperative relations, the Bush administration, overriding the objections of many in Congress, has moved to prevent the Taiwan issue overshadowing the emergence of a positive relationship between China and the United States. Concerned about the prospects for Taiwan, President Chen Shui-bian's re-election campaign raising sensitive issues about a new constitution and the Chinese missile threat, President Bush warned the Taiwanese leader: 'the comments and actions made by the leader of Taiwan indicate that he may be willing to make decisions unilaterally to change the status quo, which we oppose' (Swaine 2004, p. 1).

It can be safely assumed that it is a combination of these shifts in regional political affairs, along with a large and burgeoning trading and investment relationship with the United States and the preoccupation of the Chinese leadership with internal development, that keeps the NMD issue on a back burner. This, however, does not amount to China accepting assurances that America's NMD poses no problem for it. Given the long-term horizons involved in the development of nuclear weapons systems, the political issues associated with them tend to move to a different rhythm from that of daily politics.

What type of force structure decisions will China have to make if the Chinese government decides that US NMD will dangerously degrade its capacity to protect itself through deterrence and sustain its position on Taiwan? China has a full suite of ballistic missiles from the short range to MRBMs, IRBMs and ICBMs. The latter two have tended to be developed in small numbers consistent with a strategy of minimum deterrence (Swaine and Runyon 2002, p. 46).

As China deals with the obsolescence of systems developed in the 1960s and 1970s, it has tended to emphasize several elements in modernization: extending solid-fuel propulsion systems that substantially reduce the time taken for deployment and improve the alert status of the rockets; developing multiple warhead capabilities for rockets and decoys; developing road mobile models; and developing sea-launched systems. These changes would be reflected in any nuclear modernization program. They are also attributes important to survivability in the context of the US NMD program (Ball 2003, p. 32).

The Chinese nuclear program over the last 20 years has seen several foreshadowed systems, with much claimed for them in the West but put on hold, expanded or developed at a slower pace than assessments have suggested. The Dong Feng (DF) 41 ICBM program was aborted in favour of developing longer-range variants of the DF31. A submarine-launched ballistic missile (SLBM) was developed and placed on one submarine. There the sea-based forces have rested but a variant of the new land-based missile is being pursued in the hope of expanding a force that has proved difficult to develop.

Given China's considerable economic constraints, a decision to respond to challenges imposed by US and regional BMD would simply boil down to a question of the numbers of new missiles with the characteristics being developed anyway. In addition, thought might be given to the development of anti-satellite weapons, given their crucial contribution to US dominance in space-based sensor systems for military purposes.

What is at stake in all this for Chinese planners? As long as the Taiwan issue remains unresolved, China's strategic policymakers will remain sensitive to their level of vulnerability to US nuclear pressure. As a country fixed on its future role as a global power of the first rank, China would also be very reluctant to lose an effective deterrent capability against the United States. Both motivations are enough to drive an extensive missile-building program.

What further calculations are likely to be made about the US NMD program? First, Chinese planners would calculate that, whatever is intended with a minimal NMD, once developed the system would be capable of being rapidly expanded. Second, they would conclude from debates over the last decade that many Americans in influential positions would be quite happy if a by-product of a system directed to deal with a 'rogue state' could also diminish China's political position as its deterrent capacity became degraded. Third, Chinese planners, like all sensible defence planners, would calculate on the basis of capabilities rather than intentions. No matter what the view of the current US administration, another administration may be different and therefore what the United States is capable of constructing is what counts, rather than intentions.

The fundamental problem is that there is no strategic engagement between China and the United States. Conversations have been offered but discussions have been no more than rudimentary. The US administration responds to Chinese concerns by arguing that China's current program to enhance its ICBM force will preserve Beijing's deterrent in the face of the US NMD. If the Chinese are building bigger offensive forces anyway, the argument goes, there is no reason to blame the US NMD program for stimulating the Chinese build-up.

It is clear that it is difficult for the United States to accept China as a strategic dialogue party in any sense resembling the status that was accorded to the Soviet Union and now Russia. It is true that there is little of the clarity surrounding the development of BMD systems, or even the determinations driving the Chinese modernization program, that equates with the structure of comparative Soviet and US forces of the 1960s.

China is now the world's third nuclear power, but is not currently a power of such dimension that compels a dialogue. There is no consensus in the US foreign policy community on what status China's current and projected power accords it, nor on whether it is a US strategic competitor or partner. With such ambiguity and uncertain projections as to what the situation might be like in ten years, there appears little incentive at the moment to move towards a structured strategic dialogue with formal or informal agreements on force levels and technologies. The result is that the US–China interchange is driven largely by short-term, immediate, pressing problems.

CONCLUSION

What would be the value of commencing a structured dialogue now? First, however sanguine contemporary US politicians might be about Chinese modernization and projected force levels, it would take very little in the future to persuade decision-makers in the United States that something more sinister was underway when the build-up occurs rather than Chinese efforts to preserve a minimal deterrence. At a minimum that would undermine in the work being done in Russia and the United States to reduce the still massive number of deployed warheads.

Second, whatever its status in the mind of US decision-makers, China is firmly in the view of force planners in India. India makes its own calculations on nuclear deterrence in relation to China. It will not fail to respond to the appearance of massive increases in Chinese capability. Tension in Sino-Indian and Indo-Pakistani relations may wax and wane, but, whatever the efforts of contemporary politicians, flash-points will remain potent. The costs of miscalculation rise dramatically the more extensively the armed forces of these states are nuclearized. Preserving China's capacities for minimum deterrence at low levels affects more than just Sino-US relations – it affects the other two major nuclear powers in the region too: India and Pakistan.

Third, the more threatening China's nuclear capabilities appear, the more complicated Japan's position and forward planning will be. Japan is taking increasingly decisive steps to build its own shield, as well as towards taking advantage of a US umbrella. As the debate in Japan increases in sophistication, so will the arguments about the need for a sword as well as a shield.

Fourth, US conventional supremacy globally is based on the force multipliers it enjoys through its massively superior space-based sensor and intelligence systems. It is not in the US interest to see China turned into the sort of competitor that might start to develop active programs against those space-based systems as it struggles to find solutions for the problems of a deterrent it has lost confidence in. China already has a satellite capacity – pushing it into expanding this to a military direction is unwise.

Fifth, the United States has firmly committed itself to a substantial international anti-proliferation regime. Building on the revelations of the illicit involvement of Pakistani scientists in very dangerous proliferation activities, President Bush has presented an extensive set of steps for strengthening international collaboration to prevent proliferation. Included in the Bush agenda is a tightening of provisions of the Nuclear Non-Proliferation Treaty and other agreed international controls ('Bush's speech on the spread of nuclear weapons' 2004). China is either a signatory to or abides by several agreements on test bans, fissile material controls and missile technology transfers. Serious modernization of its forces or a sense that it is not a power included in serious nuclear dialogue may start to weaken Chinese commitments. The Nuclear Non-Proliferation Treaty was negotiated on the basis that major powers would rationalize their own affairs while they sought performance from others. Then it was the Soviet Union and the United States that were expected to enter serious arms control arrangements. Extending that now to China would be a demonstration of serious intent in contemporary terms and an indirect recognition of the importance of China in world affairs.

A seriously structured dialogue between the United States and China would establish very quickly the sensitive points on both sides. It would provide a forum for understanding the embraced new technology. It could satisfy China's aspiration to be taken seriously as a global power at quite low force levels. It could prevent over-reaction to the potential implication of technologies that ultimately are not pursued.

Finding diplomatic airspace for all of this, with the focus on regional imbroglios and defeating vicious terrorist movements, is not easy. Arms control discussions of the Cold War era took place in a framework of international relations that was more rigid. Nevertheless, international stability was well served in that era by the appearance that major players were focused on regulating their deployment of doomsday weapons. The situation is no different now.

NOTES

1. President Raegan's speech of 1973 is better known as the speech that gave rise to the 'Star Wars Program', which sought to develop a shield capable of protecting the whole of the United States from external threat or nuclear attack.
2. DSP stands for Defence Support Program. DSP satellites use infra-red detectors to locate missile and space launches and nuclear explosions.
3. In this paper Beazley distinguishes between TMD (Theatre Missile Defence) and NMD (National Missile Defence). According to Swaine and Runyon, these are the two main alternative missile defence systems: 'A NMD system would be designed to protect civilian population centres on the homeland from being attacked by nuclear-armed ICBMs and SLBMs, whereas TMD is a deployed missile defence designed to protect forces and their allies on a (likely foreign) battlefield from theater ballistic missiles' (Swaine and Runyon 2002, p. 54, note 98). [Ed.]
4. The Jindalee radar system depends on three tracking stations located at Laverton (Western Australia), Alice Springs (Central Australia) and Longreach (Queensland).

REFERENCES

Ball, Des (2001), 'Missile defence: trends, concerns and remedies', Strategic and Defence Studies Centre, Working Paper No. 360, ANU, Canberra.

Ball, Des (2003), 'Security trends in the Asia-Pacific region: an emerging complex arms race', Strategic and Defence Studies Centre, Working Paper No. 380, ANU, Canberra.

Barker, G. (2004), 'Chink in the armour', *Australian Financial Review*, 16 February.

Beazley, K. (2003), 'Inaugural Frank Broeze Memorial Lecture', *Journal of the Australian Naval Institute*, 108, 30–38.

'Bush's speech on the spread of nuclear weapons' (2004), *The New York Times*, 11 February.

'Bush: US must move beyond constraints of ABM' (2001), *People's Daily Online*, 2 May, http://english.people.com.cn/english/200105/02/eng20010502_69146.html, accessed January 2006.

Davidson, Kenneth (2003), 'Howard's latest cosying up to Bush is madness', *The Age*, 11 December, www.theage.com.au/articles/2003/12/10/1070732279583.html, accessed January 2006.

Evans, Chris (2004), media release, 14 January.

Fruhling, Stephan (2003), 'Ballistic missile defence for Australia: policies, requirements and options', Canberra Papers on Strategy and Defence, no. 151, pp. 1–142, Strategic and Defence Studies Centre, Research School of Pacific and Asian Studies, Australian National University.

House of Representatives Hansard (1987), 24 September, Parliament of Australia.

Huisken, R. (2002), 'Missile defence, the ABM Treaty and nuclear weapons – an opportunity missed', *Pacific Review*, 14 (2).

McDonald, Hamish (2001), 'Space invaders ...', *Sydney Morning Herald*, 27 July.

Mutahir, Ahmed (2002), 'Missile defense and South Asia: a Pakistani perspective', Henry L Stimson Centre Report, No. 46, July.

Department of Defense (2001), *Quadrennial Defence Review Report*, www.comw. org/qdr/qdr2001.pdf, Washington, 30 September, 4.

Romberg, Alan and Adam J. Hartman (2003), 'A new arms race with China', *South China Morning Post*, 15 March.

Senate Hansard (1991), 5 November, Parliament of Australia.

Senate Hansard (1993), 6 May, Parliament of Australia.

Senate Hansard (1995), 22 August, Parliament of Australia.

Swaine, Michael D. (2004), 'Trouble in Taiwan', *Foreign Affairs*, 83 (2).

Swaine, Michael D. and Loren H. Runyon (2002), 'Ballistic missiles and missile defence in Asia', *NBR Analysis*, 13 (3), Washington: The National Bureau of Asian Research.

Wilkening, Dean A. (2000), 'Ballistic missile defence and strategic stability', Adelphi Paper 334, May, Oxford: Oxford University Press for IISS.

18. Japan's experience with terrorism

Takashi Sakamoto

Just like the assassination of President Kennedy and the 9/11 incidents for Americans, Aum Shinrikyo's subway terrorist attack reminds most Japanese of where they were on that very day – 20 March 1995. I was an economic reporter covering the Ministry of International Trade and Industries (MITI). My morning ritual was to visit the residence of the Minister (Ryutaro Hashimoto) to ask a few questions with other reporters. His residence was located in the area of Roppongi in central Tokyo. I have always used the subway to reach his place. But that particular morning I could not make it. I felt somewhat strange when I heard the announcement at the subway station that the Hibiya Line was not operating owing to an accident. The nature of the accident was not explained. After waiting half an hour, I decided to take a cab straight to the headquarters of MITI in Kasumigasaki, not so far from Roppongi. There I heard the news that somebody had dispersed poison gas in the subway and many people were killed or injured. The Hibiya Line was one of the subway lines affected by the attack. Some victims were found between Roppongi and Kasumigaseki. I realized I would have been one of those victims if I had taken the subway a little earlier: 12 people died and about 5000 became seriously ill in response to poisoning by the nerve gas, sarin. Ten years later the victims' families and many other citizens who, like me, could have been victims, gathered at five subway stations, including Kasumigaseki, to commemorate the deaths. They prayed and placed flowers for those who were killed. Prime Minister Koizumi was present and told reporters that he promised to give full support to those survivors who continued to suffer.

The subway terrorist attack cannot be forgotten in Japan. It changed the way the Japanese think about security. They are still worried that such attacks might take place again. In a poll conducted on 10 March 2005 by *The Yomiuri Shimbun*, a Japanese newspaper, more than 80 per cent of respondents said they were concerned about similar attacks in the future. Seventy-three per cent expressed concerns over the cult group that had committed these murders – the 'Aum Shinrikyo' or 'Aum Supreme Truth'. Despite this, Aum Shinrikyo has been allowed to continue its activities under the new name of Aleph even after the attacks ('10 years on, public still fears Aum' 2005).

TERRORISM IN JAPAN BEFORE AUM SHINRIKYO

Before a series of terrorist attacks by Aum Shinrikyo, the Japanese boasted that their country was probably the safest in the world. This was a dearly held myth among ordinary citizens, but it was partially true.

First, Japan's crime rate had been remarkably low compared with other industrialized countries. According to government statistics taken in 1975, for instance, the number of murder cases per 100 000 citizens was 1.9 in Japan, while 9.6 in the United States, 4.8 in West Germany and 2.3 in Britain (Ministry of Justice 1977). The figures for 2001 confirm that this is a long-term difference: the number of murders per 100 000 citizens is still very low in Japan at 1.1, compared with to 5.6 in the United States, 3.2 in Germany and 2.3 in Britain (Ministry of Justice 2003). Second, the small number of terrorist acts that took place in Japan after World War II did not affect the lives of ordinary citizens in most cases. The majority were committed by political fanatics of the extreme left or right and they had specific targets: politicians, high officials and big business executives.

A few terrorist incidents had involved ordinary citizens. In 1970 members of the Red Army faction hijacked a Japan Airlines plane, taking 131 passengers hostage. The hijackers defected to North Korea (Takarajima 2004, p. 32). All passengers were released unharmed. After this first hijacking, several other extreme groups hijacked Japanese and non-Japanese aeroplanes in a similar way (ibid.). In 1972 another group of extremists, the Japanese Red Army, sent gunmen to Israel to support the Popular Front for the Liberation of Palestine (PFLP). Those gunmen produced machine guns from their luggage and opened fire in the arrivals terminal at Ben-Gurion Airport in Lod, Israel. Twenty-six people, including 24 gunmen, were killed (ibid., pp. 30–31).

The most serious terrorist act before Aum Shinrikyo was probably the series of bombings of Japanese big business by the independent group called the 'East Asia Anti-Japan Armed Front'. They bombed 11 company buildings between 1974 and 1975, including the Mitsubishi Heavy Industries office in Tokyo's central business district. Eight innocent citizens were killed on that site (Takarajima 2004, pp. 62–3).

After these incidents, leftist extremists lost the support of the Japanese people. Extremism became even weaker after the end of the Cold War. The new calm contributed to the growth of the myth that Japan was the safest place in the world. Many Japanese people believed that myth until Aum Shinrikyo started a totally new kind of terrorism.

THE EMERGENCE OF AUM SHINRIKYO

The founder of the Aum Shinrikyo cult, Shoko Asahara, was sentenced to death on 27 February 2004 for masterminding 13 crimes that resulted in the death of 27 people. His crimes included two sarin gas attacks – on the Tokyo subway system and in the Nagano prefecture. A total of 189 people were indicted and Asahara was the twelfth person sentenced to death in the series of Aum Shinrikyo-related crimes. Who is Asahara and what does he represent?

The real name of Shoko Asahara is Chizuo Matsumoto. He was born in Kumamoto, on Kyushu, the southern island of Japan, in March 1955. He was the fourth son of a poor *tatami* mat-maker. When Chizuo was six years old, he was sent to a government-owned boarding school for the blind in Kumamoto. According to Japanese press reports, he was not totally blind at that time and he complained about not being able to attend the local primary school. But the students at the school for the blind were given government scholarships that paid for school supplies, meals and transportation costs to and from home. No doubt his poor parents found this an attractive way of giving their son a basic education. But he was bossy and violent in the school, and made protégés of the submissive junior students who were totally blind or weak ('Humble beginnings shed light on Aum cult leader' 2004). He often forced his classmates to fight each other. Although he called this 'wrestling', if he found that one of them was not fighting with sufficient enthusiasm, Asahara himself would punch the opponent ('A man called the Guru' 1995).

After graduating from this boarding school, Asahara went to Tokyo to prepare for the entrance examination of Tokyo University. He failed but remained in Tokyo and opened a Chinese herbal medicine and acupuncture clinic in the suburbs. As his business expanded, he was gradually attracted to religion. He participated in the religious activities of a neo-Buddhist sect, 'Agon Shu'. It was also at this time that his criminal activities began. In 1982 he was arrested for selling bogus medicines; he was compelled to pay a fine of 200 000 yen (about US$2000). Two years later, he left Agon Shu and founded his own sect, 'Aum Shinsen No Kai'. It was started as a yoga training centre but later became the base of the cult group Aum Shinrikyo ('A chronology of Shoko Asahara' 1995; 'humble beginnings shed light on Aum cult leader' 2004).

Around 1989–90 Aum Shinrikyo began to change from a minor religious group into a violent cult. The organization was registered by the Tokyo metropolitan government as a religious corporation in 1989. By then Asahara had about 3000 to 4000 young followers. He claimed to be the only enlightened person in Japan and insisted on being called 'guru'.[1] Aum Shinrikyo gained some legal status and much financial benefit by being officially recognized as a religious corporation. Behind the scenes, however, Aum Shinrikyo began a strategy of violence. In November 1989 they killed Tsutsumi Sakamoto (a lawyer) and his family because they felt threatened (for further details see below). Sakamoto had provided assistance to Aum Shinrikyo followers who wanted to leave the cult. In 1990 Shoko Asahara and his disciples ran in Japan's general election. They believed that political clout was needed to expand their organization. Asahara and his colleagues were resoundingly defeated in February 1990 ('The summary of the ruling' 2004).

Electoral failure was no surprise for the Japanese public but it came as a great shock to Asahara. He was very angry about the result and accused the government of rigging the election. Many police officials and journalists believe that it was at this time that Asahara started thinking about gaining power through illegal means. He stopped teaching non-violence and predicted that Japan would sink into the sea. He also claimed to be the last messiah of the century. Finally, in April 1990 he told senior followers: 'From now on we will employ *Vajrayana*. We will disperse botulinus all over the world.' Asahara had in effect declared Aum Shinrikyo's objective of indiscriminate mass murder, which he sought to pass off as legitimate '*poa*' ('The summary of the ruling' 2004). He ordered senior followers to cultivate botulinus, the poisonous bacterium that causes botulism. In the process, Asahara corrupted the Buddhist tenet of *Vajrayana*, and thus debased the primary idea of compassion in Buddhism.[2]

While Aum Shinrikyo described itself as a Buddhist cult, others have claimed that Aum Shinrikyo's teaching was a 'distorted version of Buddhism and Hinduism steeped in apocalyptic theology' (Larimer 2002). Asahara borrowed the concept of Armageddon from Christian visions. He even referred to the visions of Nostradamus, and wrote in the January 1988 issue of *Mahayana*, the Aum Shinrikyo magazine, 'the terrible Armageddon by nuclear weapons is waiting for us' (Akimoto 2002). Despite the criticisms, it remains true that many young and talented Japanese were attracted to Asahara. Some belonged to the Japanese elite; for example, a lawyer who graduated from Kyoto University, an engineer from Tokyo University Graduate School and a medical doctor who graduated from Keio University. For the sake of their faith in Asahara, they sacrificed almost everything. They left their family and job, donated all their income and assets to Aum Shinrikyo and became 'priests' of the cult.

The number of Aum Shinrikyo's followers continued to grow. In 1995, just before the subway attack, it had 14 000 followers, 1400 'priests' and millions of dollars of assets. It was also active beyond Japan through its branches in Moscow, New York and other major Western cities. It was said that it had 35 000 followers in Russia alone. It even had a base in Australia, on a remote sheep farm some 375 miles north-east of Perth, the capital city of Western Australia (Minority Staff of the Permanent Subcommittee on Investigations 1995).

TERRORIST ACTS BY AUM SHINRIKYO

Aum Shinrikyo's crimes were not restricted to mass murder by sarin gas. Asahara and his followers killed and injured many other people in different ways. An overview of their crimes can be best obtained by studying the list of indictments against Asahara, who masterminded most of these serious offences. He was indicted as a co-principal in 13 criminal cases because he had ordered these acts to be carried out. He was found guilty of all the following:

- Tokyo subway gas attack (murder, attempted murder) – on 20 March 1995 Aum Shinrikyo members released sarin nerve gas on Tokyo subway trains, killing 12 people and seriously injuring 14 others.
- Sarin nerve gas attack (murder, attempted murder) – on 27 June 1994 Aum Shinrikyo members sprayed sarin gas in Matsumoto, Nagano Prefecture, killing seven people and seriously injuring four others.
- Murder – on 4 November 1989 Aum Shinrikyo members killed Tsutsumi Sakamoto, 33, a lawyer helping people with complaints against Aum Shinrikyo, his wife Satoko, 29, and their son Tatsuhiko, one, at their home in Yokohama.
- Abduction and murder (abduction and confinement resulting in death, damage to corpse) – on 28 February 1995 Aum Shinrikyo members abducted Kiyoshi Kariya, 68, the chief clerk at the Meguro Public Notary Office, on a Tokyo street, to question him about the whereabouts of his sister, who wanted to leave the cult. Kariya was given general anaesthesia, which led to his death from heart failure. His body was burned in a microwave heating device.
- Murder – in early February 1989 Aum Shinrikyo members killed Shuji Taguchi, 21, who had wanted to leave the cult, at its complex in Fujinomiya, Shizuoka Prefecture.
- Murder (murder, damage to corpse) – on 30 January 1994 Aum Shinrikyo members killed Kotaro Ochida, 29, who had helped a female member escape from the cult's complex in Kamikuishiki, Yamanashi Prefecture. His body was burned in a microwave heating device.
- Murder – in early July 1994 Aum Shinrikyo members killed Toshio Tomita, 27, who the cult suspected was spying against it, at its complex in Kamikuishiki.
- Murder – on 12 December 1994 Aum Shinrikyo members killed Tadahito Hamaguchi, 28, who the cult suspected was a spy, with highly toxic VX gas on an Osaka street.
- Attempted murder – on 2 December 1994 Aum Shinrikyo members attempted to murder Noboru Mizuno, a parking lot owner, with VX gas,

owing to his assisting the family of an Aum Shinrikyo member who wanted to leave the cult.

- Attempted murder – on 4 January 1995 Aum Shinrikyo members attempted to kill Hiroyuki Nagaoka, head of the cult's victims' association, by splashing VX gas onto his neck on a Tokyo street.
- Attempted murder – on 9 May 1994 Aum Shinrikyo members attempted to kill lawyer Taro Takimoto by injecting sarin nerve gas into the ventilator of his car in a parking area outside a district court while he was attending a hearing of a civil suit against the group.
- Construction of a sarin nerve gas production plant (murder preparation) – Aum Shinrikyo members completed construction of a chemical plant to mass-produce sarin nerve gas by December 1994 at the Kamikuishiki complex. This was to kill a large number of people.
- Manufacturing of guns (violation of law regulating gun production) – Aum Shinrikyo members produced gun parts and one prototype gun in 1994 and 1995 as part of a failed attempt to mass-produce automatic rifles.

('The list of indictments against Japanese cult leader' 2004)

THE THREE MOST SERIOUS CASES

Three cases in the above list deserve careful analysis. They demonstrate that Aum Shinrikyo changed the concept of terrorism in Japan.

First, the murder of lawyer Sakamoto, his wife and baby son in 1989 compelled people to pay attention to the dark side of Aum Shinrikyo. Until the bodies of the Sakamoto family were recovered, as a result of confessions by Aum Shinrikyo members, the Sakamotos were believed to be missing. However, there had been a strong suspicion that Aum Shinrikyo was involved in some way because Sakamoto had had confrontations with it. Sakamoto's friends and supporters strongly urged the police to investigate the 'disappearance' of the lawyer and his family more thoroughly, but police were unable to collect enough evidence to charge Aum Shinrikyo. Shoko Egawa, a freelance journalist who had been covering the Aum Shinrikyo story, expressed her frustration with the police investigations in a story published just after her friend Sakamoto went missing (Egawa 1995, pp. 78–93). This was the situation at the time of the sarin gas attack in the Tokyo subway. Until then, because the followers of Aum Shinrikyo were unaware of the truth behind these disappearances, the organization, increasingly confident, continued to resort to murder when they needed to rid themselves of their enemies.

The second case – the Matsumoto sarin gas attack, a year before the Tokyo subway attack – had mystified the Japanese public. Matsumoto is a middle-sized provincial city in the Nagano Prefecture. It is located in the centre of

Honshu Island. Here Asahara ordered members of Aum Shinrikyo to kill the judges of the local court and spray sarin about. This was in retaliation for Aum Shinrikyo being sued by residents for opening a local branch. The court ordered Aum Shinrikyo to reduce the size of its branch building. This made Asahara very angry. He decided to test sarin gas locally in preparation for his eventual take-over of the whole of Japan ('The summary of the ruling' 2004). This attack was the first time a terrorist group in the country had used weapons of mass destruction to achieve its ends. Initially, the local police believed that the resident who reported the incident to the police had unintentionally leaked the poisonous gas made of agricultural chemicals. His pleas of innocence were largely ignored by the police and public. His wife was also hospitalized as a result of the attack. She did not recover, and even ten years later remained bedridden and unable to eat ('Sarin victims suffering from severe hangover' 2004). More than five months passed before some officials in the national police headquarters and self-defence forces came to recognize that the disaster had been caused by sarin, a chemical weapon, and that it may have been the product of Aum Shinrikyo's secret factory. By then it was too late to prevent another such attack.

The third and most important incident was the attack on the Tokyo subway. In understanding Asahara's motives, it is essential to see that he intended to topple the secular government of Japan and establish his own kingdom. That vision became clear after his defeat in the general elections of 1990. Participating in that election was a peaceful means for achieving the same goal, but after the defeat Asahara began to plan to take Japan by force. He ordered his followers to buy assault weapons and study the production of biological and chemical weapons. They even purchased a military helicopter from Russia ('The summary of the ruling' 2004).

By February 1994 Asahara's messianic delusions were well established. He told the cadres of the cult:

> I will be the king of Japan in 1997. Most of the world will be under the control of Aum Shinrikyo by 2003. We have to kill those who get in the way as soon as possible.

He renamed each section of the cult, which became a 'ministry', and appointed 'ministers' to head each one. In this way he began to replicate the legitimate organs of government in Japan. However, in late 1994 it seemed as if this conspiracy was about to end. The police detected sarin residue near the Aum Shinrikyo compound at the foot of Mt Fuji. Police also began to link the Matsumoto sarin case to Aum Shinrikyo. *The Yomiuri Shimbun* broke the news about those findings on 1 January 1995. Aum Shinrikyo then learned that the police were after them and their plans were threatened. Asahara decided to pre-empt the police raid and the Tokyo subway attack followed ('The summary of the ruling' 2004).

When one of Asahara's followers proposed using sarin gas to attack the Tokyo subway, Asahara said, 'It could create a big panic' ('The summary of the ruling' 2004). He authorized the plan. The opportunity was a good one because the police force was overwhelmed by the large earthquake in the west of Japan that January. Among other things, the city of Kobe had been devastated. Relief activities absorbed precious police time, diverting attention from their investigation of the Aum Shinrikyo case. Asahara counted on this confusion to make his own preparations. The scientists working in Aum Shinrikyo produced sarin on 19 March. Five members were chosen to carry out the attack. Each received two or three packs of sarin packed in a plastic bag. They were told to break the bags in the subway train with the tips of their umbrellas. On the morning of 20 March, those five men boarded different trains that formed part of the rail subway system of the central district of Tokyo. At eight in the morning, almost simultaneously they stuck their umbrellas into the plastic bags and let the sarin leak out. The 'terrorists' each escaped at the next station; none of them was injured ('The summary of the ruling' 2004).

The Police Response

Police raided the Aum Shinrikyo headquarters at the foot of Mt Fuji two days after the subway attack. That day's raid had been planned before the attack. Police knew Aum Shinrikyo was producing sarin and that it had allegedly used it in Matsumoto. But it took time to prepare for the search of the cult's headquarters – it was assumed that Aum Shinrikyo followers could be armed with chemical weapons. When Aum Shinrikyo learnt that an investigation was under way it 'pre-empted' the police by the attack on the Tokyo subway. That was why a high official of the National Police Agency in charge of the investigation reportedly shouted, 'We are defeated', when he heard that the Tokyo underground had been subjected to a sarin attack (Aso Iku 1997, p. 165). Since then, there has been strong criticism that the attack could have been averted had the police acted more quickly.

When it came, the police raid was a massive affair involving some 1500 policemen supported by the anti-chemical weapons team of the Japanese Self-Defense Force (SDF). Their information was that Aum Shinrikyo had not only chemical weapons but also biological weapons, assault rifles and handguns. The raid was televised live. Viewers were shocked to see thousands of policemen wearing heavy, protective, spacesuit-like clothing. Some of them held canaries in their hands to detect any changes in air quality that might be caused by chemical or biological substances.

The raid took an entire day. Most of the buildings of the Aum Shinrikyo headquarters were thoroughly searched, but Asahara was not found. At the end of the day, some 600 policemen remained behind to continue. This was followed by a major police operation against Aum Shinrikyo, lasting for several months, throughout Japan. The search climaxed when police found Asahara sealed in a secret room within the compound of the Aum Shinrikyo headquarters. The image of the handcuffed 'guru' provided the Japanese public with the much-needed relief that the Aum Shinrikyo cult had finally been defeated. By then, Aum Shinrikyo was known to be responsible for other crimes, including the mysterious disappearance of the Sakamoto family and the Matsumoto sarin attack.

In total, the number of arrested cult members is now more than 500. Some of them were rounded up for petty crimes such as stealing a bicycle and released later without any charge. One hundred and eighty-eight followers of Asahara have been indicted. The original trial found all of them guilty except one. Twelve were sentenced to death. Asahara himself was sentenced to death on 22 February 2004.

THE LESSONS LEARNED

Aum Shinrikyo's terrorist acts not only destroyed the myth about Japan's safety but also changed conventional thinking about terrorism in general. What lessons can Aum Shinrikyo teach us?

Weapons of mass destruction can be employed by terrorists Aum Shinrikyo was the first terrorist group to develop and use weapons of mass destruction. According to the ruling on Shoko Asahara, they committed mass murder twice by spreading sarin nerve gas – in Matsumoto and Tokyo. They also produced and used VX gas, another chemical weapon, at least three times and killed one person. Besides sarin and VX gas, investigators found Aum Shinrikyo had tried to produce phosgene. As for biological weapons, Aum Shinrikyo had developed and produced anthrax and botulin. They had even spread anthrax in Tokyo in 1992 but their 'experiment' failed to have any impact on anyone. This failure reportedly made Aum Shinrikyo shift from biological weapons to chemical weapons. They were also interested in nuclear weapons. Their followers managed to steal data on uranium enrichment from Mitsubishi Heavy Industries.

Another horrific dimension to Aum Shinrikyo is that they even studied developing weapons of mass destruction that had never been produced before. Aum Shinrikyo's published documents referred to weapons such as laser beam guns and plasma weapons. In theory, plasma weapons destroy only living organisms by exposure to powerful microwaves. Even the US military has only been able to 'develop' these weapons in research labs. Aum Shinrikyo never succeeded in producing such weapons, but they did get as far as building a box-shaped microwave-generating device called a 'Power Unit'. They used that device to burn at least three of the victims they killed.

Asahara's followers believed that they were preparing for Armageddon. There is nothing surprising about their attempts to create evil weapons. What is surprising, however, is that they actually succeeded in producing at least some of them.

Why were they able to do this? First, they had enough labour and financial resources, and they were different from political extremists – Aum Shinrikyo followers constituted a religious congregation. A substantial number of scientists and medical doctors devoted themselves to Aum Shinrikyo. It was their religious duty to develop these deadly weapons. Aum Shinrikyo earned billions of dollars from its private business interests in areas such as computer manufacturing and sales. In addition, a huge volume of resources took the form of donations from Aum Shinrikyo's followers. None of this income was taxable because Aum Shinrikyo was a registered not-for-profit religious corporation.

Second, the spread of advanced technologies and knowledge made it easier to develop and produce weapons of mass destruction. According to Tadao Inoue, a former WMD expert at Japan's Self-Defense Force (SDF), chemical weapons could be produced by any scientist with a masters degree in chemistry provided he or she were able to work in a well-facilitated laboratory. The same applies to biological weapons. Both chemical and biological weapons can be developed more readily and more cheaply than nuclear weapons (Inoue 2003).

On the other hand, experts maintain that Aum Shinrikyo's WMD were not sophisticated. Rather, commentators such as Kyle B. Olson, the prominent WMD expert in the United States, notes: 'The Aum Supreme Truth's actions were successful in part because there is no effective defense against a clandestine chemical or biological attack'. At the same time, Olson warned that after Aum Shinrikyo terrorist attacks would become more deadly. He predicted that Aum Shinrikyo's actions 'provide a bloody roadmap for others who will certainly follow in pursuit of these weapons' (Olson 1995). The example of Aum Shinrikyo continued to resonate in policy circles. In 1996, one year after the Tokyo subway attack, US Senator Sam Nunn sponsored American legislation to prepare local, state and federal authorities to defend against a chemical or biological attack. He said, 'There is a high likelihood that a chemical or biological incident will take place on American soil in the next several years ... We do not want a domestic Pearl Harbor' ('US Senate OK's bill on chemical, biological attacks' 1996). After almost 10 years, Aum Shinrikyo remains the only non-governmental organization that has ever used weapons of mass destruction for terrorist purposes. But something similar to a 'domestic Pearl Harbor' did occur on 11 September. Despite this, US President

Bush repeatedly warns against the possibility of terrorists obtaining WMD from one of those 'rogue countries'. Clearly, Aum Shinrikyo changed our perceptions of terrorism forever.

Anyone can be a target Political extremists always have clear targets when they engage in acts of terrorism – the assassination of a particular politician, for example. But, Aum Shinrikyo was different. Aum Shinrikyo declared total war against the rest of the world. Its followers believed that the world was in crisis and that they were the ones who had to save it by fighting against Armageddon. They rationalized killing innocent people by distorting the Tibetan Buddhism concept of *poa*. Asahara taught his followers that Aum Shinrikyo could wash away all human sins and send people to a happier afterlife by killing them. Ikuo Hayashi, a medical doctor who belonged to Aum Shinrikyo and one of the perpetrators of the Tokyo underground attack, confessed in his autobiography: 'I felt terrible when I was asked to spread sarin in the subway car. But I had to do it to protect Aum' (Hayashi 2001).

Terrorists can operate from anywhere Aum Shinrikyo was a registered religious corporation exempted from income taxes. It was open to anyone, no matter who. The number of followers in Japan rose to 14 000 when Aum Shinrikyo was at its height. By that time it had become an international movement. All members appeared to be average, normal and ordinary citizens. Apart from the 'priests' there was nothing to tell them apart from other members of the public. They also came from extraordinarily diversified socioeconomic backgrounds. Among the file disks that the police found during their raid on Aum Shinrikyo headquarters, there were lists of some 1115 priests and followers with all their particulars. Almost every occupational group and class in Japanese society was represented – even the police, the SDF and the media. This diversity itself made it very difficult for the police to undertake their work because there was no particular target for their investigations.

HOW JAPAN RESPONDED

In the ten years that have passed since the Tokyo subway attack, has Japan made sufficient effort to prevent the next sarin attack? The answer is yes and no. The Japanese government has introduced many preventive measures against serious terrorism incidents such as those that occurred in the underground. At the same time, public opinion has condemned the government for failure to develop an overall anti-terrorism strategy.

The immediate task for the Japanese government after the subway attacks was to stop Aum Shinrikyo from committing further, similar acts. Almost immediately, some 400 Aum Shinrikyo followers were arrested. The protection afforded Aum Shinrikyo by the Religious Corporation Law was suspended. By 1996 Aum Shinrikyo was declared bankrupt. Despite this, Aum Shinrikyo members were not prohibited from pursuing their religious activities. They changed the name of the cult from Aum Shinrikyo to Aleph, and most of them still continue to worship Asahara as their guru. Some observers have even suggested that the number of followers is increasing.

Apart from its appeal to a certain number of people, the most important reason for Aum Shinrikyo's survival during the last decade has been the Japanese government's failure to apply the Anti-Subversive Activities Law to it. This law provides the only legal means for the government to disband Aum Shinrikyo. The law was enacted in 1952, largely to target leftist extremism. The purpose of the law is to control violent and subversive organizations promoting communism and other political causes designed to topple the government. The law can be applied only if two conditions are met: (a) if an organization is involved in violent and subversive activities and (b) if that organization is deemed likely to continue and repeat such illegal activities in the future. So far this law has not been applied to any Japanese group in recent times.

In January 1997 a government request to invoke the Anti-Subversive Activities Law to outlaw Aum Shinrikyo was rejected by the Public Security Examination Commission. The independent commission concluded that the cult's power had diminished after it was ordered to disband as a religious corporation and declared bankrupt. Thus it concluded that there was no good reason to believe that the cult would consider further violent and subversive actions in the future ('Aum escapes disbandment' 1997). That was a big setback for the Japanese government. The Chief Cabinet Secretary Hiromu Nonaka was loud in his condemnation of the Law: 'The Anti-Subversive Activities Law has no reason to exist if it cannot be applied to issue an order to dissolve a brutal organization' ('Shady groups targeted in government law revision bill' 1999).

A new law was therefore passed – the Subversive Organizations Control Law. Its main purpose was to restrict the activities of Aum Shinrikyo. However, this law is also limited by its lack of any provision that permits the government to disband the cult. As a result, the cult has been tolerated, although it remains under police surveillance. *Yomiuri* has asserted that there are about 1650 Aum Shinrikyo followers active at 26 branches in 17 Japanese prefectures. Trouble between cult members and local residents continues to be a problem. Another index of the survival of Aum Shinrikyo has been the return to the fold of some 100 of the 400 Aum Shinrikyo members who were arrested and indicted in 1995. These data are based on the records of Japan's Public Security Investigation Agency ('Matsumoto to be sentenced on February 27' 2004).

Japan's Contingency Plans

Although the Japanese government has been unable to disband Aum Shinrikyo, they have made some progress in dealing with the new kind of terrorism that the Tokyo underground attacks gave rise to, namely the usage of WMD.

At the time of the sarin gas attacks, the Japanese police were not at all prepared. The police did not know how to handle a situation involving chemical warfare. They asked the SDF to help. The SDF dispatched special taskforces to each of the subway stations along the main line, but the stations were crowded with victims, subway staff, policemen and firemen. SDF taskforces had no experience of how to handle the confusion that awaited them at the stations or in the hospitals, where the situation was even more chaotic. Most doctors and nurses had never seen patients affected by chemical weapons. An SDF doctor sent to one of the hospitals treating the victims had just finished a course of training in chemical warfare. He brought along a textbook that was a translation of the manual used by NATO and American forces. He and his colleagues were able to treat the victims according to the instructions in this text (Aso Iku 1997). Recently there has been some effort to prepare for attacks by chemical weapons such as sarin. The Tokyo Metropolitan Fire Department has created three special taskforce units to deal with terrorism using WMD. The National Hospital also has a large stockpile of 'PAM', a drug that can reduce the effect of a sarin attack. It also has other medicines for bio-chemical attacks (Tu 2005, pp. 131–3).

The Japanese government also quickly introduced new legislation to prohibit the production of chemical weapons. Until then, there were no laws of this kind in Japan. Had such legislation not been passed, Aum Shinrikyo or any other terrorist group could have developed chemical weapons again without fear of being charged. The bill passed the Japanese parliament (Diet) exactly one month after the attack in Tokyo. The law was called the 'Sarin Law'.

The government also created a new high authority to be responsible for the management of such crises in future – the post was at the level of deputy chief cabinet secretary. The secretary's first duty was to assist the prime minister in emergency situations. In 2001 the duties of this office were expanded as part of a counter-terrorism program drawn up by the government. The program stipulates that, in the case of a terrorist attack using nuclear, biological or chemical weapons, the deputy chief cabinet secretary and bureau chiefs of the concerned ministries and agencies should gather at the Crisis Management Center in the prime minister's office. The main purpose of this is to collect and share information in order to design a proper response strategy. Under the program the prime minister is authorized to set up and chair Japan's antiterrorism headquarters. As a result of these initiatives, Japan now has a rudimentary framework for responding to terrorism.

Even so, these initiatives hardly constitute an overall anti-terrorism program. On balance, the Japanese government has been more reactive than pre-emptive. They are still not for pursuing and apprehending would-be terrorists before those people actually do some damage. In fact, the government tends to be more concerned with natural disasters like earthquakes than with terrorism. After 9/11 the Japanese government has again been compelled to review and reorganize its anti-terrorism policies, largely in response to the US government's insistence that Japan cooperate against international terrorism.

Public Perceptions of Terrorism

As stated at the beginning of this chapter, Aum Shinrikyo destroyed the myth of a safe Japan. But the broken myth did not lead the Japanese public to a better understanding of what needed to be done about potential terrorist threats. By contrast, there was a much better grappling with these issues in the West, especially among Americans, who appreciated how Aum Shinrikyo's activities had redefined 'terrorism' as something that could be initiated by religious fanatics armed with weapons of mass destruction and fighting for global, messianic causes. Long before President Bush declared the 'war on terror', the Clinton administration had taken a special interest in Aum Shinrikyo. It recognized the possibility that citizens in other big cities in the world could be threatened by terrorist attacks similar to those by Aum Shinrikyo in Tokyo. President Clinton often referred to the Tokyo subway attack when he emphasized the importance of an anti-terrorism policy.

In Japan the terrorist acts by Aum Shinrikyo were thought to be terrible but isolated incidents. Numerous press stories and books were written about Aum Shinrikyo. However, many of them focused on the nature of the individual followers of Aum Shinrikyo. Alternatively they tried to analyse the impact of this religious cult on Japanese society. Very few discussed Aum Shinrikyo's terrorist acts from the viewpoint of social or national security, nor did they ask how society might be defended against such attacks in future. According to Miyasaka (2004), during the 1990s only one Japanese scholar wrote a thesis about terrorism; in America 268 did so and in Britain 75 scholars were focused on this subject. In other words, Japanese people, including the media, did not make enough effort to study Aum Shinrikyo's style of terrorism or how Aum Shinrikyo's methods were reflected in international terrorist organizations. This is indeed a curious omission, given that Japan experienced many terrorist attacks on its embassies and citizens based in foreign countries; for example, there was the shootout in Luxor (Egypt), the Peruvian guerrilla take-over of the Japanese Embassy in Lima (Peru), and the 9/11 incident claiming the lives of 23 Japanese.

NORTH KOREA AND 'STATE-SPONSORED TERRORISM'

The abduction of Japanese citizens by North Korean secret agents was another bitter experience that the Japanese have had of terrorism. This particular kind of terrorism was as unthinkable to the Japanese public as a religious cult using chemical weapons to attack innocent people.

Most Japanese people did not know that dozens of citizens had been abducted by North Korean agents during the 1970s and 1980s until the North Korean leader Kim Jong-Il admitted to these abductions during a visit to Pyongyang by the Japanese Prime Minister Juninchiro Koizumi in 2002. There had been rumours that North Korean spies had something to do with those missing men and women. But very few people believed that state-sponsored terrorism of this kind was possible. Some of those who went missing were lovers who had been walking along the beach. One of them was a high school girl who never returned home from school. The Japanese government had compiled a list of the missing citizens and repeatedly asked the North Korean government whether they knew anything about these persons. The North Koreans continued to deny their involvement until Mr Koizumi met with Mr Kim. So it was a great shock for Japanese people when Mr Kim admitted that, without his knowledge, his spy agencies had kidnapped 14 Japanese and that five of them were still alive. The Japanese government was especially surprised when the North Koreans told them that they had abducted one woman who was not even on the Japanese government's list of missing persons. She eventually married an American soldier who had escaped to North Korea from the south.

The abduction of Japanese citizens by North Korean spies acting on the orders of the North Korean government can rightly be described as state-sponsored terrorism. However, the abductions are very different from the attacks by Aum Shinrikyo, so some scholars insist that they should not be discussed as if they belonged to the same group of problems. Moreover, some observers argue that the abductions are not likely to be repeated; they note that Kim Jong-Il himself regretted these incidents and said that this sort of thing would never happen again. Regardless of the debate, Japanese people today feel more insecure in their daily lives. After the Aum Shinrikyo incidents, they can never escape the fear of being attacked in the streets or in the subway at any time. Now they also realize that the threat could come from a neighbouring country. The Japanese media appreciate this change in public outlook and have exploited this fear to attract more viewers or readers. Ratings, it seems, depended on reporting something about the North Korean abduction issue in every TV news show.

The Japanese government has now demanded a full explanation of each abduction case. They do not believe the North Korean claim that the majority of abductees have died. As a result, a full resolution of the abduction issue has now become a top priority in Japanese diplomacy towards North Korea, along with the nuclear and missile issues. The dialogue aimed at normalizing relations between Japan and North Korea is now less likely to advance because of the abductions. According to an opinion poll taken in January 2005, 85 per cent of the Japanese supported the economic sanctions imposed on North Korea as punishment for the abductions ('More than 80% support sanctions on North Korea' 2005). State-sponsored terrorism has, in this case, become a major setback for Japan–North Korea relations.

CONCLUSION

Three Aum Shinrikyo members are still on the run. Their names appear on the list of Japan's 'Most wanted', posted by the National Police Agency. Two of them are wanted in connection with the Tokyo subway sarin attack. A reward of two million yen (roughly US$19 000) for each suspect has been offered by the police, who in Japan rarely offer rewards. Police remain eager to pursue Aum Shinrikyo. The Japanese public, on the other hand, has learned to live with the fear of terrorism.

After an absence of five years (1996 to 2001) I returned to Japan and noticed many differences. On commuter trains, nobody puts their bags on the overhead shelf anymore – bags are held on people's laps. All bags need to be identified with the persons who own them; in this way, daily travel imitates the new security standards being applied at international airports. Since April 2005 all subway stations in Japan have had new transparent plastic rubbush bins. After the Tokyo attacks, all rubbish bins were removed because they posed the danger that they could be used to hide WMD. Transparent plastic rubbish bins are a good compromise between safety and the need to dispose of rubbish. These modest changes show that the Japanese public is learning to live with the threat of terrorism.

NOTES

1. The Indian word 'guru' for teacher is also used in the Japanese language. It presumably came to Japan through Buddhism.
2. Vajrayana is the third path of Buddhist practice towards enlightenment. It enables the process of acquiring 'experience' to be fast-tracked by the use of tantric methods. The Buddhist notion of 'poa' allows the forcible extraction of consciousness from a dying person in order to propel that consciousness to another. Both concepts are complex and subtle, and far removed from the crudity and violence promoted by Asahara. [Ed.]

REFERENCES

'10 years on, public still fears Aum' (2005), *The Daily Yomiuri*, 18 March.
'A chronology of Shoko Asahara' (1995), *The Mainichi Shimbun*, 2 June.
'A man called the Guru' (1995), *The Asahi Shimbun*, 23 October.
Akimoto, Haruo (2002), *AUM Kagakuteki Kiroku (AUM – The Scientific Observation)*, Tokyo: Souzou Shuppan.
Aso Iku (1997), *Gokuhi Sousa (The Secret Investigation)*, Tokyo: Bungei Shunju.
'Aum escapes disbandment' (1997), *The Daily Yomiuri*, 1 February.
Egawa, Shoko (1995), *Aum Shinrikyo Tsuiseki 2200 Nichi (2200 Days to Pursue Aum Shinrikyo)*, Tokyo: Bungei Shunju.
Hayashi, Ikuo (2001), *Aum to Watashi (Aum and I)*, Tokyo: Bungei Shunju.
'Humble beginnings shed light on Aum cult leader' (2004), *The Daily Yomiuri*, 13 February.
Inoue, Tadao (2003), *Tero Wa Nihon Demo Kakujitsuni Okoru (Terrorist Acts Surely to Occur in Japan)*, Tokyo: Kodansha.
Larimer, Tim (2002), 'Cult shock: yearning for spiritual leadership, Japan has spawned a rash of apocalyptic religious and ominously popular sects', *Time Asia*, 8 July.
'Matsumoto to be sentenced on February 27' (2004), *The Daily Yomiuri*, 20 February.
Ministry of Justice (1977), *White Paper on Crime*, Government of Japan.
Ministry of Justice (2003), *White Paper on Crime*, Government of Japan.
Minority Staff of the Permanent Subcommittee on Investigations (1995), 'Global proliferation of weapons of mass destruction: a case study on the Aum Shinrikyo', Senate Government Affairs Permanent Subcommittee on Investigations, cited at Federation of American Scientists, Intelligence Resource Program: 1995 Congressional Reports, 31 October, Staff Statement, www.fas.org/irp/congress/1995_rpt/aum/part06.htm accessed January 2006.
Miyasaka, Naoshi (2004), *Nihon wa Tero wo Husegeruka (Can Japan Prevent Terrorism?)*, Tokyo: Chikuma Shobo.
'More than 80% support sanctions on North Korea' (2005), *The Yomiuri Shimbun*, 21 January.
Olson, Kyle B. (1995), 'Aum attack extension of terrorism trend', *The Daily Yomiuri*, 31 December.
'Sarin victims suffering from severe hangover' (2004), *The Asahi Shimbun,* 25 February.
'Shady groups targeted in government law revision bill' (1999), *The Daily Yomiuri*, 23 May.
Takarajima, Bessatsu (2004), *Nihon Tero Jikenshi (The History of Terrorism in Japan)*, Tokyo: Takarajima.
'The list of indictments against Japanese cult leader' (2004), Kyodo News Service, Tokyo, 4 February.
'The summary of the ruling handed down on Chizuo Matsumoto (a.k.a. Shoko Asahara) by the Tokyo District Court, February 27, 2004' (2004), *The Yomiuri Shimbun, The Asahi Shimbun, Kyodo News*, 28 February.
Tu, Anthony T. (2005), *The Truth of Sarin Incident*, Tokyo: Shinpu-sha.
'US Senate OKs bill on chemical, biological attacks' (1996), *The Daily Yomiuri*, 29 June.

Index